AF580958

Highlights of the Art Institute of Chicago

Edited by James Rondeau

The Art Institute of Chicago
Distributed by Yale University Press, New Haven and London

First edition
Printed in Italy
31 30 29 28 27 26 1 2 3 4 5
Authorized representative in the EU:
Easy Access System Europe, Mustamäe tee 50, 10621 Tallinn, Estonia
gpsr.requests@easproject.com

ISBN: 978-0-300-28853-7 (hardcover)

Library of Congress Control Number: 2026930973

Published by
The Art Institute of Chicago
111 South Michigan Avenue
Chicago, IL 60603-6404
artic.edu

Distributed by
Yale University Press
302 Temple Street
P. O. Box 209040
New Haven, CT 06520-9040
yalebooks.com/art

Edited by Kati Woock
Production by Elizabeth Upenieks with Lauren Makholm
Photography research by Kristie Kahns
Proofreading by Juliet Clark
Indexing by Jane Friedman
Design by Christine Zavesky with Kristin Best
Separations by Echelon, Los Angeles
Printing and binding by Verona Libri, Verona, Italy

Publishing, the Art Institute of Chicago
Katie Reilly, Associate Vice President, Publishing
Lisa Meyerowitz, Editorial Director
Lauren Makholm, Director of Production

Imaging, the Art Institute of Chicago
Bonnie Rosenberg, Director of Imaging
Nathan Keay, Associate Director, Photography
Elyse M. Allen, Associate Director, Production

Cover: Detail of Edward Hopper, *Nighthawks*, 1942 (entry 142). Photo by Robert Lifson.

This book was made of material from well-managed FSC®-certified forests and other controlled sources.

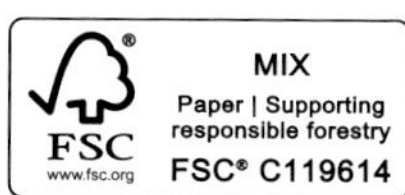

Contents

Foreword

"It is impossible to look forward to the work of the next year and of future years without enthusiasm and even excitement—With a collection and a school which already command the respect of all well informed persons, with a recent gift of pictures surpassing in munificence any which has preceded it, and with a museum building which we fully believe to be as good for its purposes as any ever built, standing ready and receptive at the opportune moment when the most various and valuable collections are close at hand, our condition and our opportunities are such as rarely present themselves to any institution—There is reason to apprehend that the new building, large as it is, will hardly be large enough for our uses when we come into full possession of it."

—Director William M. R. French, 1893 Annual Report

With these prescient words William M. R. French, the museum's first director, captures a keen understanding of the distinctive elements that define the Art Institute of Chicago: an institution made of both a school and a museum, a celebrated collection formed from the generosity of forward-thinking collectors and patrons, and a spirit of continual growth, which has led to the expansion from a singular, now-iconic structure to a campus of nine buildings and the second-largest art museum in the United States.

As French's statement also suggests, the Art Institute began as a daring, aspirational civic experiment. In reality, these museum leaders built its first permanent home to *attract* a collection rather than to *house* an existing one. The Chicago French and others envisioned would be not only a manufacturing and transportation hub—a city of grain, livestock, and trains—but also a center of culture and learning. The trustees chose a location at the intersection of Michigan Avenue and Adams Street in the heart of the city with the hopes that the museum's growth would parallel that of Chicago and contribute to its development and reputation as a world-class city. Designed in the Beaux-Arts style, the museum's 1893 building is fashioned as a "temple to culture." A working drawing of the elevation of the west facade reveals that the architectural firm Shepley, Rutan, and Coolidge reserved the entablature for an inscription (fig. 1) to be determined by museum leaders. In the Art Institute archives is a working list of artists' names for the new building (fig. 2) along with notations—"Japanese?" "American?"—alluding to other considerations. Ultimately

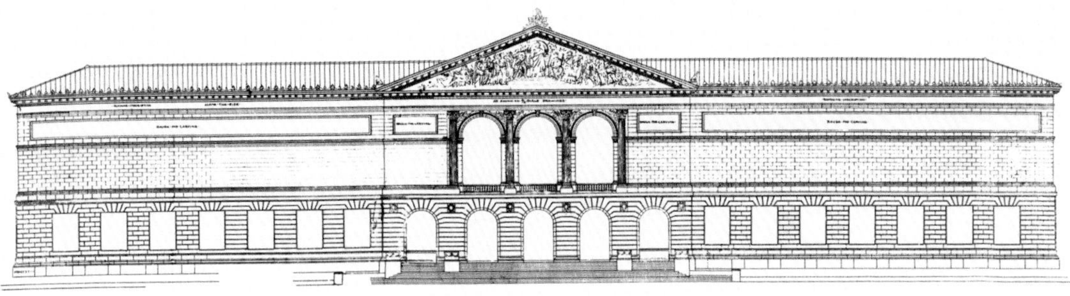

Fig. 1. Shepley, Rutan, and Coolidge (American, 1886–1914). Elevation of the west facade of the Art Institute of Chicago, 1892. Building and Renovation Files, Design and Construction, Institutional Archives, The Art Institute of Chicago.

thirty-two names of classical and European painters and sculptors were chosen, such as Michelangelo, Praxiteles, Rembrandt, and Turner, as well as the ninth-century Japanese painter Kose Kanaoka. The carved names served as a public and permanent expression of the museum's intentions to collect works of the greatest art historical significance.

Nearly 140 years later, the museum proudly counts many of these artists' works among its holdings, and yet the Art Institute's collection has expanded radically and purposefully beyond these initial aspirations. Today the museum holds more than 300,000 objects that span six continents and five millennia. Given the institution's enormous growth, one might wonder how to understand the defining characteristics of the Art Institute's collection today.

Poignantly relevant to the Art Institute's current institutional thinking is the work of American, Cuban-born artist Felix Gonzalez-Torres, who offered a framework for self-definition, both collective and individual, that is ever-changing:

> *When we think of who we are, we usually think of a unified subject. In the present. An immutable entity. . . . We are not what we think we are, but rather a compilation of texts. A compilation of histories, past, present, and future, always, always shifting, adding, subtracting, gaining.*

In 1989 Gonzalez-Torres composed a nonrepresentational portrait, *"Untitled"* (fig. 3), of words and phrases matched with dates—some public or historical and others private and personal. Installed along the top of a gallery wall just below the ceiling, *"Untitled"* borrows its compositional structure from traditional friezes carved on the faces of public buildings, like the Art Institute's. This portrait, which the artist at times referred to as a self-portrait, occupies a commemorative form normally reserved for institutional use. In contrast to what is literally carved in stone, *"Untitled"* is malleable; it can and should change each time it is installed, creating an obligation on the part of the Art Institute, as its owner, to consider adding to (or subtracting from or rearranging) history. Events preceding and occurring during the artist's life intertwine with more recent identifiable public events: Grant Park 2008, Obergefell 2015, Palm Springs 2022. Identity, like history, is constantly being rewritten, expanded, and recontextualized. Gonzalez-Torres offered a newly concrete model, transforming the ancient typology of the frieze from something that celebrates the intractable and the permanent to something flexible, elastic, multivocal, and evolving.

Highlights of the Art Institute of Chicago utilizes a framework similar to Gonzalez-Torres's *"Untitled,"* bringing together permanent and objective elements of the museum's collection and history with the evolving and subjective. Rather than one institutional "voice," texts have been written by numerous authors—curators, conservators, interpretation staff, artists, architects, and poets—representing a wide range of perspectives. The catalogue presents approximately two hundred entries on works of art selected from across all of the museum's curatorial departments. The object entries are arranged chronologically, intermixing geographies, cultures, and media and encouraging readers to make unexpected connections between objects. An illustrated timeline of the history of the Art Institute discusses major moments in the expansion of the museum's buildings and collections as well as in popular culture. Complementing the entries are nine brief essays highlighting collection strengths and addressing areas of curiosity for our visitors.

From the objects, images, dates, events, and themes presented in this catalogue, one could construct the Art Institute's own conceptual portrait as a frieze: Chicago Fire 1871, Chicago Academy of Fine Arts 1879, World's Columbian Exposition 1893,

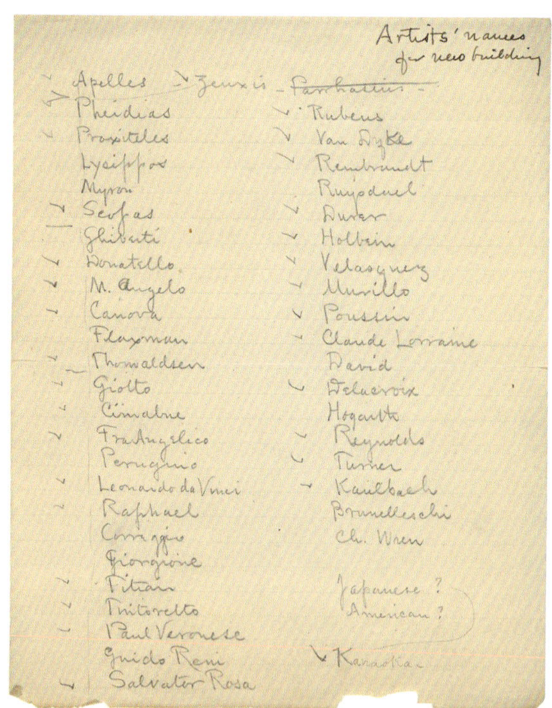

Artists' names for new building

Apelles Zeuxis

Pheidias	Rubens
Praxiteles	Van Dyke
Lysippos	Rembrandt
Myron	Ruysdael
Scopas	Durer
Ghiberti	Holbein
Donatello	Velasquez
M. Angelo	Murillo
Canova	Poussin
Flaxman	Claude Lorraine
Thorwaldsen	David
Giotto	Delacroix
Cimabue	Hogarth
Fra Angelico	Reynolds
Perugino	Turner
Leonardo da Vinci	Kaulbach
Raphael	Brunelleschi
Correggio	Ch. Wren
Giorgione	
Titian	Japanese ?
Tintoretto	American ?
Paul Veronese	
Guido Reni	Kanaoka
Salvator Rosa	

Fig. 2. List of artists' names for the new building, 1892. Board of Trustee and Committee Files, Secretary's Office, Institutional Archives, The Art Institute of Chicago.

Fig. 3. Felix Gonzalez-Torres (American, born Cuba, 1957–1996). *"Untitled,"* 1989. Enamel paint on wall; dimensions vary with installation. The Art Institute of Chicago, bequest of Carolyn Spiegel; Watson F. Blair Prize, Muriel Kallis Newman, Sara Szold and Modern and Contemporary Discretionary funds; Samuel and Sarah Deson and Oscar L. Gerber Memorial endowments; and the San Francisco Museum of Modern Art, Accessions Committee Fund Purchase: gift of Jean and James E. Douglas Jr., Carla Emil and Rich Silverstein, Collectors Forum, Doris and Don Fisher, Niko and Steve Mayer, Elaine McKeon, and Danielle and Brooks Walker Jr., 2002.80.

Kemeys's Lions 1894, The Armory Show 1913, Buckingham Collection 1924, La Grande Jatte 1926, Steiglitz Collection 1949, Arms and Armor 1982, Modern Wing 2009, Edlis Neeson 2015, Grainger Center 2027. The words and dates may change iteratively or radically depending on the year or person(s) compiling them. And yet, certain defining characteristics of the Art Institute emerge as a result of its history and remain constant: a collection shaped by Chicago as the birthplace of the modern city and the skyscraper, a dual commitment to collecting art of the past *and* the present, and a position as a place for training and inspiring the artists of the future. Ultimately the central ideals of the Art Institute's mission reinforce its commitment to steward and share its collections with Chicago and the world, to continually and dynamically engage with the art, to foster the exchange of ideas, and to inspire an expansive, inclusive understanding of human creativity. Operating under these principles, we present these collection highlights not as a definitive list of objects but as an iterative and flexible guide.

Like the Art Institute's expanding collection, the visitors who walk through its doors and into its galleries continue to evolve and change, and the meaning and inspiration each person gleans from the range of human imagination and ingenuity inherent in these objects changes too. The artists and objects that make an impression at one moment may give way to new sources of personal connection, ensuring that the museum is not merely a permanent monument to culture, but a living institution shaped by and reflective of the people who experience it.

James Rondeau
President and Eloise W. Martin Director
The Art Institute of Chicago

Acknowledgments

Highlights of the Art Institute of Chicago reimagines our long-standing signature publication on the collection, the *Essential Guide*, to reflect the spirit and singularity of the Art Institute today. We rebuilt the publication from the ground up, striving to meet the needs of our visitors who are curious not only about the most important works in the collection, but also about our buildings, history, and areas of unique strength. Choosing two hundred objects from our holdings of more than 300,000 was challenging. After soliciting recommendations from our curatorial teams, Kate Tierney Powell, Executive Director of Communications and Research; Sarah Guernsey, Deputy Director and Senior Vice President, Curatorial Affairs; and Jacques Schuhmacher, Executive Director of Provenance Research, were instrumental in evaluating and selecting works. I am also grateful for Kate's rich and engaging timeline, a labor of love of hers for many years. Our colleagues in Retail, Heather Reinholtz, Jennifer Evanoff, and Kaleb Sullivan, helped shape the vision for this publication, ensuring that it will be an enduring resource for our visitors and for art lovers around the world. The enthusiastic guidance of Sarah Kelly Oehler, Field-McCormick Chair and Curator, Arts of the Americas, and Vice President of Curatorial Strategy; David Nacol, Senior Vice President, Philanthropy; Katie Rahn, Senior Vice President, Marketing and Communications; Emily Benedict, Vice President, Campus Operations; Amy Allen, Vice President, Engagement; and Aaron Andersen, Associate Vice President, Financial Planning and Analysis, has been equally crucial.

We are indebted to the authors (all ninety-two of them listed on pp. 267–68), who offered insightful, sometimes personal, and often unexpected takes on works in our collection. Each of the museum's eleven curatorial departments contributed their expertise, including recommending objects, coordinating new photography, and carefully proofing object information. This publication would not have been possible without the efforts of: in Applied Arts of Europe, Christopher Maxwell, Ellenor Alcorn, Madeleine Hazelwood, Mairead Carney Horton, and Jonathan Tavares; in Architecture and Design, Irene Sunwoo, Anna Burckhardt Pérez, Alison Fisher, and Craig Lee; in Arts of Africa, Constantine Petridis, Ashley Arico, and Elizabeth Benge; in Arts of the Americas, Sarah Kelly Oehler, Lois Taylor Biggs, Andrew James Hamilton, Annelise K. Madsen, Sofia Martinez, Elizabeth McGoey, Elizabeth I. Pope, and Kate Weinstein; in Arts of Asia, Tao Wang, Kris L. Anderson, Yeonsoo Chee, Madhuvanti Ghose, Janice Katz, Keely Morgan, and Seung Hee Oh; in Arts of Greece, Rome, and Byzantium, Lisa Ayla Çakmak and Katharine A. Raff; in Modern and Contemporary Art, Paulina Pobocha, Makayla Bava, Giampaolo Bianconi, Annika Bohanec, Jay Dandy, Caitlin Haskell, Tamar Kharatishvili, Kate Nesin, Thea Liberty Nichols, Tacy Wagner, and Isabel Waring; in Painting and Sculpture of Europe, Gloria Groom, Emerson Bowyer, Jena Carvana, Jacquelyn N. Coutré, Rebecca J. Long, Andrea Morgan, and Megan True; in Photography and Media, Matthew S. Witkovsky, Antawan I. Byrd,

Grace Deveney, Alexandra Kader Herrera, Jamie Vaught-Karasek, Grant Williams-Yackel, and Yechen Zhao; in Prints and Drawings, Kevin Salatino, Mel Becker Solomon, Jay A. Clarke, Jamie Gabbarelli, Charlotte Healy, Alex Jen, Felipe Villada Ruiz, and Emily Vokt Ziemba; in Textiles, Melinda Watt, Katherine Andereck, Janet Marion Purdy, and Stephanie R. Caruso; and Jill Bugajski and Castor Santee in the Research Center.

The department of Conservation and Science provides ongoing care for and research on these works and supported this project in particular by contributing their own insights; we thank Francesca Casadio, Chris Brooks, Kelly Keegan, Allison Langley, Emily Mercer, Charles Pietraszewski, and Giovanni Verri. We are also indebted to the extraordinary team in Interpretation and Gallery Activation, who spearheaded an earlier audience research study that informed the scope and approach of this publication and contributed their own interpretations to works in this volume. We particularly thank Emily Fry, Molly Bryson, Nancy Chen, Marielle Epstein, Ginia Shubik Sweeney, Loren Wright, and former intern Sarah Ahmed.

In Publishing, Katie Reilly prompted a reimagining of our signature collection publication; along with Lauren Makholm and Lisa Meyerowitz, she orchestrated the many collaborative conversations needed to give it shape and bring it to fruition. Kati Woock took on the herculean task of organizing and editing the hundreds of contributions, with assistance from Lisa Meyerowitz, Kit Shields, and Reagan Stevens-Keller. Elizabeth Upenieks produced this beautiful publication, with assistance from Lauren Makholm. Kristie Kahns obtained photography rights, while Isella Sandoval coordinated the many contracts and administrative details.

Christine Zavesky in Visual Design created the publication's clean and inviting design, harkening back to our own publishing history while embracing our current brand identity. Kristin Best skillfully laid out the interior, bringing our stunning holdings to life. Many of the works reproduced here were captured by members of the Art Institute's Imaging department, led by Bonnie Rosenberg; our particular thanks go to photographers Nathan Keay, Robert Lifson, Jonathan Mathias, Juan Molina Hernandez, and Joe Tallarico; and in production, Elyse Allen, Kaitlyn Fultz Campion, and Hayley Hinsberger.

And finally, a special thank-you to our guest authors, who include artists, educators, and writers from right here in Chicago and across the country. This diverse group shares a deep knowledge and appreciation for art, and we are grateful for their unique reflections. Each entry shows the enduring impact of our collection upon our community and throughout the art world. We hope that these pages inspire you to look closely at some of your favorite artworks and perhaps discover something new.

James Rondeau
President and Eloise W. Martin Director
The Art Institute of Chicago

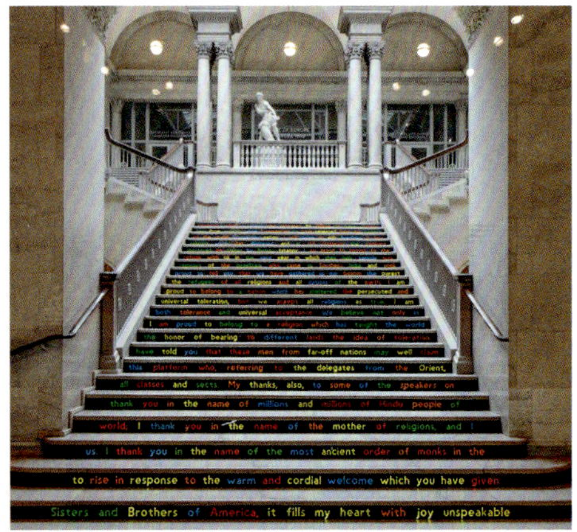

1893 At the World's Parliament of Religions, held in the future home of the Art Institute, Swami Vivekananda gives a powerful speech calling for an end to religious fundamentalism, intolerance, and bigotry. Jitish Kallat's site-specific installation *Public Notice 3* (2010) runs the text of the speech across the risers of the Woman's Board Grand Staircase.

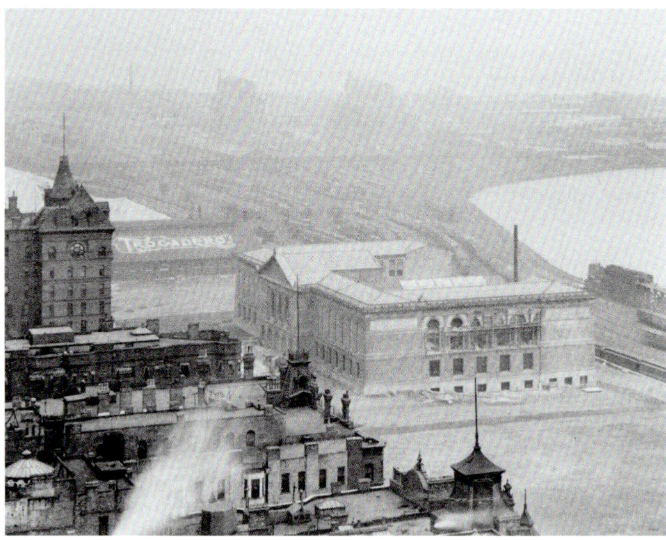

1893 The *Chicago Tribune* describes the new museum building and its holdings as "transformations that delighted the public and afford magnificent views [with] masterpieces from the days of Moses to the present time."

A History of the Art Institute of Chicago

Kate Tierney Powell

1871

Located at the edge of the original shoreline of Lake Michigan, the Art Institute of Chicago site occupies a landfill created in the 1870s with debris from the Great Chicago Fire of 1871. These artificial lands encroach on the waters of Lake Michigan—a name derived from the Ojibwe word *mishigamaa*, meaning "large water." The museum is located on the traditional, unceded homelands of the Council of the Three Fires: the Ojibwe, Odawa, and Potawatomi nations.

1879

On May 24, the Academy of Design, which had been established in 1866 by a group of artists, changes its name to the Chicago Academy of Fine Arts. It is renamed the Art Institute of Chicago in 1882, and the School of the Art Institute of Chicago (SAIC) name follows. The institution occupies a site at the corner of Michigan Avenue and Van Buren Street.

1892

In February construction begins on a new building on Michigan Avenue at Adams Street. Designed by Boston architectural firm Shepley, Rutan, and Coolidge and planned in cooperation with the 1893 World's Columbian Exposition, the Allerton Building, as it will later be named, first hosts the World's Congress Auxiliary of the Columbian Exposition.

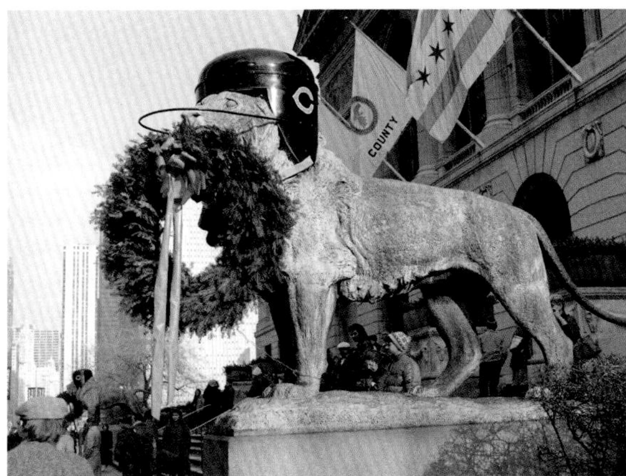

1894 Edward Kemeys's lion sculptures are installed at the Michigan Avenue entrance. The Art Institute lions have long been a celebrated mascot of the city. Here, they wear football helmets made from Weber grills to support the Chicago Bears as they advance toward their Super Bowl XX win, December 1985.

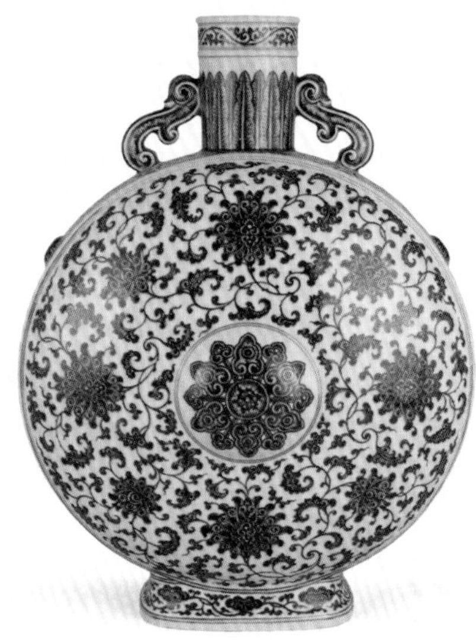

1900 Samuel Nickerson gives *Moon Flask* (Bianhu) *with Lotus Scroll and Central Floret, Ruyi Mushrooms and Plantain Leaves* (1736–95), a Chinese porcelain vessel from the Qing dynasty.

1893

The new building hosts the 1893 World's Parliament of Religions where Hindu monk Swami Vivekananda gives his famous "Sisters and Brothers of America" speech, calling for religious tolerance. Visitors make pilgrimages to the site to this day. After the World's Columbian Exposition closes on October 31, the Art Institute occupies the building, which formally opens on December 8. Surrounded by later wings, it continues to serve as the main entrance to the museum.

1894

Within a year of opening at its new location, the Art Institute receives its first major gift, a collection of French paintings presented by Florence Lathrop Field Page. Two bronze lions by sculptor Edward Kemeys are installed at the Michigan Avenue entrance. Modeled in active poses, the lion on the north pedestal is "on the prowl," while the south lion is "in an attitude of defiance."

1895

Between March 18 and March 28, the Art Institute hosts Claude Monet's first-ever solo exhibition held in a museum.

1898

Fullerton Hall is added to the north side of the museum's main-floor lobby in an area that had once been an open court. Louis Comfort Tiffany designed the exquisite stained glass dome, which still illuminates the auditorium today.

1900

Chicagoan Samuel Nickerson, who traveled to China and Hong Kong, building an impressive, eclectic collection, donates Chinese and Mughal jades, Chinese ceramics, and Japanese decorative arts, one of the largest early gifts to the museum.

1901

Ryerson Library, designed by Shepley, Rutan, and Coolidge (architects of the Michigan Avenue building), opens. It occupies a former light court of the 1893 structure. Louis J. Millet designs the skylight.

1905

The Assumption of the Virgin by El Greco (see p. 65) comes on the market and artist Mary Cassatt, an admirer of the altarpiece, campaigns to find a home for it in an American museum. Over the course of nineteen months, board president Charles Hutchinson persuades his fellow board members to authorize the acquisition by this then-obscure artist.

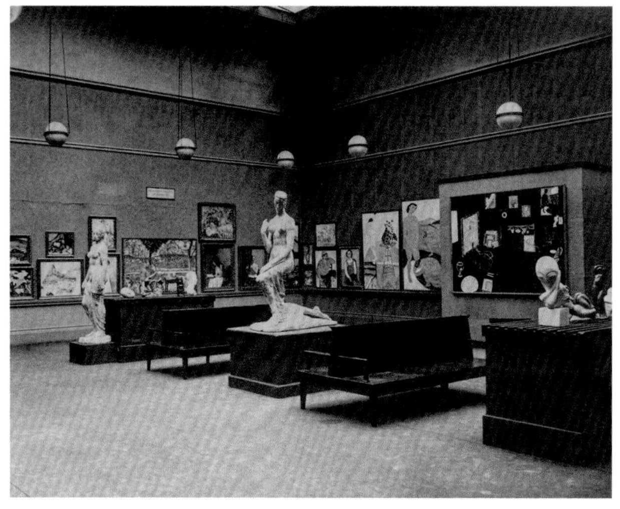

1913 *The Art Institute Bulletin* defends the museum's presentation of the controversial Armory Show: "Question has been raised in some quarters whether the Art Institute does right in exhibiting the strange works of the cubists and post-impressionists. . . . The policy of the Art Institute, however, has always been liberal, and it has been willing to give a hearing to strange and even heretical doctrines, relying upon the inherent ability of the truth ultimately to prevail."

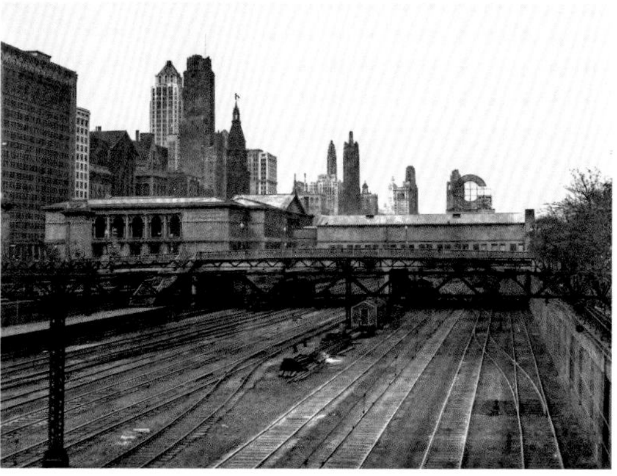

1916 Gunsaulus Hall increases gallery space significantly, enabling the Art Institute to share 40 percent more of its permanent collection and creating a dedicated space for temporary exhibitions.

"The value of an Art Institute should be measured by the services it renders to the community in which it stands. . . . The Art Museum of the past has been set aside. It has been transformed from a cemetery of bric-a-brac to a museum of living thought. The Museum of today is democratic in the best sense of the word."

—President and Director Charles Hutchinson, "The Democracy of Art," 1916

1906

Henry Ossawa Tanner's *Two Disciples at the Tomb* wins a prize at the Annual Exhibition of American Art and becomes the first painting by an African American artist to enter the collection.

1913

From March 24 to April 16, the Art Institute hosts the controversial International Exhibition of Modern Art, better known as the Armory Show. The Armory Show scandalizes visitors in both New York and Chicago, introducing the United States to avant-garde European art. Exhibited the previous month at the Sixty-Ninth Regiment Armory, New York, it is the most comprehensive assemblage of European modern art held in the United States to date and attracts 188,650 visitors in Chicago.

1914

In December the Board of Trustees formally awards Bessie Bennett the title Curator of Decorative Arts, effectively making her the first woman curator in a major museum in the United States.

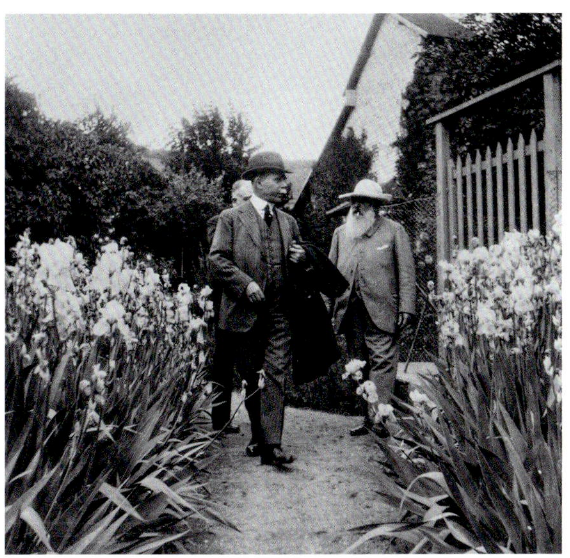

1920 Martin A. Ryerson walks with Claude Monet in the artist's garden at Giverny, France. Ryerson traveled widely through Europe assembling his transformative collection.

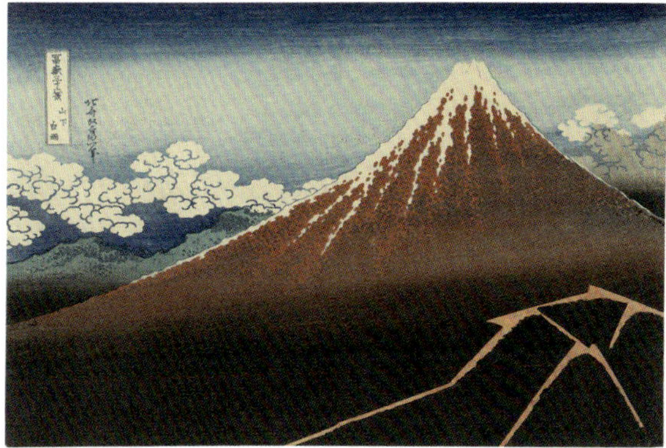

1925 The museum receives the Clarence Buckingham Collection. A highlight of the gift are works by Katsushika Hokusai, the great Japanese artist famous for his woodblock prints of scenes of Mount Fuji.

1916

The museum again expands in order to suitably display a collection that now includes nearly every artistic medium. The bold solution is Gunsaulus Hall, designed by Shepley, Rutan, and Coolidge, a two-story bridge addition over the Illinois Central Railroad tracks bordering the Art Institute's east wall.

1921

Joseph Winterbotham makes an initial gift of $50,000 to the Art Institute with an unusual stipulation: The money will be invested, and the museum will use the interest to build a collection of thirty-five European paintings. Once the first group of thirty-five is assembled, any of these can be sold or exchanged to ensure that "the purchase of paintings, as time goes on, is toward superior works of art and of greater merit and continuous improvement."

1922

Four years after Bertha Honoré Palmer's death, museum leaders and Palmer's sons Honoré Palmer and Potter Palmer II select works from her collection. The museum acquires these works with money she left for this purpose. Her sons also present the museum with works they inherited from their mother. Along with works by French Romantic and Barbizon artists, the Palmer gift brings the first major holdings of French Impressionist art to the museum's collection.

1924–25

The Hutchinson Wing galleries are added east of the Illinois Central Railroad tracks. Additional museum galleries and classrooms are built and include memorials to two young men who died in World War I: the George Alexander McKinlock Jr. Memorial Court (1924) and the Kenneth Sawyer Goodman Theater (1925).

Museum patron Kate Sturges Buckingham donates her collection of medieval sculpture and decorative arts to the museum along with a significant Chinese art collection in honor of her sister Lucy Maud and her brother Clarence's renowned Japanese prints, helping make the museum's Asian collection world-class. In 1927 she also gives Chicago the iconic Buckingham Fountain and establishes a fund for its upkeep.

1926

As a memorial to his second wife, Helen Birch, Frederic Clay Bartlett presents the Art Institute with *A Sunday on La Grande Jatte—1884*, along with over twenty other significant Post-Impressionist paintings. Upon purchasing *La Grande Jatte*, Bartlett reports to museum director Robert Harshe that he has acquired "almost by a miracle . . . the finest modern picture in France." Bartlett will both add to and subtract from the collection in the late 1920s.

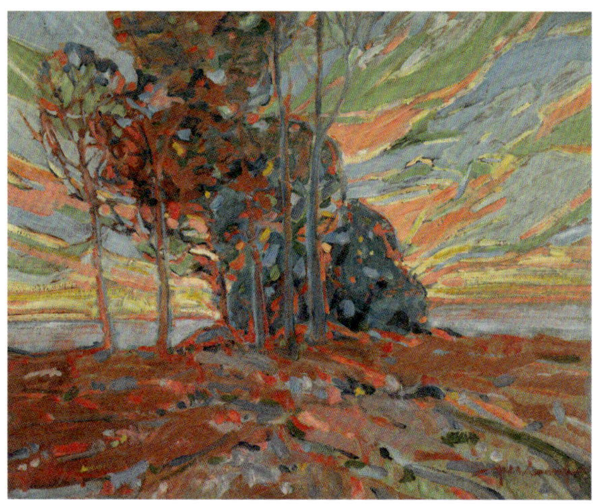

1927 Hale Woodruff's painting *Twilight* (about 1926) is included in an exhibition dedicated to African American artists and to traditional artworks from Africa. The work is eventually acquired by the Art Institute nearly seventy years later.

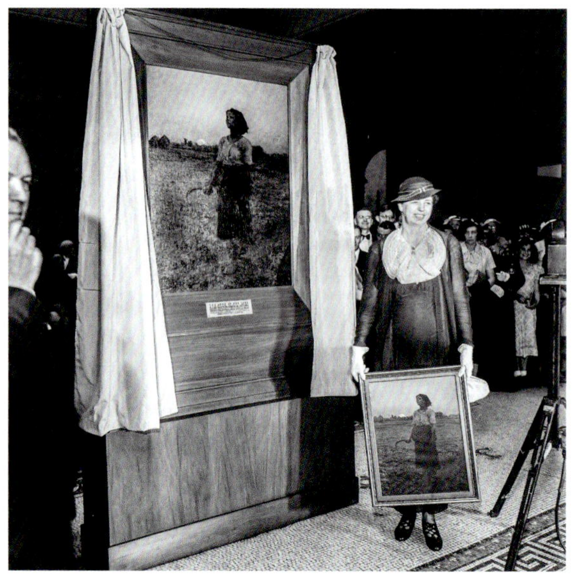

1934 First Lady Eleanor Roosevelt unveils Jules Breton's *Song of the Lark* (1884), named the most popular painting in America in a *Chicago Daily News* contest.

1927

The museum hosts an exhibition dedicated to local and national African American artists, including Henry Ossawa Tanner, Aaron Douglas, and Hale Woodruff. Their paintings are displayed along with traditional African artworks, several of which are purchased and gifted to the museum; these are among the first sub-Saharan African objects to enter the collection.

1931

The Art Institute receives twenty-three objects, including paintings by Expressionists Vasily Kandinsky and Franz Marc, from the estate of Arthur Jerome Eddy, a prominent Chicago lawyer and a pioneering champion of modern art.

1932

Annie Swan Coburn bequeaths to the museum more than one hundred paintings, pastels, and watercolors, many of which are important American, Impressionist, and Post-Impressionist works, including Pierre-Auguste Renoir's *Two Sisters (On the Terrace)* (see p. 129) and Edgar Degas's *Millinery Shop* (see p. 126).

1933

Upon Martin A. Ryerson's death, the Art Institute receives the initial bequest of the Mr. and Mrs. Martin A. Ryerson Collection. This unprecedented gift—totaling over two hundred European and American paintings in addition to textiles, European decorative arts, sculptures, prints, and drawings—remains the greatest single donation of art in the museum's history.

In conjunction with the Century of Progress Exposition commemorating Chicago's centennial, the Art Institute organizes an exhibition of one-thousand-plus works of art from the early Renaissance to the present. The exhibition attracts 1.5 million visitors over five months, making it the highest-attended show in the Art Institute's history. Assembled primarily from North American collections, the show illuminates the progress of art collecting on this side of the Atlantic.

1934

The Century of Progress Exposition proves so popular that it reopens the following year. The Art Institute responds by staging a second loan exhibition, from June 1 to November 1.

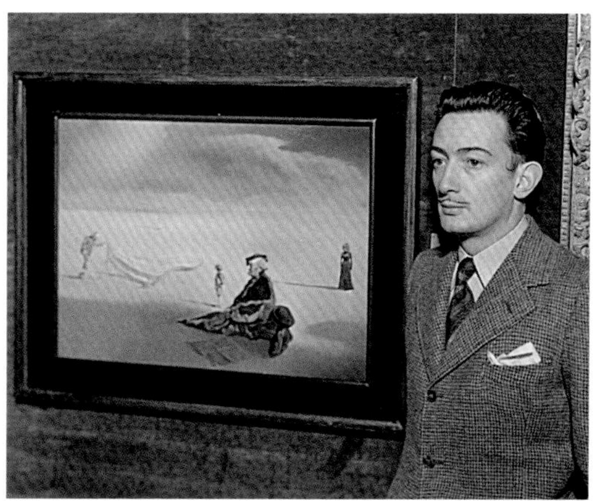

1937 Salvador Dalí poses with his painting *A Chemist Lifting with Extreme Precaution the Cuticle of a Grand Piano* (see p. 189) during a visit to the museum.

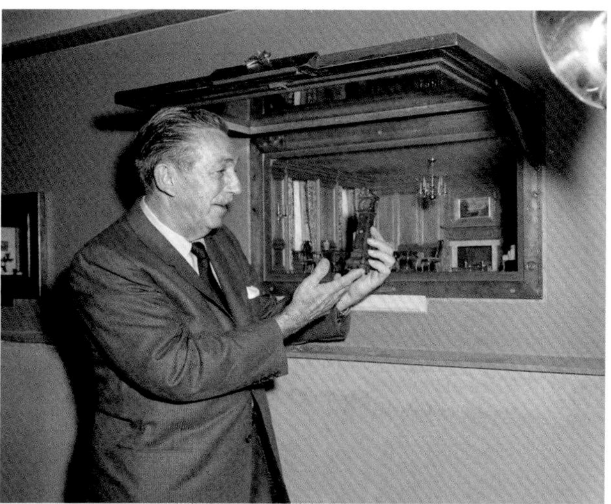

1940 Narcissa Niblack and James Ward Thorne donate the Thorne Miniature Rooms to the Art Institute (see pp. 90–93). Chicago-born Walt Disney, himself a collector of miniatures, takes a peek inside in 1960.

1938

In his first report to the board, Art Institute director Daniel Catton Rich spells out his objectives, which include strengthening the program of museum education and assembling more trained curatorial staff. An advocate of education, he later states that museum education should be made "the core rather than the fringe of a museum program." He believes that education at the museum needs to place greater emphasis on looking at art and less on art history, and that art should be explained in accessible terms.

1940

The museum creates the Society for Contemporary American Art with a mission to collect living American artists, and early gifts from the society include Jackson Pollock's *Greyed Rainbow* (1953) and Joan Mitchell's *City Landscape* (see p. 210). In 1967 it broadens its focus to include international art and becomes the Society for Contemporary Art.

Narcissa Niblack and James Ward Thorne donate the Thorne Miniature Rooms (see pp. 90–93). First exhibited at the Century of Progress, these sixty-eight miniature period rooms designed by Narcissa interpret the history of design and applied arts from the 1200s to 1940. The museum permanently installs them in 1954.

1942

The museum acquires Edward Hopper's *Nighthawks* (see p. 187) the same year it is painted. Hopper writes to Director Daniel Catton Rich, very pleased that *Nighthawks* will join the Art Institute's collection and sharing that he believes it is "one of the very best things I have painted."

1943

An exhibition devoted to Black Chicago artists includes works by Marion Perkins, as well as SAIC alumni Eldzier Cortor, Archibald Motley Jr., and Charles White.

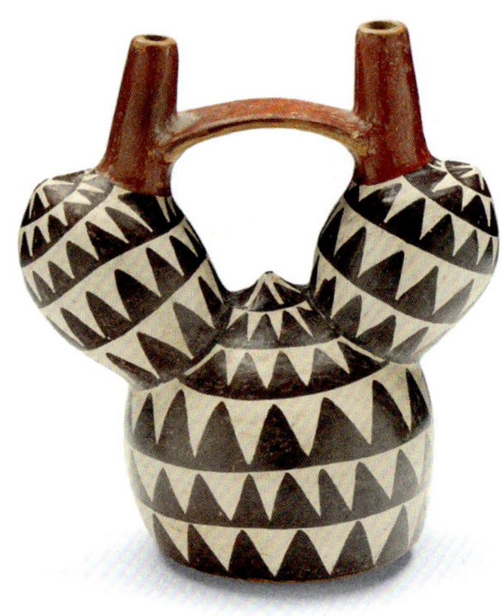

1955 A foundational group of Andean ceramics, textiles, and metalwork enters the Art Institute with the purchase of the Edward Gaffron Collection—then one of the largest private collections of antiquities in Peru. Gaffron, a German ophthalmologist, assembled much of the collection while working in Lima in the late 1800s.

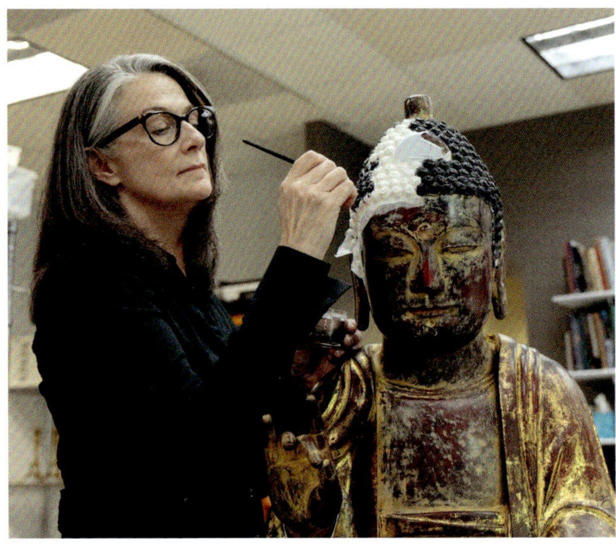

1956 The museum officially establishes a conservation department. Conservator Lisa Ackerman paints the Buddha's recreated hair on this eighteenth-century Korean sculpture in 2024.

"The tradition of the institute since its beginning has been that art is something alive and going on, rather than finished and dead. If it comes to a choice, we would rather have an art merry-go-round than an art morgue.... In much that we have done we have shown contemporary art, with its strange forms and new ideas. This inevitably has resulted in controversy. But this museum, which bought the first El Greco and the first Matisse in America, which hung the first Van Goghs, and installed the first room of modern art in the United States, is not afraid of controversy. It welcomes discussion as a sign of life."

—Director Daniel Catton Rich, 1951

1949

Georgia O'Keeffe gives a transformative gift of modern American art: the Alfred Stieglitz Collection (see p. 163), which effectively seeds the museum's photography collection. The gift also features paintings by O'Keeffe and her circle, along with key modernists such as Diego Rivera. O'Keeffe had been the subject of a major retrospective at the museum in 1943, the museum's first solo exhibition of a female painter.

1952

A group of dedicated women raise money to establish the Art Institute's Emergency Fund for the maintenance of the museum campus and then establish the Woman's Board of the Art Institute, which is devoted to helping the museum be more accessible and responsive to its community, especially to young people.

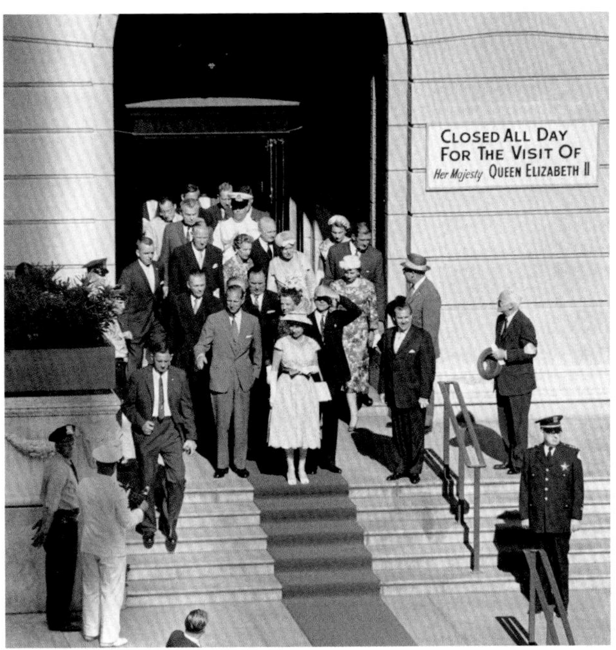

1959 Queen Elizabeth II tours the Art Institute.

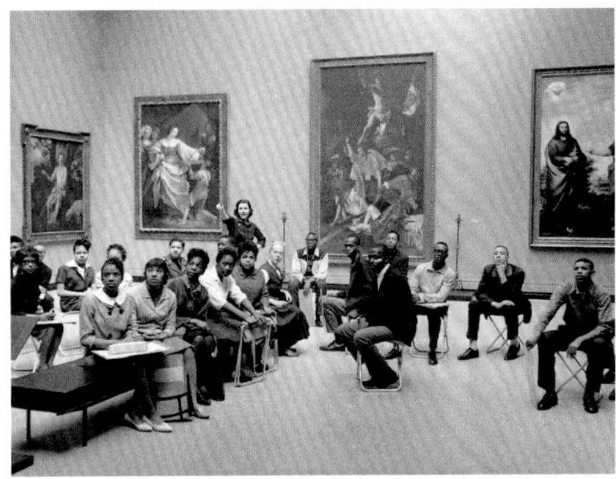

1959 Margaret Dangler, supervisor of children's education, looks at European paintings with a group of Chicago Public School students. Museum education for children increases greatly at this moment, with the museum welcoming more than 21,000 students for gallery tours.

1955

The Art Institute purchases the Edward Gaffron Collection of ancient Peruvian art from his children. In the late 1950s and early 1960s, over 300 ancient Peruvian ceramics from Chicago businessman and museum trustee Nathan Cummings further strengthen the Art Institute's holdings of ancient Andean art, making it the largest collection in a US art museum at that time.

1956

The museum hires its first full-time paintings conservator, Louis Pomerantz, and establishes the department of Conservation. Facilities for paper (1970), textiles (1977), photography (1980), objects (1985), conservation science (2003), and time-based media (2020) come later, along with a growing staff of conservation experts in twelve specialties who are responsible for the preservation, research, and treatment of all objects in the collection.

1957

The museum's first major exhibition dedicated solely to African art features objects from Chicago-based collector Raymond Wielgus, who goes on to donate more than forty works. The Art Institute establishes a new department dedicated to arts of Africa, the Indigenous Americas, and Oceania.

1958

The growth of the professional staff leads to the completion of the first major new structure in more than twenty years: the B. F. Ferguson Memorial Building. These office suites are situated to the north of the original 1893 structure.

A major retrospective of the art of Georges Seurat, including *La Grande Jatte*, travels to the Museum of Modern Art, New York. During the exhibition at MoMA, a fire breaks out in the galleries. Although the painting is unharmed, the Art Institute's trustees decide never to let it leave the museum again.

1959

During a trip to Canada for the official opening of the Saint Lawrence Seaway on June 26, Queen Elizabeth II comes to Chicago, the only United States stop on her itinerary. Over two million spectators gather to catch a glimpse of the queen and Prince Philip, who visit the Art Institute among other sites.

1960

The North Garden, designed by Holabird, Root & Burgee, opens at the corner of Michigan Avenue and Monroe Street.

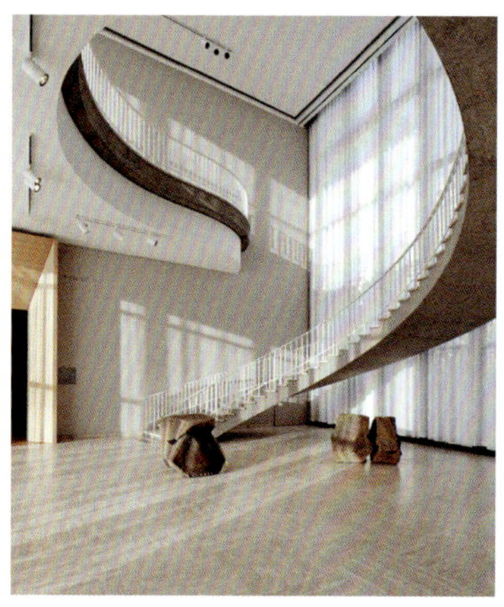

1962 A new two-story, glass-walled gallery enclosing a helical staircase designed by Shaw, Metz, and Associates connects Gunsaulus Hall and east wing galleries with the Morton Wing.

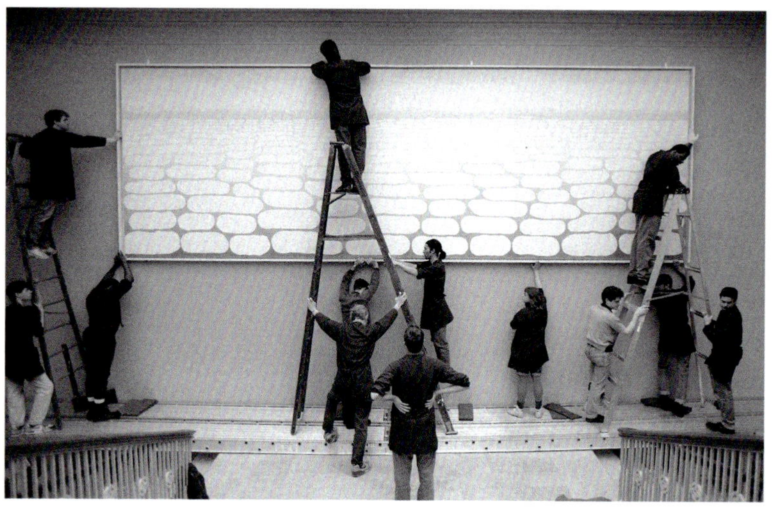

1965 Georgia O'Keeffe finishes *Sky Above Clouds IV*, the largest painting she ever made. She writes, "I painted a painting eight feet high and twenty-four feet wide—It kept me working every minute from 6 A.M. till 8–9 at night. . . . Such a size is of course ridiculous but I had it in my head as something I wanted to do for a couple of years so I finally got at it and had a fine time . . ." The painting comes to the Art Institute in 1983, in part as a gift of the artist.

"A museum isn't here to teach art history; it does something much more important than that. Art is [an] intense personal experience, and the essential thing is to understand the meaning of that experience."

—Director James Wood, 1980

1962

Shaw, Metz, and Associates of Chicago design the Morton Wing, erected to the south of the Michigan Avenue building, to house the expanding modern art collection and restore symmetry to the complex.

1964

Under the leadership of John Maxon, director from 1958 to 1965, the Art Institute acquires Gustave Caillebotte's masterpiece *Paris Street; Rainy Day* (see p. 119), which quickly becomes an Art Institute favorite.

1965

The Stanley McCormick Memorial Court (South Garden), designed by Dan Kiley, opens. A centerpiece of the garden is Lorado Taft's *Fountain of the Great Lakes* (1907–13), which is moved from its original location, facing south closer to the intersection of Jackson Drive and Michigan Avenue.

1974–76

The museum creates the departments of Classical Art, Photographs, and American Arts to support well-established collections in those areas.

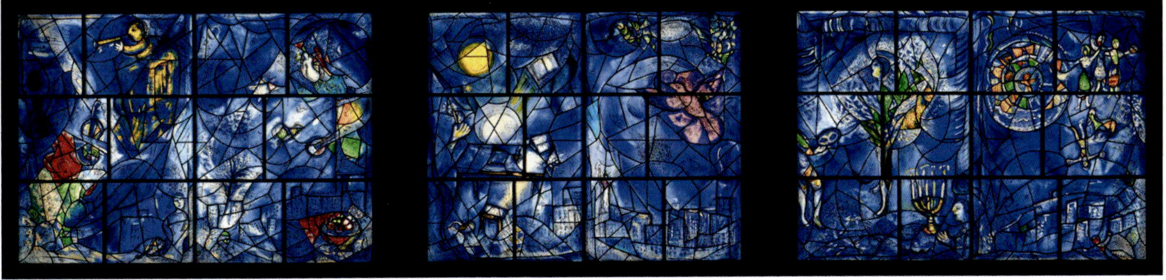

1977 In honor of the United States' bicentennial in 1976, Marc Chagall's stained-glass *America Windows* celebrate the country's artistic achievements across disciplines and include national icons like the Statue of Liberty alongside the Chicago skyline.

1977

An entirely new east side expansion includes new studios, classrooms, and a film center for SAIC as well as new public spaces for the museum. This addition also houses a reconstruction of Louis Sullivan's original Chicago Stock Exchange Trading Room, portions of which were saved from demolition in 1972 and acquired by the museum.

In May the stained-glass *America Windows*, designed by Marc Chagall to commemorate the US Bicentennial and celebrate the arts, freedom, and liberty, are first installed in the west wall of the upper-level McKinlock Court galleries.

1981

The museum establishes the department of Architecture in 1981—only the second of its kind in an American fine arts museum. The newly formed department selects 40,000 drawings "judged to be of artistic value" from the Burnham Library and architectural fragments from existing collections at the museum.

1982

The George F. Harding Collection comes to the Art Institute. The collection consists of decorative arts, American and European paintings, and most famously arms and armor (see pp. 54–57), including exceptional examples that once belonged to Austrian emperors, the royal house of Saxony, the Russian czars, the princes of Liechtenstein and Radziwill, and the English royal family.

1985

Arthur M. Wood Sr., trustee of the Art Institute for several decades and chair of the board from 1978 to 1981, donates Claude Monet's *Stacks of Wheat (End of Summer)* to the Art Institute in honor of his late wife, Pauline Palmer Wood, granddaughter of Potter and Bertha Honoré Palmer. This gift adds a sixth *Stacks of Wheat* canvas to the Art Institute's collection, making it the largest group from a single Monet series to be owned by any museum in the world (see pp. 122–25).

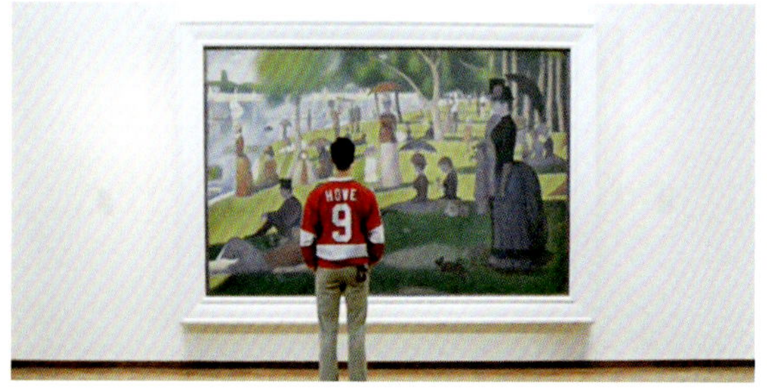

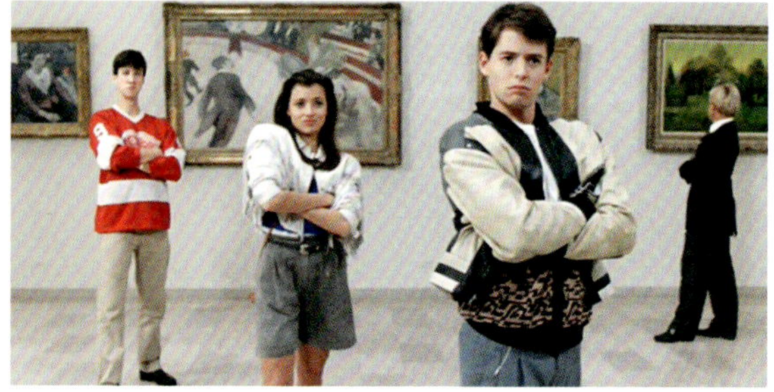

1986 In the film *Ferris Bueller's Day Off*, the titular character and his friends spend time visiting the museum and viewing its collection. Director John Hughes stated that the Art Institute was a "refuge" for him when was in high school. Hughes remarked, "This was a chance for me to go back into this building and show the paintings that were my favorite."

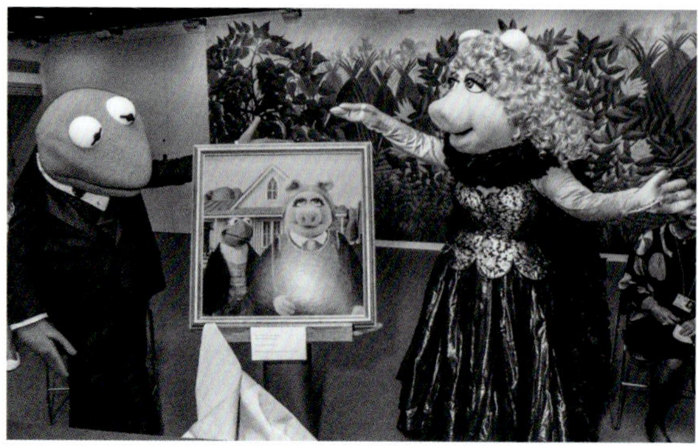

1992 The Junior Museum transforms into the newly renovated Kraft Education Center in 1992. At the opening, Kermit the Frog and Miss Piggy unveil *American Gothique*, a Muppet-inspired version of Grant Wood's famous painting.

1986

The Art Institute has a definitive moment in pop culture when John Hughes's film *Ferris Bueller's Day Off* is released, featuring iconic scenes in the galleries.

1987

The Art Institute's galleries of European Art reopen to the public after a two-year renovation overseen by Chicago architectural firm Skidmore, Owings & Merrill. With the reinstallation, works on paper can be exhibited in the corridor galleries adjacent to the daylit spaces where paintings and sculptures are displayed. This new arrangement of rooms allows viewers to appreciate the work of an artist in a variety of media. The project also includes a renovation of the Art Institute's lobby and Grand Staircase by Chicago architect John Vinci.

1988

The dramatic growth of the contemporary art collection and the popularity of large traveling exhibitions leads to the construction of the Daniel F. and Ada L. Rice Building, which opens in 1988. This expansion houses the museum's largest special exhibition space, Regenstein Hall, until 2026.

1991

On the occasion of the reinstallation of the modern art galleries, trustee Lindy Bergman and her husband Edwin give seventy-seven major works of Dada and Surrealist art, establishing the Art Institute as a major center for Surrealism (see pp. 188–91).

Renovation of the North Garden, designed by landscape architects Hanna/Olin, includes the installation of Alexander Calder's *Flying Dragon*.

1992

Famed Japanese architect Tadao Ando designs his first American space, a gallery for Japanese screens, as part of a new suite of galleries to house the Asian arts collection. The Ando Gallery evokes a traditional Japanese interior with sixteen freestanding wooden columns in a darkened room, framing the art objects displayed in cases around the room's perimeter in an entirely modern way.

1993

The Art Institute celebrates the centennial of its iconic Michigan Avenue building with a story of its greatest works in the exhibition *Chicago's Dream, a World's Treasure: The Art Institute of Chicago 1893–1993*.

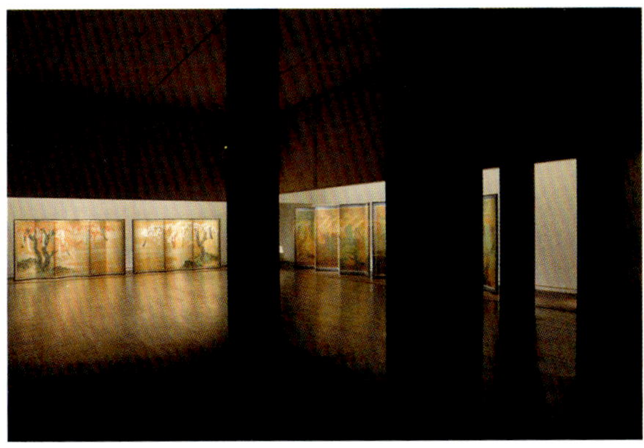

1992 Gallery 109, designed by Japanese architect Tadao Ando, is completed.

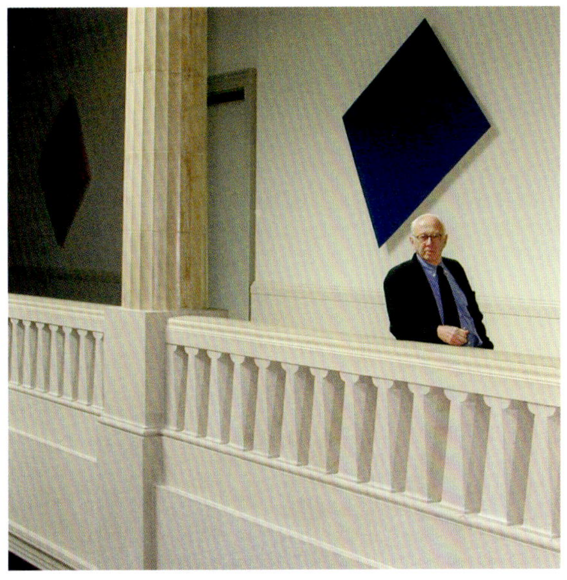

1999 American artist Ellsworth Kelly redefines the second-floor courtyard of the Rice Building with the installation of his six *Chicago Panels*.

1995

Claude Monet: 1840–1926 is seen by nearly one million visitors, making it the second-best-attended exhibition in the museum's history.

2004

Hero, Hawk, and Open Hand: American Indian Art of the Ancient Midwest and South opens. It helps foster a deeper connection between the museum and Indigenous tribes and brings renewed attention to Native American art and archaeology of the United States.

2005

Spurred by the ever-growing permanent collection, the Art Institute begins planning another major expansion. Working with Renzo Piano and his firm, Renzo Piano Building Workshop, the museum breaks ground on the site of the Goodman Theater in 2005 to build the Modern Wing facing Millennium Park.

"To say this is a historic moment in the history of the Art Institute is almost an understatement. What we celebrate on May 16 is nothing less than the reinvention of the Art Institute. With an entire new building devoted to the museum's collection of twentieth- and twenty-first-century art and design, we can now take our place as one of the leading encyclopedic collections in the country that has also remained steadfastly committed to the collecting the art of our time."

—President and Eloise W. Martin Director James Cuno, on the opening of the Modern Wing, 2009

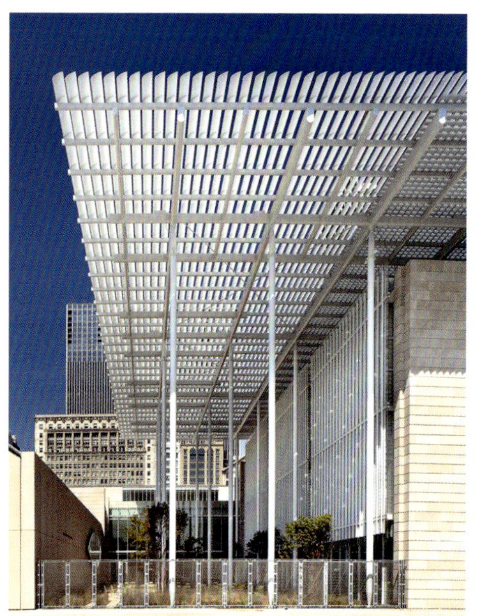

2009 The Modern Wing—the largest expansion in the museum's history—increases the size of the Art Institute to more than one million square feet, making it the second-largest art museum in the United States.

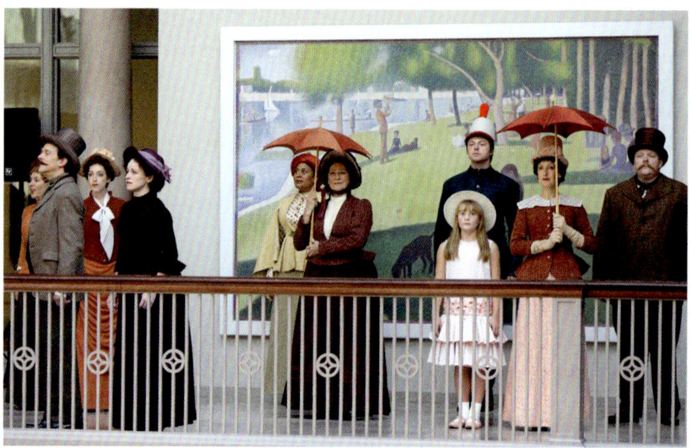

2012 The cast of Chicago Shakespeare Theater's *Sunday in the Park with George* performs at the top of the Grand Staircase in front of a reproduction of Georges Seurat's *Sunday on La Grande Jatte—1884*, the painting that inspired Stephen Sondheim's musical.

2009

The Modern Wing opens. At 264,000 square feet, the addition increases the museum's total size by nearly 35 percent, allowing each curatorial department to display more of their permanent holdings. This addition houses the museum's collections of twentieth- and twenty-first-century art, architecture, design, and photography as well as the Ryan Learning Center, two restaurants, the Bluhm Family Terrace for commissioned installations of contemporary sculpture, and the Nichols Bridgeway, which links the third floor of the Modern Wing to Millennium Park. In concert with the Modern Wing, the former home of the museum's collection of arms and armor is transformed into a sculpture court for Indian and Southeast Asian art, also designed by Renzo Piano.

2010

In the summer, space formerly devoted to contemporary art becomes the new home of galleries dedicated to Native American and pre-Columbian art, as well as galleries focusing on art from across sub-Saharan Africa, presenting the rich diversity of these superb collections in substantially larger spaces.

Redesigned Japanese art galleries open in the new Roger L. and Pamela Weston Wing.

2012

The Mary and Michael Jaharis Galleries of Greek, Roman, and Byzantine Art open. This suite of galleries encircles McKinlock Court with artworks that trace the development of Western art from the dawn of the third millennium BCE to the time of the great Byzantine Empire.

2013

Under the leadership of Director Douglas Druick, the Art Institute receives nearly one thousand works of art in a single gift from Dorothy Braude Edinburg. The Harry B. and Bessie K. Braude Memorial Collection includes approximately 800 works on paper—primarily European prints and drawings from Baroque to modern—and 150 Chinese and Japanese works of art.

2015

Stefan Edlis and Gael Neeson donate forty-four paintings, sculptures, and photographs—including works by Jasper Johns (see p. 212), Takashi Murakami, Robert Rauschenberg, Cindy Sherman, and Andy Warhol—making the Art Institute's contemporary art collection one of the most important in any encyclopedic institution in the world.

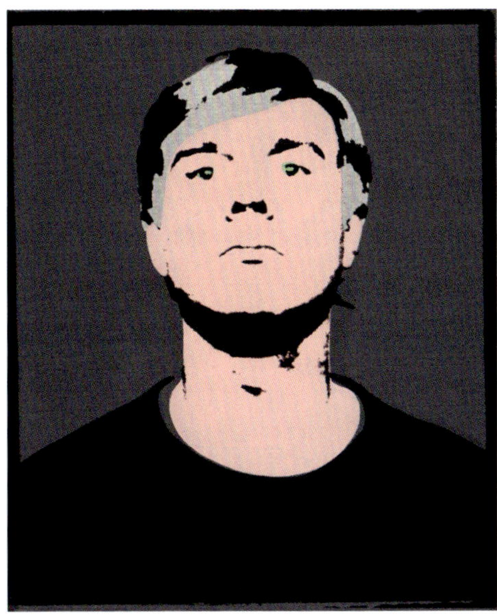

2015 The Edlis Neeson Collection of contemporary artworks, including this 1964 self-portrait by Andy Warhol, is gifted to the Art Institute.

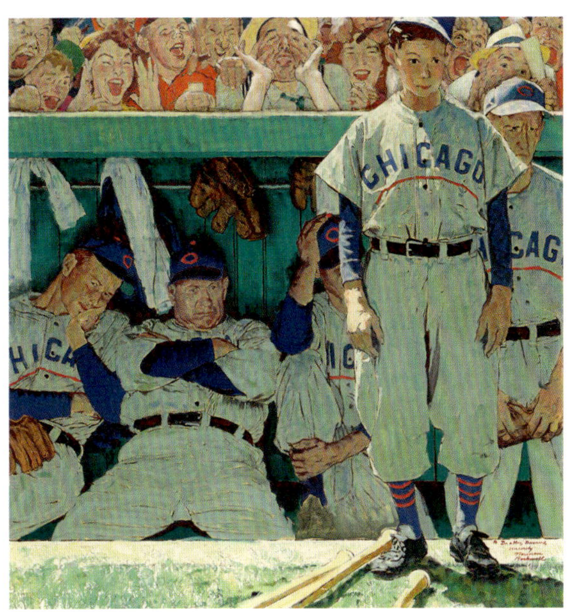

2025 The Art Institute acquires Norman Rockwell's 1948 large-scale study for *The Dugout*, a memorable image of the Chicago Cubs that served as a *Saturday Evening Post* cover that same year. It is the first work by the acclaimed twentieth-century American illustrator to enter the collection.

2018

The Deering Family Galleries open in the Morton Wing, offering an immersive experience of medieval and Renaissance life, including the visitor-favorite arms and armor galleries, with full-size horse sculptures illustrating armor in action (see pp. 54–57).

2019

Looking to the future, President and Eloise W. Martin Director James Rondeau engages the Barcelona-based architectural firm Barozzi Veiga to assess the needs and opportunities for growth for the Art Institute's museum campus.

2025

Working closely with Spanish architecture firm Barozzi Veiga, the Art Institute opens the newly redesigned Eloise W. Martin Galleries featuring highlights of European furniture, silver, ceramics, and glass made between 1600 and 1900.

The Art Institute announces the future Grainger Center of Conservation and Science. Scheduled to open in late 2027, the facility will feature labs, study rooms, and spaces for public viewing.

> "Together with our committed board and exceptional staff, we're ready to guide the Art Institute toward an even more ambitious future—one defined by how creatively we find new and relevant ways to meet our global audiences' expectations, and to empower them to meaningfully engage with works of art."
>
> *—President and Eloise W. Martin Director James Rondeau, 2024*

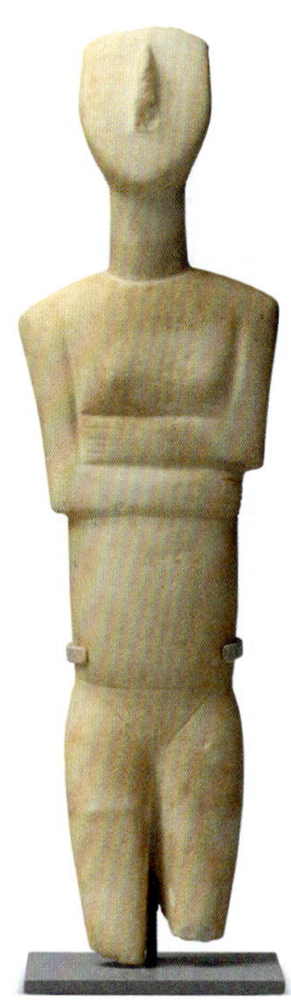

1. **Statuette of a Female Figure**, 2600–2400 BCE, probably island of Keros

This ancient marble sculpture is nearly five thousand years old; yet it feels strikingly modern, perhaps due to its minimal, abstract form. Cycladic (from Greek islands in the southern Aegean Sea) sculptures like this one were a source of inspiration and fascination for early modern artists such as Constantin Brancusi and Amedeo Modigliani, who admired their stark simplicity. But this sleek sculpture's age has disguised its true appearance. Statuettes like this one once had hair, eyes, jewelry, or other ornaments added in red, blue, and black paint, which has long since faded away.

There is another interesting and often overlooked detail missing from this example: its feet. Cycladic figurines of this type typically have pointed toes—like a Barbie doll—making it impossible for them to stand upright on their own. Even so, many museums, including the Art Institute, choose to display them this way. What then was the original function of such a sculpture, if it couldn't stand on its own? Although the original findspot of this sculpture (and almost all others of its kind) has been lost, they are thought to come from graves. Perhaps such sculptures were meant to sleep for eternity along with the deceased? We may never know. *Lisa Ayla Çakmak*

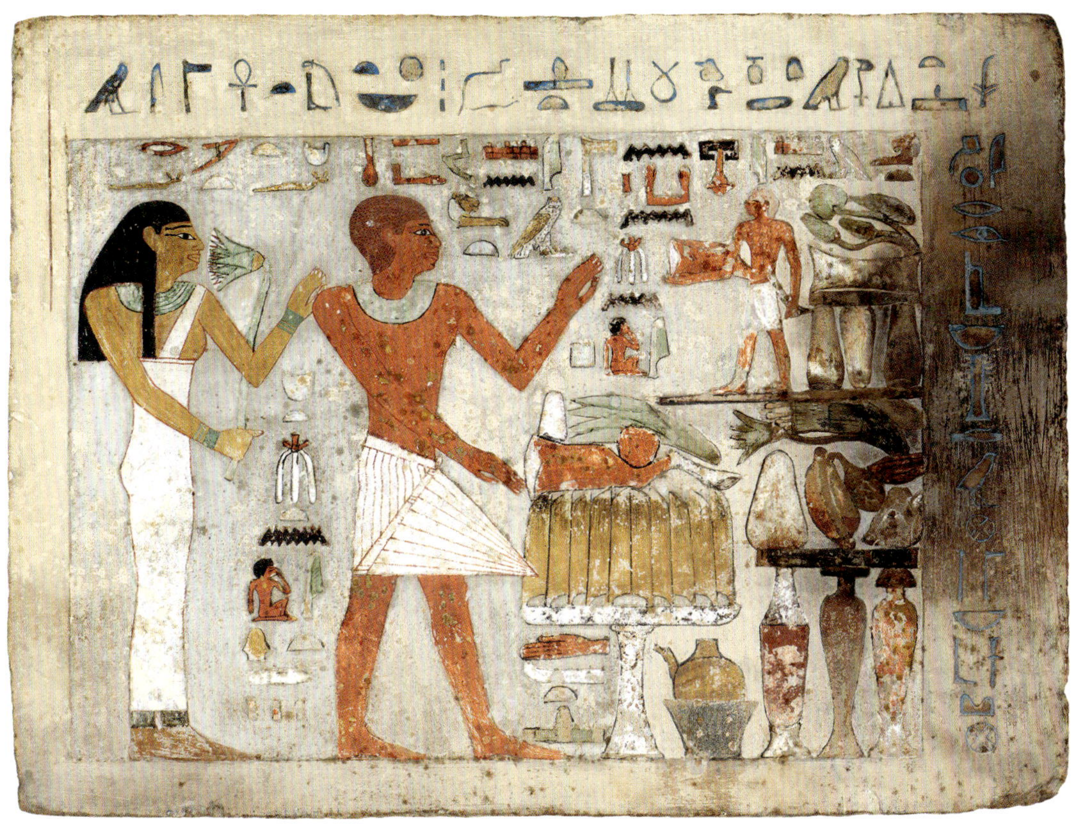

2. **Stela of Amenemhat and Hemet**, about 1956–1877 BCE, Egypt

Standing behind a table laden with tall loaves of bread and other food, Hemet rests her hand on her husband Amenemhat's shoulder on this stela designed to commemorate and sustain the couple for eternity. Hieroglyphs—each painted as an individual image—record the identities of the figures they surround. Following ancient Egyptian artistic conventions, the man presenting the couple with a foreleg of beef in the upper right corner (also named Amenemhat) is proportionally rendered using a smaller scale, underscoring his status secondary to the couple who are the primary focus of this scene.

Carved in shallow raised relief, the signs and images on this stela retain the colorful pigment that is often lost to time, including details such as the stippled texture of Amenemhat's short hair and the feathers on the small owl above his hand, which represents the second *m* sound in his name. Around the upper and right side of the image, sunk relief hieroglyphs filled with Egyptian blue pigment write out the traditional offering formula that, when recited by those viewing the monument, would provide Amenemhat and Hemet access to goods that supported existence in the afterlife, including bread, beer, oxen, and fowl. *Ashley Arico*

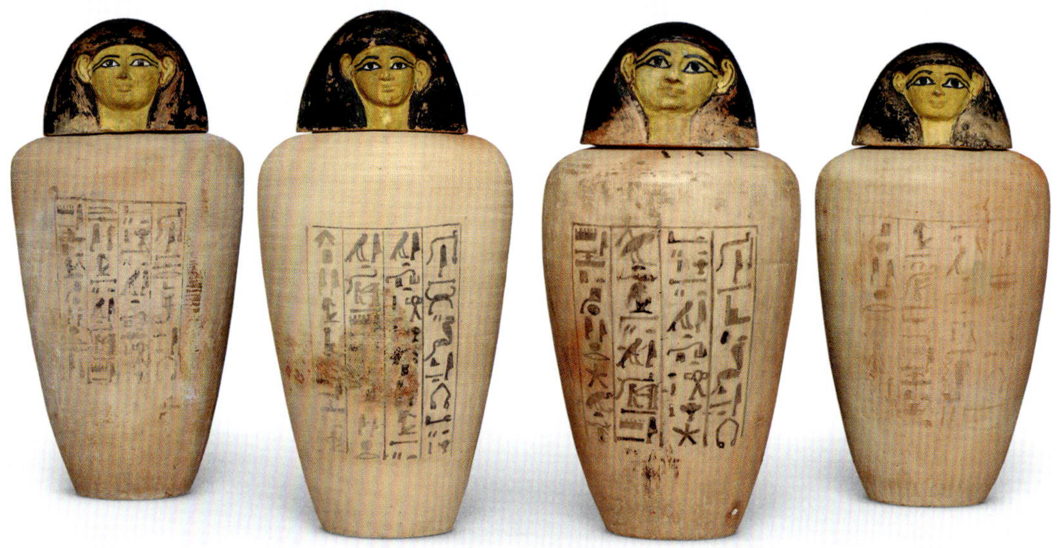

3. **Canopic Jars of Amenhotep**, about 1427–1400 BCE, Egypt

Produced in sets of four, canopic jars safeguarded a deceased Egyptian's intestines, liver, lungs, and stomach, which embalmers removed during the mummification process. On each jar in this complete set, hieroglyphs record a promise to protect the jar's contents uttered by a goddess—Isis, Neith, Nephthys, or Serket—adding an extra layer of defense. Now empty, these jars belonged to the Overseer of the Builders of (the god) Amun Amenhotep, who was buried in Thebes (now Luxor) more than three thousand years ago.

Dome-shaped stoppers, fashioned in the form of human heads with deep black wigs or hair, yellow skin, and large eyes accentuated by elongated cosmetic lines, seal the jars. Sculptors fashioned the ceramic stoppers by hand, lending each face a charming, individual character. An ink notation on the inner rim of each stopper names the goddess whose speech is recorded on the exterior of the corresponding jar. Hidden from view, these brief texts served as a key to ensuring that the stoppers were placed on the correct jars, giving insight into how these funerary objects were produced and used in ancient times. *Ashley Arico*

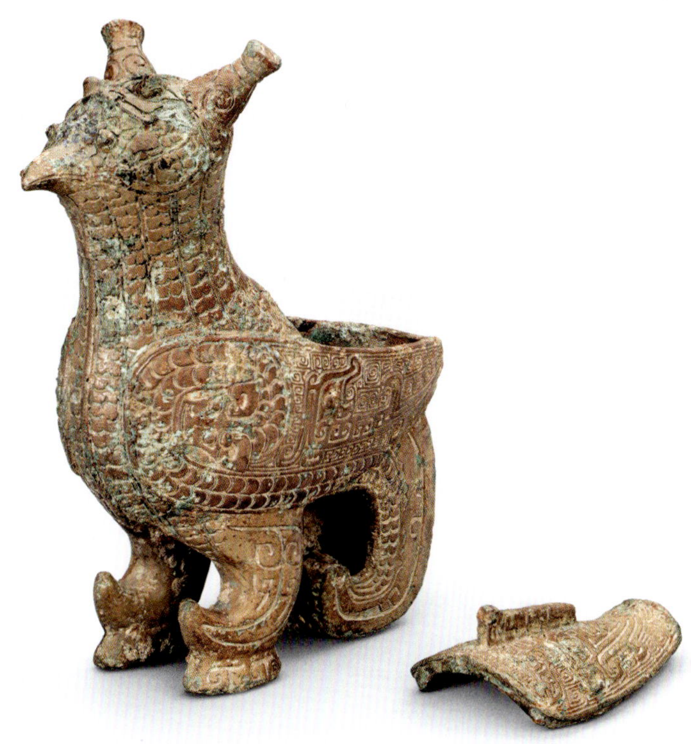

4. Bird-Shaped Container (*Zun*), 13th century–1046 BCE, China

Animal-shaped ritual vessels are among the rarest and most striking bronze objects from the Shang dynasty. This *zun* container takes the form of a fantastical bird, and its body combines naturalistic and imaginative elements. The scale pattern on the neck and tail represents feathers, but the rest of the decoration is richly symbolic rather than lifelike. The bird's overall form may refer to an owl, an animal often associated with mystery or the spirit world and one of the few real animals that appear frequently in Shang bronze design. On its head, the creature has two antennae and the open mouth of a tiger. Each wing is adorned with a dragon in profile and a coiled serpent—creatures often linked to mythical power and transformation. The lid and head feature stylized *taotie* (a monster depicted as a masklike creature), common in Shang ritual art.

Used in ceremonies to honor ancestors or deities, vessels like this zun carried visual messages about sacrifice, reverence, and the supernatural. The layered imagery and sculptural form underscore the significance of ritual and ancestral worship in the early dynasties of ancient China.
Seung Hee Oh

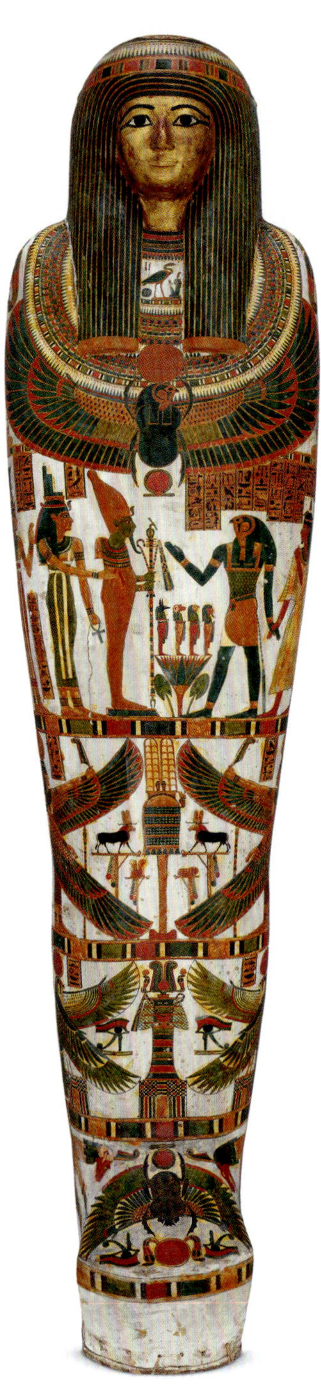

5. **Coffin and Mummy of Paankhaenamun**, about 924–889 BCE, Egypt

Stylishly dressed in a white kilt and sheer pleated tunic, the Doorkeeper in the Temple of (the god) Amun Paankhaenamun walks hand-in-hand with the falcon-headed god Horus, who extends his right arm to introduce the deceased to Osiris, the ruler of the underworld. The scene is painted across the torso of the cartonnage (layers of plaster and textile) coffin case that envelops the mummified Paankhaenamun. For ancient Egyptians, preserving the body through mummification (a ritual process that included desiccation, wrapping with strips of linen, and anointing) helped ensure the deceased's continued existence in the afterlife.

A rich decorative program incorporating deities and hieroglyphic signs—such as the *wedjat* eye (𓂀), which conveys wholeness, and the *djed* pillar (𓊽) representing stability—provides added layers of protection for the deceased during his transition from the realm of the living to the land of the blessed dead. Atop the coffin's feet a winged scarab beetle pushes the dawn sun into a new day. Oriented toward the coffin's gilded face (its color a reflection of Paankhaenamun's new semidivine state), the potent image represents the sun's daily journey of death and rebirth, and expresses the hope that Paankhaenamun too will be reborn. *Ashley Arico*

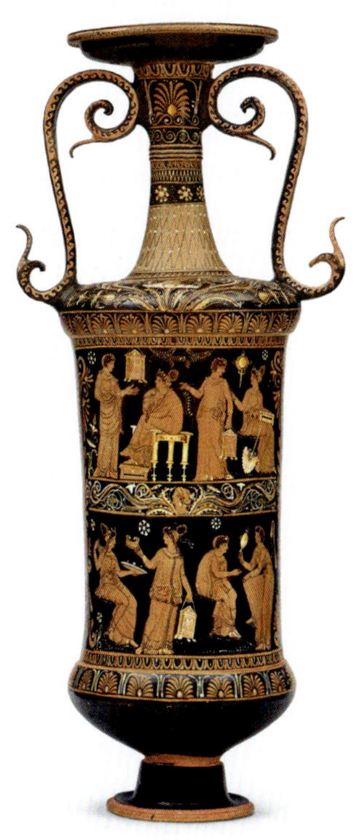

6. Attributed to the Varrese Painter, **Container for Bathwater** (*Loutrophoros*), 350–340 BCE

This type of elegant, elongated vessel, known to ancient Greeks as a *loutrophoros*, was designed to hold water for the sacred bathing of a bride on her wedding day. On one face of the vase, friends and family surround a seated woman, likely the bride. The objects they hold—hand mirrors, jewelry, and perfume flasks—represent the bridal ritual of beautifying and preparing, a practice still carried out today. This vase, however, reveals a tragic alternative. On the opposite side, the four women who prepared the bride reappear surrounding a *naiskos*, a templelike structure that often marked ancient Greek graves, and at the center of the tomb monument stands the bride.

Getting married and raising a family were considered essential parts of an elite woman's life in ancient Greece. When a young woman died before reaching these milestones, a loutrophoros like this one could offer a glimpse into what should have been. The deceased could thus enter the world of the dead having realized society's ambitions for her earthly life. In depicting both her wedding and her funeral, this loutrophoros melds the rituals that defined this young woman's adulthood into a single moment, offering rare insight into the lives of ancient women. *Lisa Ayla Çakmak*

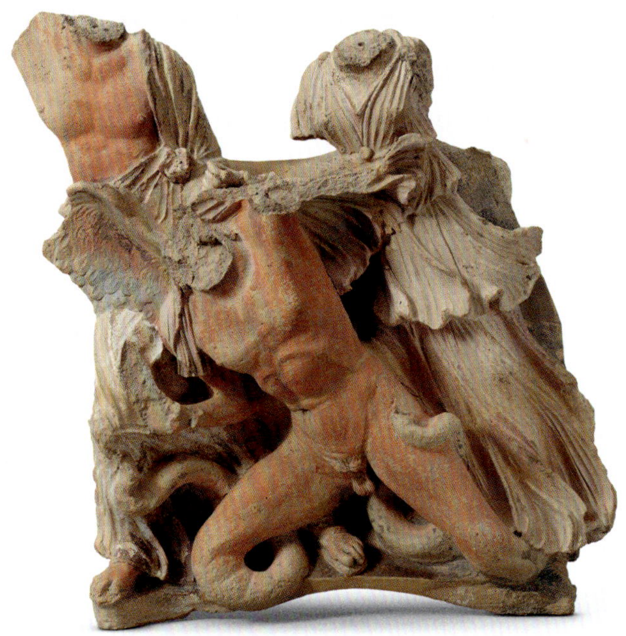

7. **Architectural Relief Depicting the Gigantomachy** (**Battle Between Gods and Giants**), 3rd–2nd century BCE, Etruria

Olympian gods and giants—a mythical race characterized by strength and violence—battle for control of the cosmos in this relief showing a gigantomachy. Two gods struggle with a slender, serpent-legged giant. The artist showed the gods' vigorous movement through their billowing clothing and oblique position. Terracottas such as this one likely adorned the roofs of religious buildings in Etruria, an ancient region of central Italy. Color enlivens the scene, and some remnants of pigment are still visible to the naked eye: ruddy skin tones, vivid purples, blues, cyans, oranges, reds, and pinks. But there is more than the eye can see. Luminescence imaging revealed an exhilarating discovery: A pigment called Egyptian blue covers the dots on the serpent legs of the giant.

For centuries, depictions of the battle between the gods and giants have inspired artists. Scholars have often interpreted this iconography as a symbol of the struggle between order and chaos, divine justice and brute force. As early as the first century BCE, however, the Roman philosopher Lucretius reversed this interpretation. He considered the giants misunderstood heroes challenging the tyranny of superstitious beliefs. This relief is an ancient reminder that the interpretation of art can differ depending on the viewer's perspective. *Giovanni Verri*

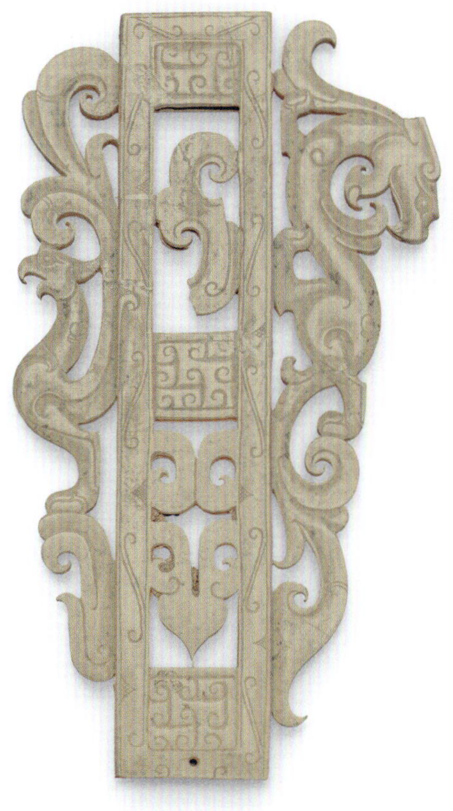

8. **Sheath with Bird and Feline or Dragon**, 3rd–2nd century BCE, China

Carved from one of the most precious materials in ancient China, this finely worked nephrite (jade) sheath reflects the technical mastery and imaginative artistry of the late Warring States period to early Han dynasty. Despite nephrite's extreme hardness, the artisans achieved remarkably fluid lines and subtle modeling using slow, labor-intensive abrasion with tools and mineral paste.

The sheath was once fitted with a single-edged blade inserted into the central channel, creating two layers of visual ornament. On either side of the central opening appear animated mythical creatures: one a long-plumed bird, the other a feline-like dragon. Their mirrored limbs and curling forms suggest both symmetry and vitality. Such fantastical animals were strongly associated with the ruling elite and likely conveyed authority or spiritual protection. Too delicate for combat, this object may have served a ceremonial, decorative, or funerary purpose, intended to reflect the wealth and status of its owner. *Seung Hee Oh*

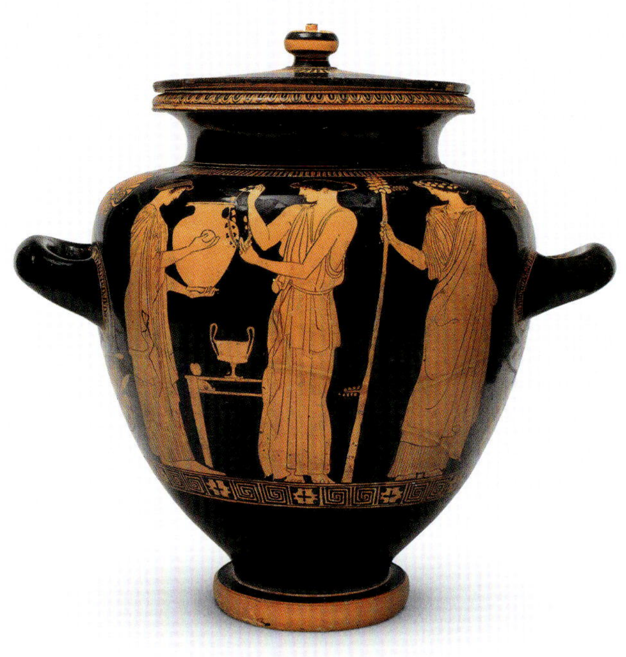

9. Attributed to the Chicago Painter, **Mixing Jar** (*Stamnos*), about 450 BCE

How did an artist living and working in Athens in the fifth century BCE get the name of a city half a world away? It's thanks to one man with an uncanny ability to discern individual artists' styles from the smallest details of their work. Sir John Beazley was single-handedly responsible for hundreds, if not thousands, of artist attributions.

Since most of the painters of ancient Athenian pottery were anonymous, Beazley had to invent a naming system. One system was to select the best example (in his opinion)—the so-called name vase—and name the painter after the city or museum that held that vase. According to Beazley, Chicago held the best example of the Chicago Painter's corpus.

Beazley's work paved the way for many more attributions, which has allowed scholars to understand artists' particular styles. The Chicago Painter often opted for serene scenes of women gathering. Here, we see a group of Greek women or maenads, female participants in rites celebrating Dionysus, the god of wine. But unlike the frenzied and whirling figures of other Greek vases, these women convey a sense of calm, even elegance. The Chicago Painter's pensive subjects refrain from engaging their companions. Instead, they impassively focus on their individual activities. *Lisa Ayla Çakmak*

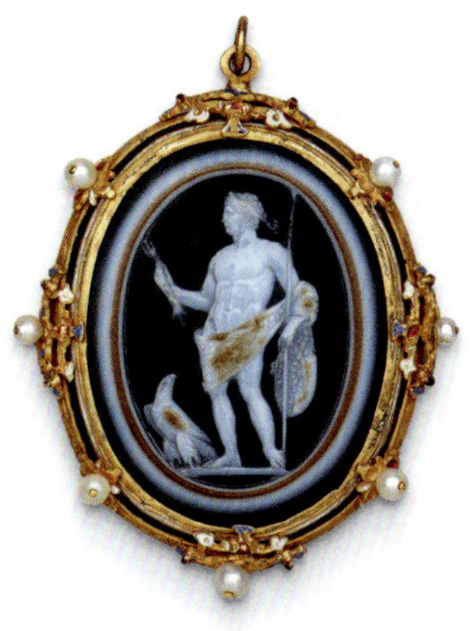

10. **Cameo Portraying Emperor Claudius as Jupiter**, mid-1st century, Rome

Most ancient art is rediscovered by archaeologists after it has been buried for hundreds or thousands of years. In contrast, this cameo (carved gem) has likely been in the hands of collectors continuously since its creation. Carved gems were among the most luxurious art forms in antiquity, prized possessions for individuals to admire or donate as offerings to temple treasuries. This remained true in the Renaissance, when the 1492 collection inventory of leading art patron Lorenzo de' Medici valued some ancient cameos at 500 to 2,000 florins apiece, compared to a Sandro Botticelli painting at ten florins. We can trace the ownership history of this cameo back almost 400 years to a British aristocrat, Thomas Howard, 21st Earl of Arundel.

To make this cameo, a gem carver expertly shaved through a piece of sardonyx with three layers of colors—brown, semitranslucent white, and black—to reveal an image of the Roman god Jupiter. We can identify him by the eagle at his foot and the thunderbolt in his right hand. The exquisite carving even enables us to recognize a portrait in the face of Jupiter—the emperor Claudius (reigned 41–54). I wonder who else might have owned this cameo during its long life—perhaps even the emperor himself? *Stephanie R. Caruso*

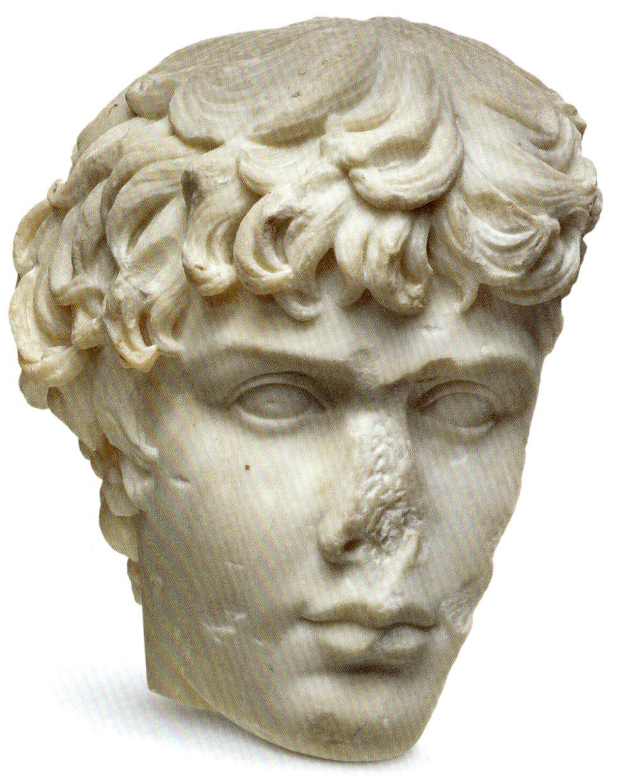

11. Portrait Head of Antinous, about 130–138, Italy

Described in an ancient inscription as a "beautiful youth," Antinous, who lived from about 111 to 130, was the companion and lover of Emperor Hadrian (reigned 117–138). Born in the Roman province of Bithynia in present-day Turkey, he appears to have joined Hadrian's entourage on the emperor's journeys throughout the far-reaching provinces. On a fateful trip to Egypt in 130, Antinous died under mysterious circumstances, perhaps an accidental drowning, while traveling up the Nile River. Devastated by the untimely death, a grief-stricken Hadrian declared Antinous a god—a privilege typically reserved only for the emperor and the imperial family—and instituted religious rites devoted to his worship. Hadrian also founded a city in the youth's honor on the east bank of the Nile, naming it Antinoupolis, or "Antinous-city."

With the spread of Antinous's cult came the production of his portrait in great numbers. He is consistently represented with a set of distinctive features, including an oval face, almond-shaped eyes, full lips, and a tousled hairstyle of thick, wavy locks. These features were essential to his identification in antiquity and remain so today: The Art Institute's portrait, although fragmentary, can be identified as the deified youth based solely on these elements.
Katharine A. Raff

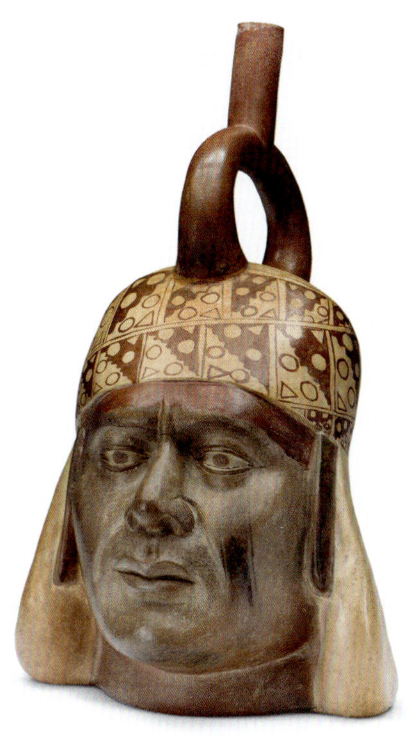

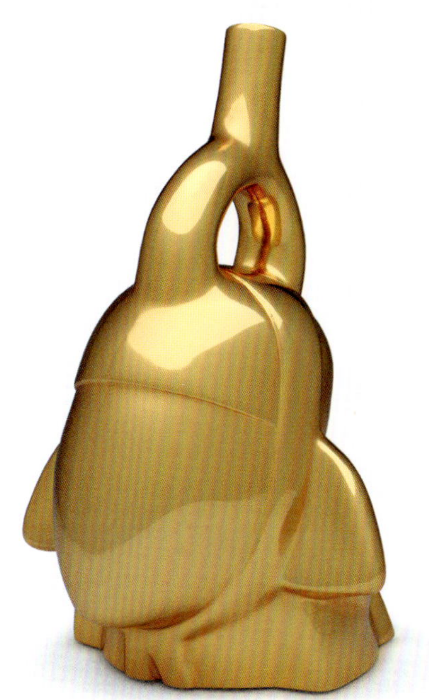

12. **Portrait Vessel**, 600–700, Peru

13. Ana De Orbegoso, **Neo-Huaco #3**, 2017

One of the most remarkable types of ancient Andean ceramics are head-shaped vessels made by Moche artists—such as the very famous example in our collection (left). These vessels may be a rare example of Indigenous portraiture in the Andes. In Peru, such pots are often called *huacos*, derived from the Quechua word *huaca*, which the Incas used for sacred objects and places. In turn, pot-hunters are often called *huaqueros*. While these activities are now prohibited, for much of the twentieth century pot-hunting was a critical livelihood, especially in poorer areas.

Ana De Orbegoso's "new huaco" recalls this complicated past, asking how Peruvians should now relate to their history. Its faceless form recreates a Moche portrait vessel. The mirrored surface allows Peruvian viewers to gaze upon the object and see their own reflection, offering an embodied connection to their ancestors. By transforming the traditional ceramic into a gleaming metallic surface, De Orbegoso calls to mind the lust for gold and silver that fueled Spanish colonialism. This material also alludes to the commodification of Andean antiquities and the contemporary art market. As De Orbegoso has stated, "That's how culture transcends, transforming the past while keeping the roots." *Andrew James Hamilton*

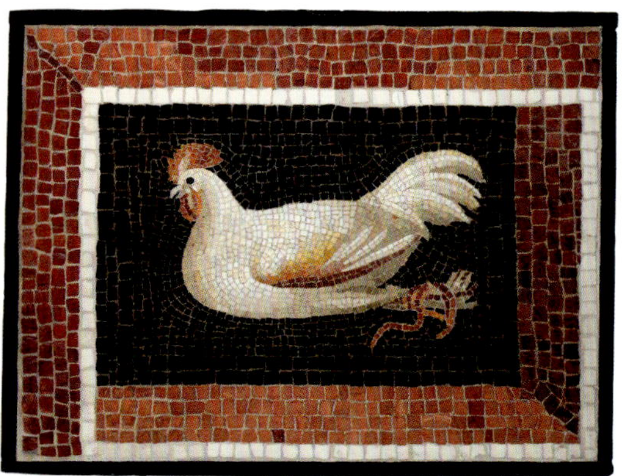
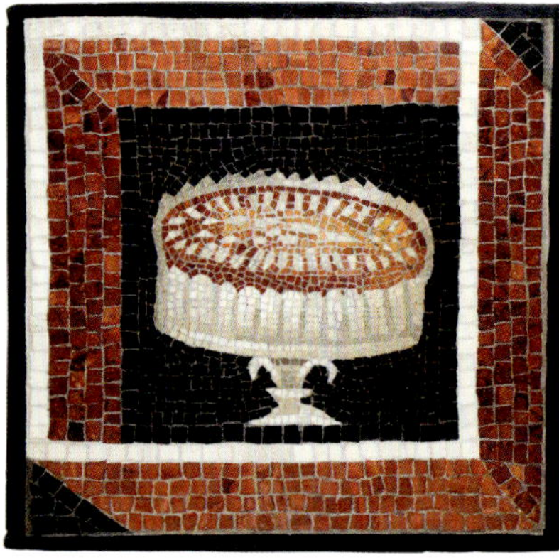
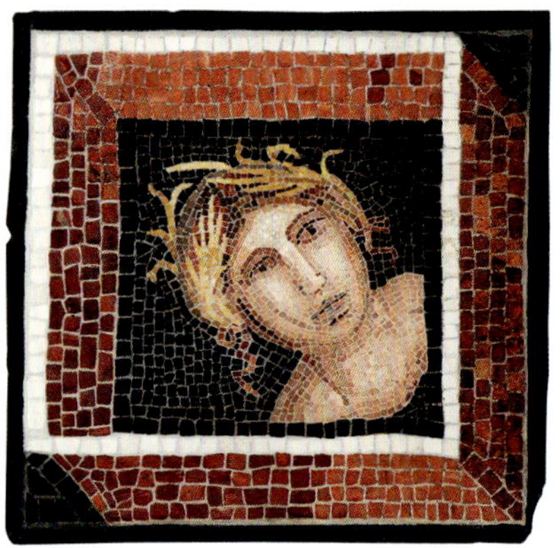
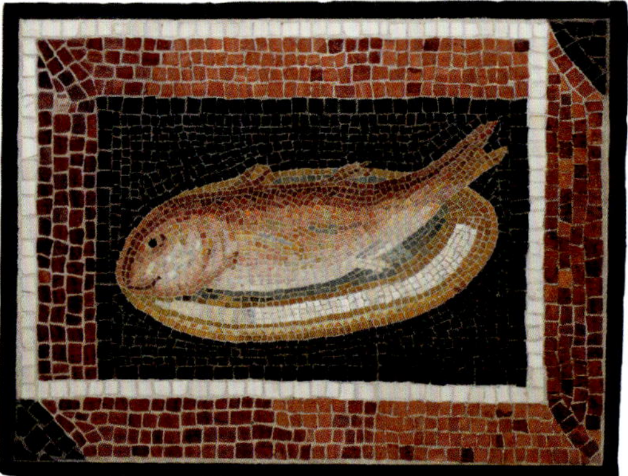

14. **Mosaic Floor Panels**, 2nd century, Rome

Ancient Romans loved a good dinner party. Known as the *convivium* (Latin for "living together"), the banquet was an important social practice among elite Romans, who would entertain friends, colleagues, and business partners in their lavishly adorned homes. Elaborate cuisine was such a critical component of the banquet that the artworks adorning Roman reception spaces often depicted foods and the tableware on which they were served.

These mosaic panels, with their naturalistic rendering and subtle use of color, once belonged to a much larger floor found in Rome in the 1800s. The bust of a female figure, with her crown of grain stalks, is thought to represent autumn. With the other seasons, she might have evoked the renewal of nature. The almond cake, which would have required elaborate preparation by a cook, might reflect the host's prosperity. The two panels depicting animals are my favorites among the group. The trussed rooster might allude to livestock raised on the owner's estates. The fish is a red mullet (*Mullus barbatus*) on a costly metal platter. Red mullets were eaten at extravagant meals and were even raised as pets in private fishponds. For ancient Romans, images like these potentially offered a playful nod to what was on the menu while also conveying a broader message of the hospitality of the host. *Katharine A. Raff*

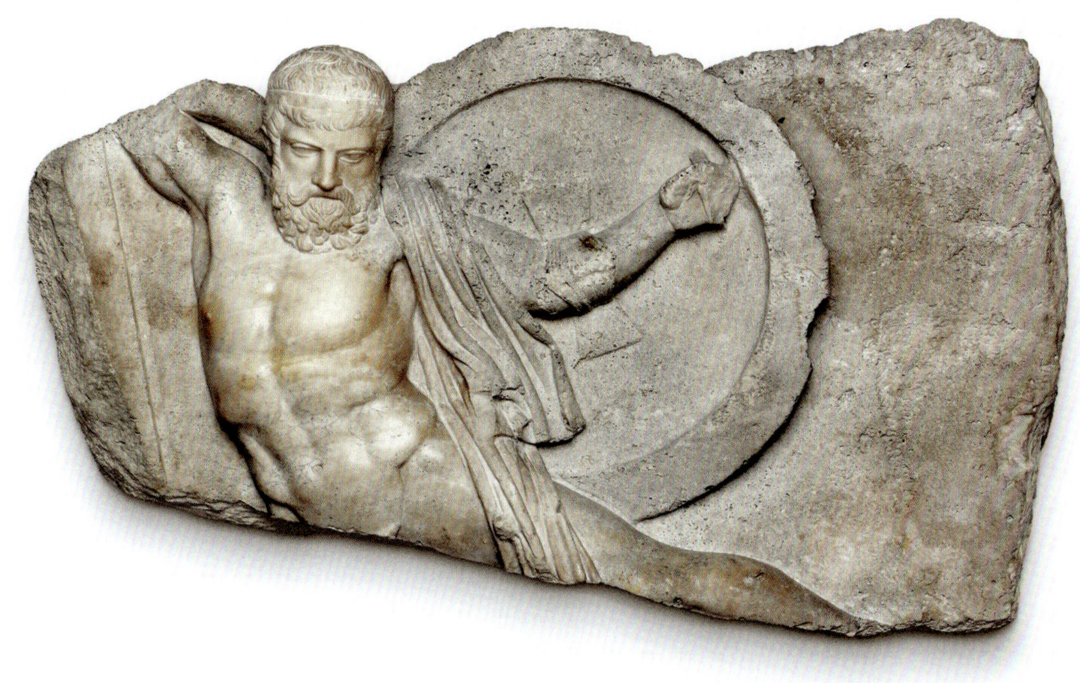

15. **Relief of a Falling Warrior**, 2nd century, Greece

The figure of a wounded Greek warrior seen on this relief originated in the fifth century BCE in Athens, where it first appeared in a mythical scene of Greek soldiers battling the legendary Amazon female warriors. The scene decorated the shield of the monumental cult statue of the goddess Athena, located in the Parthenon. Six centuries later, the same figure was adapted from its original Greek religious context for use on this Roman architectural relief, likely intended for display in a public building or a lavish home. The sculpture never made it to its final destination, however: It was found off the coast of Athens around 1925, centuries after the ancient ship on which it was traveling was presumably destroyed.

Today, the relief's surface bears traces of its extended exposure underwater. Marine organisms bored into the stone and pockmarked the surface of the warrior's left arm, cloak, and shield as well as the relief background. In contrast, much of the figure's muscular torso is strikingly well preserved. This is likely the result of the object's face-down orientation on the seabed, as the higher relief of the torso was pushed deeper into the marine sediment by the weight of the stone.
Katharine A. Raff

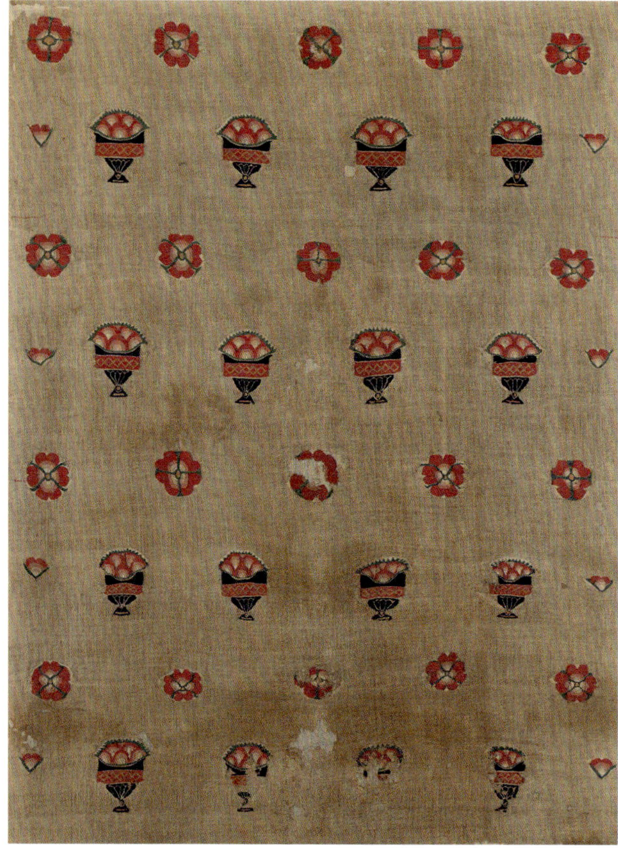

16. **Curtain**, 6th century, Egypt

Byzantine textiles once used in everyday life as clothing or architectural adornment were first discovered in the mid-1800s in Egyptian desert cemeteries, reused to bury the dead. These textiles were deposited in private and public collections but not before most of them were cut up and divided into many smaller pieces. This curtain is a rare example of a Byzantine textile not split after its discovery; the complete width of this textile remains intact as indicated by its preserved edges.

Imagine my surprise to find a matching textile panel in a collection in Karlsruhe, Germany. Not only do the patterns of rosettes and vases filled with fruit or flowers match, but they are also identical in terms of width, weaving technique, and thread count. The German panel helped us understand the missing top of our curtain, which would have included a winged figure holding up a wreath encircling half a portrait. The curtain panels from Germany and Chicago are essentially mirror images. They would have been carefully aligned at the top and hung for the split portrait to be legible. Out of the hundreds of thousands of surviving Byzantine textile fragments, this is only the second-known complete mirrored pair, and it is also the largest. *Stephanie R. Caruso*

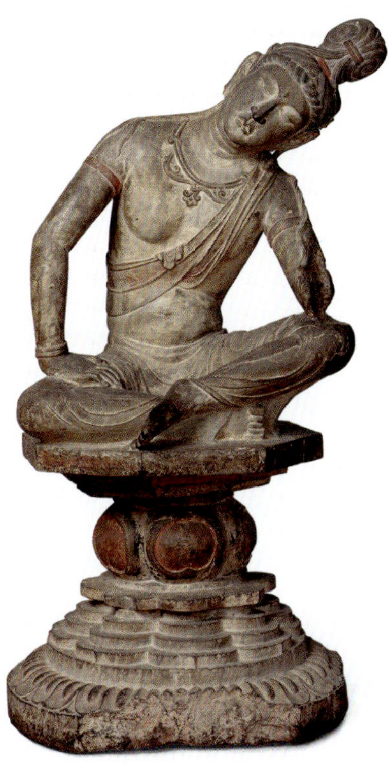

17. Bodhisattva, about 725–50, China

This sculpture reflects a shift in eighth-century China, when Buddhist art began to embrace more humanistic and graceful forms with strong Chinese characteristics. The figure represents a bodhisattva—an enlightened being who chooses to remain in the world to help others achieve spiritual awakening, symbolizing compassion and wisdom. Unlike the more formal and restrained depictions of the Buddha, this bodhisattva is characterized by gentle curves, refined carving, and an elegant sense of movement.

Traces of pigment suggest the figure was once brightly painted, enhancing its lifelike presence. The bodhisattva's missing left arm likely rested lightly against their face in a classic pensive pose, evoking deep contemplation. This pose draws from early images of Prince Siddhartha meditating on human suffering before renouncing his princely life. Over time, such imagery came to be associated with Maitreya, the Buddha of the future, particularly in East Asian traditions. The sculpture's intricate detail and serene posture exemplify the blend of spiritual devotion and artistic innovation that defines Tang dynasty Buddhist art. *Seung Hee Oh*

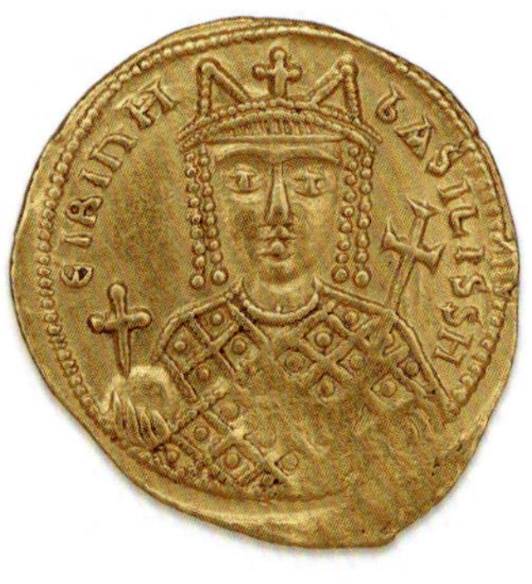

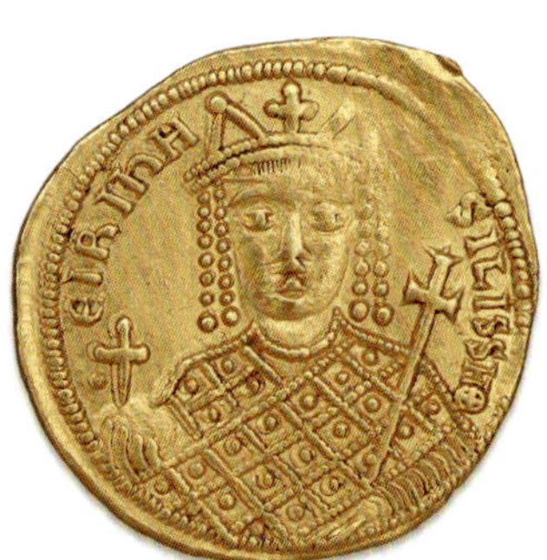

18. Coin (Solidus) of Empress Irene, 797–802, Constantinople

This coin commemorates the first and only time that a woman ruled the Byzantine Empire alone. To emphasize this fact, Empress Irene, who reigned from 797 to 802, took an exceptional approach to coin design. Upon the death of emperor Leo IV (reigned 775–800), Irene became regent for, and then co-ruler with, her son Constantine VI (reigned 780–97) before becoming sole ruler upon his death. Typically, the front (obverse) of a coin portrayed a portrait of the ruler, while the back (reverse) represented a value, deed, or project for which the ruler wanted to be remembered. In this case, the coin design portrays Irene identically on both sides and frames the portrait with an inscription that identifies her as *basilissa*, or empress. This straightforward, frontal portrayal emphasizes Irene's exclusive authority in a medium that would have been seen by many, as coins circulated widely across the empire.

In the ancient world, coins were a critical mode of disseminating messages of imperial authority. As court-sanctioned works of art, coins give us insight into how rulers wanted the public to view them. They were particularly powerful images during the Iconoclastic Controversy (730–843), when few figural representations were produced.
Stephanie R. Caruso

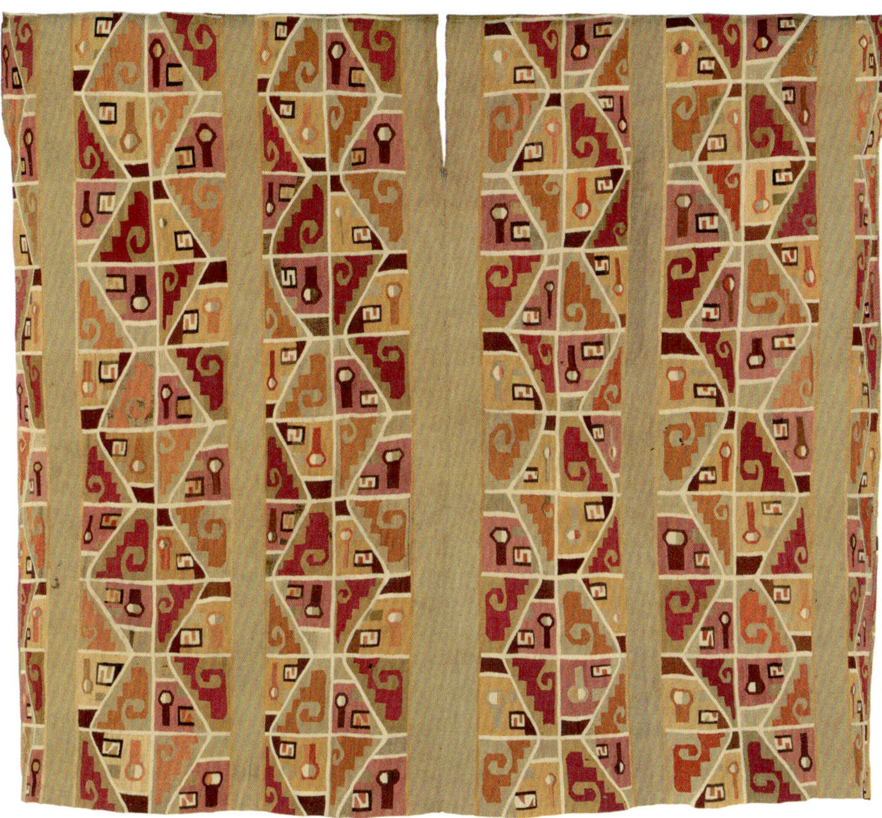

19. Tunic, 600–800, Peru

With its inventive abstractions, this tapestry-woven tunic from the Nazca Valley in Peru showcases the incredibly complex and sumptuous fabrics for which artisans of the Wari Empire were known. Wari textiles have some of the highest thread counts of any handwoven fabric made anywhere in the world. A weaver used an average of seven miles of yarn for each tunic, and the finest examples could contain up to eighteen miles of yarn, far exceeding the density of tapestries created in sixteenth-century Europe.

Tapestry-woven textiles were considered prestige goods in the cosmopolitan and diverse Wari state, along with ceramics and jewelry inlaid with shells, stones, silver, and copper. Their creation required the technical expertise and skills of highly accomplished spinners, dyers, and weavers. Men of the ruling class wore these garments and other adornments in official ceremonies, with specially designated colors, designs, and styles to indicate status and visual alignment with the state. The tunics also served as diplomatic gifts to valued allies. Painted ceramics from the same period show parading warriors who wear tunics of similar design. This could indicate that the symbols and patterns may have carried military or sacrificial significance. *Janet Marion Purdy*

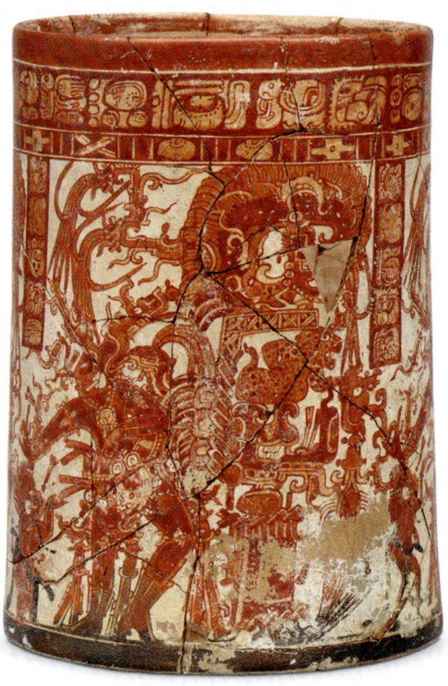

20. Aj Maxam, Vessel with Dancing Maize Gods, 780–810

Ancient Maya kings and elites drank chocolate from tall cylindrical vessels and gifted them as tangible signs of their relationships. These ceramics carry images of royal court activities, mythological events, and otherworldly beings. The painting on this vessel is the work of Aj Maxam from the kingdom of Naranjo (Sa'aal; in present-day Guatemala). Aj Maxam is one of the few ancient Maya artists who inscribed his name on a work of art, and he claimed the title *its'aat*, or "wise person," the same word used to identify supernatural painters and sculptors, suggesting that artists shared the generative power of the gods.

Separated by short, vertical hieroglyphic texts are three nearly identical depictions of the Maya Maize God, whose distinctive elongated forehead is shown in profile. The god's body is overshadowed by his regalia of jade beads, flowing quetzal feathers, a cut-shell belt, and a backrack in which he carries emblems of the cosmos. He raises his left heel and gestures elegantly, signaling that he is dancing. This image recalls a pivotal moment in Maya mythology when the deity emerged out of the earth's surface as a mature maize plant, bringing sustenance to the newly created world. Maya kings regularly associated themselves with the Maize God, embracing the deity's life-giving powers as part of their own claims of rulership. *Elizabeth I. Pope*

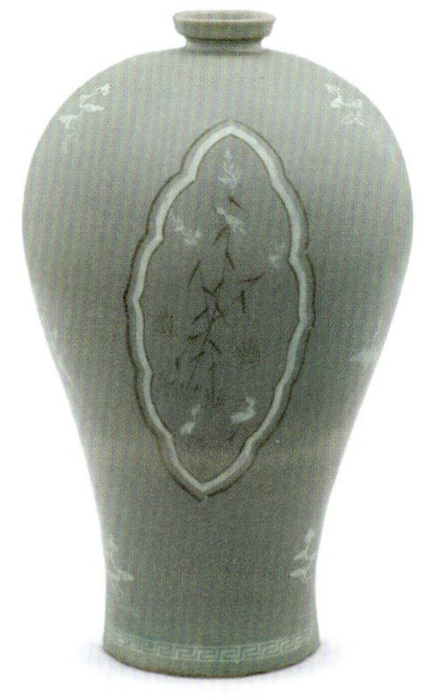

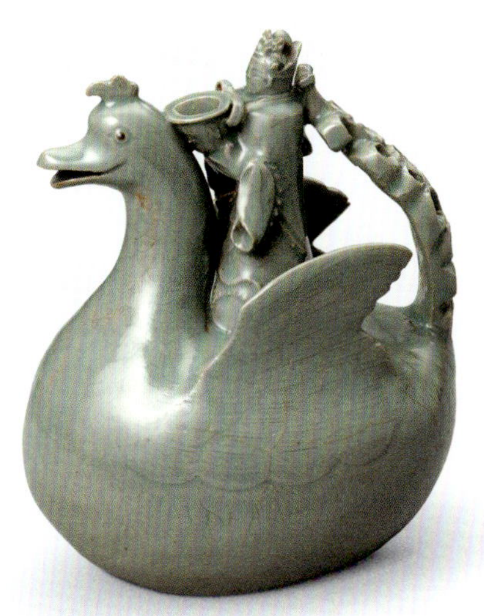

21. **Plum Vase (*Maebyeong*)**, late 12th century, Korea

22. **Duck-Shaped Ewer with Daoist Priest**, 12th century, Korea

Celadon, a grayish stoneware, is a prime example of the exceptional craftsmanship and refined aesthetic sensibilities achieved during the Goryeo dynasty (918–1392) in Korea. This *maebyeong* (plum vase), in particular, exemplifies two distinctive features of Goryeo celadon—the serene jade-green glaze known as *bisaek* and *sanggam*, an inlay technique. The artist used sanggam to decorate the vase: They carved cloud-and-crane motifs and children playing beneath bamboo and willow trees, which represent wishes for longevity and fertility, onto the surface and filled them with colored slip (liquefied clay), before firing the vessel twice.

Goryeo artisans also excelled at making forms modeled after animals, plants, and human figures. This ewer, for example, depicts a priest on a duck with outstretched wings and a raised tail forming a handle. A subtle smile on the bird's face allows wine to flow out. The complex structure of the ewer demonstrates advanced technical skills while its liveliness reflects the Goryeo people's sense of humor. In its carefully rendered details, innovative composition, and beautifully translucent color, this vessel is both a technical tour de force and a playfully charming object for admiration and delight. *Yeonsoo Chee*

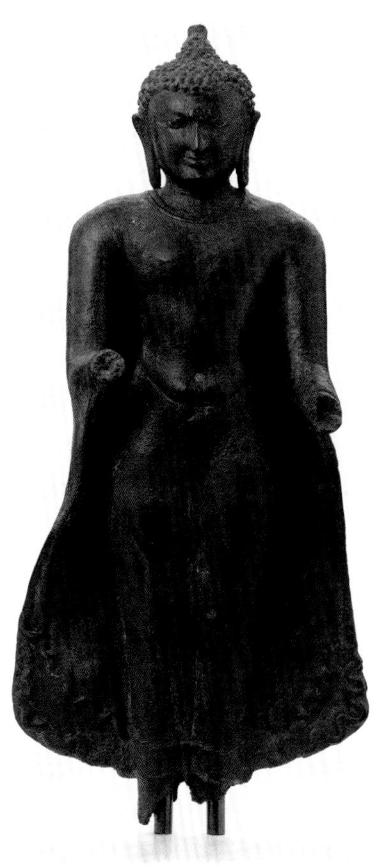

23. **Standing Buddha**, about 12th century, Burma

This standing bronze Buddha, with rare inlaid silver eyes and navel, comes from Pagan, the capital city of an eponymous kingdom that flourished in Burma (now Myanmar) between the ninth and thirteenth centuries. Situated along the Irrawaddy River, Pagan (now Bagan) was once home to thousands of Buddhist temples, monasteries, and stupas (reliquary shrines).

This Buddha has suffered damage to its extremities: The remains of the *ushnisha*, the flame-topped protrusion atop his head, indicate that it would have had a five-pointed flame representing wisdom. The Buddha's missing right hand would probably have been in the gesture of reassurance, and the left hand would have held the ends of his robe. This sculpture reflects similar portable bronze images cast in southeastern India around the same time. The frilled, flaring double hem of the Buddha's monastic robe commonly appears on Buddhist processional bronzes from the trade hub of Nagapattinam on the Coromandel coast of southeastern India. This sculpture attests to robust networks of exchange across the Indian Ocean even one thousand years ago. *Madhuvanti Ghose*

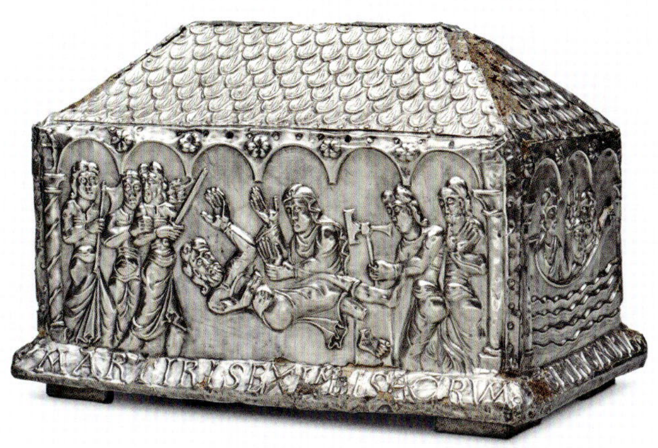

24. Reliquary Casket of Saints Adrian and Natalia, 1100–50, Spain

"Sacred [relic] of the exalted martyr" proclaims a portion of the Latin script at the base of this silver mausoleum-in-miniature. The metal, fluidly hammered and tooled over a wooden casket, captures images that are as sublime as they are hauntingly violent. They tell the tale of Saint Adrian, a fourth-century Imperial Roman guard who converted to Christianity before, as one panel shows, being brutally executed, his limbs hacked off with an axe. Amidst this horror, the central scene shows a tender moment where Adrian's wife, Natalia, rescues his severed hand from the flames of a pyre. On the left side, Natalia is depicted crossing the sea, transporting this now holy hand.

The faithful believed that a portion of Adrian's hand—a relic—was once contained in this chest. This reliquary would have been the focus of prayer and meditation, visited by travelers seeking a miracle or a connection to the holy. The silversmith harnessed the malleability of this material to heighten the experience of those who beheld the reliquary: Its figures are bold, their eyes telling, and their actions visceral. When under the flickering light of a candlelit chapel, it is as if the silver captures movement itself. The story is powerful, and the emotion timeless.
Jonathan Tavares

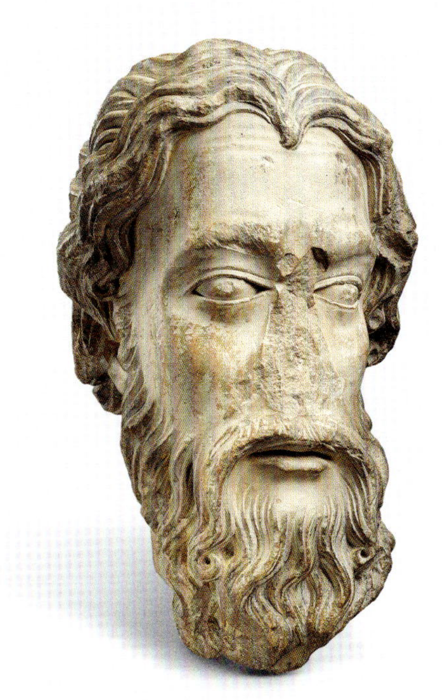

25. **Head of an Apostle**, about 1210, Paris

This elongated head—with its piercing, almond-shaped eyes and prominent mouth with parted lips—projects a commanding presence in limestone, despite its absent body. The unidentified subject likely represents an apostle from the biblical New Testament: Such full-length and larger-than-life-size depictions of Jesus's followers often decorated columns or door jambs in Gothic cathedrals. The stylistic qualities of this head correspond to the architectural decoration produced for the west facade of Notre-Dame Cathedral in Paris around 1200. The symmetry of the head, the locks carved into cascading waves, the leanness of the cheeks, and the physical grandeur lacking emotional content, all resemble sculptures on that part of the building.

The missing nose attests to the head's storied history. It was allegedly excavated in the mid-1800s during the modernization of Paris; revolutionaries might have deliberately damaged and buried it half a century earlier because of the cathedral's long association with the monarchy. This provenance, however, remains unsubstantiated. Neutron activation analysis has shown that the limestone used for this object derives from the same quarry as other figures from Notre-Dame, as well as the cathedral at Sens, about seventy-five miles from Paris. This sculpture awaits further technical, stylistic, and provenance research to verify its origins. *Jacquelyn N. Coutré*

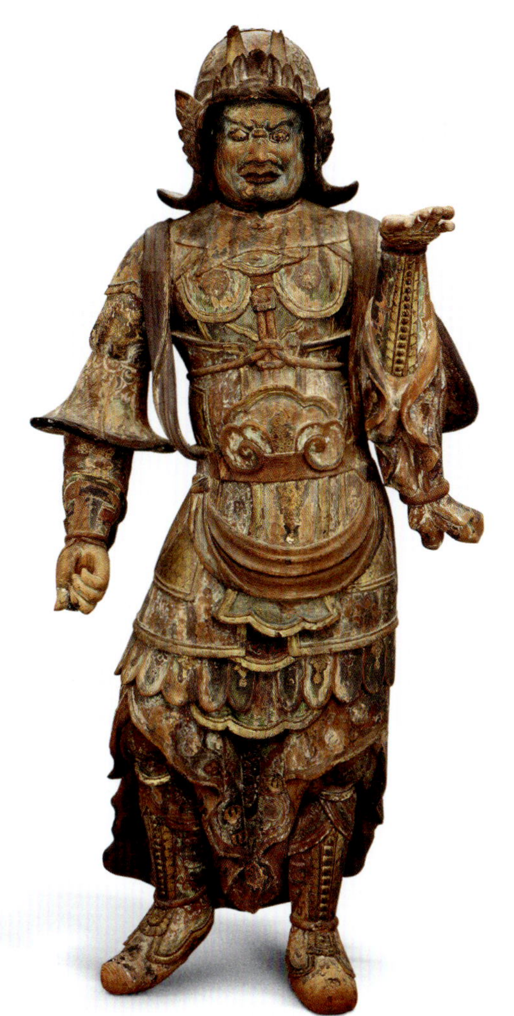

26. **Bishamon**, 11th century, Japan

Due to its early date and great condition, this is one of the Art Institute's most prized works of Japanese Buddhist sculpture. Bishamon (also known as Tamonten or Vaisravana) is the chief of the four guardian deities who protect the cardinal directions in a Buddhist sanctuary. Together, they defend the entire world against evil and promote the seeking of enlightenment. Originally an Indian folk deity later adopted by Buddhism, Bishamon wards off harmful influences to the north.

Glaring at those who pose danger to the Buddhist law, Bishamon is clothed in full armor, ready to take on the Buddha's enemies. The figure is carved from wood in an intricate style that conveys action while also attending to the smallest details of his costume. The dynamic representation of Bishamon's figure—the sway of his hips and the opposing movements of his arms, with his sleeves swinging as if caught in a divine breeze—effectively expresses the guardian's strength and determination. The plated armor is elaborately decorated with dragons, flowers, and other patterns depicted in gold and bright colors, traces of which remain. Bishamon once held a miniature reliquary in the upturned palm of his left hand and a spear in the right, symbolizing his duty to defend the Buddhist law. *Janice Katz*

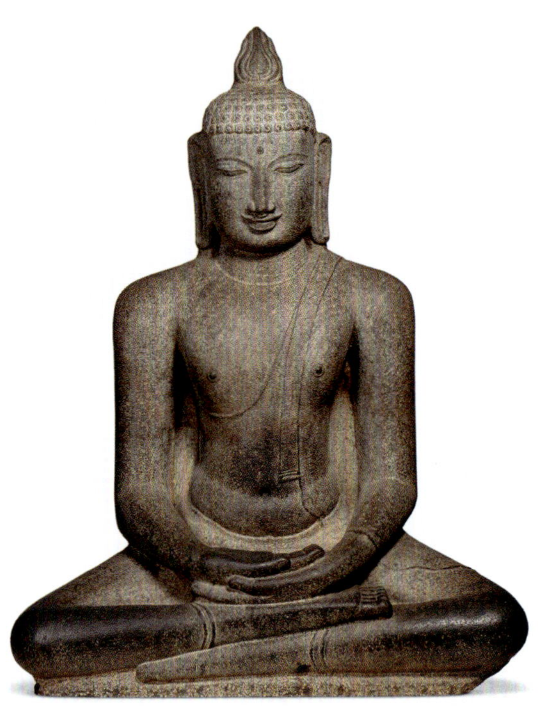

27. Buddha Shakyamuni Seated in Meditation (*Dhyanamudra*), about 12th century, India

This Buddha—with his elongated earlobes, wheel marks on his palms, *urna* (tuft of hair) between his brows, and cranial protuberance covered in snail-shell curls—sits in the posture of meditation with his hands resting on his lap (*dhyanamudra*). He wears a seemingly transparent monastic garment visible only at its edges. This meditating Buddha Shakyamuni comes from the southeastern coast of India, near Nagapattinam. Nagapattinam had a bustling community of monks and merchants from across the Buddhist world; it was an important center of Buddhism from about the eighth to at least the fifteenth century. It was also the primary port and commercial center of the imperial Chola dynasty. As in other images from Nagapattinam, a five-pointed flame emerges from the top of Buddha's head, signifying his wisdom.

This monumental granite sculpture originally would have graced a monastic site, but the weathered Tamil inscription on its back reveals a later, more commonplace use. The recently reinterpreted text indicates that by the seventeenth century this Buddha was being used as a signpost by a pond. It had become simply a surface for a prohibitory notice, its original Buddhist context long forgotten. *Madhuvanti Ghose*

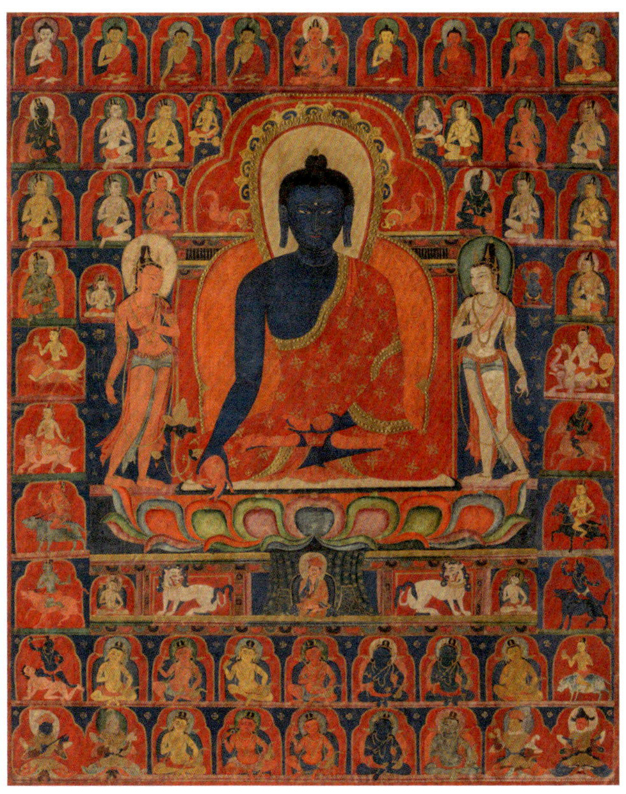

28. Painted Banner (*Thangka*) of the Medicine Buddha (Bhaishajyaguru), 1300s, Central Tibet

Bhaishajyaguru, the Medicine Buddha, presides in this portable scroll painting (*thangka*). The Medicine Buddha is a popular patron of healing in Tibet and a manifestation of the Buddha as master physician who cures suffering caused by the three poisons of desire, aversion, and ignorance.

Bhaishajyaguru's brilliant blue body is reflected in his full title, which means "King with Lapis Lazuli Radiance." The color blue links him to the sky: He is as blue—and his wisdom and compassion are as vast—as the heavens. His left hand rests in his lap in the gesture of meditation (*dhyanamudra*) while his right hand holds a medicinal myrobalan plant, his distinctive attribute. He is flanked by the red Suryaprabha and the white Chandraprabha, bodhisattvas of the sun and moon. The remaining figures are members of Bhaishajyaguru's mandala (entourage), including buddhas in monks' robes, bodhisattvas adorned with jewelry, guardians of the ten directions on animal mounts, yaksha generals bearing mongooses in their left hands, and world protectors in Central Asian dress. The Indian adept Padmasambhava appears wearing a yellow hat directly below Bhaishajyaguru, possibly linking this work to the Nyingma school of Tibetan Buddhism, in which he is honored as a founding figure. *Kris L. Anderson*

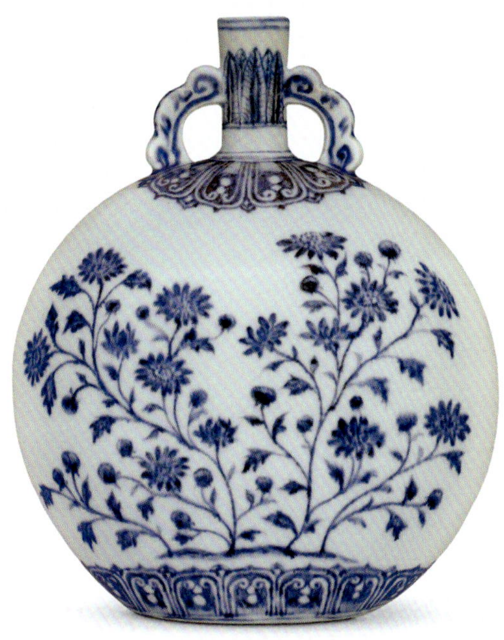

29. Moon Flask (*Bianhu*), 1403–24, China

This oval-shaped vessel, known as a moon flask, derives from a western Asian model but reflects the refined aesthetic and technical innovation of the early Ming dynasty, distinguished by high-quality cobalt pigment and elegantly composed designs. Created under the patronage of the Yongle emperor, the vessel has a graceful form, with a flattened, rounded body and delicate scroll handles, that suggests both strength and elegance.

Each side is decorated with a lush bouquet of flowers—asters on the side shown above, carnations on the other—expertly painted in vibrant cobalt blue. These blooms are framed by lotus-lappet borders, with additional decorative bands on the neck and handles. The precision of the painting and the harmony of the design speak to the exceptional skill of the imperial kilns at Jingdezhen, where such works were made for courtly use or diplomatic gifts. This moon flask's balanced proportions and richly symbolic floral motifs reflect a moment in Chinese ceramic history when artistry, imperial patronage, and foreign influence combined to produce some of the finest porcelain ever made. *Seung Hee Oh*

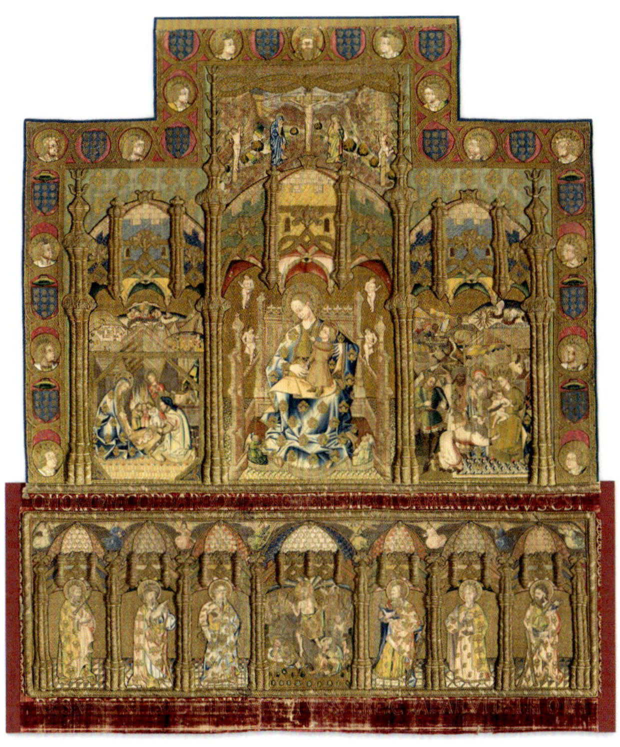

30. **Altarpiece of the Virgin and Child**, 1460–70, Spain

This monumental embroidered altarpiece is a unique survival of 1400s Spain. Altarpieces were a critical focus of worship in the fifteenth-century church. Pedro de Montoya, the bishop of Osma, commissioned this one for the Cathedral of El Burgo de Osma, in the Kingdom of Castile near Aragon. Donors like Montoya expressed their devotion by commissioning items for churches, which also helped them obtain favor in their communities. Today, we associate altarpieces with the media of painting and sculpture; however, textile altarpieces like this were the most sumptuous.

Skilled weavers, embroiderers, and painters worked collaboratively to produce in fiber the images and architecture usually made in paint and carved wood. This altarpiece is a testament to the talent of the artists who manipulated the textile medium to generate resonances with other materials. For example, areas that might have been gilded on a painted or carved altarpiece were here made lustrous with silk and velvet. Artists wrapped silk threads in gilt strips and painstakingly incorporated tiny pearl beads (now mostly lost) to enhance the work's luminosity. These features strengthened the artwork's ability to generate a connection between its patron, the altarpiece's viewers, and the divine. *Stephanie R. Caruso*

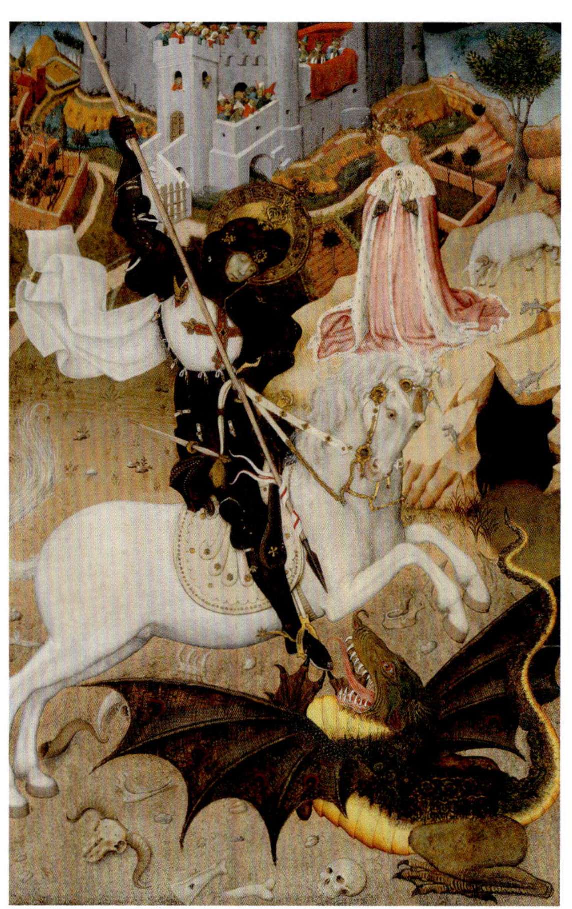

31. Bernat Martorell, **Saint George and the Dragon**, 1434–35

As a model of Christian knighthood, Saint George was a popular figure in the Middle Ages. Artists most frequently represented the episode from his legend in which he slays a dragon and rescues a beautiful princess set to be sacrificed to the beast. The Catalan painter Bernat Martorell included a wealth of detail in his version of the story. Animal and human bones litter the foreground. Lizards—or perhaps baby dragons—crawl around the opening of the dragon's cave. The princess's parents and throngs of onlookers crowd the town's battlements to view the action. Martorell enlivened the physical surface of the painting as well: He richly modeled George's halo and armor and the scaly body of the dragon with raised gesso decoration, and he gave granular texture to the depiction of the sandy foreground.

Saint George and the Dragon was the central panel of an altarpiece devoted to the saint and was originally surrounded by four smaller narrative panels showing his martyrdom (now in the Musée du Louvre, Paris). Martorell probably painted the altarpiece for the chapel of the Barcelona palace of the government of Catalonia, a region whose patron is Saint George. *Rebecca Long*

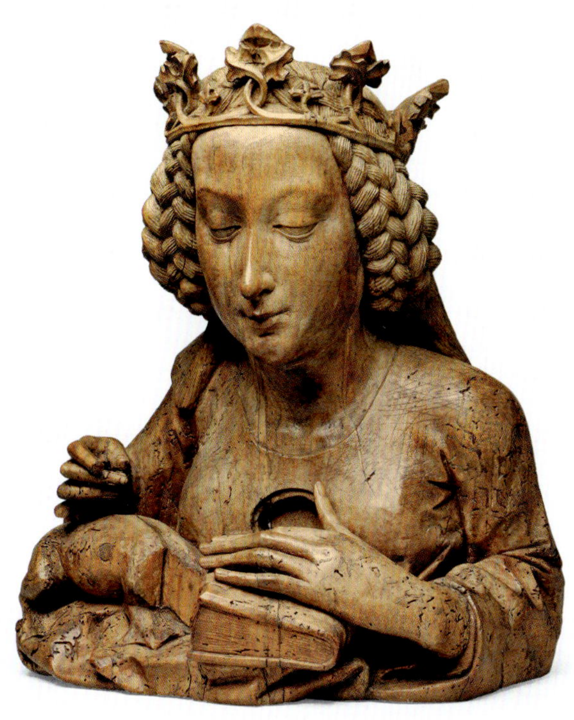

32. Niclaus Gerhaert, **Reliquary Bust of Saint Margaret of Antioch**, about 1470

The now empty space in the chest of this bust of Saint Margaret of Antioch once displayed a relic—an object associated with a saint or martyr. Margaret's hands rest on a book, a symbol of her piety, and a dragon, an allusion to her struggle with Satan disguised as a beast. According to legend, a dragon swallowed her whole after her conversion to Christianity, but after making the sign of the cross, she burst forth from the dragon's belly. She later became the patron saint of women in childbirth. Niclaus Gerhaert, whose female depictions are often characterized by an oval face ending in a round, dimpled chin, introduced an unconventional naturalism into his sculptures, thereby bringing sacred figures closer to the realm of the fifteenth-century viewer.

In its original setting—the Abbey Church of Saints Peter and Paul in Wissembourg, France—this bust was likely accompanied by three others of early martyred women: saints Barbara and Catherine (now in the Metropolitan Museum of Art, New York) and Agnes (Anglesey Abbey, Cambridgeshire, UK). Both Margaret and Agnes are carved in walnut and lean forward with inclined heads, suggesting that they were originally installed next to each other and intended to be seen from below. *Jacquelyn N. Coutré*

Are the Horses Real?

Jonathan Tavares

Questions echo in the gallery: How did they move in those things? Did they really use these? How heavy is that? Were they shorter then? Are those horses real?

With its connection to our own body—designed to either protect, defend, or indeed to assault—there is no wonder the Art Institute's collection of European arms and armor (see fig. 1) draws attention and curiosity.

Armor may seem foreign to our lives, but it is worn today, from tactical vests and firefighting gear to athletic equipment for sports like football, hockey, and lacrosse. Firefighters wear gear that weighs as much as a full armor—around thirty to eighty pounds—although it is not handcrafted or given the same aesthetic considerations as in the sixteenth century. Modern athletic equipment, meanwhile, merges fashion and function much like armor of the past.

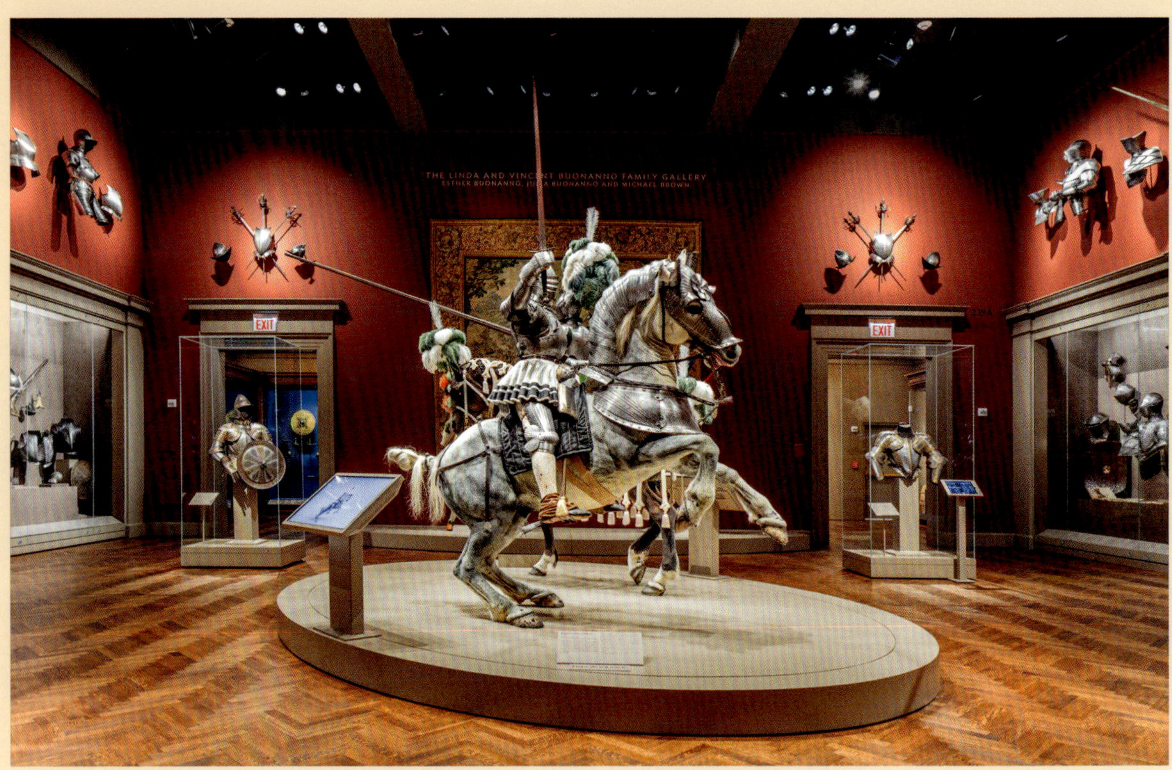

Fig. 1. The Linda and Vincent Buonanno Family Gallery of Arms and Armor, Gallery 239A.

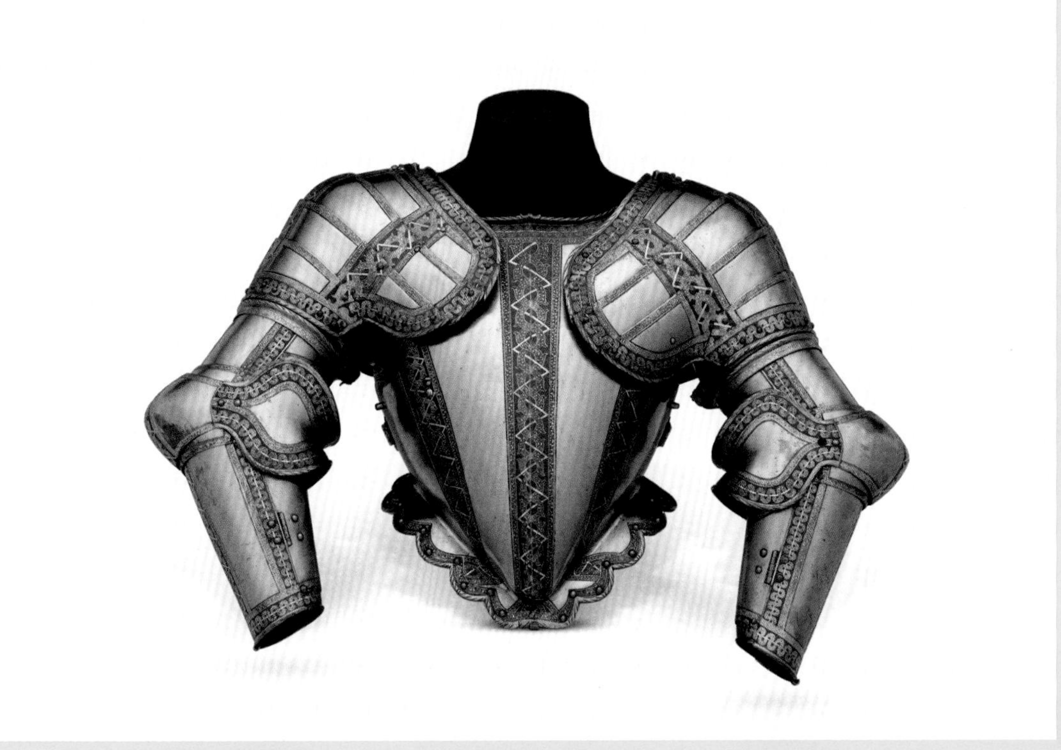

Fig. 2. Portions of a Field Armor, about 1588. Jacob Halder (English, 1558–1608); Royal Workshops of Greenwich, England. Steel, brass, gilding, leather, and silk velvet textile; h. (mounted with arm defenses): 61 cm (30 in.); wt. 17.97 kg (39 lb. 10 oz.). George F. Harding Collection, 1982.2241a–f.

Consider the portions of an armor produced in the Royal Workshops of Greenwich, England, under the reign of Elizabeth I (fig. 2). Its bulbous, long-bellied breastplate with a slim, high waist and broad shoulders demonstrates the peak of fashion in Europe in the 1580s. The extended belly made it impossible to bend over, but this was not just a concession to fashion—the acute angle improved the armor's ability to withstand gunfire. This armor was meant to be used: Its owner, likely William Compton, the Earl of Northampton, would have worn it if the Spanish Armada's invasion of 1588 had reached land, confident in its ability to protect his body as much as promote his status. Incidentally, this armor fits the average five-foot-eight man; indeed, anthropologists have demonstrated that people were in fact not generally smaller several centuries ago!

Form also follows function on tournament armor. One of the rarest pieces in the collection is a massive, twenty-pound jousting helmet from about 1480 (fig. 3). It was once part of an ensemble of armor for the joust, which was fought on horseback with heavy lances. The sport's objective was for the jouster to hit his mounted opponent on the head or a shield-like target worn on the left shoulder.

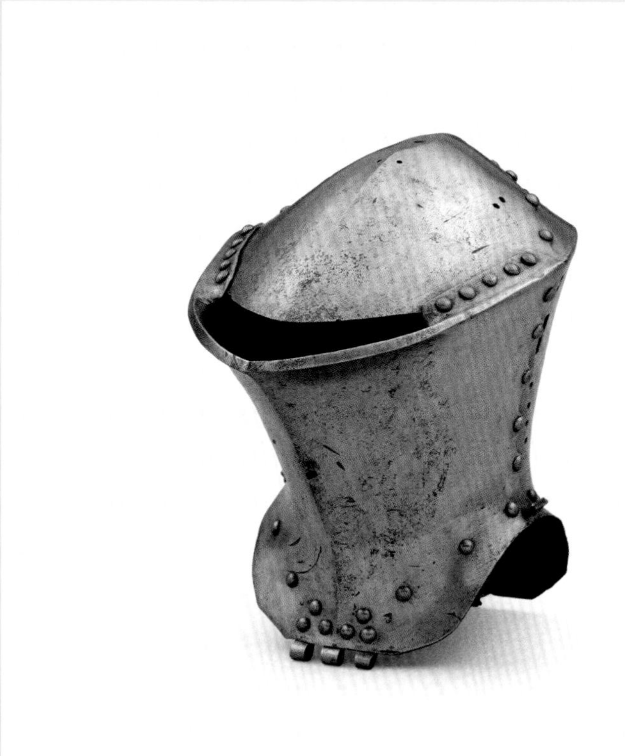

Fig. 3. Jousting Helm (*Stechhelm*), 1480–90. Christian Spor (Austrian, 1464–1495); Innsbruck, Austria. Steel, brass, and paint, 44.5 × 31.8 × 40.6 cm (17½ × 12½ × 16 in.). George F. Harding Collection, 1982.2445.

This helmet, or helm, has large gouges over its prow-shaped front and its vision slit, telltale marks of the blows its wearer endured. The helm, "frog-shaped" and up to half an inch thick, could only be used for jousting—its shape and weight would have been far too limiting in movement, ventilation, and peripheral vision to be worn in battle. It is as much a piece of steel sculpture as it is late medieval sports equipment.

In addition to armor, the Art Institute has one of the finest collections of European luxury firearms in America. There are pieces from the gun cabinets of such rulers as King Louis XIII of France and the Habsburg dynasty. A large group of arms comes from the former collection of the German dukes of Saxe-Weimar-Eisenach. A highlight of these is a carved pair of ivory-stocked pistols produced in Maastricht, the Netherlands, around 1660–70 (fig. 4). There are no more than one hundred known pairs of pistols with similar stocks, and this pair is among the most exuberant. The carvings feature imaginative, fleshy grotesque monsters and, on the butts, bold helmeted heads of the god of war, Mars. African elephant ivory seems an impracticable medium for a working gunstock, as is evidenced by the cracks and losses the pistols have suffered, but the wear on the gunlocks suggests they have been shot.

Almost all of the Art Institute's collection was formed by a Chicagoan, George F. Harding Jr., who acquired many objects from princely collections that were dispersed in Europe in the early 1900s. Active in both real estate and politics, Harding was Chicago's answer to a modern feudal lord who built a castle addition to his home in Hyde Park and opened it to the public as a museum. The walls of his "castle" were dripping with romantic trappings of the past: paintings, sculpture, furniture, and even a cane collection. Most of Harding's museum came to the Art Institute in 1982; the principal treasure was the arms and armor collection, which the museum has preserved for the city of Chicago ever since. The galleries' dioramas of combat on horseback and on foot, the panoplies of arms high on the walls, and the paneled gun cabinets are imbued with the spirit of Harding's legacy.

To answer one last question: the horses in the gallery are not taxidermy. They are fabricated sculptures intended to bring these objects—which were designed to be in motion—to life. These scenes spur our imaginations, allowing us to better understand the fusion of art, fashion, history, politics, science, sport, and technology inherent in arms and armor. Thanks to works like these, a walk in the galleries is a stroll through time and a mirror to our own humanity.

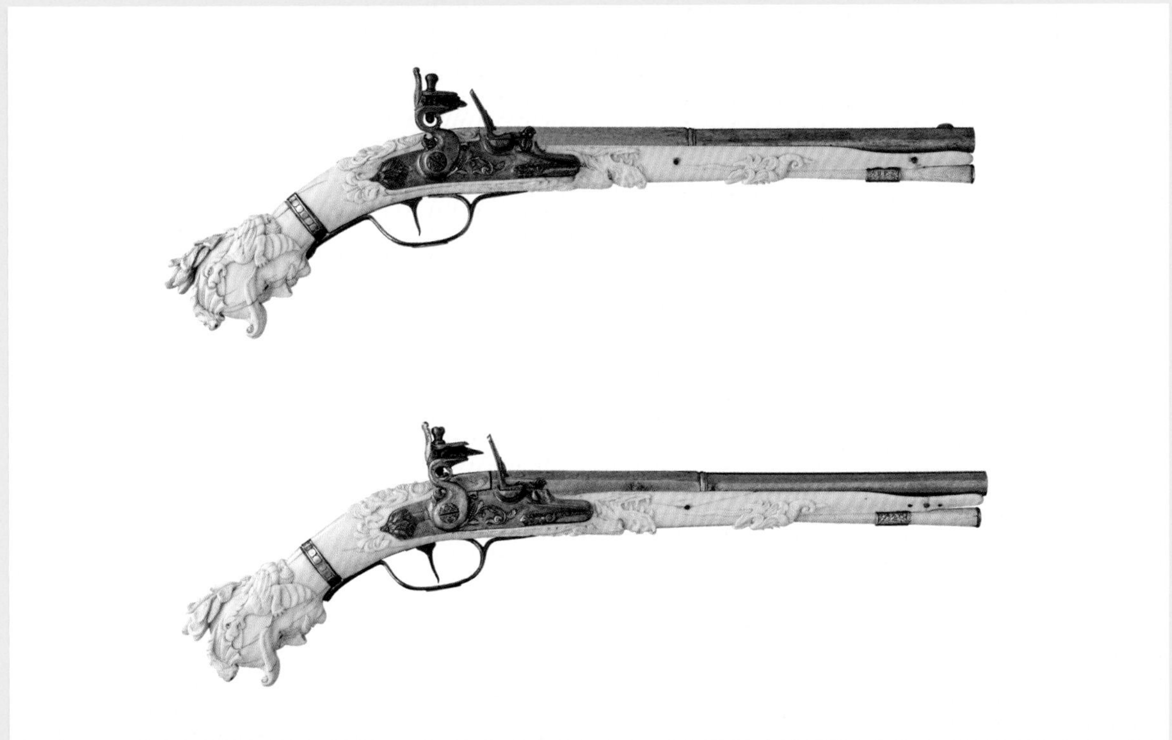

Fig. 4. Pair of Flintlock Pistols, 1660–70. Maastricht, Netherlands. Steel, silver, ivory, ebony, leather, and flint; h.: 45.6 cm (17 15⁄16 in.). George F. Harding Collection, 1982.2324a–b.

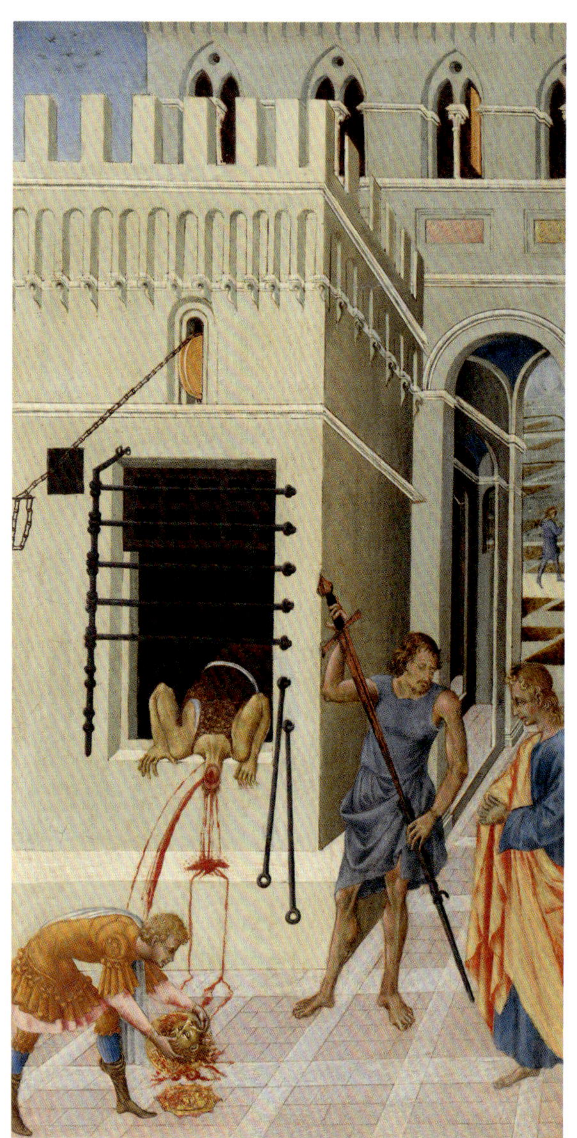

33. Giovanni di Paolo, The Beheading of Saint John the Baptist, 1455–60

Blood spills from Saint John the Baptist's freshly severed neck as a henchman places his head on a golden platter. Sienese painter Giovanni di Paolo illustrated the life of John the Baptist in a twelve-part series; this panel depicts the moments just after John's beheading, ordered by King Herod at the request of his daughter, Salome. The gruesome details contrast with the other figures' placid expressions and the executioner's casual pose as he returns his sword to its scabbard. The building itself, with its strict geometry, is likewise at odds with the rivulets of blood that pour over the patterned street.

Other panels in the series include scenes of John's birth, his departure for a hermit's life in the wilderness, his prophecy of Christ's coming, performing Jesus's baptism, and his imprisonment. The complex, detailed settings exploit the narrow proportions of the panels and set off the figures' expressive poses. Throughout the series, the artist repeated background elements, colors, and patterns to create a unified, easily legible narrative. Assembled in three rows, the original ensemble probably served as doors for a shrine containing a sacred relic (probably a body part) associated with John the Baptist. Of the eleven panels that survive, six are at the Art Institute.
Rebecca Long

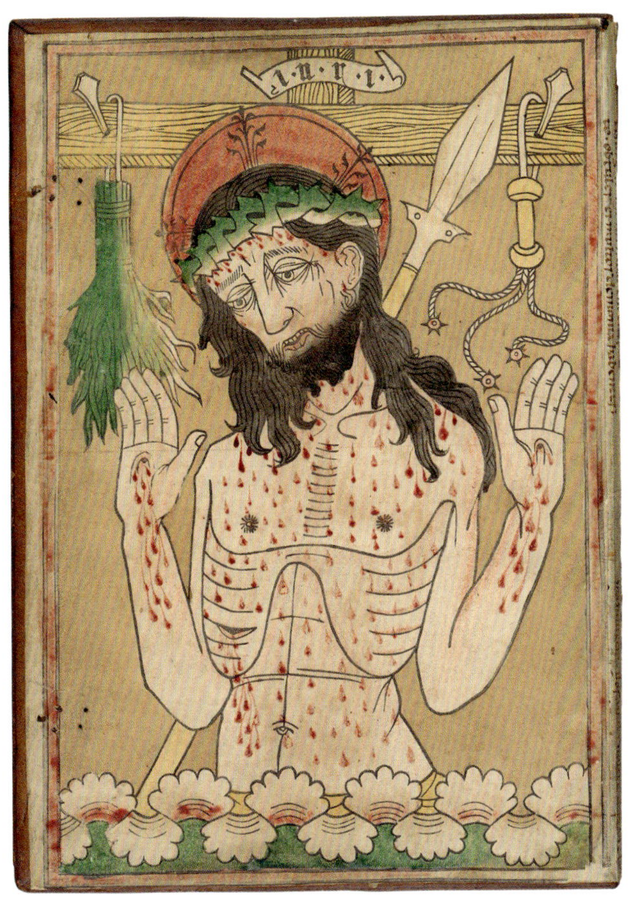

34. Man of Sorrows, 1465–70, Germany

Imagine opening the cover of an oversize book and coming face-to-face with a nearly life-size picture of the naked, blood-splattered, wounded body of Jesus Christ. Still glued to the hefty, hand-tooled leather cover of a book, this striking devotional image represents the suffering Christ known as the Man of Sorrows. The term comes from the Bible, which describes the coming of the Messiah: "He is despised and rejected of men, a Man of sorrows, and acquainted with grief" (Isaiah 53:3). Objects of torture appear behind Christ as he rises above a row of puffy clouds, hands upheld, silently imploring the viewer to prayer or contemplation.

Nearly contemporary with the first printed book, the Gutenberg Bible, this is an exceptionally early mechanically produced image. It was made from a massive block of wood carved in relief, then inked and pressed onto a sheet of thick paper. A skilled painter carefully hand-colored the black-and-white impression with brown, green, red, and yellow watercolors. Retrieved from the rubble during the bombardment of London in 1945, this unique and pristine work of art survives as a masterpiece of print culture at the dawn of the Renaissance. *Sandra Hindman*

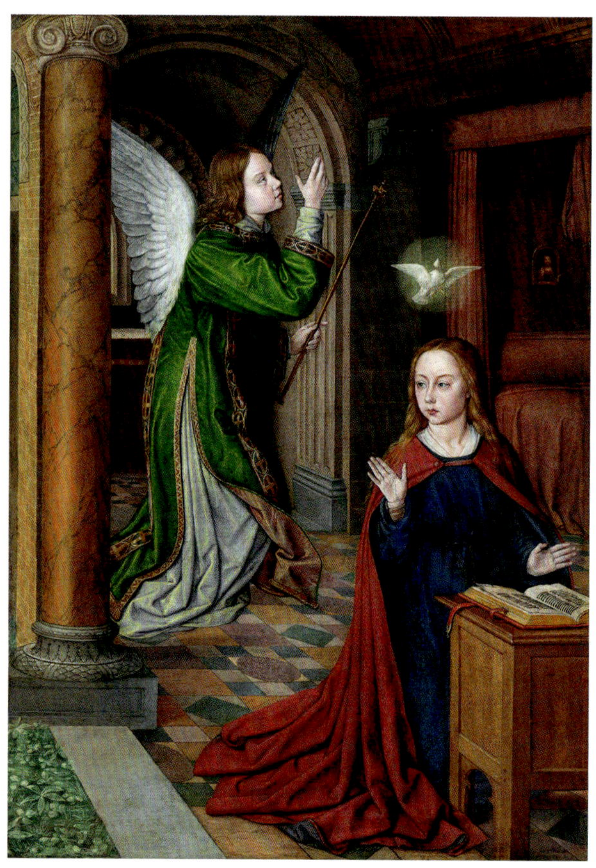

35. Jean Hey, The Annunciation, 1490–95

This scene—the archangel Gabriel's announcement to Mary that she will give birth to Jesus, the son of God—may appear to be complete, but it is actually a fragment of a larger altarpiece. X-radiography and infrared reflectography indicate that a figure originally stood along the left edge. At some point before 1906, this figure was scraped out and painted over.

The painting served as the right wing of an altarpiece; scholars have identified the left wing as a painting depicting the meeting of Mary's parents (about 1491–94; National Gallery, London). Not only do both panels have figures painted with the precious pigment ultramarine along one of their edges, but they are united in theme: The London panel represents the moment in which Mary is conceived, while the Chicago panel illustrates the moment of Jesus's conception.

Jean Hey, court painter to Pierre II, Duke of Bourbon, and his wife, Anne of France, may have made this altarpiece to celebrate the birth of their only child. The sumptuous palette and crisp definition of form echo Franco-Flemish manuscript painting, while the barrel vault and marble column—reflecting a blossoming interest in antiquity in the late 1400s—imbue this scene with a timeless quality. *Jacquelyn N. Coutré*

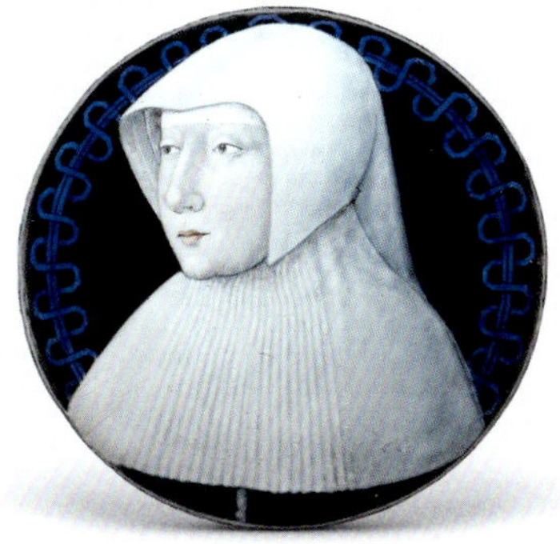

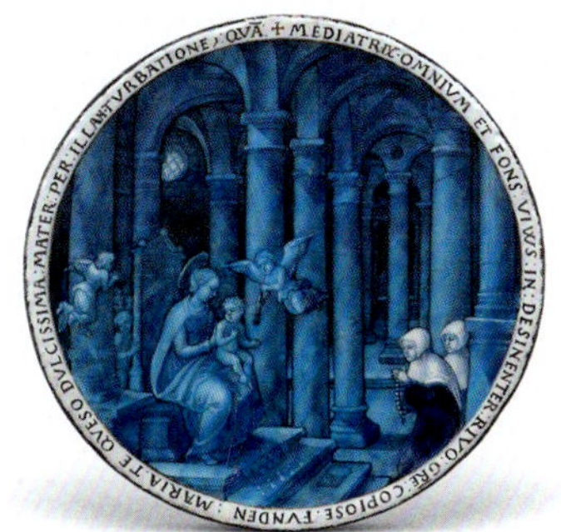

36. Attributed to Léonard Limosin, **Medallion**, about 1530–40

Does the tranquil beauty of this small medallion come from the exquisite skill of the enamel painter or from the subject, a widow wearing the headdress of mourning? The two—artist and subject—seem to be in perfect unity. The subject's calm face, mature but unlined, apparently glows from within, suggesting a profound inner peace that the painter seems to have felt deeply. The portrait is painted primarily in grisaille (shades of gray and white), but touches of color on her lips and cheek lend a haunting character to her pious profile. The reverse bears a scene of the Virgin and Child with two nuns holding rosaries in an intricate, receding architectural space. The painter exploited the translucency of the brilliant blue enamel, layering it over a white base in a complex technique that required as many as eight firings.

The medallion's subject is probably Margaret of Lorraine, a French aristocrat and widow of the Duke of Alençon. She established several convents, and upon her husband's death she entered the Order of Poor Clares in 1518. This piece belongs to a small group of medallions bearing Margaret's image, which devoted followers might have worn around their necks for inspiration and as an aid to religious contemplation. *Ellenor Alcorn*

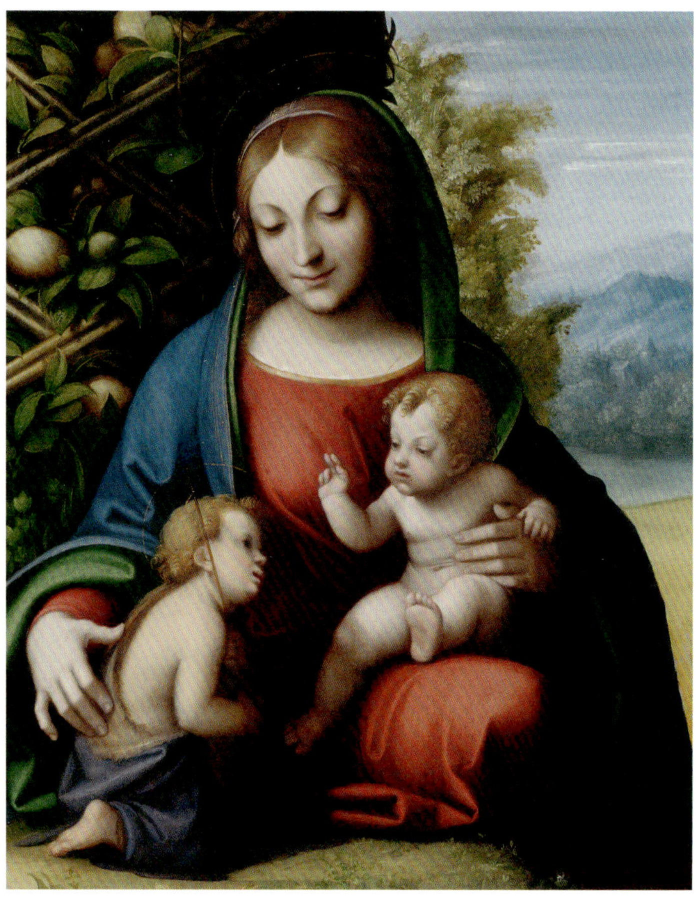

37. Correggio, **Virgin and Child with the Young Saint John the Baptist**, about 1515

In this intimate devotional panel, the young Correggio demonstrated his own evolving style while also assimilating lessons from other great painters of his era. The work's pyramidal grouping of figures reflects the style of Raphael, while their soft outlines and the Virgin's enigmatic smile recall the work of Leonardo da Vinci. The landscape in the background adds to the painting's charm and demonstrates the artist's knowledge of Northern European precedents. The gentle sensuousness of the figures and the tenderness they show one another, however, are unique to Correggio. The artist used color, light, and shadow to bathe the image in a gentle glow, with skin and fabrics taking on a velvety texture.

Correggio lived and worked in the northern Italian city of Parma, executing a body of work that is remarkable for its inventiveness and sophistication given his remove from the artistic centers of Rome, Florence, and Venice. This small panel is in his earliest style, but its idyllic quality presages the radiant ceiling frescoes of Correggio's maturity, especially those in Parma's cathedral (1526–30). *Rebecca Long*

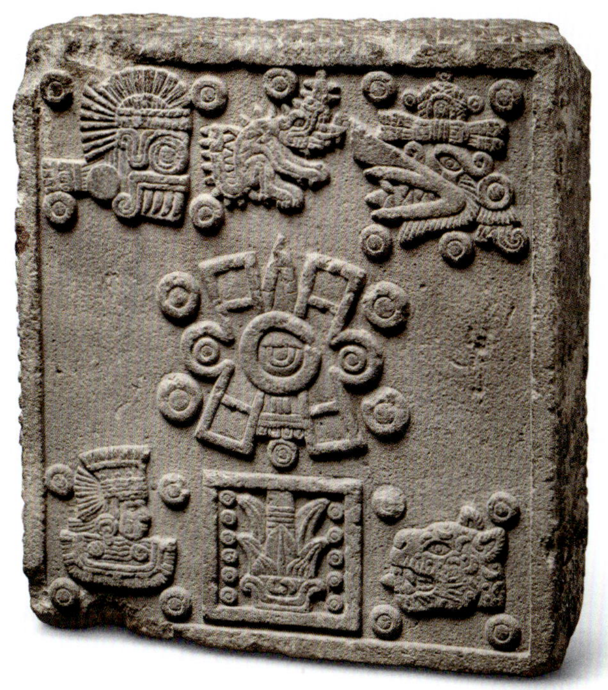

38. Coronation Stone of Moctezuma Xocoyotzin, about 1503, Tenochtitlan

This monument records the entire history of the Mexica universe up to 1503 through glyphs, or symbols. On the back, a glyph scholars call *1 Rabbit* represents the beginning of time. The sides are carved with representations of the earth goddess Tlaltecuhtli, squatting and holding up the front of the stone. In its corners are the end dates of the four previous cosmic eras: *4 Jaguar* (lower right), *4 Wind* (upper right), *4 Rain* (upper left), and *4 Water* (lower left). The current cosmic era is inscribed in the center with *4 Movement*. The final date on the monument is July 15, 1503, represented by *1 Crocodile* above *11 Reed* (in the square frame). That was the date of Motecuhzoma (Moctezuma) Xocoyotzin's coronation; he ruled until 1520, when he was killed during the Spanish invasion led by Hernán Cortés.

Just as these glyphs reappeared throughout the urban landscape of imperial Tenochtitlan, the former Mexica capital lying beneath modern Mexico City, they can also be found throughout Chicago. *4 Movement* appears in a mural on the platform of the Eighteenth Street "L" stop, as well as on manhole covers in the Pilsen neighborhood—long home to Chicago's vibrant Mexican community. *Andrew James Hamilton*

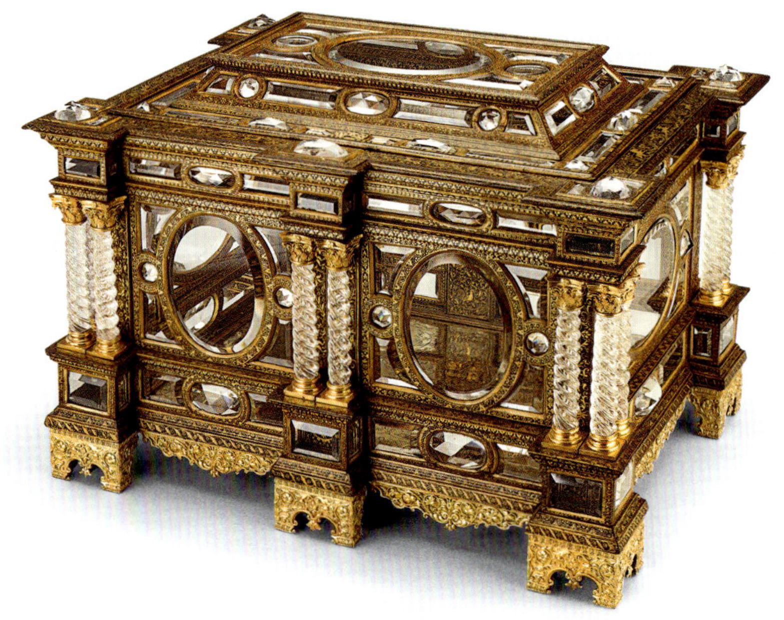

39. Casket, about 1595, Italy

Have you ever received a gift and thought the box it came in was nicer than the gift itself? That was possibly how the recipient of this crystal casket felt. Pope Clement VIII likely presented it to Anne of Austria, Queen of Poland, the mother of the future King Ladislaus IV of Poland, on the occasion of his birth in 1595. It contained blessed linens for the royal baby, with a Latin inscription declaring "To the good Mother—Use it with luck." The delicate linens are long gone, but this precious receptacle remains. It is one of nearly a dozen similar caskets produced in Venice for the pope to give to Catholic royal families.

The casket is a collaborative work between a goldsmith, a woodworker, and a hardstone cutter, who was responsible for grinding and polishing the 184 panels of alpine quartz crystal that form its walls. In today's postindustrial world where crystal-clear, machine-beveled glass is commonplace, the impossible grandeur of this work is difficult to grasp. No sixteenth-century glass could approximate the clarity of natural crystal. The casket's transparency and golden frame would have seemed like a minute piece of heavenly architecture, an appropriate gift from the pope to a royal family. *Jonathan Tavares*

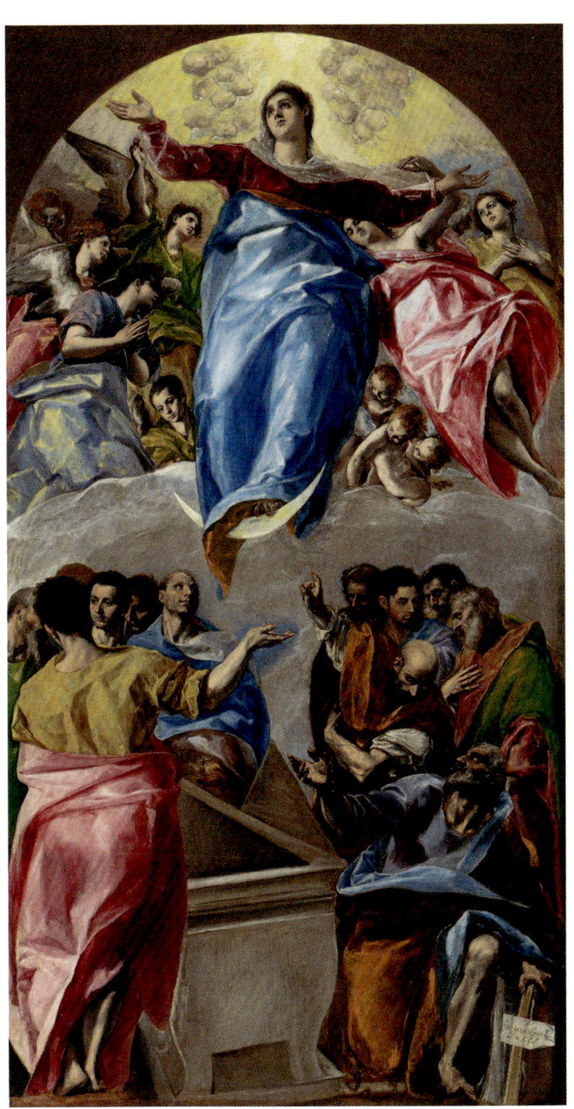

40. El Greco, **The Assumption of the Virgin**, 1577–79

The Assumption of the Virgin was the central image of El Greco's first major commission, an altarpiece for the Church of Santo Domingo el Antiguo, a convent in Toledo, Spain. The painting's subject, the raising of the Virgin Mary's body into heaven, relates to the function of the church as the funerary monument of a wealthy noblewoman, Doña Maria de Silva; the iconography of the entire commission focuses on death and salvation.

El Greco used broad, free brushwork, flickering hues, rich color harmonies, and bold figural arrangements to arouse devotional fervor in the viewer and impart a deep sense of faith. The composition is divided into two zones: the earthly sphere of the apostles and the celestial realm of the angels. El Greco masterfully compressed many figures into a tall and narrow format: In the earthly zone, the apostles' faces and gestures express a range of emotions through their dynamic, agitated gestures and poses. They are so individually considered that it seems El Greco studied actual studio models. In contrast, the angels in the heavenly scene above are calm, graceful, and direct in their focus toward the looming figure of the Virgin Mary as she rises into their realm. *Rebecca Long*

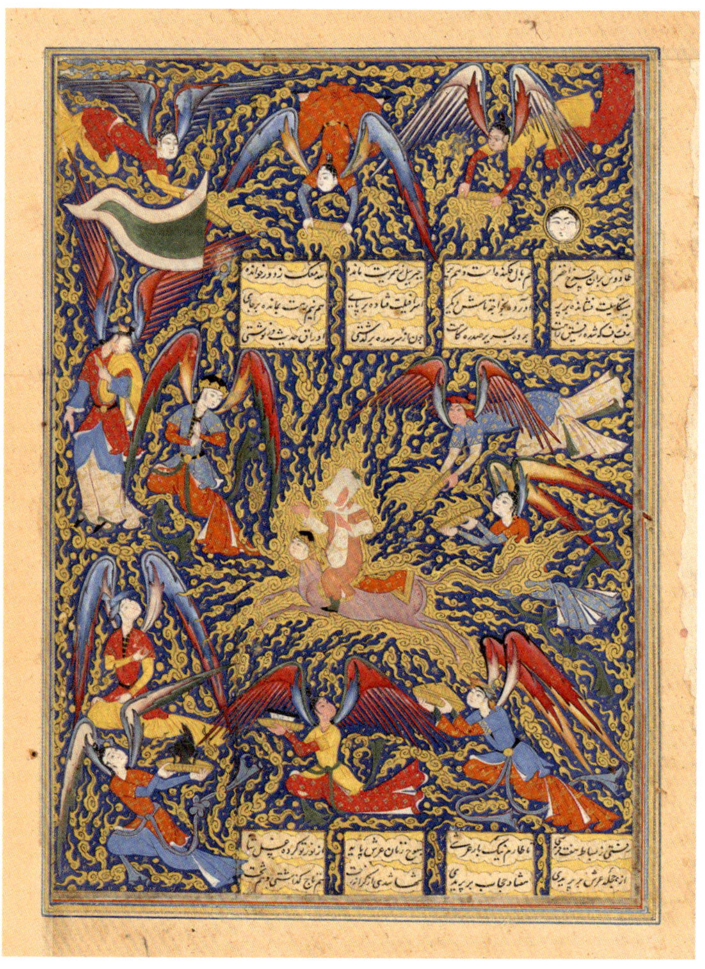

41. The Ascent of the Prophet to Heaven, about 1600, Iran

The *mi'raj* (ascension) and *isra* (night journey) of the Prophet Muhammed is a favorite subject in Islamic painting. A scene from early in the story is illustrated on this page from a Safavid-era copy of the *Khamsa* (quintet) of Nizami, a celebrated twelfth-century Persian poet. A flaming halo surrounds the Prophet, his face respectfully veiled, as he rides a mythical human-headed steed named Buraq (lightning) against the dark-blue sky. Muhammed is being carried up to heaven to behold the majesty of God. The golden swirls are fire illuminating the night sky, and angels bend to offer gifts to the Prophet as he rides past, led by the angel Gabriel bearing a green banner. Despite Islamic tradition, which holds that religious figures are too sacred to be depicted, there are some images of Muhammed and other sacred figures from around 1600, particularly within the Iranian cultural sphere where pre-Islamic traditions of figural painting were still prevalent. *Madhuvanti Ghose*

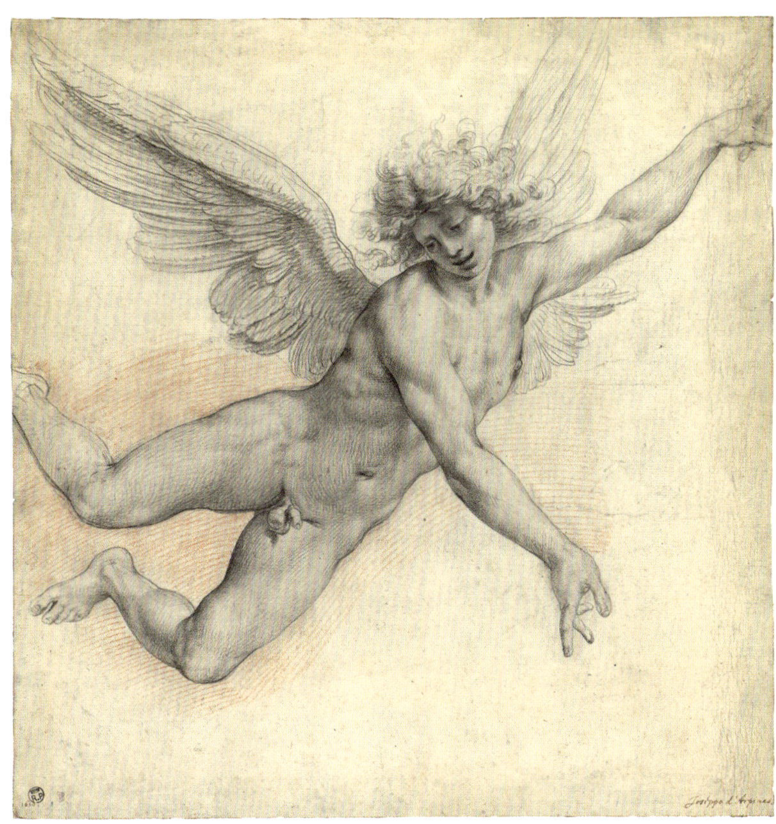

42. Giuseppe Cesari, An Angel in Flight, about 1599–1600

An angel—his pose a starburst of diagonal lines—emerges like an apparition from the otherwise blank sheet. His rapidly sketched wings and windswept curls suggest swift movement, his meticulously drawn body a tactile sense of presence. His expression is tinged with melancholy. The combination of the torqued, muscular body, influenced by Michelangelo's dynamic nudes, with ethereal sweetness, derived from Raphael's limpid facial types, lends the figure an idealized, androgynous beauty befitting a supernatural being. Few works embody the refinement and elegance of late sixteenth-century Italian drawing as vividly as this sheet by Giuseppe Cesari.

Cesari was admitted to the Roman drawing academy at just fifteen—the youngest member ever. By thirty-one, when he made this drawing, he was leading a major papal commission to design and oversee fresco decorations in the Lateran Palace and the adjacent Basilica of San Giovanni. This drawing is a preparatory study for a fresco in that church's transept, depicting the Ascension of Christ flanked by two hovering angels.

Although less known today, Cesari was among the most prominent artists of his time; the young Caravaggio even briefly worked in his studio. The elegant draftsmanship and seductive beauty of this drawing prove that his reputation was well deserved. *Jamie Gabbarelli*

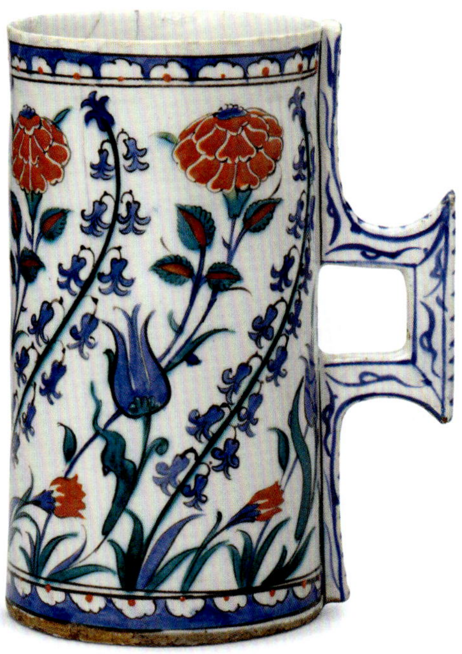

43. Tankard (*Hanap*) with Tulips, Hyacinths, Roses, and Carnations, late 1500s, Turkey

Potters in Iznik, Turkey, southeast of Istanbul, created fine ceramics like this cylindrical tankard (*hanap*) during the late 1500s. Characterized by its white body, brilliant transparent glaze, and distinctive decoration, Iznik pottery is among the most technologically refined and aesthetically arresting traditions in the history of Islamic ceramics. Hyacinths, carnations, blue tulips, and red roses decorate this tankard. The artist fully realized the rhythmic potential of alternating floral forms, exploiting the vessel's tall, cylindrical surface to create a feeling of motion.

Though imported Chinese blue-and-white porcelain inspired the Iznik tradition, by the 1550s Iznik pottery flourished in its own right. Working in collaboration with the imperial Ottoman atelier in Istanbul (*nakkash-hane*), Iznik potters created a style that epitomized the empire and was eventually sought-after outside Turkey. The popular tulip-and-carnation motif appears on book bindings, paper borders, and textiles made for the Ottoman court. The craze for tulips was not limited to ornament: The real flowers were cultivated in Istanbul's gardens, and the bulbs exported to Europe. The size of this tankard suggests that it may have once been used as a flower vase, perhaps to hold the very blossoms it depicts. *Madhuvanti Ghose*

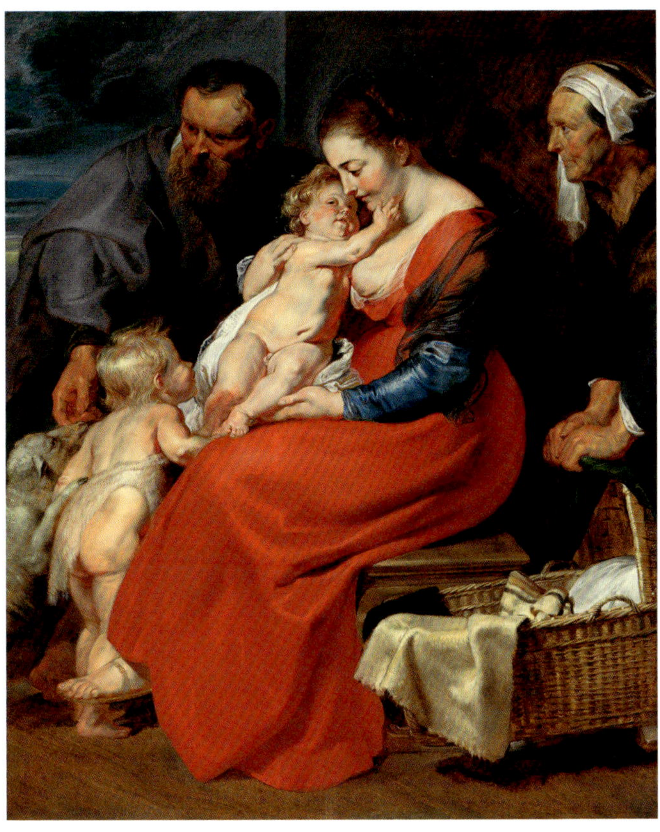

44. Peter Paul Rubens, The Holy Family with Saints Elizabeth and John the Baptist, about 1615

Peter Paul Rubens's distinctive blend of fleshy figures and heroic actions dominated the artistic ethos of Antwerp (in present-day Belgium) for much of the 1600s. Here, he translated a sacred subject into vernacular language. The infant Jesus cuddles on the lap of his mother, Mary, whose exposed breast serves as a visual reminder of the human needs of Jesus, also the child of God. Her elderly cousin Elizabeth and Elizabeth's son, John the Baptist, look on in wonder and awe, and Joseph, Mary's husband, tends to a lamb, a symbol of Jesus's eventual self-sacrifice. Notably, not one of these figures bears a halo, and they are all wearing contemporary dress. Furthermore, not one engages with the viewer; rather, they participate in a series of interlocked gazes that ultimately lead back to Mary. Rubens energized the European art market with his robust and monumental forms, inspired by those of Michelangelo and Raphael that he had seen in Italy. A consummate businessman, Rubens not only directed assistants to paint multiple variants of this composition, but he also commissioned engravings after it. It was an early success for the young, ambitious painter, who achieved a harmonious blend of emotional tenderness and moral strength within each figure. *Jacquelyn N. Coutré*

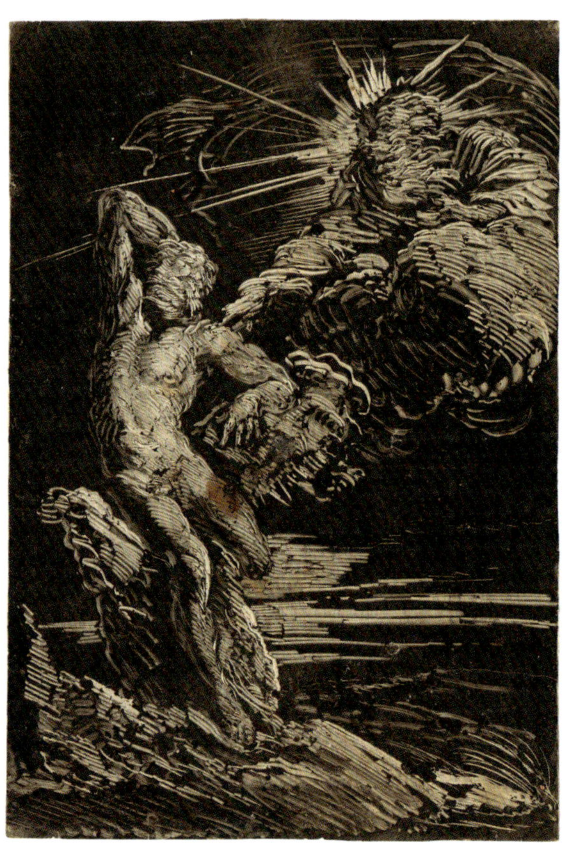

45. Giovanni Benedetto Castiglione, The Creation of Adam, about 1645–50

The Creation of Adam is both a print and a unique work. The word monotype—"single printing"—was coined in the 1800s to describe this technique, which the painter-etcher Giovanni Benedetto Castiglione is often credited with inventing. He created around two dozen images using this process in the mid-1600s.

Here, Castiglione began by covering a blank copper plate with a mixture of printing ink and oil paint. He then removed the pigment using various tools, pulling the composition into being from the dark, prepared ground. Once he was satisfied with the design, he placed a blank sheet of paper on the plate and passed it through a printing press, producing this singular impression. The white lines are the paper showing through the areas where the ink was removed. This experimental technique was ideally suited to the subject of divine creation—the coming into being out of nothing. Castiglione's forceful and fragmented strokes heighten the raw visual drama of his image. The result is startling: It looks like nothing that had come before it.

Formerly part of the prestigious collection of the Dukes of Devonshire, this is the only Castiglione monotype in the Western hemisphere. It remains one of the most significant print acquisitions ever made by the Art Institute. *Jamie Gabbarelli*

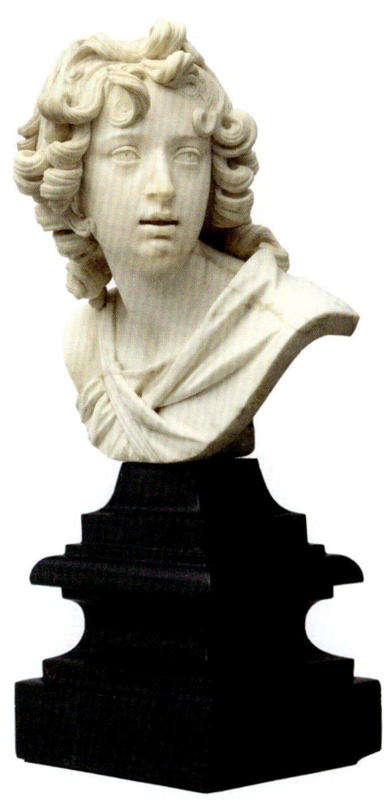

46. Francesco Mochi, **Bust of a Youth (Saint John the Baptist)**, 1630–40

This work might appear to be a portrait, but the costume and expression indicate that it represents a mythological or biblical figure. The young man is shown in the act of speaking, his mouth open as if caught mid-sentence. This detail suggests that the figure is likely Saint John the Baptist; one of his roles was that of a preacher who foretold the coming of Jesus Christ. The dramatic turn of the youth's head suggests that he is addressing an unseen conversant, a dynamic and inventive means of engaging with the viewer. The sculpture's small scale indicates that it was likely made for private contemplation.

The figure's deeply carved corkscrew curls, soft skin, and parted lips are all characteristic of the sculptor Francesco Mochi, whose work is notable for its energetic lines, dramatic movement, and subtle psychology. One of the most talented and individual sculptors in seventeenth-century Rome, Mochi possessed an extraordinary technical aptitude both in carving marble and in depicting carefully nuanced expression in his figures. *Rebecca Long*

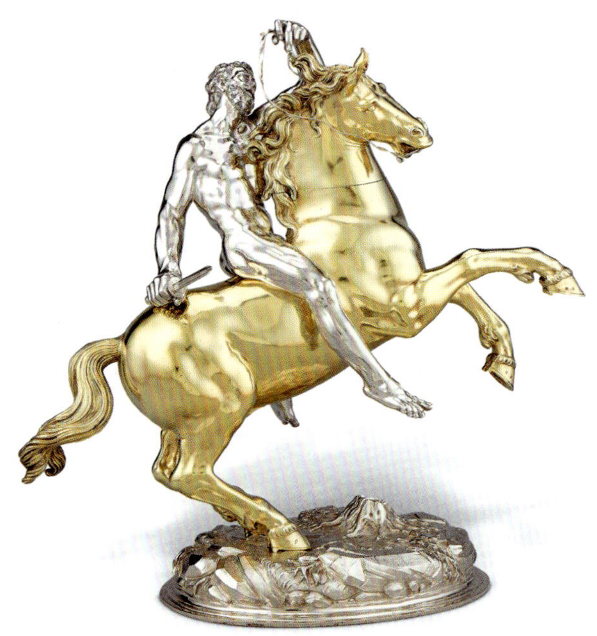

47. Hans Ludwig Kienle, Cup in the Form of a Horse and Rider, 1630

The silversmith Hans Ludwig Kienle was justly proud of this sculpture, engraving his name, his city (Ulm, Germany), and the date on the base's underside. The dynamic posture of the figure is beautifully rendered, his power equal to that of his magnificent mount. During the Renaissance, artists working in small-scale bronze revived the subject of the heroic male figure astride a horse, known from monumental Greek and Roman sculpture. Kienle's work belongs to a tradition of intricate silver vessels that represent wondrous animals, incorporate rare materials, or have an engaging twist: The rider and horse's head can be removed so that its hollow body can be used as a cup. Such pieces were often displayed as works of art rather than actually used, evidence of the erudition and taste of their often-princely owners.

Kienle initially modeled the sculpture in wax, the first step in the technically challenging lost wax process. The fluid handling of the horse's mane and tail, the rider's delicately rendered toes, and the horse's flaring nostrils retain their waxy quality, which Kienle enhanced after casting with sensitive tooling and gilding. The finished work transcends the laborious process of its manufacture, and the composition reads as a perfectly integrated whole, balanced and animated from every angle. *Ellenor Alcorn*

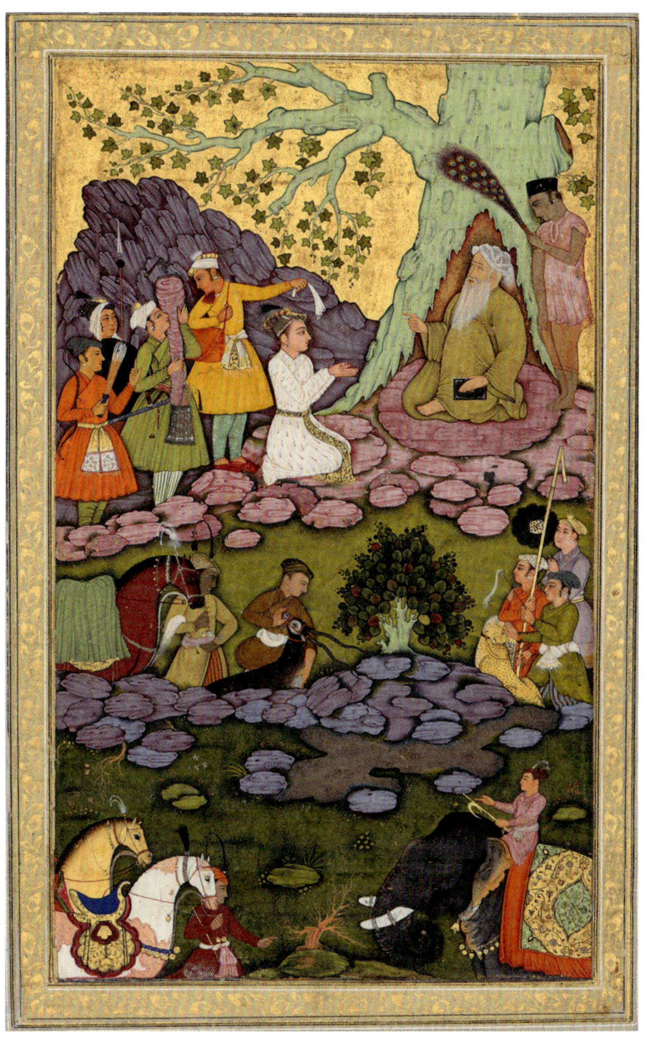

48. **Prince Visiting an Ascetic During a Hunt**, about 1625–50, India

In this rare painting from Kashmir, a young prince detours his hunting party to pay homage to a famous holy man seated in the wild. The holy man appears to be Muslim, perhaps a Sufi. This theme is common in Mughal painting, particularly in works produced during the reigns of emperors Jahangir and Shah Jahan during the first half of the seventeenth century. The prince's status is apparent: The men behind him carry his weapons, a servant shoos flies from above his head, and the royal elephant occupies the lower right corner. Although the theme of this painting is essentially Indian, it was executed under an Iranian stylistic influence, apparent in the fantastic rendering of the rocks and tree and in the color palette. The patron surely had a penchant for the older, more conservative style of painting related to Safavid Iran rather than the newer style of the Mughal court. *Madhuvanti Ghose*

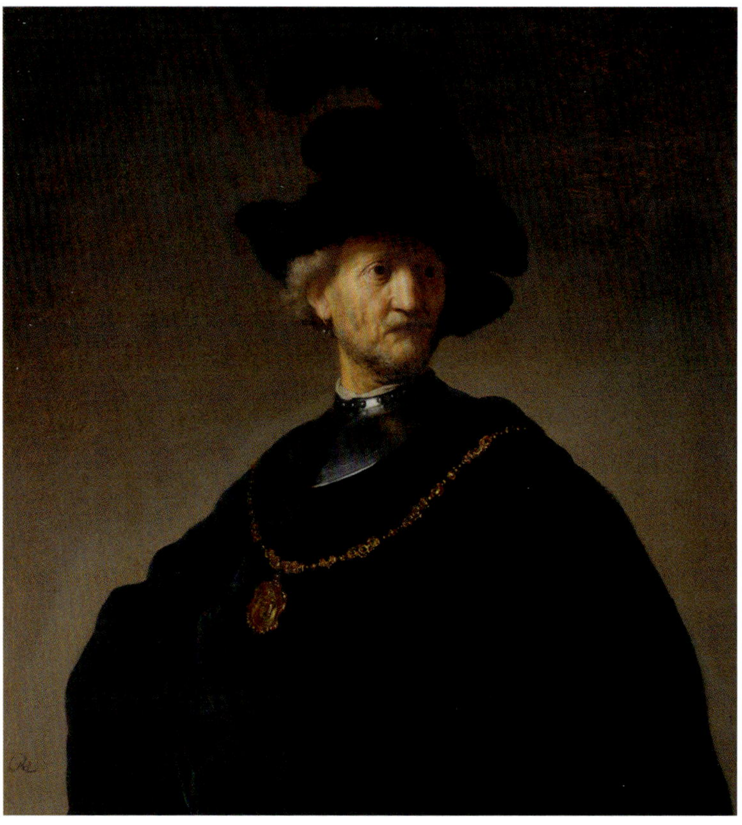

49. Rembrandt van Rijn, **Old Man with a Gold Chain**, 1631

This compelling figure—fancifully adorned with a steel gorget (armor protecting the throat and upper chest), golden chain, and plumed beret—represents a new commodity on the Northern European art market: a *tronie*, or character study. While artists had created such studies since the 1500s, Rembrandt and his colleague Jan Lievens made these images into more affordable alternatives to portraits, heightening their appeal by introducing bold visual elements like dramatic lighting, whimsical costumes, and dynamic poses. Rembrandt and his colleagues painted this model frequently; although he has been called "Rembrandt's father," recent research suggests that the "Old Man" may have been the keeper of an almshouse in Leiden, the Netherlands.

Although tronies were less expensive than commissioned portraits, Rembrandt invested just as much skill in them. The attention given to the folds of flesh beneath the eyes, the prickly, tightly trimmed beard, and the highlights in the gorget and gold chain reveal a talented painter engaged in the joys of painting. The prominent gold chain appears in several works from Rembrandt's Leiden and Amsterdam periods: He must have had one in his studio. But unlike his acclaimed peers Peter Paul Rubens and Anthony van Dyck, Rembrandt never received one as a gift from a royal patron. *Jacquelyn N. Coutré*

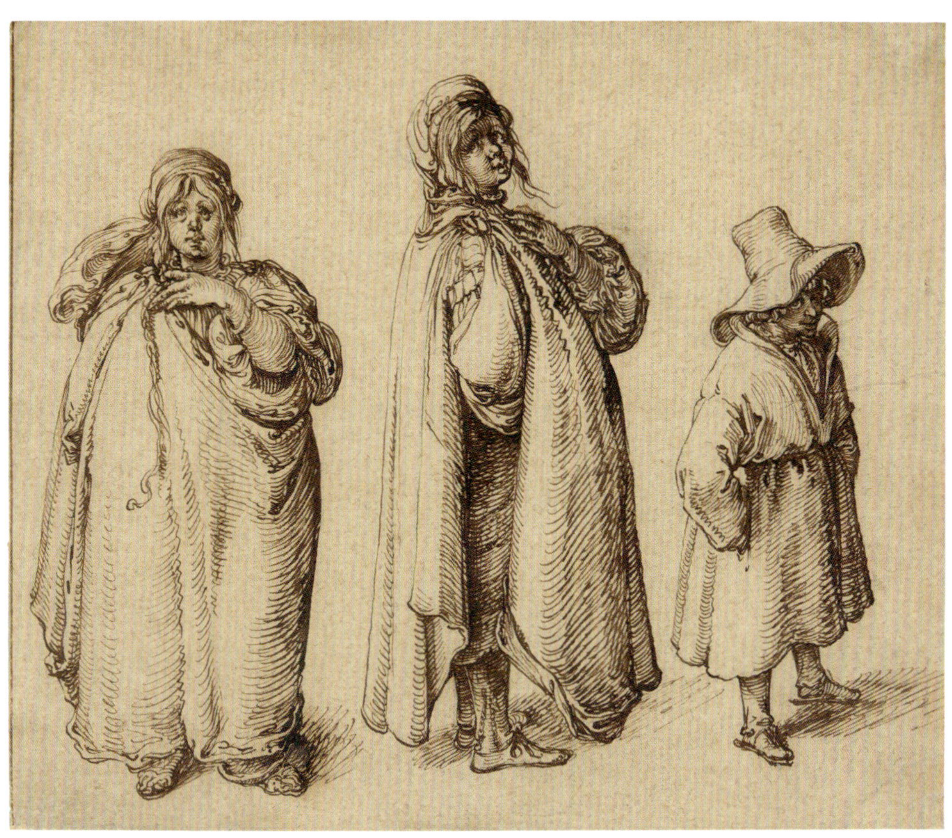

50. Jacques de Gheyn II, *Two Studies of a Roma Woman and a Roma Boy in a Large Hat*, about 1605

With characteristically fluid strokes of the pen, Jacques de Gheyn depicted three figures—a boy and two girls—recognizable by their clothing as members of the Roma people, a nomadic group of Asian origin who had been migrating through Europe since the 1300s. European artists, who viewed the persecuted and marginalized Roma with a mix of fear and fascination, exoticized them in their work. Here, de Gheyn focused on their clothing rather than their individuality. Look at their generic features: Did he draw two girls, or the same figure from two angles?

While this drawing is a sketch from life, de Gheyn reused the central figure's dress and the boy's profile in a print showing an unkempt Roma woman reading the palm of an elegant Dutch lady. He transformed observed details into ciphers for social types: The "Roma fortune teller" became a cliché in art of the time. It is in this fraught interplay of observation and stereotype—of curiosity and othering—that the drawing's power lies. In addition to its technical and aesthetic merits, it offers a timeless glimpse into human attitudes toward "outsiders" at times of migration and rapid social change. *Jamie Gabbarelli*

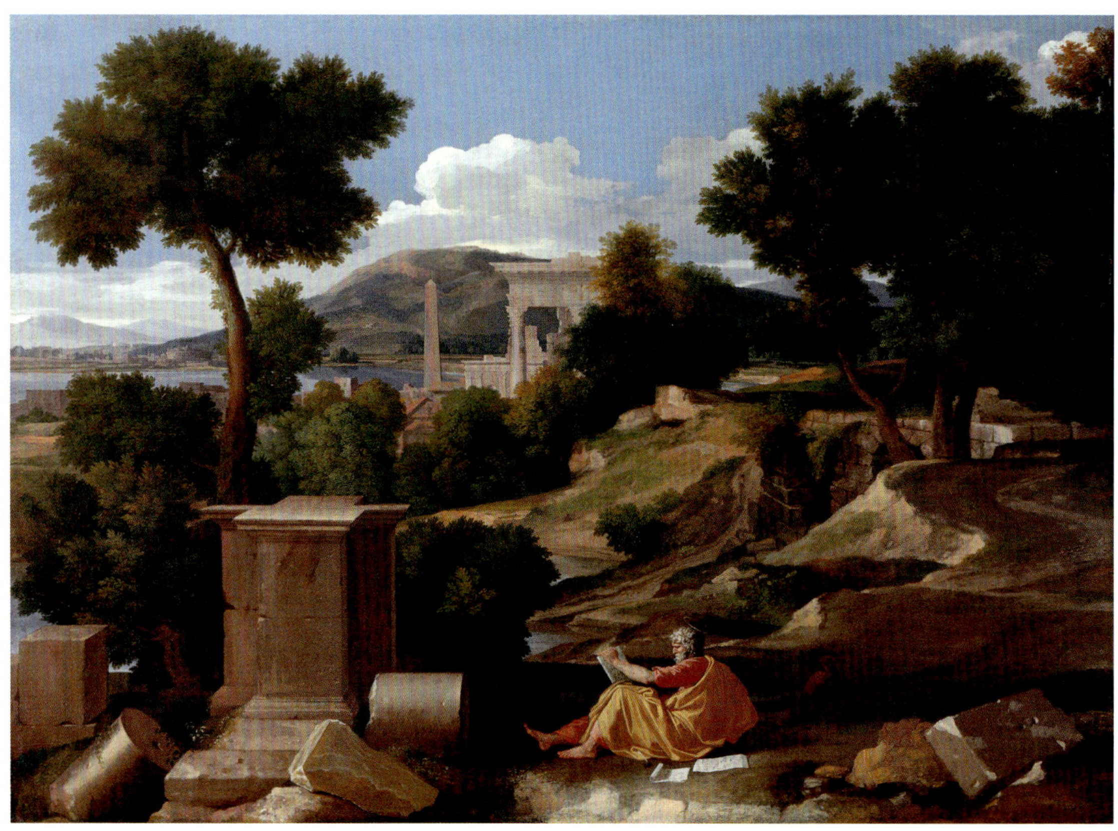

51. Nicolas Poussin, Landscape with Saint John on Patmos, 1640

In Christian tradition, Saint John the Evangelist is thought to be the youngest of Christ's twelve disciples—but Nicolas Poussin depicted him here as an elderly man. The disciple has retired to the Greek island of Patmos to write the Gospel of John and the Book of Revelation; he is shown at work with his attribute, an eagle, just behind him. Poussin constructed an idealized landscape, shaping natural forms according to geometric principles and reinforcing the measured order of the composition by arranging them parallel to the picture plane. The resulting serene setting is replete with references to Greco-Roman civilization, including column fragments, an obelisk, and a temple. For Poussin and his friends and patrons, Christianity was closely linked to Stoic philosophy, which emphasized reason, unity, and serenity.

Scholars now regard Poussin's art, more than that of any other seventeenth-century European artist, as synonymous with classicism, the philosophy that prized the model of ancient Greek and Roman art and architecture. Born in France, Poussin spent most of his career in Rome, painting for an educated elite. Along with *Landscape with Saint Matthew* (Gemäldegalerie, Berlin), painted the same year, *Landscape with Saint John on Patmos* may have been part of a planned series including all four evangelists. *Rebecca Long*

52. María Josefa Sánchez, Crucifixion, 1646

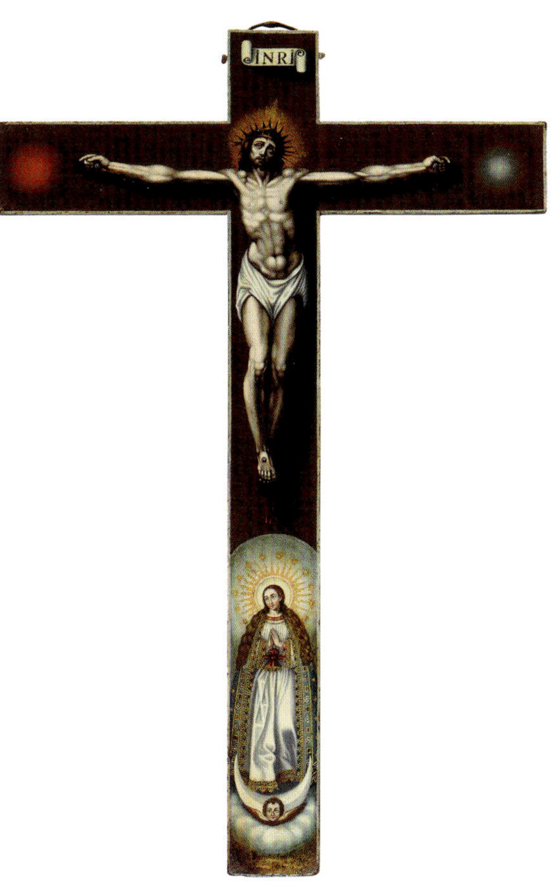

This small, painted crucifix is exceptional not only for its artistry, but also because it is signed by a woman artist: María Josefa Sánchez. Sánchez worked roughly from 1639 to 1649, probably in Castile, Spain, but little else is known about her. Women rarely worked as professional artists in seventeenth-century Spain, where laws and customs discouraged them from entering professions. Laws also prohibited women from serving as apprentices or signing official documents. The few women who became artists usually trained in their fathers' workshops. Some women artists of the period, Sánchez included, might have been nuns who produced devotional works within monastic communities.

Sánchez depicted Jesus alive on the cross, an iconographic type known as *Christus triumphans*. His graceful pose contrasts with his agonized expression, and carefully rendered drops of blood spill from his hands and feet. The orbs near his hands represent the sun and moon, a reference to an eclipse at the moment of Christ's death by crucifixion. At the foot of the cross, Jesus's mother, Mary, portrayed as a young girl wearing white and blue robes, is crowned with stars and standing atop a crescent moon. These attributes identify her as the Virgin of the Immaculate Conception, an atypical subject for a Crucifixion image. *Rebecca Long*

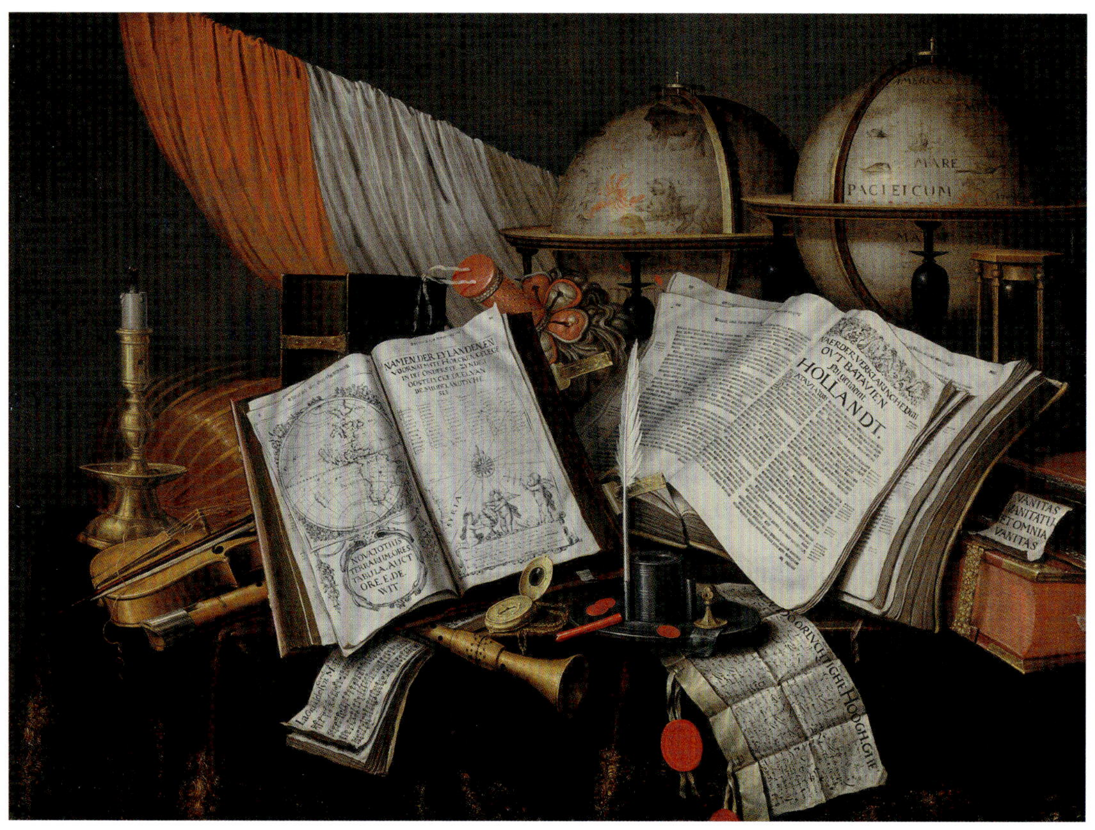

53. Edwaert Collier, A Vanitas Still Life with a Flag, Candlestick, Musical Instruments, Books, Writing Paraphernalia, Globes, and Hourglass, 1662

This ambitious still life conjures the complexities of Dutch colonization and cartography in the 1600s. Casually arranged on a table are a book about seafaring, which includes a map of the Americas copied from a 1660 print; a volume on the history of Holland (Oud Batavia), a clever reference to the Dutch Republic's new territory in Indonesia (Batavia); and the terrestrial and celestial globes, positioned to show the Pacific Ocean and lands the Dutch had newly reached. While the inscriptions on the globes and the scrap of paper at right are in Latin, the other documents are in Dutch; the Dutch presence is reinforced by the flag in the background.

By 1662 the Netherlands had ceded its territory in New Holland (now Brazil) to the Portuguese, and it was also fighting with the British for New Amsterdam (now New York) in North America. The tenuous nature of these conquests is amplified by ephemeral allusions. The extinguished candle, violin with a broken string, pocket watch, and hourglass all represent the biblical passage from Ecclesiastes at far right: *Vanitas vanitatum et omnia vanitas* (Vanity of vanities, all is vanity). With his striking ability to paint the printed word, Collier raised questions about the permanence of worldly accomplishments and the ambitions of humankind. *Jacquelyn N. Coutré*

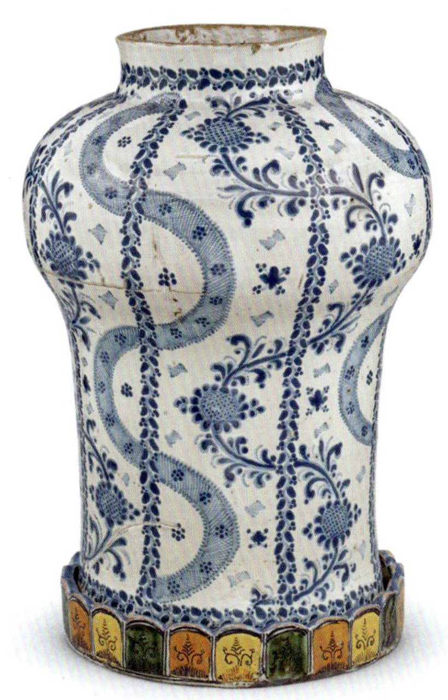

54. Jar (*Tibor*), 1700–1750, Viceroyalty of New Spain

The Americas have always been a site of rich cultural exchange—especially for Indigenous ceramic traditions. The European invasions of the hemisphere introduced shiny vitreous glazes, which local ceramists quickly incorporated. Spanish imperial networks also connected the Americas to their colonies in the Philippines. Ships called Manila galleons sailed across the Pacific to Acapulco, bringing goods including blue-and-white porcelain from China. The foreign wares were unloaded and carted across Mexico to Veracruz, where they were loaded onto new boats to sail across the Atlantic to Spain. As a result, peoples of the Americas saw all the fashionable commodities headed to Europe well before Europeans did.

In Puebla, southeast of Mexico City, Spanish colonists started making their own glazed ceramics—like this one—called Talavera Poblana, which both resembled those from Talavera de la Reina in Spain and emulated blue-and-white motifs from Asia. The Art Institute stewards one of the most important collections of Talavera Poblana ceramics in the United States. This particular jar also draws on floral designs from European textiles—another important trade item. This vessel is one of a pair; an identical vessel is in the collection of the Museo Franz Mayer in Mexico City. *Andrew James Hamilton*

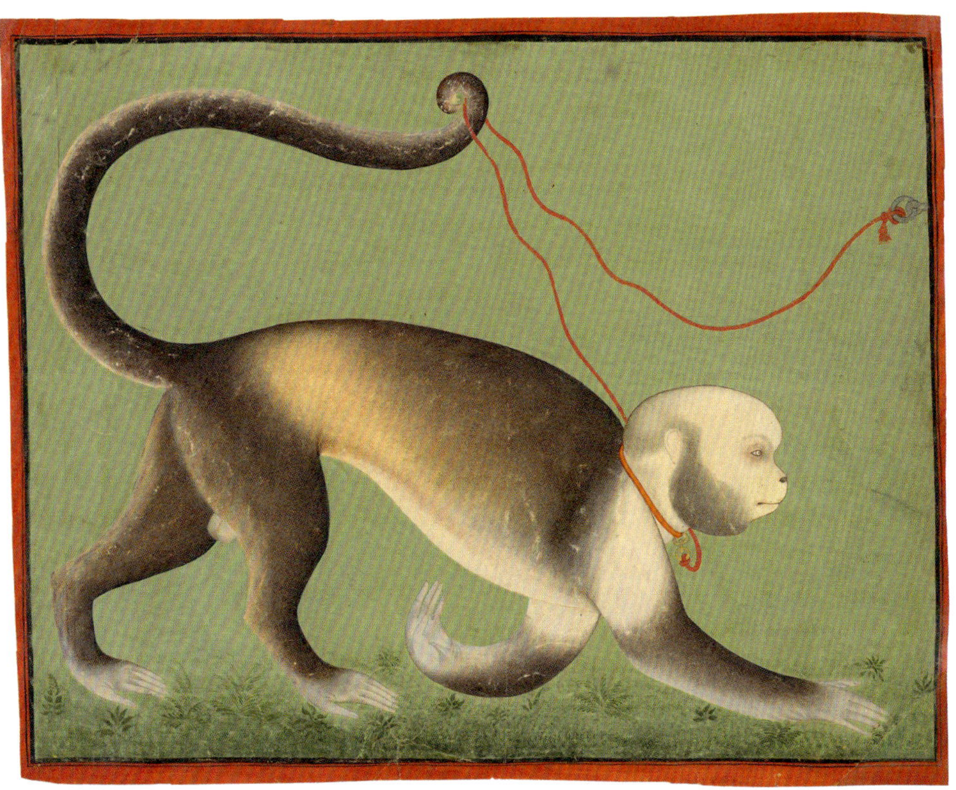

55. Attributed to the Stipple Master, A Monumental Portrait of a Monkey, about 1705–10

Except for the monkey-god Hanuman, monkeys are rarely portrait subjects in India. The monkey's human features—a beard, pale eyes, and long, slender hands—make this painting even more unusual. On the reverse, an inscription states that the monkey is named Husaini and "comes from" Nawab Davad (or Daud) Khan. This likely refers to Daud Khan Panni, a powerful nobleman and *faujdar* (military commander and territorial administrator) who served the Mughal emperors in the late seventeenth and early eighteenth centuries. He kept a menagerie and around 1705 obtained an unusual monkey—possibly a bonnet macaque from southern India—that died only a few days after its arrival. It is possible that the nawab's disappointment inspired this portrait.

An anonymous artist now called the Stipple Master probably painted this portrait between 1705 and 1710. Along with his patron, Maharana Amar Singh II (reigned 1698–1710), the Stipple Master initiated a new painting style in Mewar, a princely state in Rajasthan, around 1700. Traditional Mewari painting is characterized by bold colors, shallow pictorial space, and idealized figures, while this work displays a restrained palette, greater depth of field, and increased realism. Scholars now attribute a group of about forty-six paintings, including this one, to this artist-patron duo. *Madhuvanti Ghose*

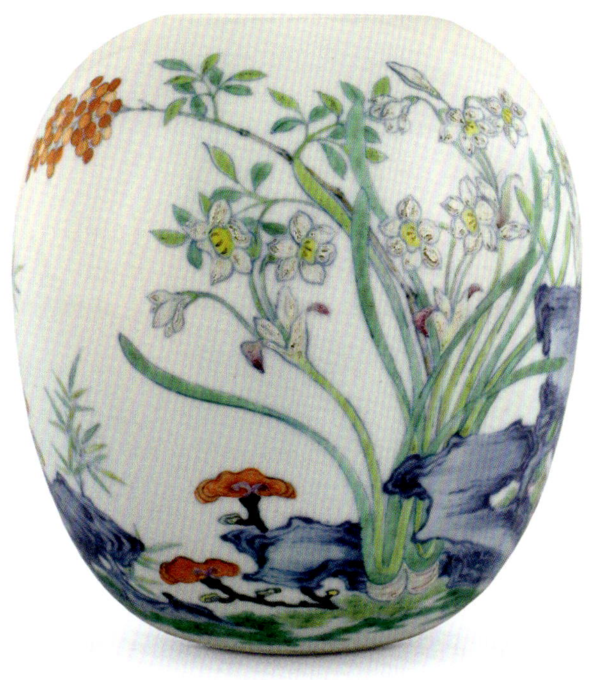

56. Jar with Narcissus, Nandina Berries, Lingzhi Mushrooms, and Rocks, 1723–35, China

This small porcelain jar showcases the elegance and technical brilliance associated with the imperial kilns of the Qing dynasty. During the reign of the Yongzheng emperor—an avid patron of the arts—porcelain production reached new heights of refinement. Designs were carefully drawn in cobalt blue underglaze, then delicately filled with soft, translucent overglaze enamels. This precise technique is known as *doucai*, meaning joined colors.

The decoration on this jar is both visually harmonious and symbolically rich. The narcissus, nandina berries, lingzhi mushrooms, bamboo, and rocks are more than natural motifs—they are visual puns and auspicious symbols. Nandina berries evoke abundance, while the narcissus and lingzhi mushrooms suggest immortality. The resilient natures of bamboo and evergreens represent morality and integrity. Together, these elements form a layered message of enduring joy and vitality, themes that resonated strongly within the court culture of the time. *Seung Hee Oh*

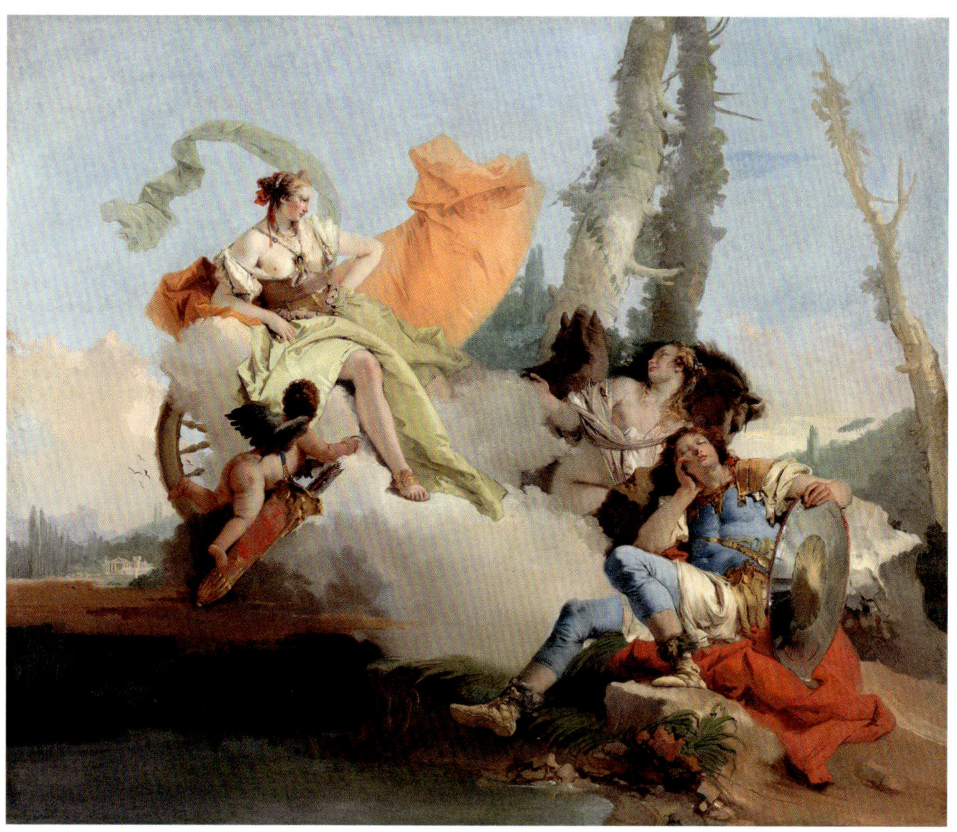

59. Giovanni Battista Tiepolo, Armida Encounters the Sleeping Rinaldo, about 1742–45

This painting likely once graced a large hall at the Palazzo Corner in Venice along with several others. The suite illustrates the ill-fated love of Armida and Rinaldo from Torquato Tasso's 1581 epic poem *Gerusalemme liberata* (*Jerusalem Delivered*). The story takes place during the First Crusade, an eleventh-century military expedition in which Christian knights attempted to seize control of Jerusalem and check the power of the Muslims who ruled the city. In this scene, the beautiful sorceress Armida encounters the knight Rinaldo as he sleeps and decides to carry him away on her cloud-borne chariot. When Rinaldo wakes, he immediately falls for Armida and forgets his quest in Jerusalem.

Giovanni Battista Tiepolo painted a vast, open expanse of sky and scenery and elaborately arranged the figures, draperies, clouds, and trees to animate the composition. Although Tasso's story symbolizes the conflict between love and duty, Tiepolo's depiction of a magical world—enhanced by effervescent colors and dense, creamy paint—seems to evoke only love's enchantment.

Tiepolo's paintings combine virtuosic draftsmanship with seemingly spontaneous execution, a formula perfectly suited to the large-scale works that he created to decorate palaces and churches throughout Italy, Germany, and Spain. *Rebecca Long*

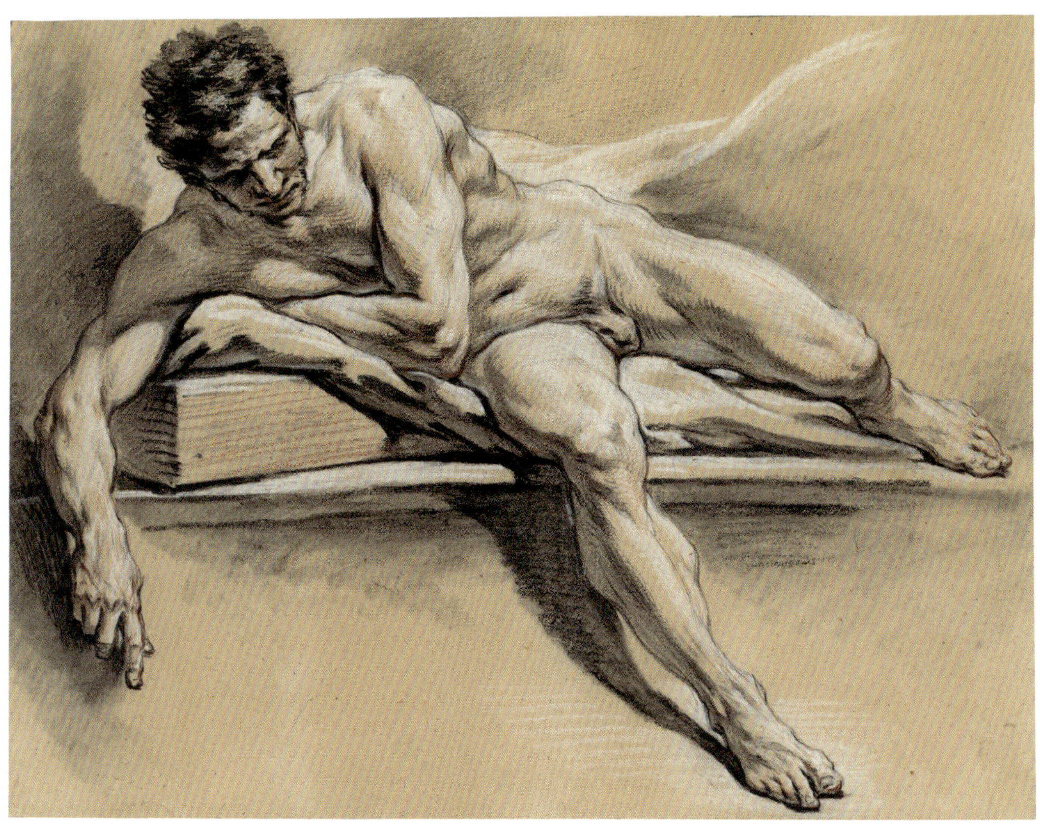

60. François Boucher, **Academic Study of a Reclining Male Nude**, about 1750

I associate François Boucher with stylized bodies: smooth squeezable flesh, pink bottoms, tiny feet, strangely long necks and arms—all luminous, ripe, touchable, and artificial. To make them this way, he folded his academic training into lush invention.

This drawing holds Boucher's rigor and simultaneously belies it. It's a tour de force anatomy lesson, but the anatomy is impossible. The dangling hand, feet, and head are all the same size, which would never be true. The arms are too long, the legs too short. All muscles tense, but the entire body slumps. Boucher's distortions reflect his attention (the large right hand) and his standards for beauty (the small right foot). I tried to draw that foot and failed. I couldn't sort out how such an economic touch gives us something so dimensional, graceful, and human.

I recommend admiring Boucher's facility six inches from the paper. Only then can you see the red. Fine, near-invisible terracotta marks sit on top of the more dramatic black and white. You'll find them on a fingertip, the bottom of the big toe, or delicately, tactilely, tracing the surface of the thigh. This warm nuance brings us back to Boucher's fundamental sensuality: that he paints glowing, blushing flesh. *Anne Harris*

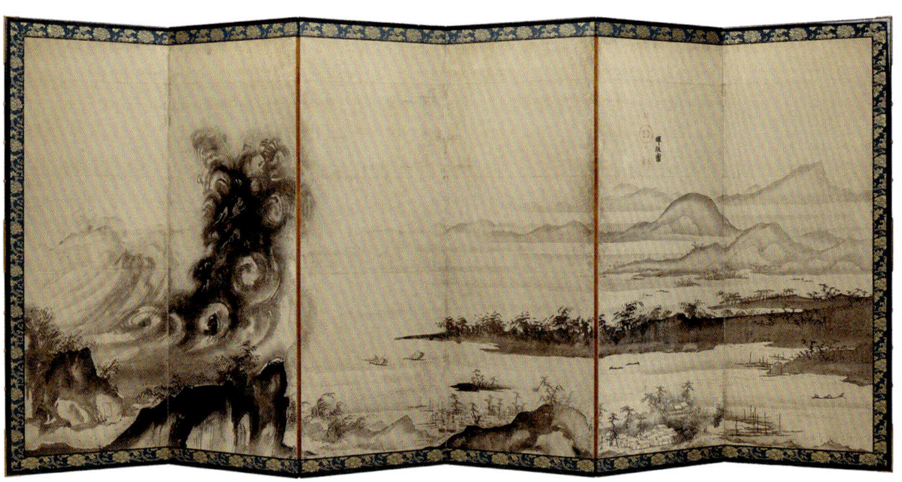

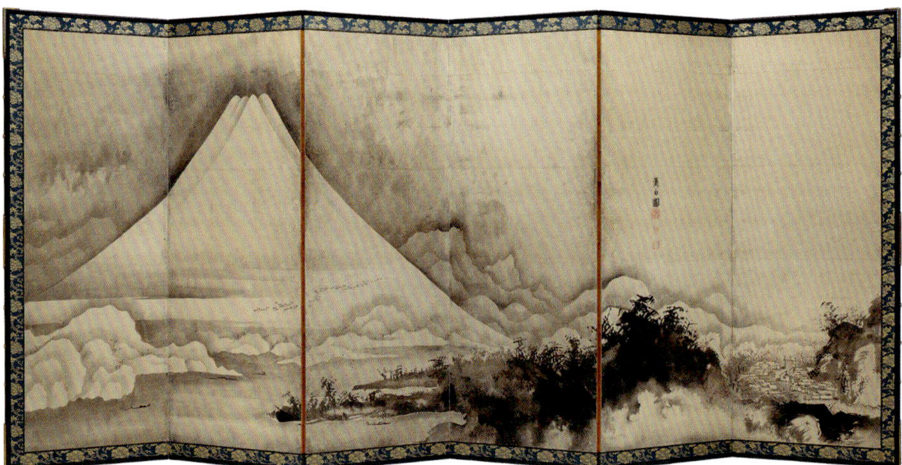

61. Soga Shōhaku, **Mount Fuji and the Miho Pine Forest**, 1761–62

Mount Fuji and its surrounding landscape are often found in Japanese art, but in this pair of screens, artist Soga Shōhaku has chosen to include an unexpected creature flying in the sky: a dragon. While Mount Fuji and the dragon would later come to be paired in painting and print, in the eighteenth century this auspicious subject was new and rare. What was commonly known at the time, however, was that homonyms in Japanese for "Fuji" and "dragon" combine to create a phrase meaning "removing all unhappiness."

During his lifetime, Shōhaku was not associated with any established school of painting; little else is known about his biography. The artist earned his reputation for his technical skills with monochrome ink painting and his irreverence for traditional norms—both qualities on display in this work. Here, Shōhaku adeptly renders lush trees, craggy rocks, and a snow-covered mountain, but also intangible atmospheric details such as wind, rain, and clouds. *Janice Katz*

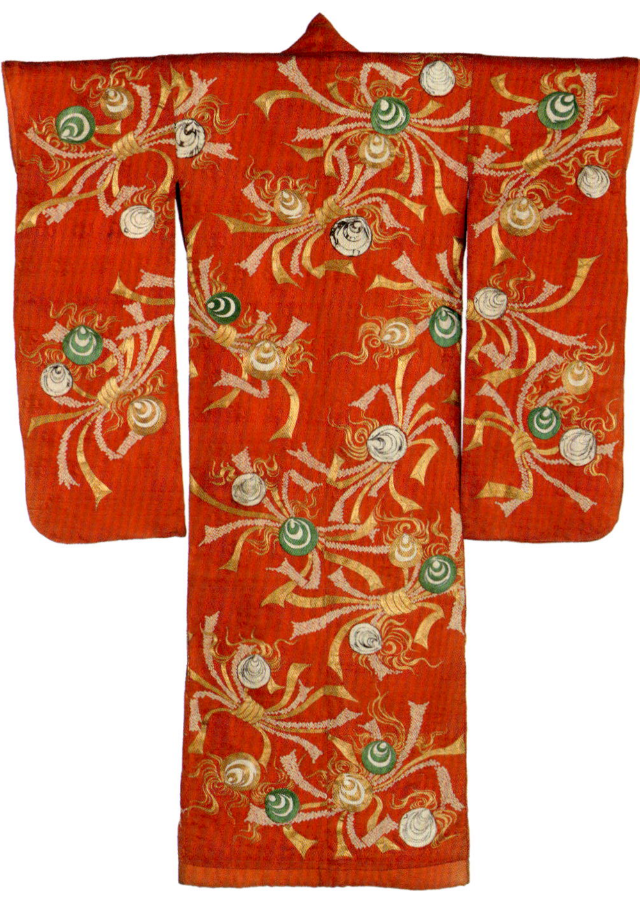

62. Uchikake, 1775–1800, Japan

An *uchikake* is a formal overgarment worn only by a bride or by an actor onstage. Uchikake are often heavily decorated, and they have a padded hemline. The garment is worn without an *obi* (belt), and the padded hem flares out and trails along the floor.

As is typical of the most precious Japanese kimono, this rare example comprises many layers of carefully considered design and decoration. The foundation textile is silk with a woven pattern of a lozenge diaper interspersed with small roundels, each containing a stylized phoenix. The woven silk was then resist-dyed with a color derived from the safflower plant. This natural dye produces distinctive and desirable shades of red and pink with yellow undertones, but it is notably unstable and fades relatively easily. The resisted areas appear as white dots. After the fabric was dyed, it was embroidered with motifs that include dried abalone—a symbol of longevity—and precious gemstones to ward off evil. Brides often wore red uchikake, and for very formal weddings this garment is still considered auspicious. Historically, among the samurai class it was also the custom to display expensive garments like this on special occasions, rather than actually wearing them. *Melinda Watt*

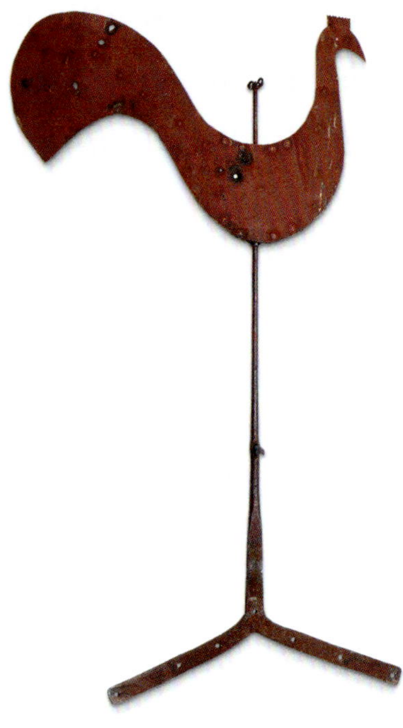

63. Peacock Weather Vane, 1800–60, Pennsylvania

For decades, this rustic peacock lived atop a building as both an architectural adornment and an instrument signaling the direction of the wind. The hand-forged weather vane's rough edges, worn red paint, and holes from a century or more of target practice speak to its history as a functional object, a relic of times past. In the early 1900s, artists, curators, collectors, and government administrators attempted to define a distinctly American visual identity through objects like these. Weather vanes were lauded as the nation's earliest examples of artistic sculpture and celebrated for their freedom and vitality—ideas that continue to shape their interpretation today.

The Art Institute acquired this weather vane in 1952 from New York gallerist Edith Halpert, who operated two galleries in the same building: the Downtown Gallery, which focused on modern American art, and the American Folk Art Gallery, the first commercial gallery dedicated to vernacular arts from centuries prior. Weather vanes were popular among Halpert's clients. She began collecting them on road trips throughout the Northeast, stopping to barter with their owners and removing them from rooftops herself. *Time* magazine reported that she "busily stripped the New England skyline of more than a hundred vanes" for sale to collectors and museums. *Elizabeth McGoey*

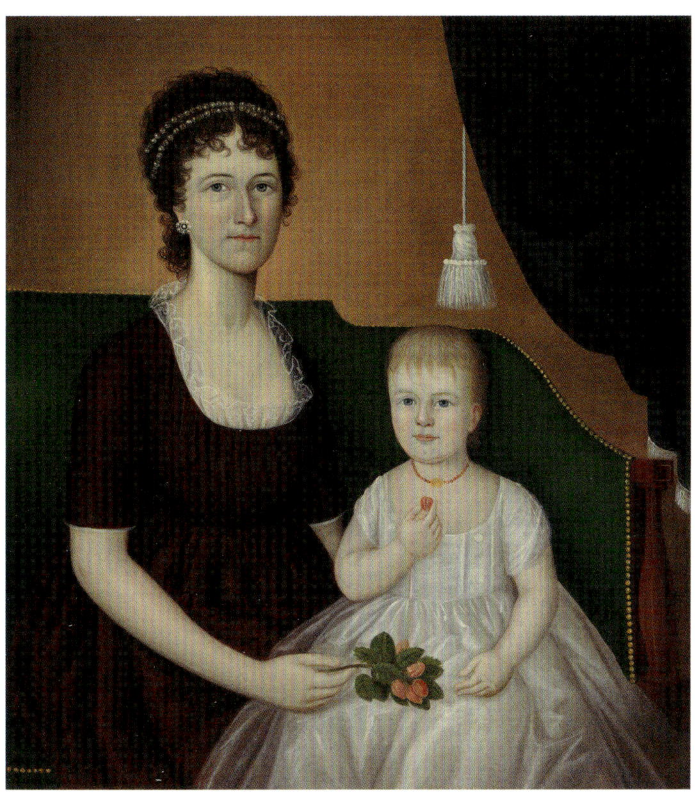

64. Joshua Johnson, Mrs. Elizabeth Grant Bankson Beatty and Her Daughter Susan, about 1805

When I visit this double portrait, the finely crackled surface draws my attention. The gentle fractures show how time erodes what we know of past lives.

The woman offers strawberries to her child, who lifts one almost to her mouth. Joshua Johnson frequently incorporated berries into his family portraits; they quietly connote a child's dependence on a parent for nourishment of body and mind. The curtain tassel reflects the girl's white dress, reminding us that from birth, society instructs children in the aesthetic and cultural codes of their environment.

Today there are fewer than one hundred extant works by Joshua Johnson, several of which portray the Beatty family. Based in Baltimore, Johnson described himself in a newspaper advertisement for his portrait painting services as a "self-taught genius" who "experienced many insuperable obstacles in the pursuit of his studies." Johnson was long speculated to be a free man of color; research has proven that he was the son of a white man and an enslaved Black woman. Sold at nineteen to George Johnson—his father—Joshua was guaranteed freedom by twenty-one. In this new light, one must imagine the "insuperable obstacles" as well as the artistic successes experienced by Johnson, the first known professional Black American painter.
Nancy Chen

It's a Small World

Christopher Maxwell

Narcissa Niblack Thorne's sixty-eight tiny rooms blend fact and fantasy. For decades, they have delighted and inspired visitors—including Walt Disney himself!

Tucked beneath the Art Institute's iconic Michigan Avenue entrance staircase is a unique gallery housing sixty-eight tiny rooms, each set behind glass and meticulously crafted at a scale of 1:12—where an inch equals a foot. These are the Thorne Miniature Rooms, and since they were presented to the museum in 1940, they have been among its most unique and enduring attractions.

Created under the direction of Narcissa Niblack Thorne, a wealthy Midwesterner living in Chicago during the architectural boom of the 1920s and 1930s, the rooms are not dollhouses or toys—they are immersive, historically inspired, and deeply researched works of art. Drawing from the architectural and interior design traditions of Europe, North America, and Asia, each room offers a window into a different world, often suggestive of centuries past (figs. 1–3).

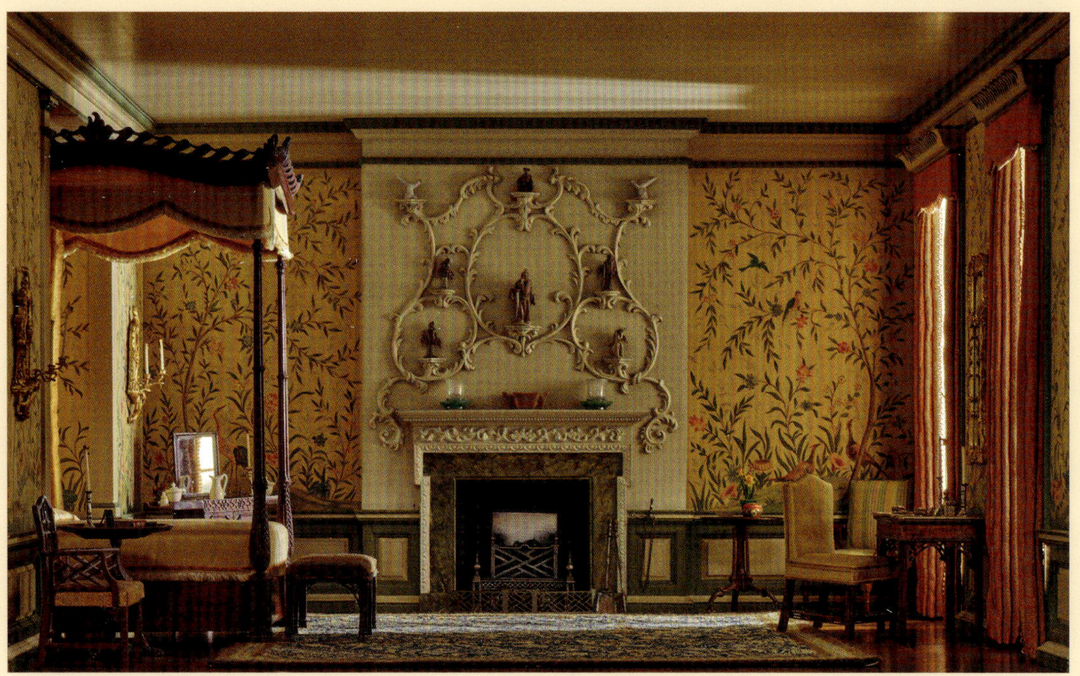

Fig. 1. Designed by Narcissa Niblack Thorne (American, 1882–1966). *E-8: English Bedroom of the Georgian Period, 1760–75*, about 1937. Miniature room; mixed media. Gift of Mrs. James Ward Thorne, 1941.1193.

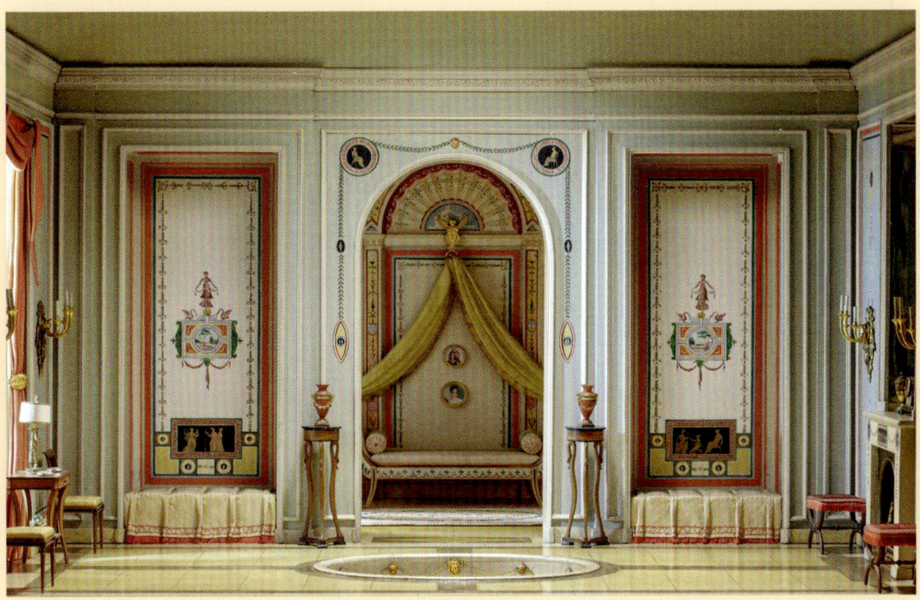

Fig. 2. Designed by Narcissa Niblack Thorne (American, 1882–1966). *E-25: French Bathroom and Boudoir of the Revolutionary Period, 1793–1804,* about 1937. Miniature room; mixed media. Gift of Mrs. James Ward Thorne, 1941.1210.

Though not formally trained as a curator or historian, Thorne was a rigorous and exacting researcher. Born in 1882, she came of age during the height of the Colonial Revival movement, which resonated deeply with wealthy Americans seeking solace in a romanticized past amidst the economic and cultural upheaval of the Great Depression and Modernism's stark rejection of familiar tradition. As a member of Chicago's globetrotting elite, she traveled widely across Europe and the United States, visiting historic homes, museums, and antique dealers. Her notebooks and files brimmed with measurements, sketches, descriptions, photographs, and postcards. She also built a comprehensive reference library of contemporary publications on decorative arts and architectural history. Thorne was especially inspired by the full-scale period rooms that had become popular in American museums during the early 1900s. These installations—often made from authentic architectural elements salvaged from historic homes—sought to immerse museum visitors in idealized recreations of the past. But while they were intended to educate visitors about the national styles of previous eras, they were often theatrical and only loosely tied to historical reality. In the same spirit, Thorne's miniature rooms are a composite of historical research and artistic license.

Back in Chicago, Thorne hired a studio of expert miniaturists, architects, drafters, and artisans to design and produce the rooms and their furnishings according to her vision. She also purchased items from specialist retailers of miniatures in Paris and New York, repurposed existing objects, and even collaborated with modern artists on the creation of contemporary works of

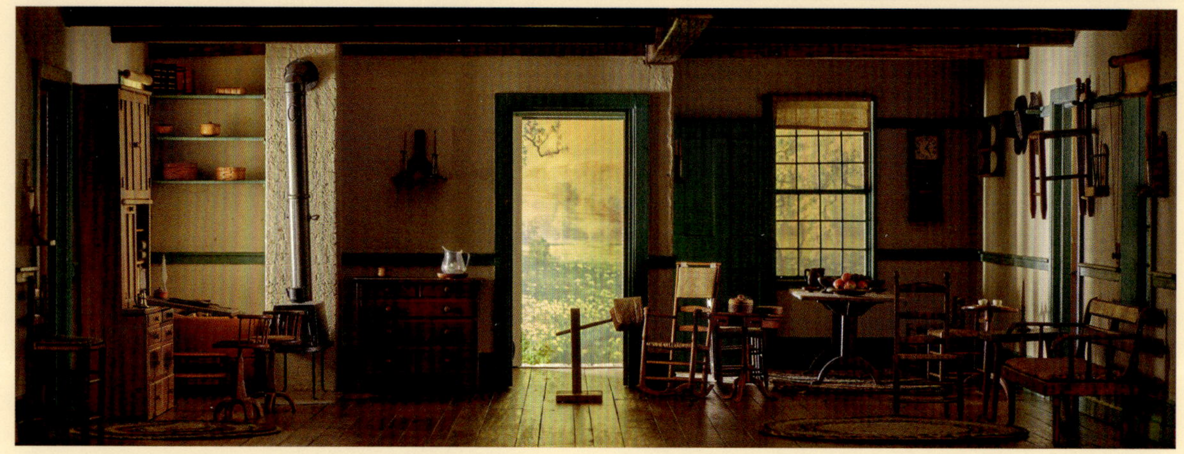

Fig. 3. Designed by Narcissa Niblack Thorne (American, 1882–1966). *A-18: Shaker Living Room, about 1800*, about 1937. Miniature room; mixed media. Gift of Mrs. James Ward Thorne, 1942.498.

art—including original paintings by Fernand Léger, Amédée Ozenfant, and Léopold Survage displayed in her modern California Hallway (fig. 4). As interior decoration became a recognized profession, Thorne likely encountered the miniature interior models used by European antiques dealers and decorators, such as Maison Carlhian in Paris, to present furnishing schemes to clients.

Thorne had presented a previous series of rooms to great acclaim at the 1933 Century of Progress Exposition in Chicago. These were joined by the Art Institute's European rooms at the 1939–40 World's Fairs in New York and San Francisco, where they caught the attention of Walt Disney, himself a collector of miniatures. Disney later visited the Art Institute to study the rooms more closely (see p. 15)—a testament to their place at the intersection of applied arts, historical interpretation, and popular imagination. Arranged with extraordinary care—external lighting, color, and scale finely tuned to evoke atmosphere—the rooms acknowledge their own virtuoso theatricality. Viewed as theater audiences would a stage set, they invite not only detailed observation but imaginative immersion.

Since ancient times, models and miniatures have served as tools for education, commemoration, and delight. During Thorne's own lifetime, Queen Mary was famously presented with a fully furnished miniature palace to showcase the finest of British design—a tribute to a way of life quickly fading in the United Kingdom in the aftermath of World War I (Thorne later received a commission from the Queen to make a miniature reproduction of a Georgian library). Similarly, Thorne's rooms preserve a vision—not only of the historical past but of the values and aesthetics of affluent white American society in the early twentieth century. They reflect both the emerging professional field of interior decoration and the long-standing cultural function of miniatures in shaping ideas of taste and domestic identity.

Today, the Thorne Miniature Rooms continue to attract thousands of visitors each month. Their enduring appeal lies in their ability to blend fact and fantasy, museum display and the applied arts, research and creativity. They don't aim to be final statements about history, but rather, to spark curiosity about it.

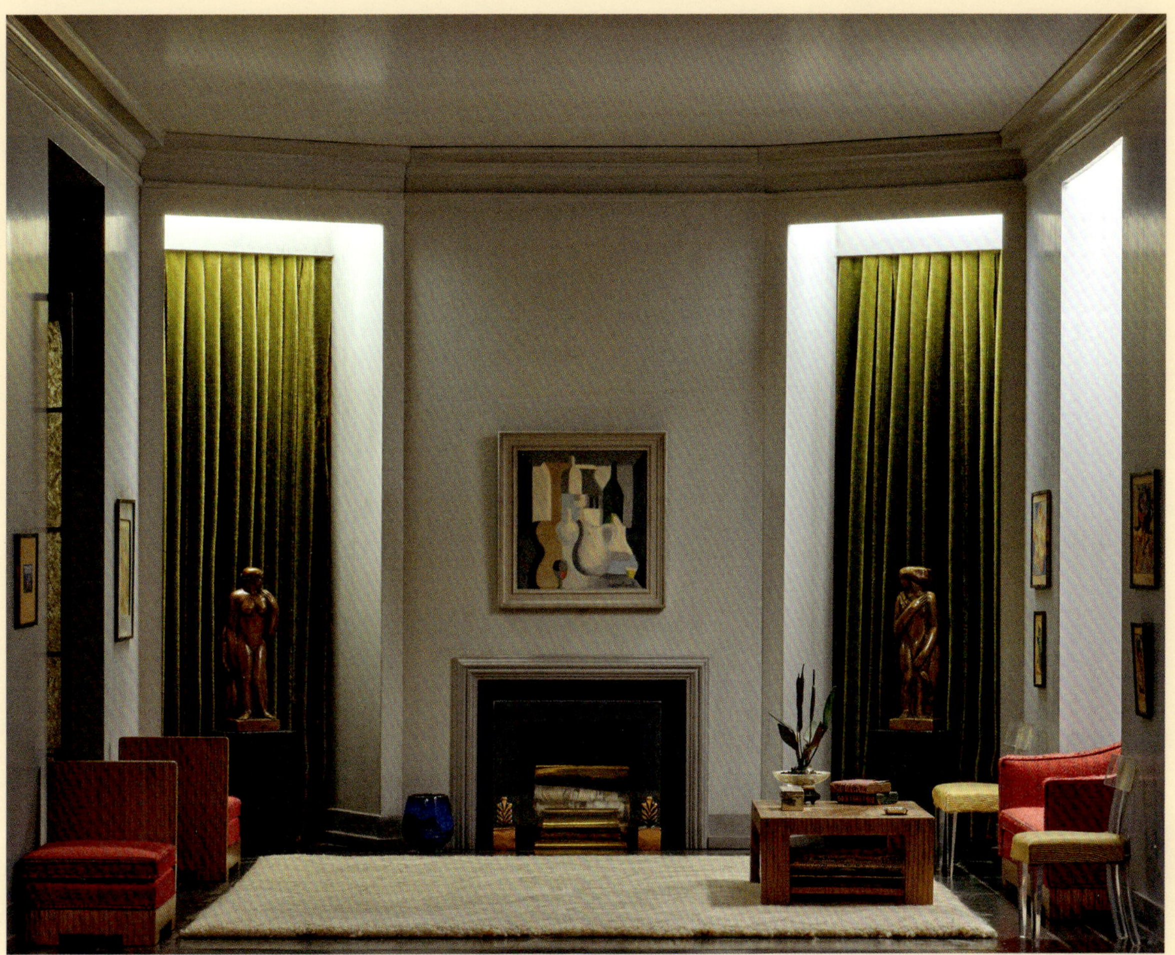

Fig. 4. Designed by Narcissa Niblack Thorne (American, 1882–1966). *A-37: California Hallway, about 1940*, about 1937. Miniature room; mixed media. Gift of Mrs. James Ward Thorne, 1942.517.

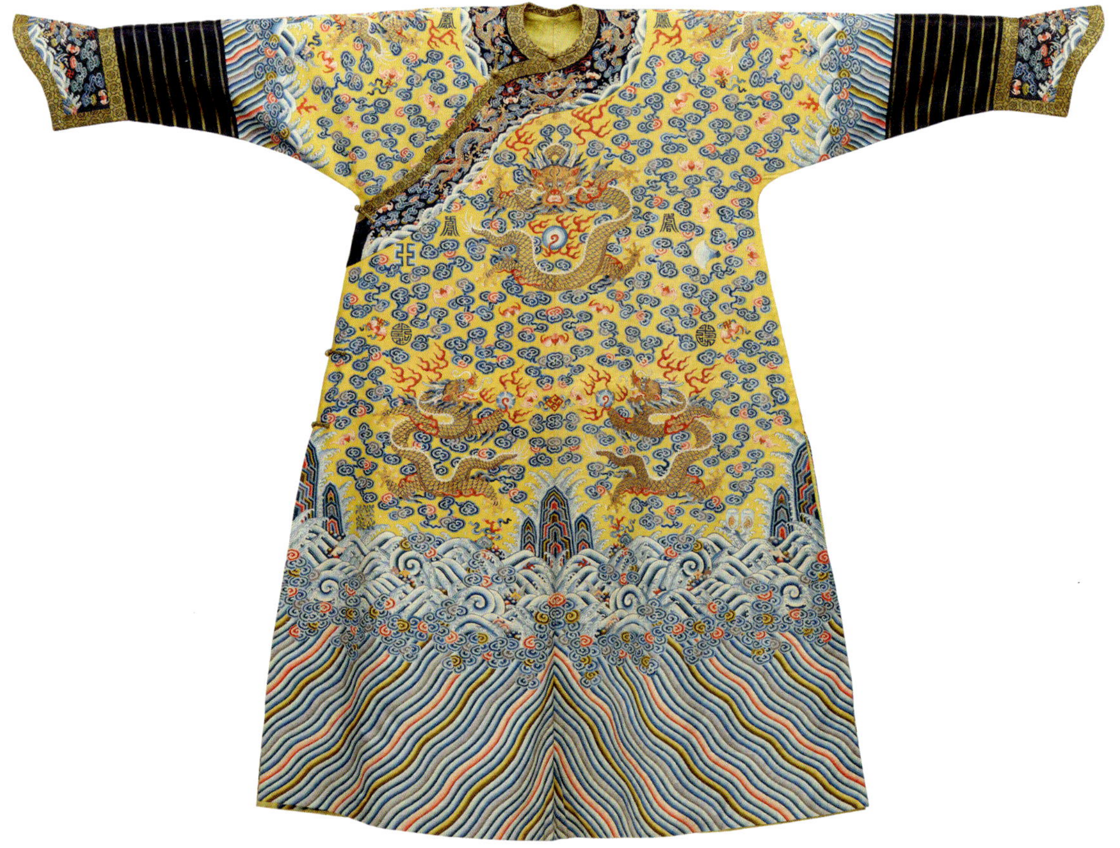

65. Emperor's Semiformal Court Robe (*Jifu*), 1790–1820, China

This garment is an emperor's semiformal court robe in the *jifu* category, meaning auspicious clothing. Jifu were worn on official occasions when business was being conducted and were meant to project the status of the wearer. Like all official garments worn by the emperor, the main body contains the twelve symbols of imperial authority: the sun, the moon, constellations, mountains, a pair of dragons, birds, ritual cups, water weeds, millet, fire, an ax, and the symmetrical *fu* symbol, which represents the emperor's ability to distinguish right from wrong. These symbols represent the emperor's right to rule over the universe. In addition, larger, five-clawed dragons are repeated on the body, a design reserved for the emperor alone. The state ensured proper use of these symbols through its tight control on the production of silk textiles.

The long Qing dynasty began in 1644, when warriors from Manchuria captured Beijing during a regional power struggle, and lasted until 1911, when global politics forced the Manchu royal family to abdicate in the name of the last emperor, who was a child of six at the time. Even well before the Qing dynasty, textiles and dress served as visual indicators of power and status within the large and complex imperial court. *Melinda Watt*

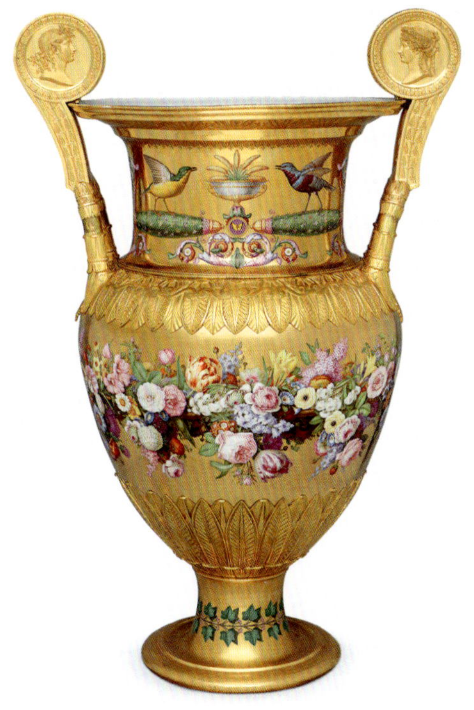

66. Sèvres Porcelain Manufactory, **Monumental Vase**, 1813, France

The Sèvres Manufactory has been France's premier porcelain manufacturer for over 250 years, renowned for its vibrant colors and sumptuous designs. Sèvres has had the uncanny ability to survive France's numerous political shifts: The national government has owned Sèvres since King Louis XV purchased it in 1759.

In the early 1800s, Sèvres embraced the Neoclassical style that was promoted during the reign of Emperor Napoleon I. The design for this vase was begun by 1810, but it was not completed until 1813 and was still in the factory in 1814 when Napoleon was exiled. Looking past the vase's imperial beginnings, the newly restored Bourbon monarch—King Louis XVIII—recognized its diplomatic potential. Charles Maurice de Talleyrand, the French foreign minister, gave the vase to Robert Stewart, Viscount Castlereagh (later the 2nd Marquess of Londonderry), the British foreign secretary. The bestowed vase was no doubt a strategic attempt by the French to curry favor with Castlereagh, as he played a key role in the Congress of Vienna, which rebalanced power in Europe following Napoleon's defeat. Today, the monumental vase is a testament to the ambition of Sèvres and the power of diplomatic gift giving. *Mairead Carney Horton*

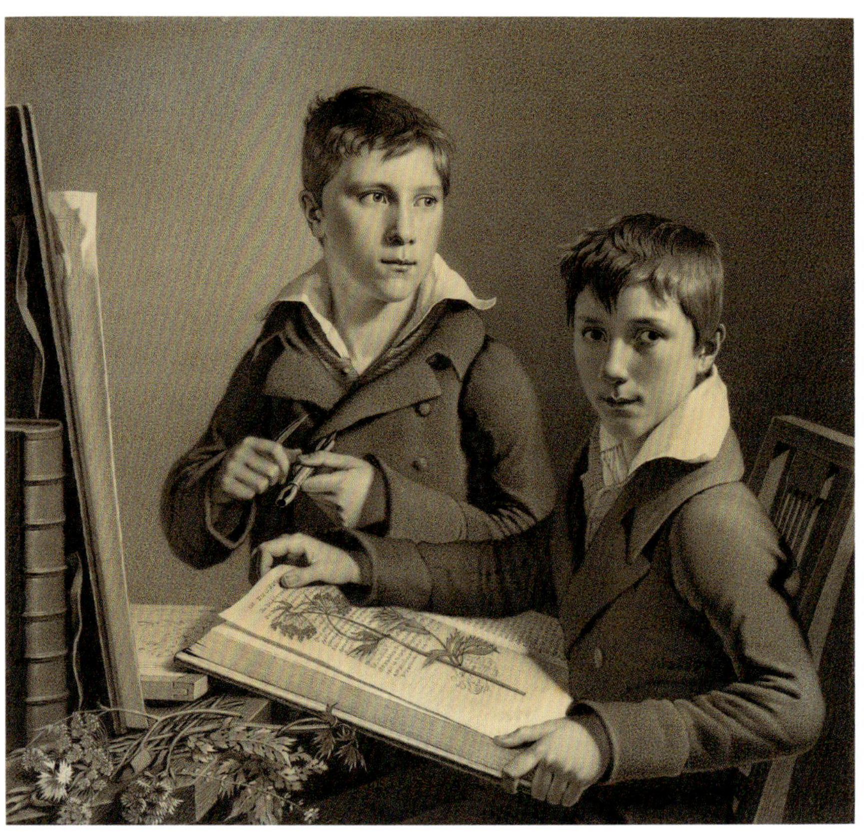

67. Hans Jakob Oeri, The Twin Brothers Ludwig and Emil Schulthess, 1818–19

The uncanny immediacy of these sitters—twin brothers Emil and Ludwig Schulthess, who lived in early nineteenth-century Zurich, Switzerland—results from the near-photorealist precision of artist Hans Jakob Oeri's technique. Oeri also placed the boys so close to the viewer that, along with the seated brother's intense outward stare, we feel as if we're in the room with them.

Emil holds a large book—an herbarium—on which a dried and pressed flower has been placed. A small pile of other flowers, apparently being prepared for the same treatment, sits at lower left. Ludwig, standing, lost in thought, holds a porte-crayon (a drawing instrument that contains black chalk on one end and red on the other), preparing to sketch the plant on the paper propped against the standing portfolio visible on the left.

This drawing celebrates the tangible and empirical, that which can be seen and observed. The artist drew Emil and Ludwig with a scientific precision similar to the way the brothers record and preserve nature within the image. This is drawing as a way of documenting the world, the scientific spirit of the Enlightenment at work. *Kevin Salatino*

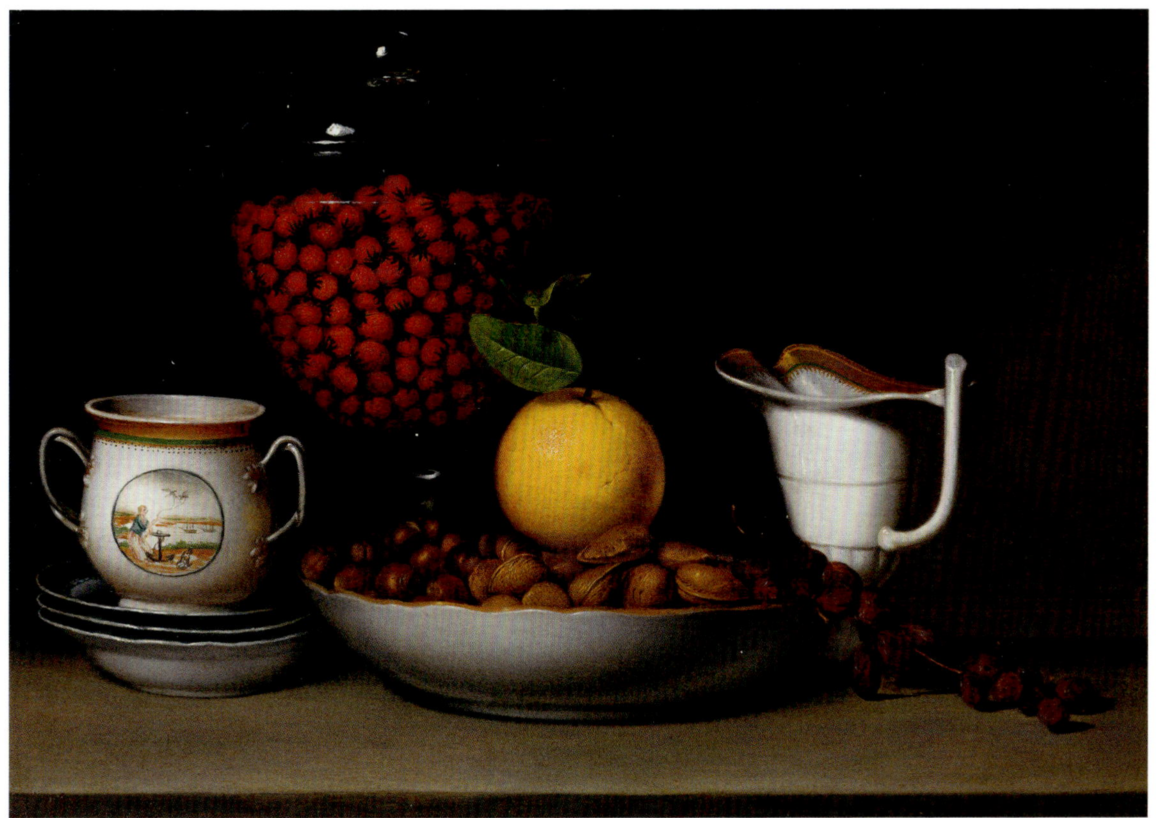

68. Raphaelle Peale, Still Life—Strawberries, Nuts, &c., 1822

Still Life—Strawberries, Nuts, &c. is a seemingly simple composition: fruits, nuts, and pottery arranged on a table. The artist Raphaelle Peale favored still lifes like this one, reveling in their pristine details but also offering subject matter meant to be decoded. Revealing Peale's layered meanings uncovers societal transformations in the nineteenth-century United States.

On the left side of the panel is a Chinese-export porcelain sugar bowl that refers to the nation's growing economy. The bowl features an allegorical figure of Hope anchored to the land but aware of the expansive possibilities of the world, shown by tethered birds and sailboats. Peale paired this allegory with fruits and nuts to symbolize the scope of what was available in Philadelphia at that time. The abundant strawberries and glistening orange cultivated in hothouses display botanical achievements, while the nuts and raisins represent familiar seasonal domestic produce. Peale carefully selected these objects for their symbolic meanings, including them in a rhythmically balanced tabletop composition that resonates with far-reaching global activities.

Peale's visual riddle reveals Hope grounded in the known world, but still looking toward the birds fluttering in the air—dreaming of a blooming new republic among the fruits and porcelain. *Sofia Martinez*

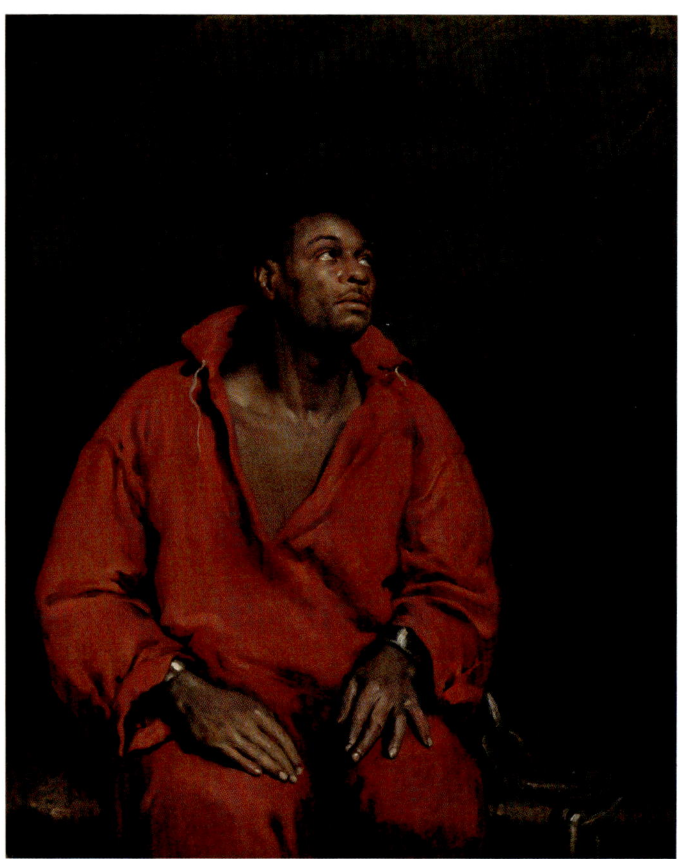

71. John Philip Simpson, The Captive Slave (Ira Aldridge), 1827

In the years leading up to the British Emancipation Act of 1833, this painting of an enslaved man constituted a timely abolitionist appeal. Set against a deeply shadowed background, the figure's upward gaze suggests a yearning for freedom as he sits manacled to a bench.

The composition echoes conventional imagery of Christian saints and martyrs; artist John Philip Simpson used familiar iconography to appeal to the sentimentality of wealthy white viewers with the requisite power to sway public policy. But the deeply moving pose also reflects the artistic contribution of the man who modeled for the figure, now identified as Ira Aldridge, a freeborn American actor famous for playing the title role in Shakespeare's *Othello*. His performance in Thomas Morton's musical drama *The Slave* may have been the immediate inspiration for Simpson's painting. Aldridge was also renowned for his impassioned speeches for the abolitionist cause.

In 1827, when *The Captive Slave* was first exhibited at the Royal Academy of Arts in London, the accompanying catalogue included the following excerpt from William Cowper's 1782 antislavery poem, "Charity": "But ah! what wish can prosper, or what prayer, / For merchants rich in cargoes of despair." *Emerson Bowyer*

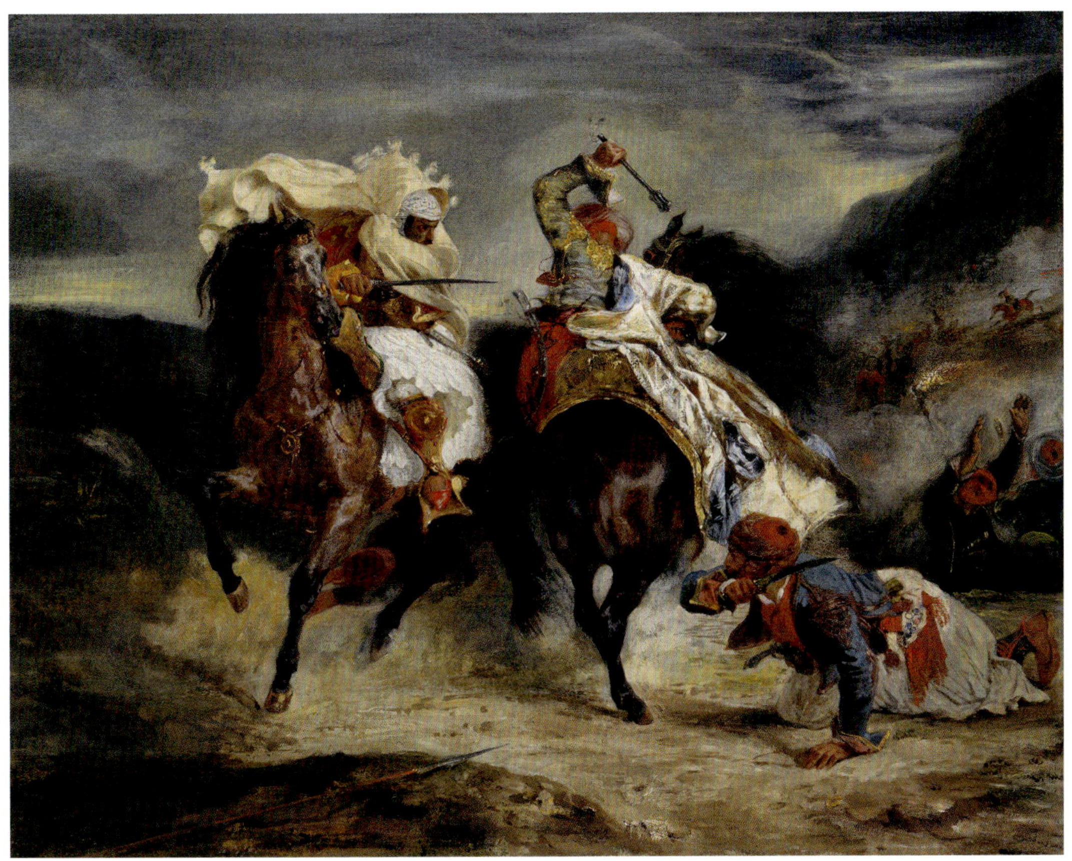

72. Eugène Delacroix, The Combat of the Giaour and Hassan, 1826

For this frenetic scene, Eugène Delacroix took inspiration from "The Giaour," a poem in a popular series of romantic tales by the celebrated English poet Lord Byron. *Giaour* is a derogatory Turkish word for a Christian or non-Muslim applied here to the warrior at left clad in swirling white drapery. Amid a violent struggle, the Giaour is avenging the death of his lover at the hands of his opponent. Delacroix mirrored the two central figures and their horses as the Giaour is about to strike the fatal blow against the faceless Turk Hassan. The artist's mastery of color is exemplified by his use of shimmering primary hues, while the loose handling of paint creates the sense of dynamism Delacroix was so capable of executing.

This painting reflects Delacroix's sustained engagement with Orientalism, the artistic representation of non-European people and places, especially North Africa, Asia, and the Middle East. Delacroix was among the first European artists to travel to Africa when he visited Morocco in 1832, shortly after he completed this painting. Widespread in the nineteenth century, Orientalism was regularly leveraged to reinforce French colonial enterprises through often fantastical, violent, or erotic depictions of the customs and cultures of faraway locales.
Andrea Morgan

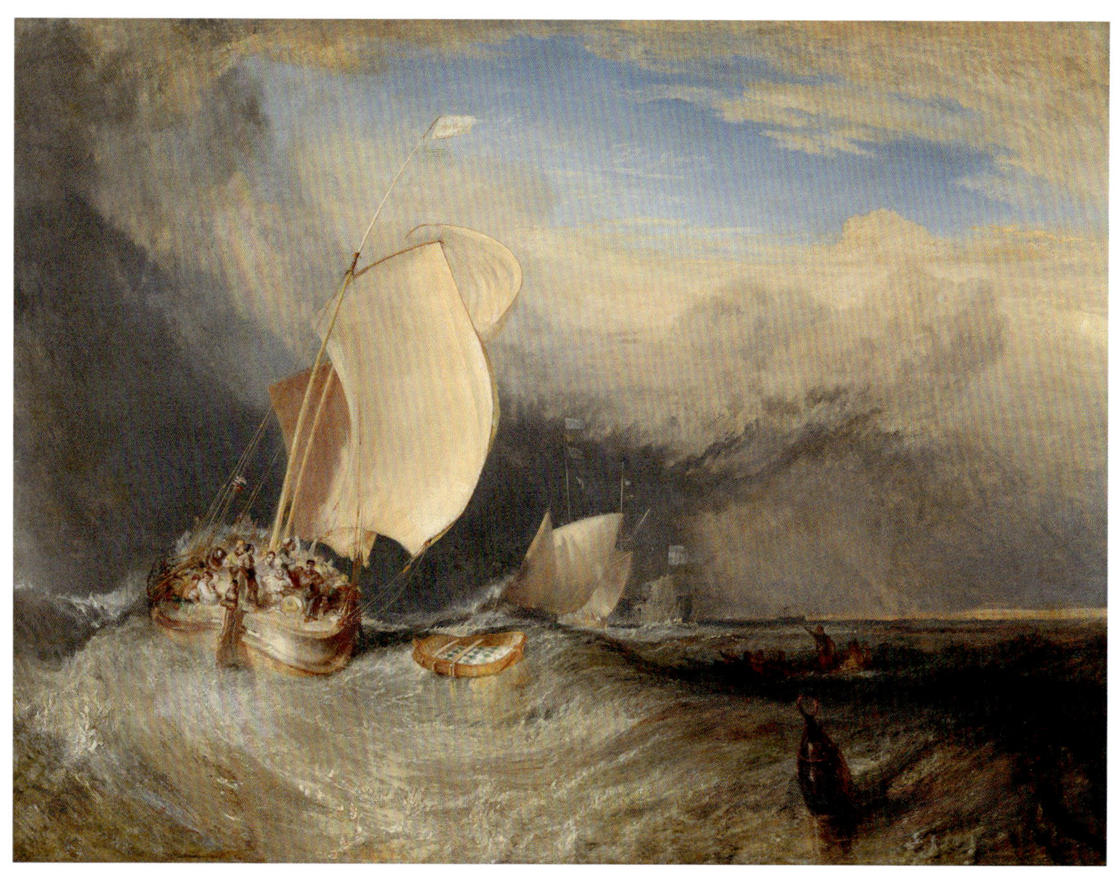

73. Joseph Mallord William Turner, **Fishing Boats with Hucksters Bargaining for Fish**, 1837–38

English artist J. M. W. Turner was fascinated by the sea. Here, a crowded fishing boat rides atop rolling, tumultuous waves. A smaller boat occupied by hucksters, or peddlers, navigates the churning waters as it approaches the larger vessel to negotiate the buying of fish to sell back at port. A steamship chugs along in the background, signaling the new industrial age.

This painting dates from a period when the artist was increasingly interested in atmospheric drama and the effects of light, exemplified here by the turbulent storm brewing in the background. The sunlit water in the foreground is dotted with a thick impasto, the heavy application of paint that results in painterly depth and surface texture. For this composition and others, Turner was inspired by the tradition of seventeenth-century Dutch marine painting and its leading painter, Willem van de Velde, whose work was popular in England. The subject itself and compositional elements such as the low horizon line are characteristic of earlier Dutch seascapes, but Turner cleverly laid claim to this painting by signing it on the white flag fluttering high on the mast of the fishing boat that pokes through to the sliver of clear blue sky. *Andrea Morgan*

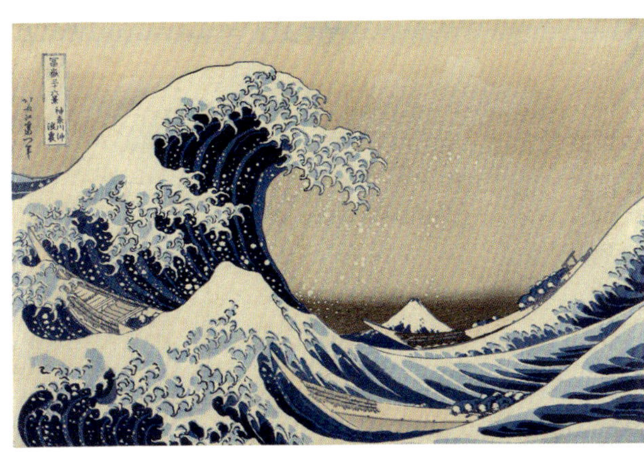

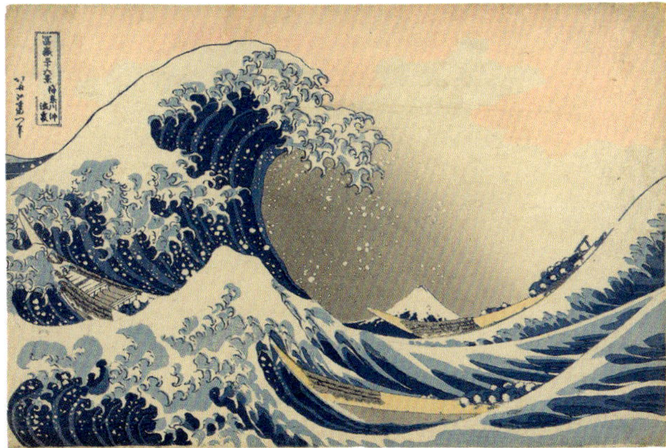

74. Katsushika Hokusai, **The Great Wave off Kanagawa**, 1830–33

The Great Wave under a pink sky? While the color has faded to a nearly imperceptible beige in almost every version of this famous print, it was part of the original design. Pink ink, made with safflower (*beni*), was particularly prone to fading. The sky retains its rosy color in the lower impression, which was made relatively late in the life of the well-known image. The shape of the light blue in the waves varies between these two works, the result of recut blocks used in later printings. Broken outlines, such as the one on the crest of the wave at far right, are an obvious sign that this was not printed when the blocks were new.

Katsushika Hokusai's prints of Mount Fuji display his masterful compositional skill—whether the volcano is visually dominant, as in many designs, or reduced in scale, as it is here. *The Great Wave* is one of the most compelling images in Japanese art. Not only do the surging breakers seem to swamp the boaters, but—to the Japanese eye, accustomed to reading from right to left—the great claw of a wave appears almost to tumble into the viewer's face. Even Mount Fuji appears fragile, about to be engulfed by the uncontrollable energy of the water. *Janice Katz*

Floating Worlds

Janice Katz

Dynamic prints illustrating Japanese life and culture have excited imaginations in Chicago for more than one hundred years.

As a curator, it is incredible to me that I can chart precisely which Japanese prints Clarence Buckingham, an early museum trustee and businessman, bought and when (and for how much!) thanks to the meticulous 1890s records kept by his personal curator and later the museum's first curator of Japanese art, Frederick Gookin. But the unparalleled collection of Japanese prints at the Art Institute is not only the product of late nineteenth-century visionaries like Buckingham: It has continually benefited from pioneering collectors and artists at key points into the twenty-first century. These individuals have impelled the museum to the forefront of displaying Japanese prints, both classical and contemporary, for over a century. Currently, the collection numbers about 15,000 single and multi-sheet works and printed books. Its strengths are in early commercial prints from the start of the eighteenth century and rare works (sometimes the only existing copy) by notable artists such as Katsushika Hokusai and Tōshūsai Sharaku. Thanks to the size and breadth of our holdings, a rotation of Japanese prints is on continuous view in the Clarence Buckingham Gallery.

Buckingham embarked on collecting only the finest Japanese prints beginning in 1894; his interest is said to have been sparked by seeing Japanese art at the World's Columbian Exposition in Chicago the year prior. I often wonder what Buckingham, who never visited Japan, thought about the images of actors and courtesans—the amusements of life in a premodern Japanese city—when he first laid eyes on these images. Japanese prints of this period are known as *ukiyo-e*, literally "pictures of the floating world." They record the popularity of stars of the stage and famous beauties, as well as just about any of the fleeting pleasures available in the most populous city on the planet at the time.

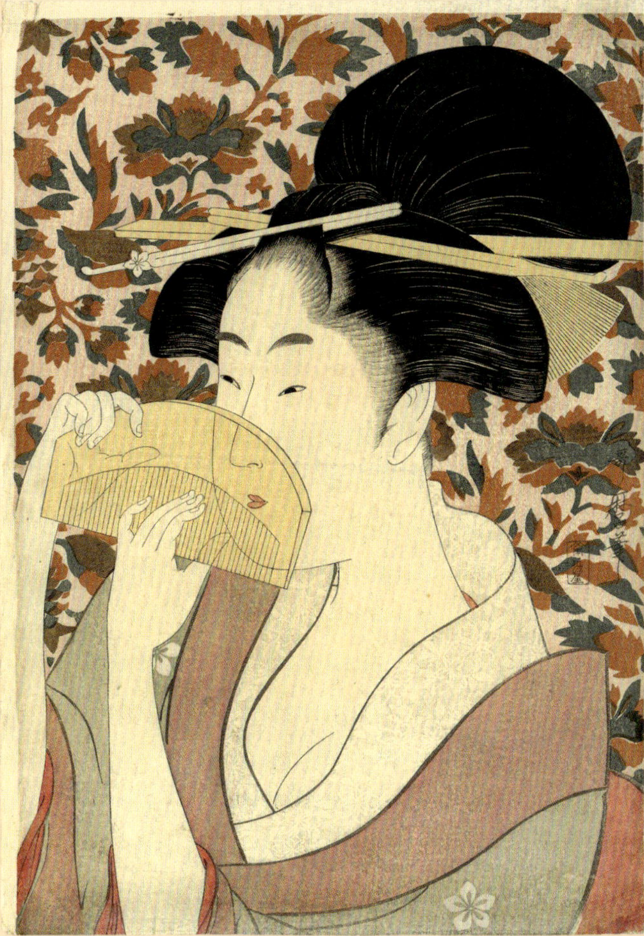

Fig. 1. Kitagawa Utamaro (Japanese, about 1753–1806). *Woman Holding a Tortoise-Shell Hair-Comb*, about 1795–96. Color woodblock print; ōban; 39.2 × 26.6 cm (15 7⁄16 × 10 1⁄2 in.). Clarence Buckingham Collection, 1925.3068.

Following Buckingham's untimely death from heart failure in 1913, his sister Kate Buckingham put the prints on loan to the museum and set up Gookin as the curator. Among the many remarkable works in this collection is one designed by Kitagawa Utamaro, whose large-head portraits attempt to capture the psychological nuances of his anonymous subjects. In *Woman Holding a Tortoise-Shell Hair-Comb* (fig. 1), the delicate facial features of the courtesan are seen through the transparency of the pale-yellow comb. Her partially hidden face and the Indian-style printed cotton behind her heighten the mystery of the woman's gesture and setting. Images of the pleasure quarters, like this one, were understandably put down in print, as the district was a rare world of color and glamour amid the drabness of the city, but they mask the harsh realities of a life lived there.

Kate continued to purchase prints in her brother's name; she never wanted her own name on the credit line. She gave some of the most famous works in the collection and provided for their exhibition and care. From the collection of Alexander Mosle, a German businessman and collector working in Japan at the turn of the twentieth century, Kate acquired Suzuki Harunobu's *Eight Views of the Parlor*, notable for its early and skillful use of multicolor printing. This particular group includes two one-of-a-kind features as well: the title wrapper (similar to an envelope) for the set as well as the signature of the project's funder and coordinator, Kyosen, written by hand on of the prints (see fig. 2). This signature might indicate that this was the very first finished set to be produced and approved. We see courtesans shaping cotton for use in hats, and the white of the fabric (beautifully embossed on the print) is meant to call to mind snow on mountains. Probably the greatest success of Kate's acquisitions to add to her brother's collection was a group of works by the master of caricature Tōshūsai Sharaku (see fig. 3) from collector Charles Chandler of Evanston, just north of Chicago. Apparently Kate did not favor Sharaku's art (and many of the artist's contemporaries in Japan shared her dislike), but she was advised (probably by Gookin) that this was a rare opportunity. While Sharaku's career lasted only ten

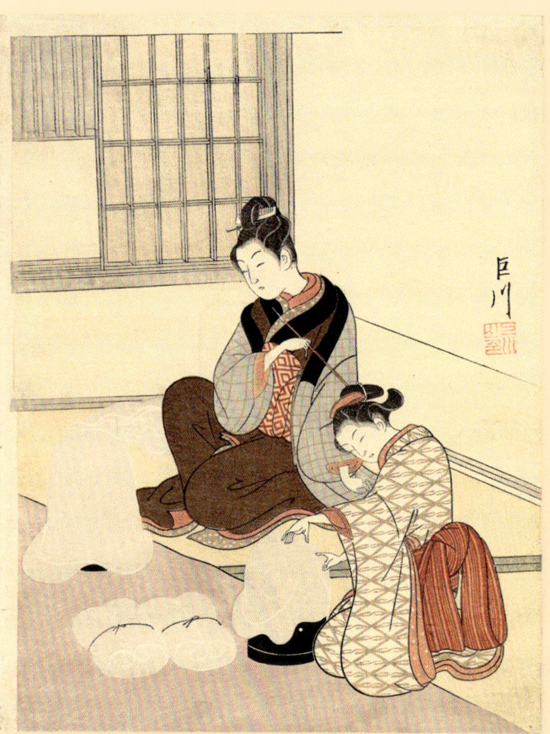

Fig. 2. Suzuki Harunobu (Japanese, about 1725–1770). *Evening Snow on a Floss Shaper* (*Nurioke no bosetsu*), from the series *Eight Views of the Parlor* (*Zashiki hakkei*), about 1766. Color woodblock print; chūban; 28.7 × 21.6 cm (11¼ × 8½ in.). Clarence Buckingham Collection, 1928.903.

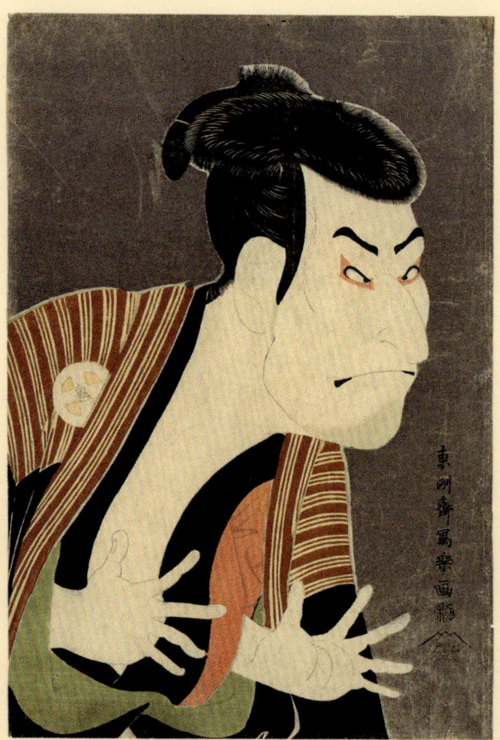

Fig. 3. Tōshūsai Sharaku (Japanese, active 1794–95). *The Actor Ōtani Oniji III as Edobei*, 1794. Color woodblock print; ōban; 37.9 × 25 cm (14 15/16 × 9 7/8 in.). Clarence Buckingham Collection, 1934.207.

Fig. 4. Onchi Kōshirō (Japanese, 1891–1955). *Object No. 2*, 1954. Woodblock and object print; 60.8 × 45.6 cm (23 15⁄16 × 48 in.). Kate S. Buckingham Endowment, 1979.629.

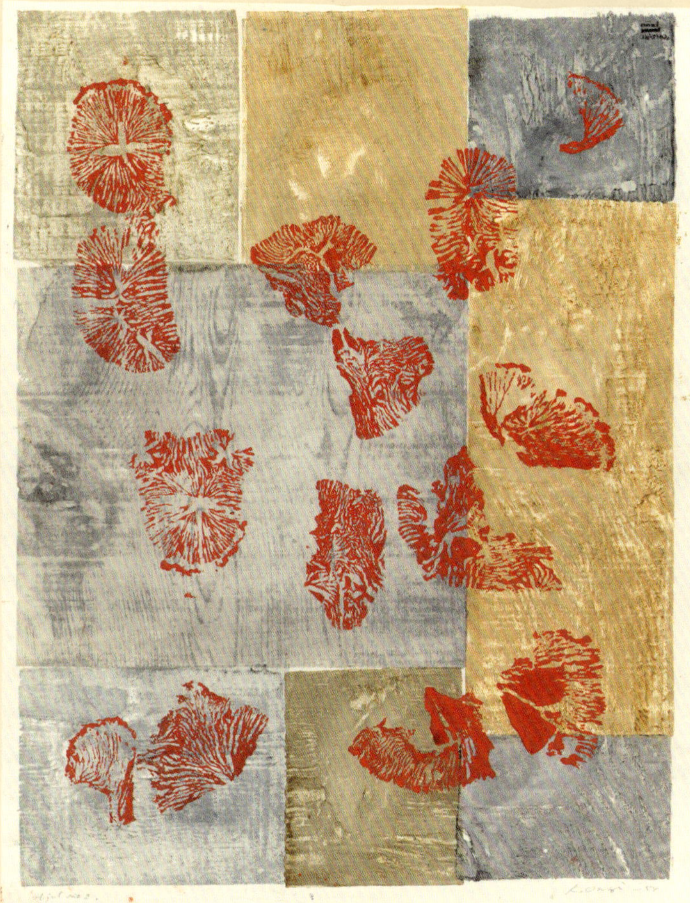

months, his images nonetheless made a strong impact with their ability to exaggerate even the drama seen on stage.

Another great period of the collection's expansion came in the 1950s and 1960s, largely due to the activities of Oliver Statler. He was one of a handful of Americans who lectured and organized exhibitions of contemporary Japanese prints during the Allied Powers occupation of Japan from 1945 to 1952. Statler was born in Illinois and attended the University of Chicago. In 1951 the museum bought its first prints from Statler, and he gave more than two hundred prints and magazines over the years. The most remarkable works to pass through Statler's hands, though, are Onchi Kōshirō's abstract prints (see fig. 4), acquired no doubt due to Statler's great friendship with the artist. It would be decades before such abstract works were appreciated outside a handful of admirers.

Because the Art Institute's collection has become a hub for Japanese prints, contemporary artists continue to gift their works directly to the collection, keeping it a vibrant record of Japanese prints up to today.

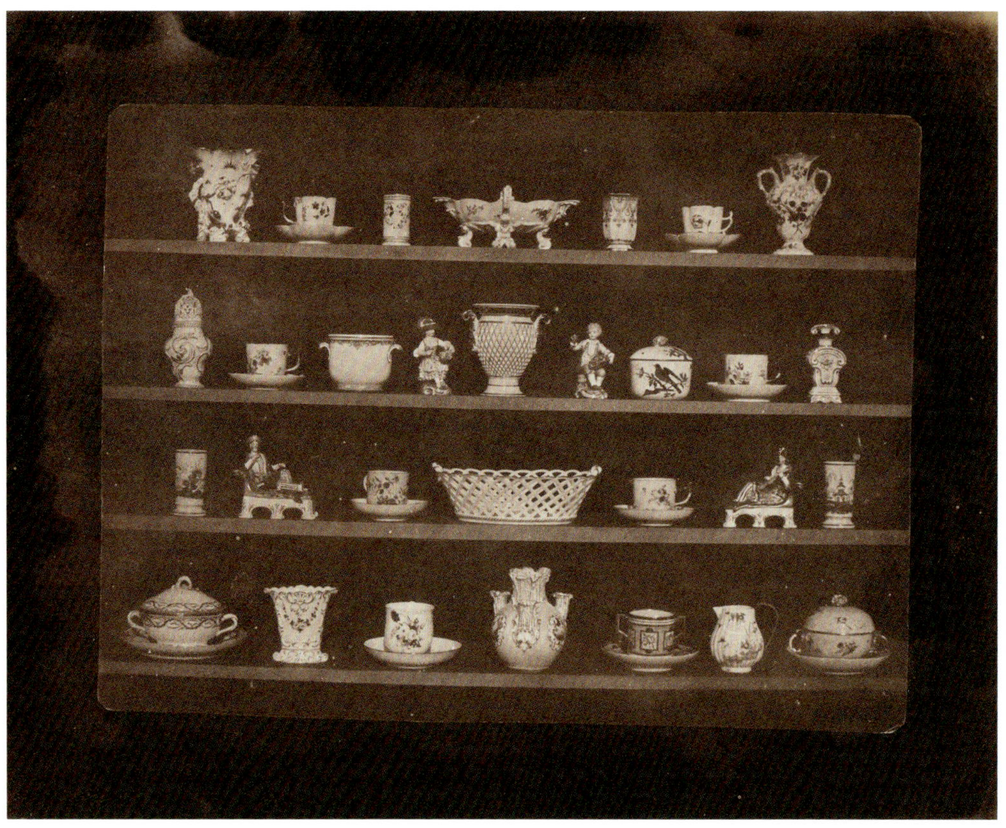

75. William Henry Fox Talbot, **Articles of China**, 1843–44

William Henry Fox Talbot printed this photograph using a process of his own invention. The salted paper print is one of the earliest forms of photography involving a negative that could generate multiple prints of the same image. Talbot coated sheets of paper with a light-sensitive mixture of table salt and silver nitrate. The negative was placed directly onto the sensitized paper and exposed to light, forming the image. Finally, the print was washed in water and "fixed" in a bath of sodium thiosulfate, making it no longer light sensitive.

Talbot elaborated on the vast potential of this new technology in *The Pencil of Nature* (1844), the first commercially published book illustrated with photographs. He included this photograph of a carefully arranged display of porcelain figures to demonstrate how accurately his new process captured the ornate details of each object, asserting that "the whole cabinet of a Virtuoso and collector of old China might be depicted on paper in little more time than it would take him to make a written inventory describing it in the usual way." Such a visual inventory, Talbot suggested, could be practical, for instance in the event of an insurance claim.
Emily Mercer

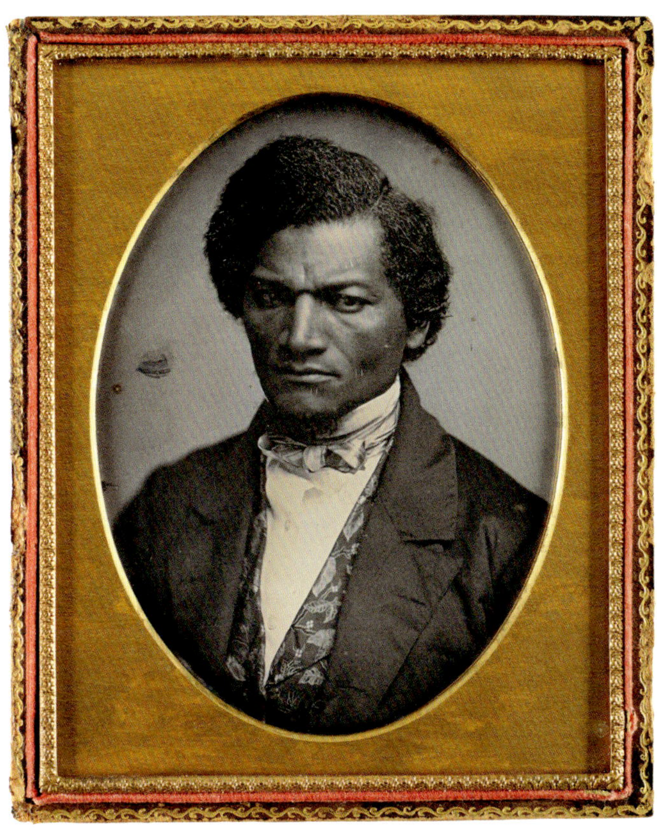

76. Samuel J. Miller, **Frederick Douglass**, 1847–52

In 1839 Louis-Jacques-Mandé Daguerre announced the perfection of the daguerreotype, a photographic process that employed a silver-coated copper plate sensitive to light. This new artistic process was celebrated for its remarkably sharp detail and praised as a "democratic art" that brought portraiture into reach for the masses. Within a few years, thousands of daguerrean portrait studios had sprung up all over the United States, among them the one that Samuel J. Miller owned in Akron, Ohio.

Although most of the likenesses made in commercial studios were formulaic and not particularly revealing of the subject's character, this portrait of Frederick Douglass—a man who escaped from slavery and became a lauded speaker, writer, and abolitionist agitator—is a striking exception. Northeastern Ohio was a center of abolitionism prior to the Civil War, and Douglass knew that this picture, one of an astonishing number that he commissioned or posed for, would be seen by ardent supporters of his campaign to end slavery. Douglass adeptly managed his public image and likely guided Miller in projecting his intensity and sheer force of character. As a result, this portrait demonstrates that Douglass truly appeared "majestic in his wrath," as the nineteenth-century feminist Elizabeth Cady Stanton observed. *Elizabeth Siegel*

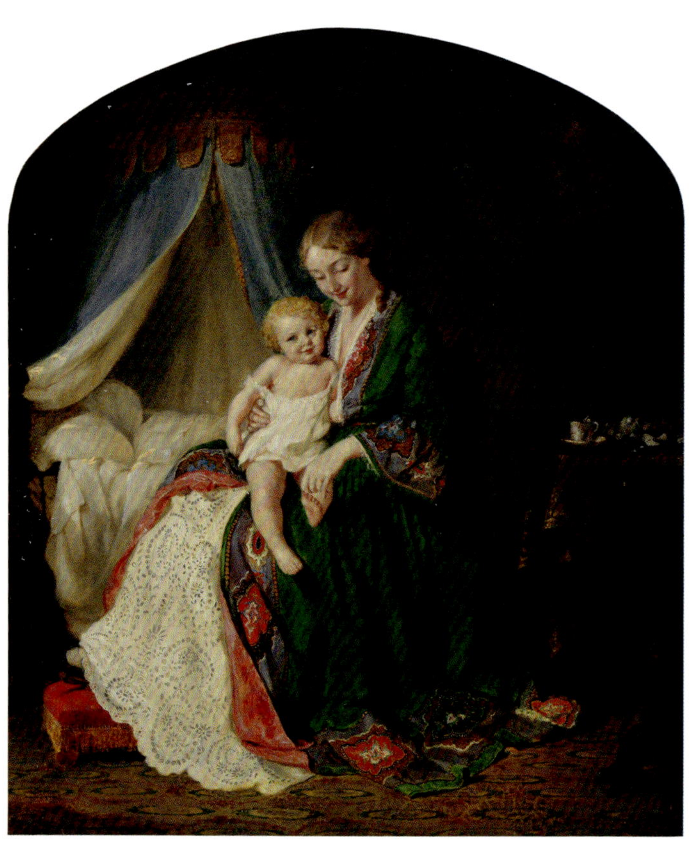

77. Lilly Martin Spencer, This Little Pig Went to Market, about 1857

Lilly Martin Spencer centered women in vivid portrayals of the everyday activities of white, urban, middle-class households like her own. *This Little Pig Went to Market* features a mother and child (probably modeled by the artist and her son William Henry) reciting the eponymous nursery rhyme. The game celebrates their emotional bond while also hinting at the larger society that the boy will eventually join.

Spencer excelled at such intricate scenes, known as genre painting, building a remarkable career in mid-nineteenth-century America. Establishing herself in Cincinnati in the 1840s, she found success the following decade in New York. A working mother (she endured thirteen pregnancies and raised seven surviving children), the artist was the breadwinner for her family. Tapping into a burgeoning US market for paintings and print reproductions, Spencer cultivated opportunities for her compositions to circulate widely. Translating her tremendous popularity into financial security, however, remained a constant struggle.

What fascinates me about this painting is its seemingly quiet, unassuming nature: a small-scale canvas depicting a moment of domestic life, a modest artwork that likely appealed to middle-class families striving to adorn their own homes. Savvy and ambitious, Spencer focused on the lived experiences at arm's reach and, in turn, opened up her world. *Annelise K. Madsen*

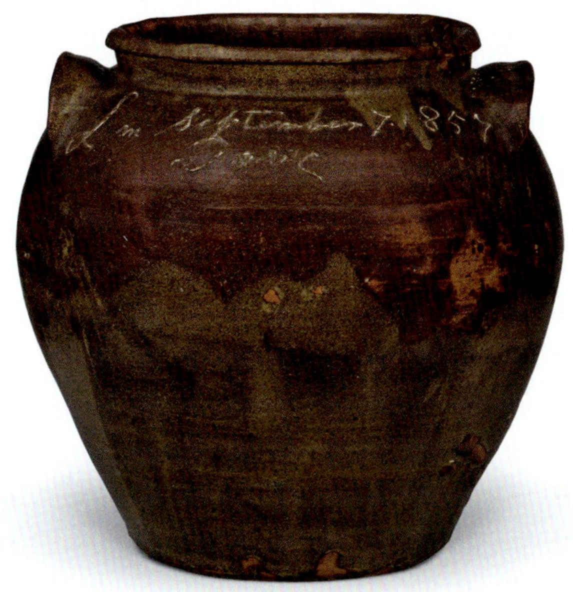

78. David Drake at Lewis Miles Stoney Bluff Manufactory (plantation), Storage Jar, 1857

It's easy to overlook the mundane, but there we can find resistance in its rawest form. David Drake made this storage jar and inscribed it "LM September 7 1857 / Dave." David was born enslaved around 1800 and learned the art of pottery in Edgefield, South Carolina. It is tempting to comment on David's exceptionalism and his defiance of mandates against his own literacy and humanity. Well intended, this praise overshadows the tiny nuances that make up the work and his life. His pieces are filled to the brim with small subtleties that can be easily missed. Taking time to follow the rhythm of his throwing marks, mimic the pour of his glazes, and trace the lines of his signature can help us discover the pieces that make up the man. You understand the context of his resistance but also the inner workings of his genius—the raw skill he innately possessed.

Being in the midst of David's work feels like meeting a distant cousin, a reconnection I did not know I had been searching for. Experiencing the presence of Black American legends, known and anonymous, reminds me that this ancestral lineage of makers is much closer than I think. And whenever I am in need, they are just a call away. *Gerald A. Brown*

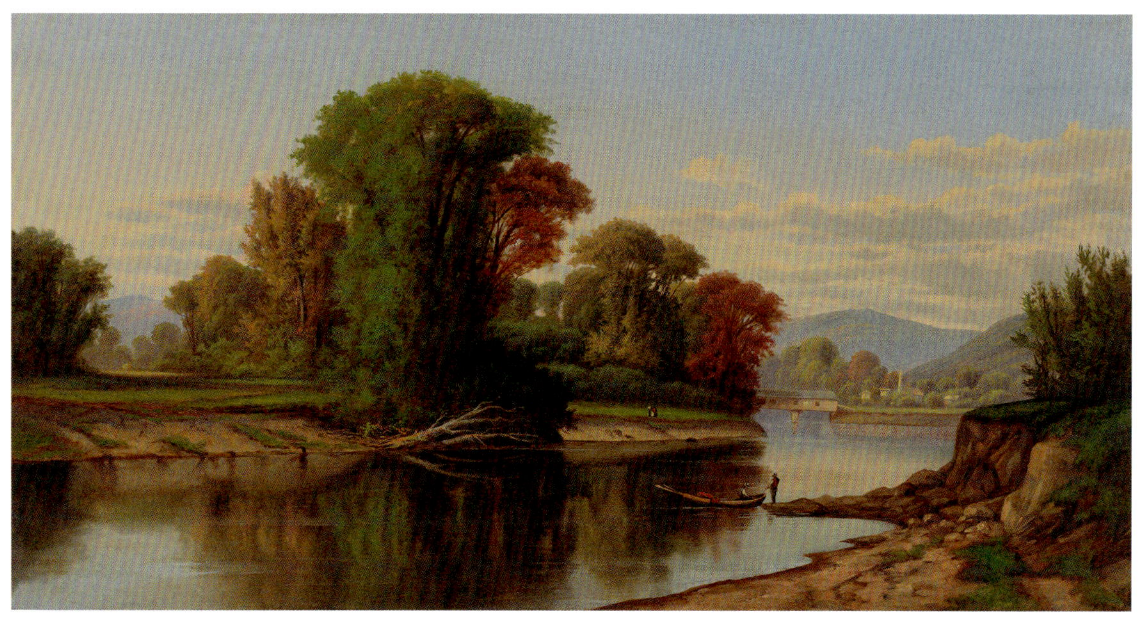

79. Robert S. Duncanson, **River Scene**, 1867–71

In this autumnal scene featuring lush foliage and luminous reflections along the water, Robert S. Duncanson employed passages of open brushwork to describe the river's placid surface and the green and russet trees along the far bank. He harmonized scenic detail with atmospheric views, from the minutely rendered figures and boat in the foreground to the jewellike tones of the sunlit terrain in the distance. *River Scene* is an immersive landscape.

A third-generation free person of color, Duncanson built a successful artistic career in antebellum America while also achieving international recognition during his lifetime. In the 1840s he settled in Cincinnati, a seat of abolitionism at the border between North and South as well as an established art center. In Ohio and on sketching trips throughout the Appalachian Mountains and the upper Midwest, he worked in the manner of the Hudson River School. The *Daily Cincinnati Gazette* declared Duncanson "the best landscape painter in the West" in 1861.

That same year, however, the artist fled the heightened racial inequities of the United States for Canada, and later spent time in Britain. After the Civil War, Duncanson returned to his studio in Cincinnati, painting *River Scene* during this late moment in his career. *Annelise K. Madsen*

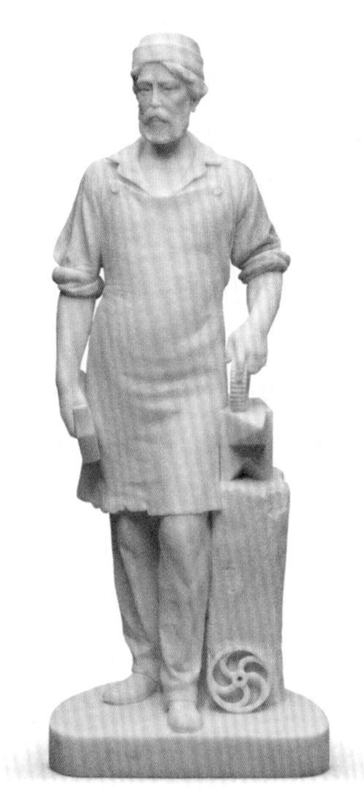

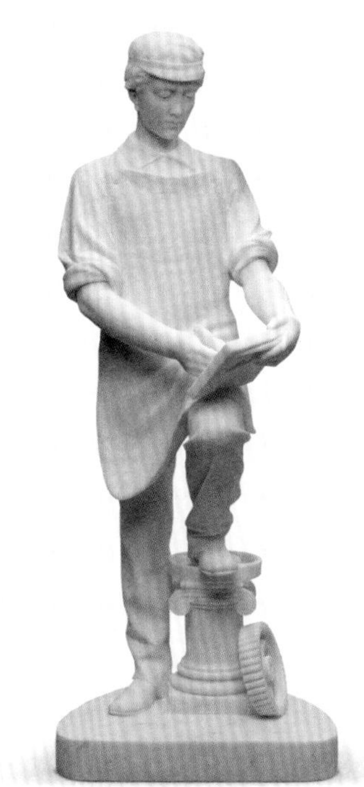

80. Emma Stebbins, **Machinist** and **Machinist's Apprentice**, about 1859

In 1856, at age forty, Emma Stebbins embarked from New York City on a life-changing trip to Europe, where she met the love of her life, renowned actress Charlotte Cushman. They decided to live together in Rome. After shifting her artistic focus from portrait drawing to sculpture, Stebbins became one of the first Americans to create public monuments in bronze, including the beloved Bethesda Fountain in New York's Central Park. Working in the neoclassical style, she also sculpted idealized marble figures inspired by ancient Greek and Roman art (see p. 34).

Machinist and *Machinist's Apprentice*, some of the earliest depictions of laborers in the history of American sculpture, blend tradition and innovation. Stebbins shows the pair making metal gears for machines—not in classical drapery or nude, but in rolled-up shirt sleeves and leather aprons. Holding a hammer at a blacksmith's anvil, the experienced older figure looks like a modern version of Hephaestus/Vulcan, the ancient god of fire and metalworking. Shielding his eyes with a visor, the earnest younger figure concentrates on manipulating his drafting tools. *Machinist* and *Machinist's Apprentice* emphasize the continuity of craft traditions and embody human skill and ingenuity during a time of rapid industrialization, technological change, and societal upheaval. *Karli Wurzelbacher*

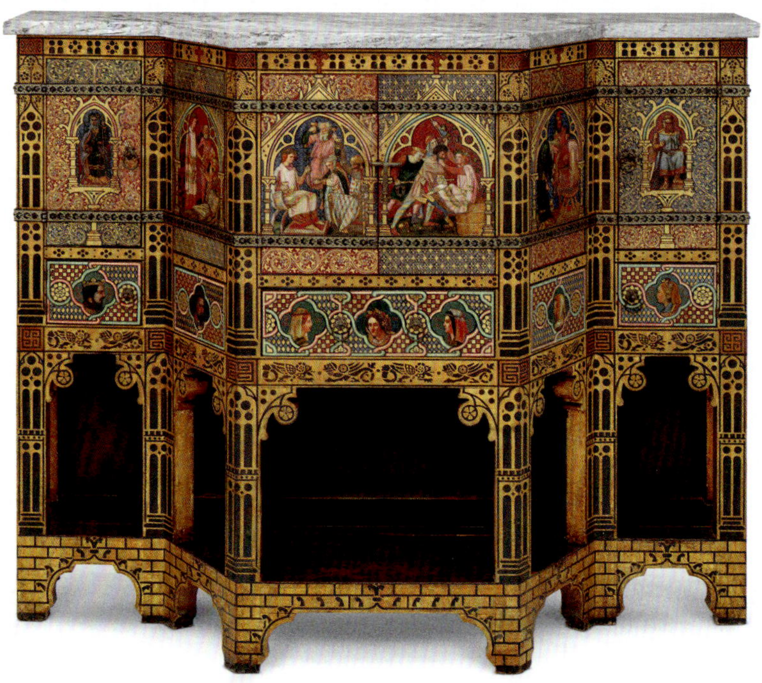

81. William Burges, Sideboard and Wine Cabinet, 1859

A story unfolds on the upper register of the projecting front of this sideboard: Across four panels, a golden-haired young man, dressed in a pink tunic and crowned in grape leaves, sits enthroned while handing out wine to needy supplicants. Then he is shoved into a barrel, where he languishes as a woman draws wine from it. This martyr is Saint Bacchus, the personification of wine from a fourteenth-century French poem called "Le martyre de saint Bacchus" (The martyrdom of Saint Bacchus) that parodies stories of the lives of Christian saints. The cabinet's celebration of wine continues in the series of seven portraits that run beneath the story of Bacchus—these are personifications of different grape varietals, from the dark-haired, crowned prince Burgundy at far left to the fair-haired maiden Champagne at far right.

The cabinet and its decoration were designed by William Burges, a member of the Gothic Revival movement who was beguiled by the art and architecture of the medieval period but who brought a distinct sense of humor to his designs. This extends to the interior of the cabinet's doors, which bear personifications of Temperance and Sobriety in a last-minute, witty reminder to pursue your wine drinking in moderation. *Mairead Carney Horton*

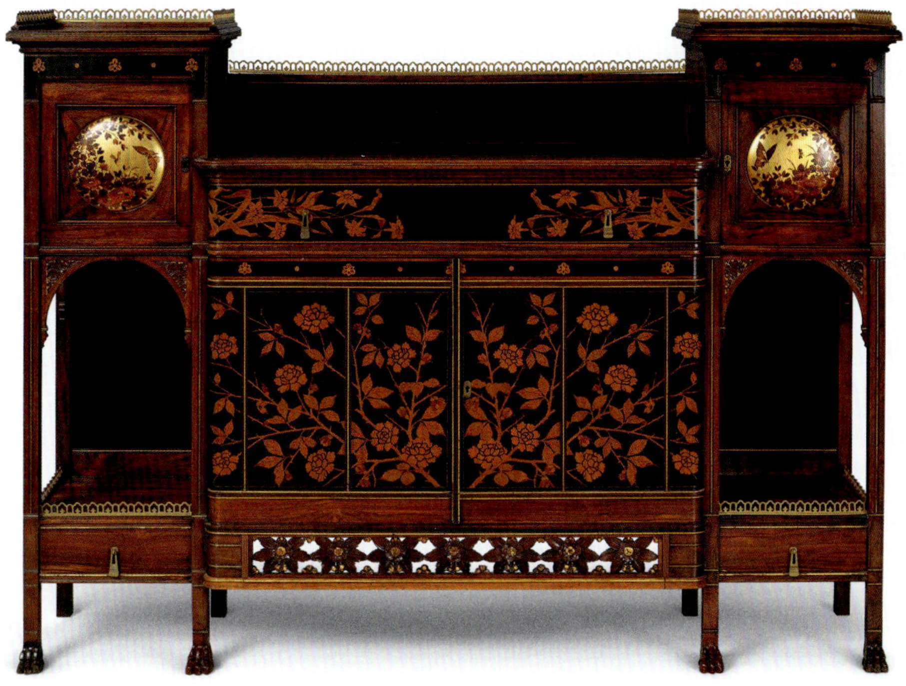

82. Herter Brothers, Cabinet, 1878–80

The influence of Japanese artistic techniques and motifs abounds in this rosewood cabinet. Butterfly roundels set into the left and right cabinet doors dazzle in gold, while stylized floral inlays on the ebonized central compartment are segmented to look like a folding screen. Japan's prolonged period of isolationism ended in 1853, and by the late 1870s, Japanese commodities and art objects proliferated throughout Europe and the United States. As a result, American designers began to incorporate such Japanese-derived elements in their designs.

Herter Brothers was one of the leading firms that designed furniture and interiors for the American upper class during the Aesthetic Movement, a cultural trend that emphasized beauty, particularly through interior design and decoration. Brothers Gustav and Christian Herter, both trained in the German furniture trade before immigrating to the United States in the mid-1800s, founded the company and employed local and migrant artisans to create furnishings that would appeal to a range of buyers. They drew on an eclectic mix of styles, materials, and cultural influences for their varied goods. This cabinet harmonizes a rectilinear furniture form and naturalistic motifs, enlivening a functional object and transforming it into a work of art intended to enrich everyday life. *Sofia Martinez*

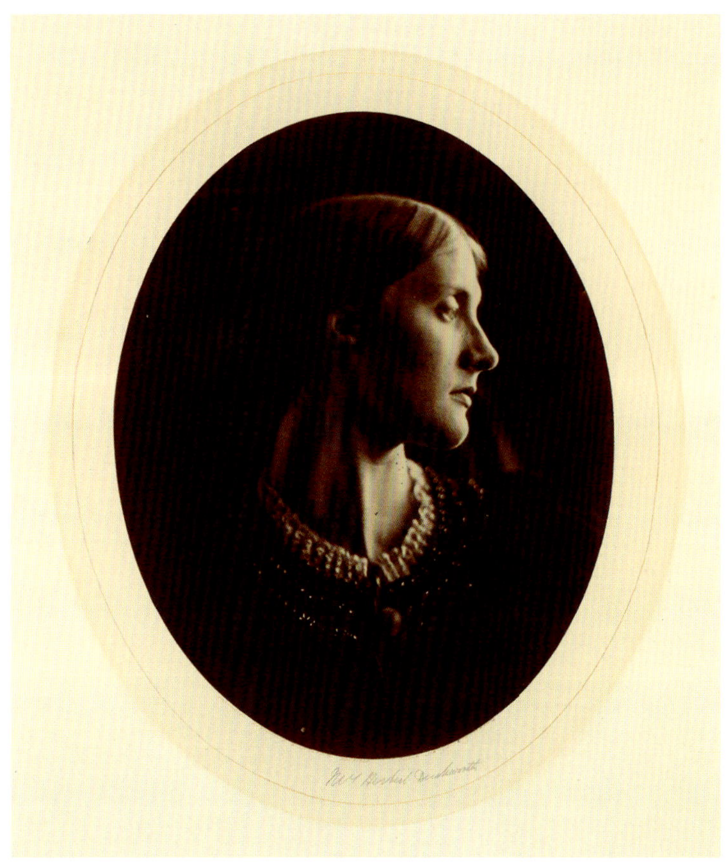

83. Julia Margaret Cameron, **Mrs. Herbert Duckworth**, 1867

In April 1867, just weeks before her niece Julia Jackson's wedding to Herbert Duckworth, Julia Margaret Cameron made a series of portraits of the bride-to-be that are remarkable for their mix of boldness and composure. Cameron titled some of the portraits, including this one, with Jackson's married name—and declared this a favorite picture of one of her favorite sitters. For Cameron, who worked in Victorian England, marital union conferred not just a change of name but also status and completeness upon a young woman.

Yet Cameron, who took up camera work at the age of forty-eight, saw photography as a means less to fix reality than to stage ideals and personalities. Jackson met Cameron's ambitions head on, posing by turns as noble, haunted, vulnerable, distant, and regal. In this photograph, Jackson appears suddenly older, with her hair pulled tight and wearing a blouse and sweater that almost recall the England of Queen Elizabeth I rather than Queen Victoria. She acts the matron that she had not yet become. Herbert Duckworth died suddenly three years later, leaving Jackson a widow with three children at age twenty-four. Her next marriage came nearly a decade later and resulted in the birth of two further remarkable women: painter Vanessa Bell and writer Virginia Woolf. *Matthew S. Witkovsky*

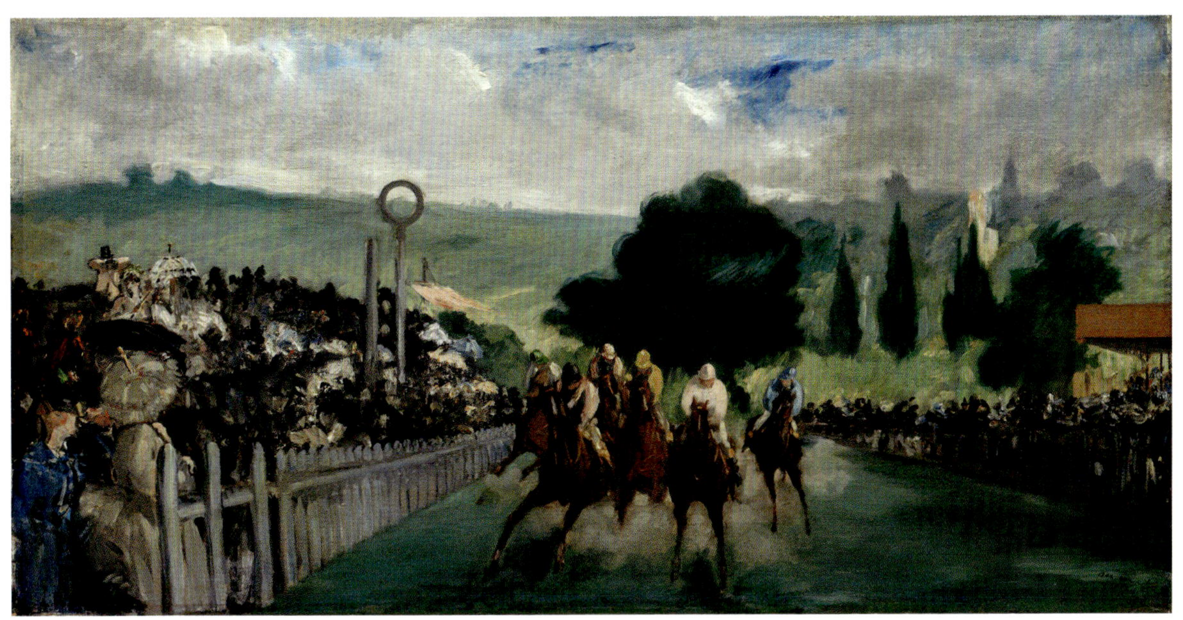

84. Édouard Manet, The Races at Longchamp, 1866

This freely executed painting captures the thrilling conclusion of a horse race at Longchamp, located at the Bois de Boulogne on the western edge of Paris. Here, Édouard Manet radically departed from conventional representations of the sport, in which races were shown from the side with the horses in profile. Instead, the competitors gallop thunderously toward the viewer, raising a cloud of turf, their pace underlined by the sweeping diagonals of the racetrack fences.

In France, horse racing became an important form of popular entertainment during the nineteenth century. Imported from England, the racetrack—with its speed, spectacle, and luxury—was a quintessentially modern space. In Manet's painting, a throng of fashionably dressed men and women press against the fences to witness the event—one man, at the upper left, uses binoculars to better observe the race.

Unlike his friend Edgar Degas, for whom the racetrack was a constant source of inspiration, Manet produced only two paintings on the theme. Originally a much larger composition, this canvas was cut down to its present scale by the artist. *Emerson Bowyer*

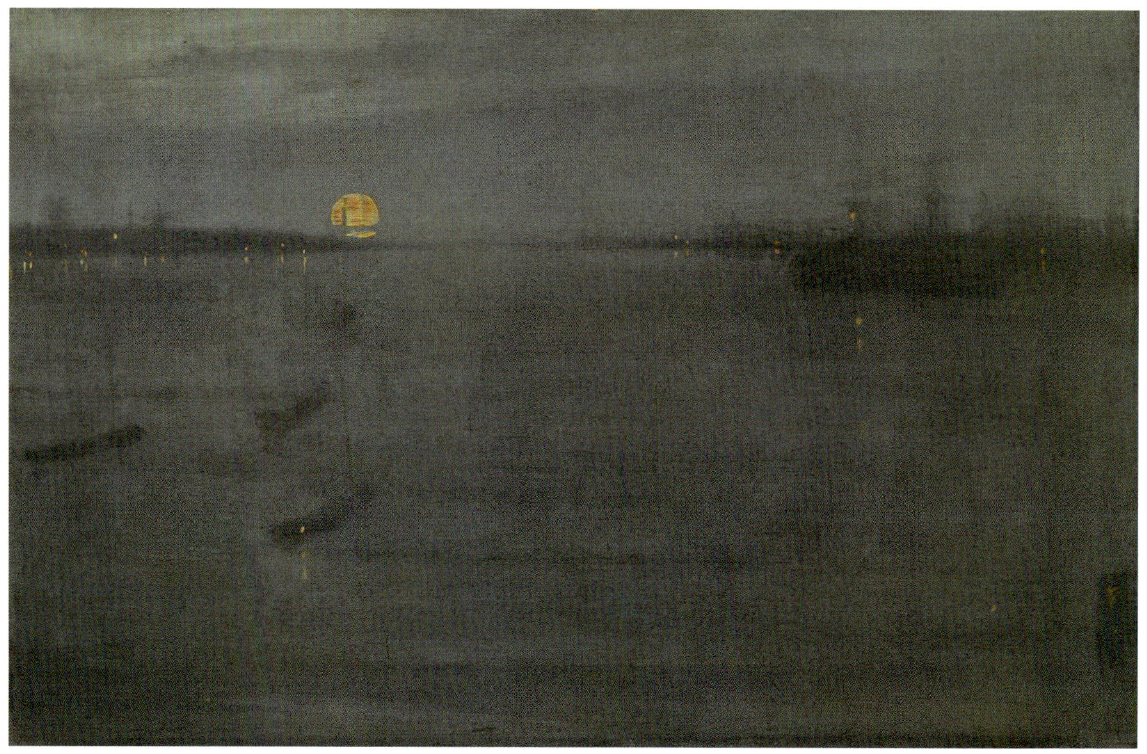

85. James McNeill Whistler, Nocturne: Blue and Gold—Southampton Water, 1872

In 1872 American expat James McNeill Whistler stunned the transatlantic art world with his *Nocturnes*, abstract nighttime scenes painted in dreamy, murky tones. The series embodied his groundbreaking "art for art's sake" ethos, conveying moods through color and form. Whistler drew the name of the series from musical terminology, compelled by music's inherent abstraction.

Whistler's *Nocturne: Blue and Gold—Southampton Water* captured moonrise over the titular British port town. The scene is blurred as if viewed in motion, yet its muted blue-gray colors evoke stillness. Gold appears in a low moon, in reflected lights dotting shorelines, and in a sole foreground boat. Dark brushstrokes form industrial structures on either side of the English Channel inlet and narrow boats in the water.

Over a century later in 1978, American rock singer and songwriter Bruce Springsteen closed his fourth studio album with an ode to ambiguity, singing the now famous line: "there's a darkness on the edge of town." Whistler, like Springsteen, takes us out past the familiar and toward dark, enchanting places that unnerve as they compel. While the former is an aesthete and the latter, a storyteller, both artists seek what goes beyond language in their respective mediums. On the edge of town, they hear the music more clearly. *Lois Taylor Biggs*

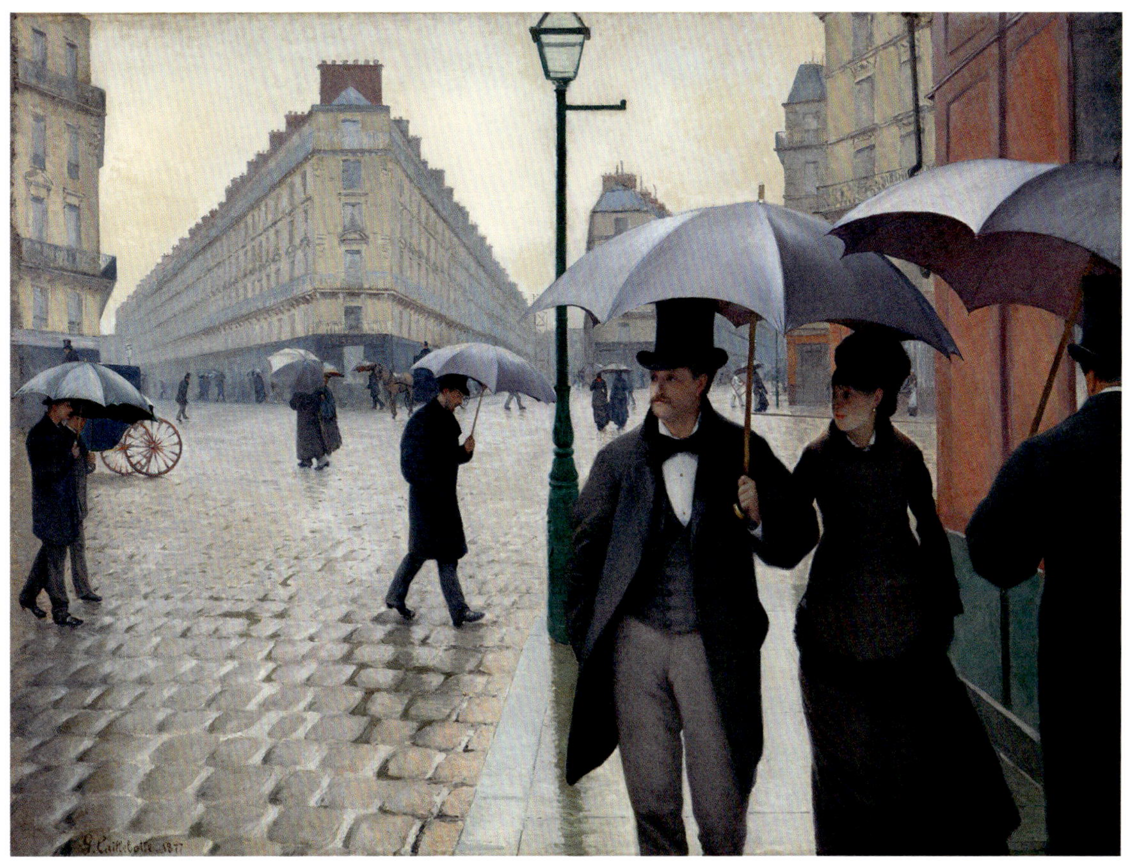

86. Gustave Caillebotte, **Paris Street; Rainy Day**, 1877

This monumental painting is Gustave Caillebotte's largest, most ambitious work and has been a visitor favorite since the Art Institute acquired it in 1964, well before the artist's contributions to the Impressionist movement were widely recognized. Caillebotte captured a busy intersection of Paris that was only a short walk from his home. In fact, his paintings of Paris rarely depict areas beyond his familiar neighborhoods.

Caillebotte demonstrated his affinity with the Impressionists through his subject of modern urban life but approached these settings with a more Realist technique. The dramatic cropping of the scene may have been inspired by the newly popularized medium of photography; the two central figures seem to be walking straight into the viewer as something captures their attention outside of the frame. At the time, artists rarely attempted to depict people in motion; Caillebotte carefully placed each of the background figures to evoke the feeling of bustling city streets. When he started exhibiting with the Impressionists, Caillebotte also focused on portraying the atmosphere of his scenes; here, instead of explicitly painting raindrops to indicate the weather, he suggests it through the incorporation of newly available retractable umbrellas and the subtle reflections on the wet cobblestones. *Megan True*

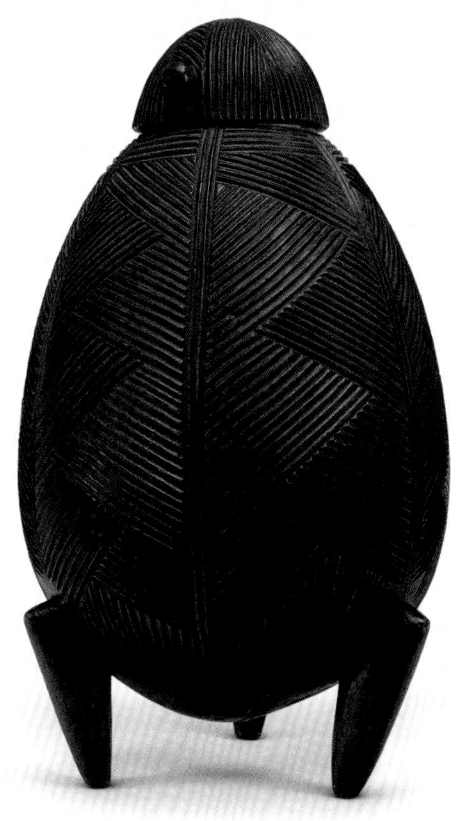

87. Attributed to Unobhadule, **Lidded Container**, mid- to late 1800s

This egg-shaped tripod vessel and its lid, all carved from the same piece of wood, closely resemble a similar object at the British Museum, London, which is said to be the work of a once famous artist named Unobhadule. Unobhadule lived near the town of Pietermaritzburg in what is today KwaZulu-Natal province, South Africa. He is associated with a number of carvings that were displayed at the 1862 International Exhibition in London, including vessels, headrests, and a meat platter. His containers, some globular and others with elaborate feet and handles, share the same surface decoration of finely gouged parallel grooves, which are often grouped in triangular sections.

European colonial collectors greatly admired Unobhadule's craftsmanship. Although vessels like this one may have been destined to serve as containers for tobacco or even water or milk, this example, like others by the same artist in collections around the world, shows no signs of use. It was probably made explicitly for sale to a foreign client—or at least sold before it was used in a traditional setting. *Constantine Petridis*

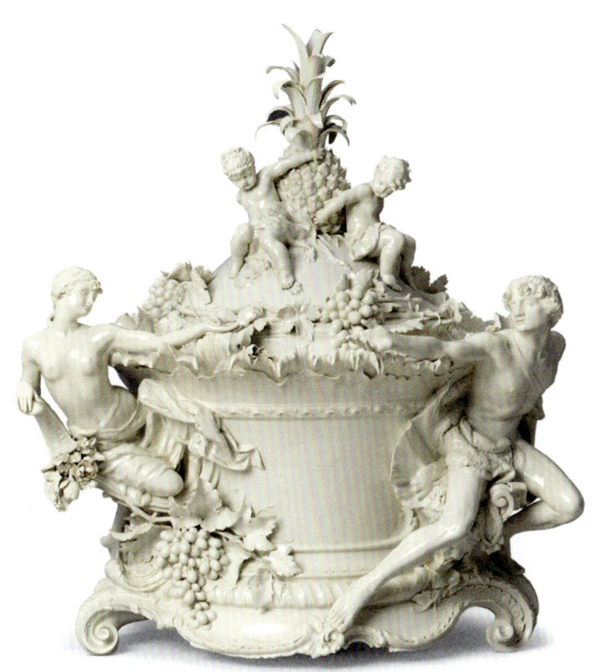

88. Berlin Royal Porcelain Manufactory, **Punch Bowl**, 1891

This exuberant porcelain punch bowl was made to impress. Designed by Alexander Kips and modeled by Ernst Wägner, it was produced by the Royal Porcelain Manufactory in Berlin (KPM) as a prototype for a piece shown at the 1893 World's Columbian Exposition in Chicago. Sculptural figures stretch around the bowl, possibly drawn from ancient mythology or symbolizing Germany's recently unified national identity. Grapevines—an homage to the Rhineland wine region of Germany—wind across the surface, while a pineapple-shaped finial, symbolizing hospitality, tops the lid, surrounded by playful putti.

Though this exact piece wasn't exhibited, it represents KPM's bold artistic vision for the fair. The manufactory's dazzling pavilion, known as the "Porcelain Porch," showcased German technical and artistic innovation in a neo-Rococo setting meant to evoke imperial grandeur and cultural pride. With over 65,000 displays from forty-six nations, the 1893 fair was a chance for the government-backed German manufactory to reach American audiences. At the time, nearly a quarter of Chicago's population was of German descent. This punchbowl is more than a decorative object—it's a sculptural celebration of ambition, identity, industry, and international exchange, and stands as a celebratory monument to the vibrant immigrant communities that shaped Chicago's history. *Christopher Maxwell*

A Stack for Every Season

Gloria Groom

Six haystacks in a row? Major gifts have made the Art Institute's Impressionism collection one of the most important outside of France.

Walking through the Impressionist galleries at the Art Institute and seeing six paintings of *meules* (French for stacks) painted by Claude Monet is not only impressive—the museum has more *Stacks* than any other museum in the world—but also a mini history of the major philanthropic campaigns of Bertha and Potter Palmer, Martin and Carrie Ryerson, and Annie Swann Coburn. Their names appear on labels throughout these galleries.

For Monet, the *Stacks* series, which he began in 1890 when he purchased his property in Giverny, France, constituted an unprecedented undertaking in both the works' making, as his first definitive attempt at a "series," and their initial exhibiting. Fifteen of the group of twenty-six known

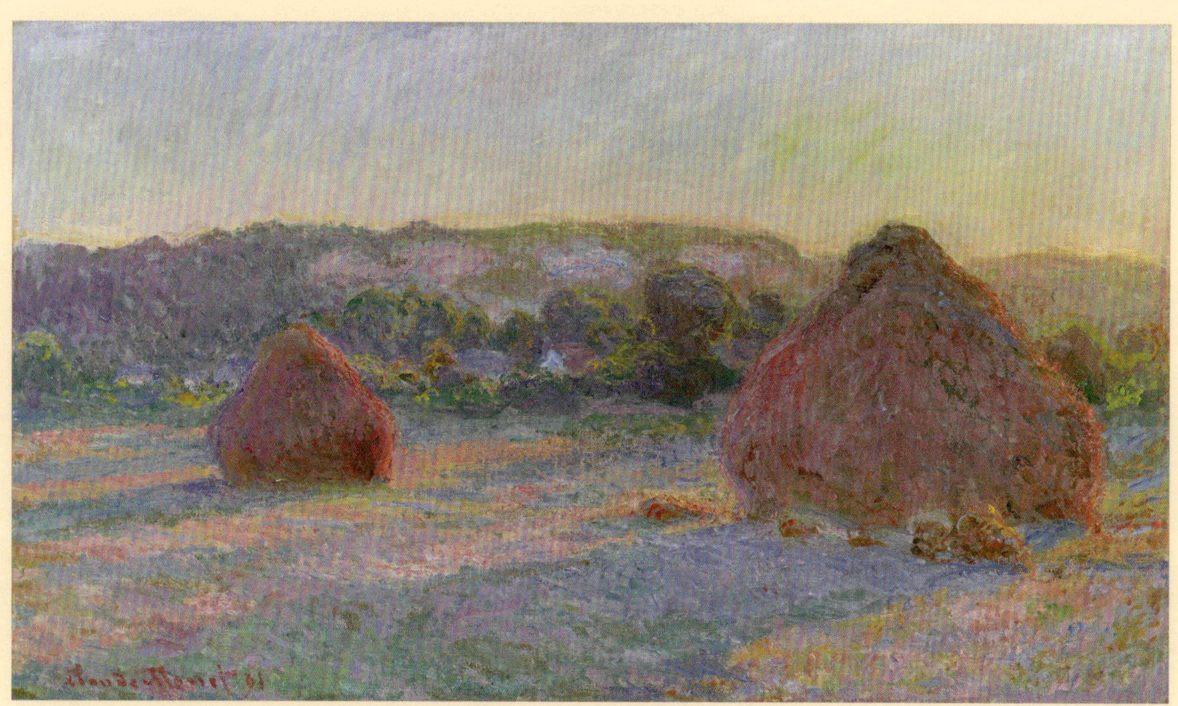

Fig. 1. Claude Monet (French, 1840–1926). *Stacks of Wheat (End of Summer)*, 1890–91. Oil on canvas; 60 × 100.5 cm (23 5/8 × 39 9/16 in.). Gift of Arthur M. Wood, Sr., in memory of Pauline Palmer Wood, 1985.1103.

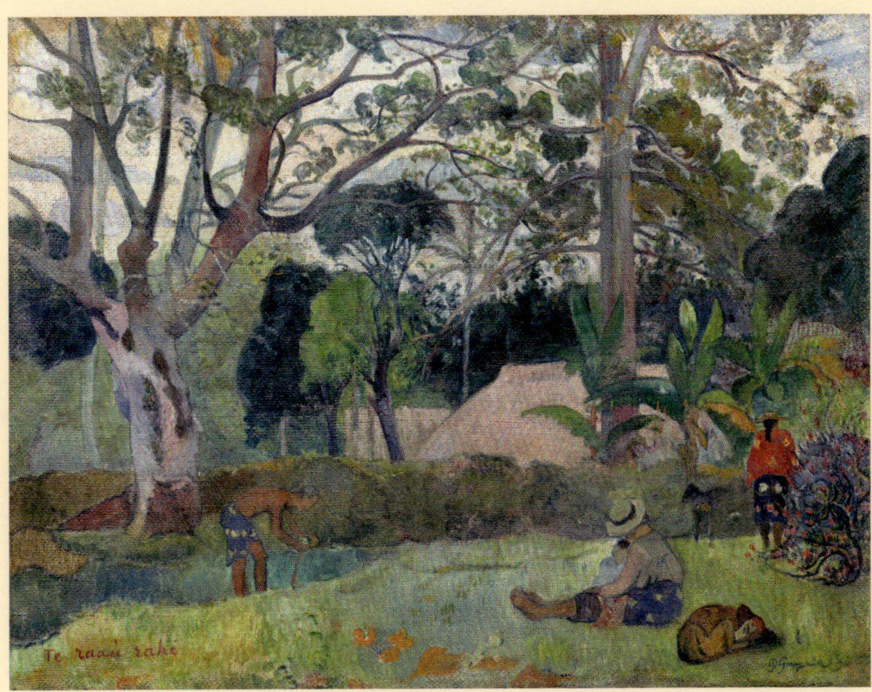

Fig. 2. Paul Gauguin (French, 1848–1903). *Te raau rahi* (*The Big Tree*), 1891. Oil on jute canvas; 72.5 × 91.5 cm ($28\frac{9}{16}$ × 36 in.). Gift of Kate L. Brewster, 1949.513.

Stacks paintings were included in a watershed exhibition at Paul Durand-Ruel's Paris gallery in 1891, when Chicago was preparing to host the 1893 World's Columbian Exposition. The year coincided with Bertha Honoré Palmer's pre–World's Fair shopping spree in Paris, where she rather exceptionally acquired several versions of Monet's *Stacks*. She eventually owned nine from the series, four of which came to the Art Institute in 1922 (see fig. 1), part of the first major group of French Impressionist works in the collection (see p. 117). Palmer returned several *Stacks* paintings to the Paris gallery between 1891 and 1893 (she had a penchant for buying and returning or exchanging Impressionist paintings in general and especially Monets); one eventually ended up with Annie Swann Coburn, a significant but little-known collector living at the Blackstone Hotel a few blocks south of the museum on Michigan Avenue. Coburn's bequest in 1933 added another *Stack,* which she had purchased by 1932, to the Impressionist collection, as well as works by Edgar Degas (see p. 126), Paul Gauguin (see p. 133), and Pierre-Auguste Renoir (see p. 129). Over the past fifty years the museum has acquired three additional stacks of wheat, including one from Arthur M. Wood, whose wife, Pauline Palmer Wood, was Bertha and Potter Palmer's granddaughter.

The Palmer, Ryerson, and Coburn bequests formed the foundation of the museum's Impressionist holdings, and by 1933 these gifts had put Chicago on the map for modern art. With thirty-three paintings by Monet, the Art Institute boasts the largest collection of the artist's work outside of France. These early collections were enriched and expanded into the twentieth century by other bequests, most notably from Joseph Winterbotham in 1925 and from Frederick Clay Barlett, whose 1926 gift of Georges Seurat's *A Sunday on La Grande Jatte—1884* (see p. 134) in memory of his wife, Helen, is a destination piece synonymous with the museum itself. Since then, many other individuals have contributed major works, although these gifts were not as numerous or as concentrated on Impressionism and Post-Impressionism. In 1947 the Kate L. Brewster bequest added Asian objects and important decorative arts; unlike the earlier collectors, she passed over Monet and instead focused on the Post-Impressionists, including Paul Cezanne, Gauguin (see fig. 2), and Vincent van Gogh (see fig. 3).

Among more recent gifts to the Impressionist collection is a painting by Berthe Morisot, one of the few women to exhibit with the Impressionists (participating in all but one of their eight exhibitions), and whose works are still largely unknown outside of France. *Woman in a Garden* (fig. 4) is among Morisot's largest and boldest compositions, contrasting dramatically in technique and

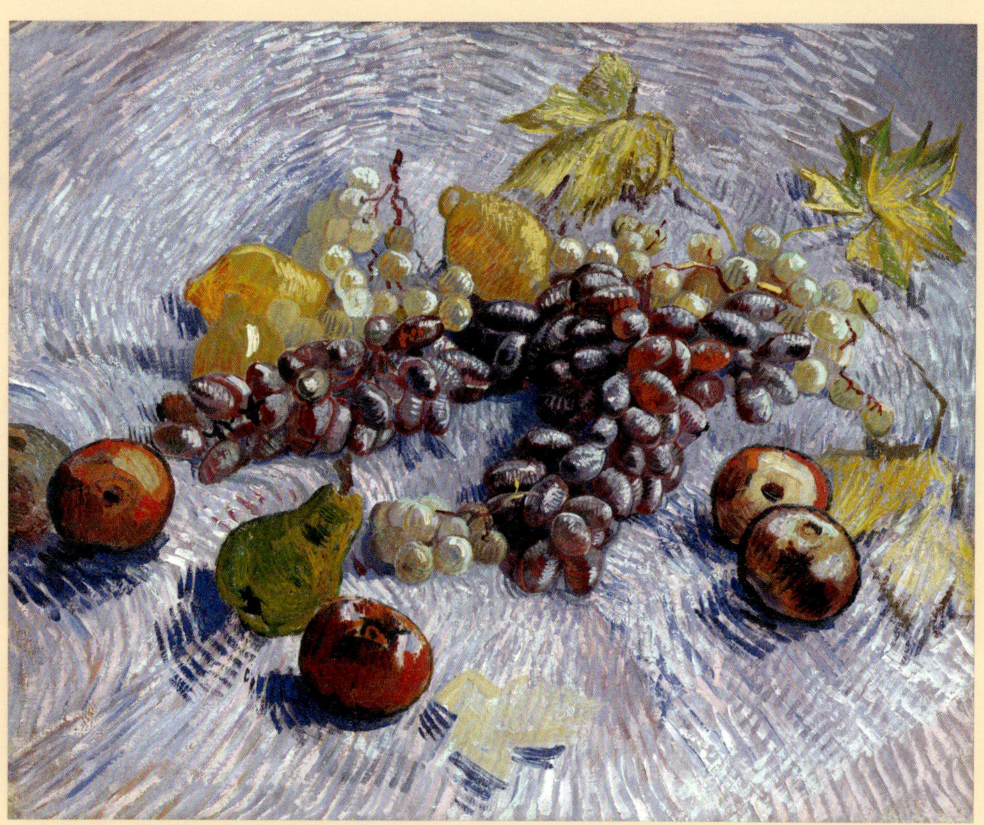

Fig. 3. Vincent van Gogh (Dutch, 1853–1890). *Grapes, Lemons, Pears, and Apples*, 1887. Oil on canvas; 46.5 × 55.2 cm (18 ¼ × 21 ¾ in.). Gift of Kate L. Brewster, 1949.215.

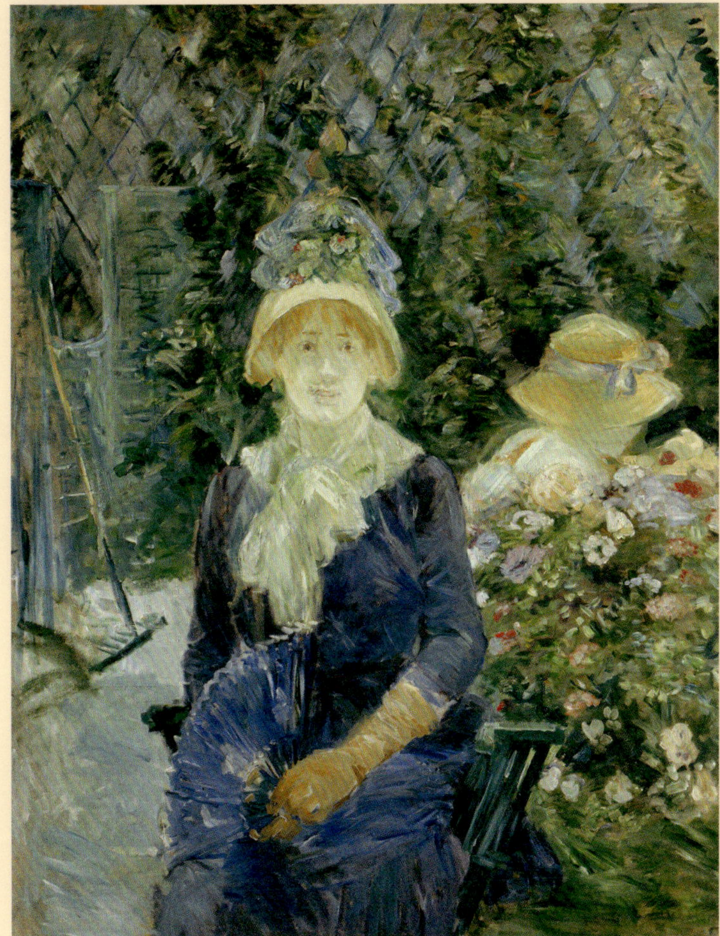

Fig. 4. Berthe Morisot (French, 1841–1895). *Woman in a Garden*, 1882–83. Oil on canvas; 123 × 94 cm (48 ½ × 37 in.). A Millennium Gift of Sara Lee Corporation, 1999.363.

intention from Renoir's similarly themed and exactly contemporary painting *Two Sisters (On the Terrace)* (see p. 129). Now one of the anchors of the Impressionist display at the museum, the painting was part of the Sara Lee Corporation's Millennium Gift to the museum. Corporations played a significant role in the postwar history of collecting in the United States. The Sara Lee gift was an important civic gesture signaling the company's strong ties to the city and to its cultural institutions. Even this corporate gift, however, can be seen as a continuation of individual philanthropic contributions to the museum's presentation of Impressionism, since the Sara Lee collection was originally part of the personal collection of the corporation's founder, Nathan Cummings.

Strengths build on strengths. The Art Institute, world renowned for its Impressionist collection, looks forward to further expansion. Names matter, not only those of the art makers, but those of the art donors, whose generous gifts and bequests are recognized on the labels of the artworks that allow us to tell the story of Impressionism in Chicago.

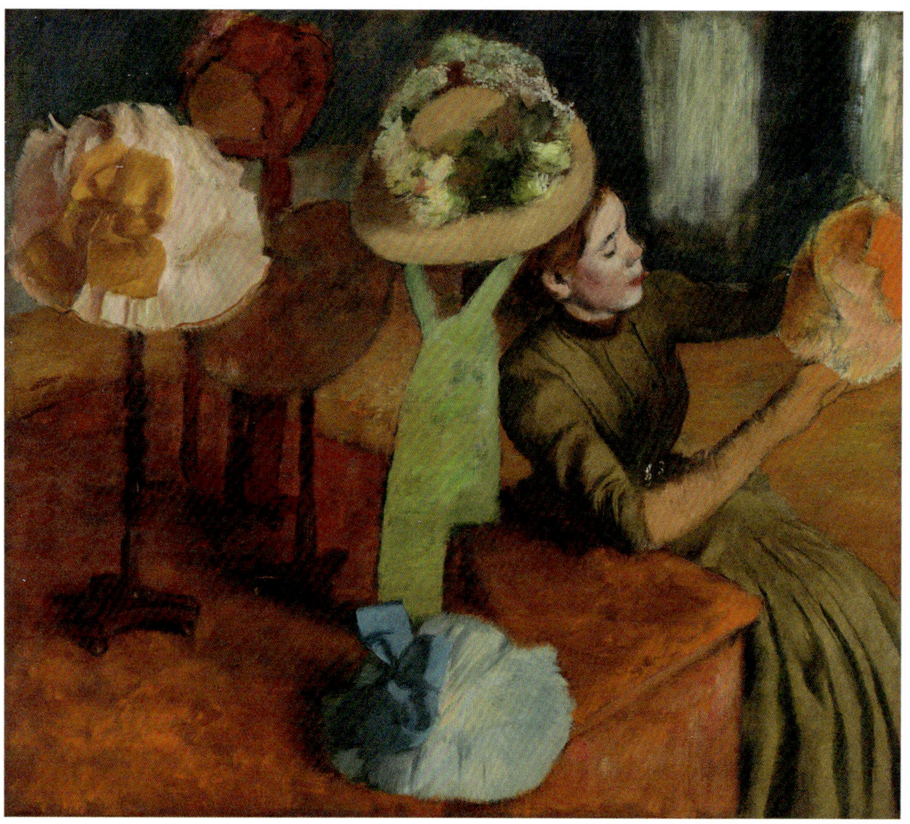

89. Edgar Degas, The Millinery Shop, 1879–86

The Millinery Shop is the largest of Edgar Degas's paintings focused on milliners, or hatmakers. He arranged the composition carefully, making multiple drawings and pastels of the lone figure, perfecting the woman's pose and experimenting with her outfit. The final composition highlights the visual ambiguities of class identity that arose in France in the late nineteenth century. The woman sits in a hat shop examining a wide-brimmed hat. She wears a fashionable green wool dress with long, elegant gloves that were just as likely to be worn by wealthy clients as by the employees of the shop. At the time, millinery work was considered a prestigious trade that required skill and taste, incrementally elevating the young women who succeeded in the business. Degas addressed this subtle shift in the class hierarchy through the subject's fashion: While her dress is nice enough to be worn by an affluent woman, she does not wear a hat of her own, which would have been expected of a high-class young lady. The artist portrayed this newfound uncertainty playfully by positioning the hat with green trimmings so it seems to sit atop the woman's head. *Megan True*

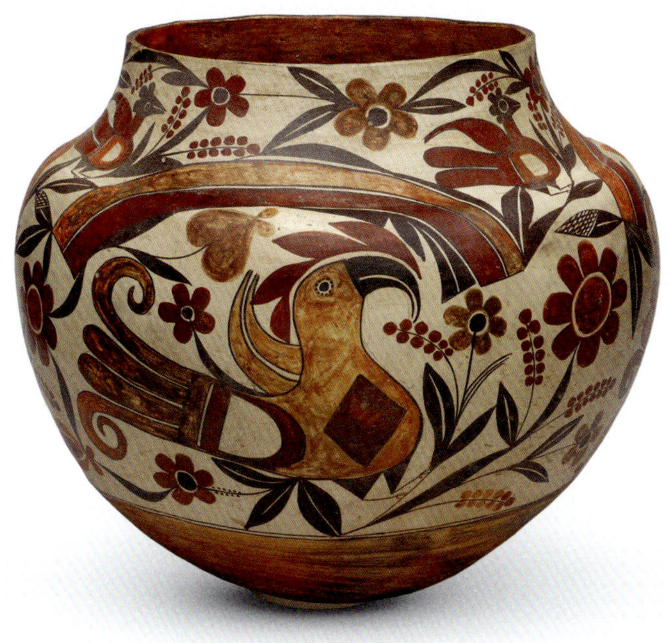

90. Parrot Storage Jar (*Olla*), 1880s, Acoma Pueblo

Thirty years ago, I saw a photograph of a woman carrying this magnificent storage jar on her head. It was taken at Acoma Pueblo in 1901. I was amazed by its size and beauty and wondered about the name of its maker. I learned it was at the Art Institute and in 2022 made plans to visit. What a great privilege it was to embrace the clay jar and to speak to it in our Acoma language.

Acoma people are descendants of the Ancestral Puebloans who settled in what is now the US Southwest, in places like Mesa Verde (in present-day Colorado) and Chaco Canyon (in present-day New Mexico). They established the Pueblo of Acoma in 1100 on top of a mesa west of Albuquerque; Acoma Pueblo is one of the oldest continuously inhabited places in the United States. The Acoma people maintain language, culture, and traditions like pottery making. Pottery is essential to daily life and is regarded as both functional and ceremonial. This jar's maker spent days processing clay and mineral-based paints before slowly forming the massive vessel by hand using the coiling method. The maker must have envisioned the elaborate design that she would paint on its expansive polished surface, exemplifying the talent and creative spirit of the Acoma people. *Brian Vallo*

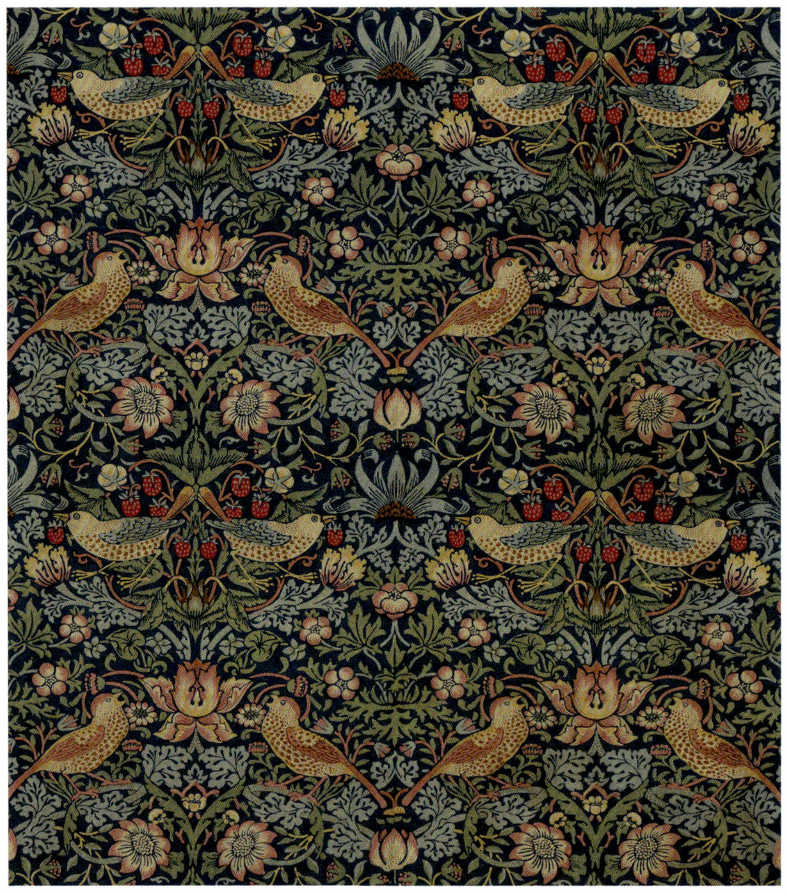

91. William Morris, Strawberry Thief, 1883

The British Arts and Crafts Movement developed as a reaction to industrialization—and William Morris was one of the movement's leading figures. He advocated for a return to handmade objects for daily life and the revival of considering artists and designers as craftspeople. Morris designed the textile called *Strawberry Thief*, intended for interior decoration, in 1883. He reportedly drew this pattern after watching birds steal strawberries from his kitchen garden. Morris was an avid student of textile history, and this pattern shows the influence of multilayered designs from the Islamic world as well as medieval European textiles that display pairs of small animals. He was also a passionate early environmentalist, advocating for the use of naturally derived dyes instead of toxic chemicals that polluted local waterways.

These small birds invading a strawberry patch have charmed consumers for more than 120 years, making *Strawberry Thief* one of the most recognizable and popular Morris & Co. patterns. Today it can be seen on wallpaper, dish towels, shower curtains, T-shirts, and teacups. It even has its own Wikipedia page and spinoff video game. *Melinda Watt*

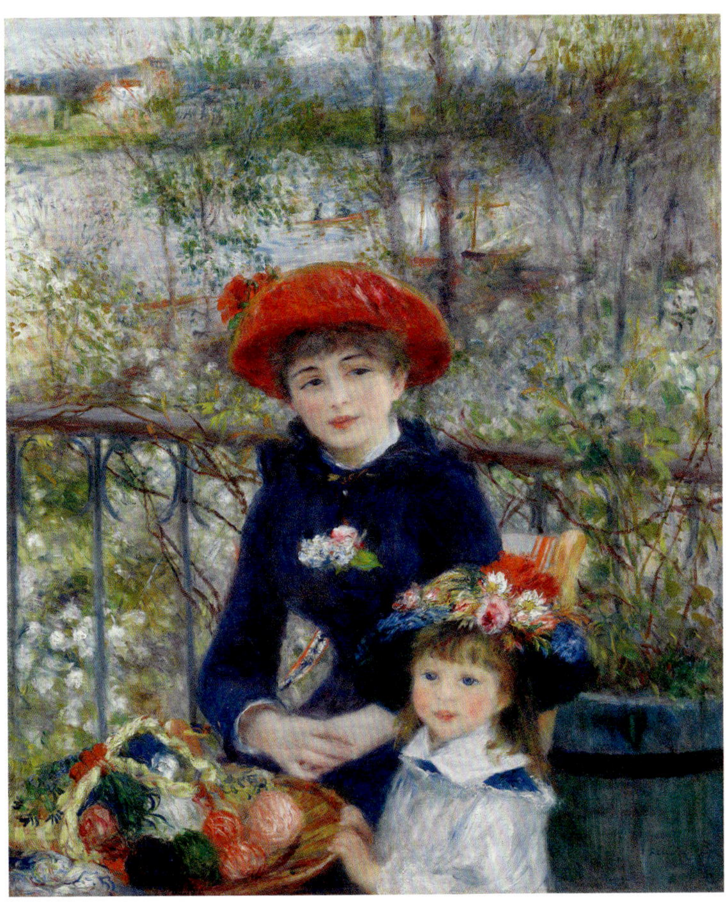

92. Pierre-Auguste Renoir, Two Sisters (On the Terrace), 1881

Pierre-Auguste Renoir considered the Restaurant Fournaise in Chatou (a village along the Seine River) the perfect spot to enjoy nature and good company away from the urban distractions of Paris. His painting *Two Sisters (On the Terrace)*, which he exhibited at the Impressionist exhibition of 1882, is among the last of his paintings set there.

Sometimes, as in his most famous work on this subject, *Luncheon of the Boating Party* (1882; Phillips Collection, Washington, DC), Renoir used his close friends as models. For *Two Sisters*, however, despite the title of the painting, he paid unrelated models to create this intimate and perfectly balanced pairing of youth and nature. The older girl, wearing the blue flannel of a female boater's outfit, sports a luxurious red hat, but it is her younger companion who captivates. Her oversize headdress composed of a floral bouquet is echoed in the brightly colored skeins of yarn in the basket that she gently touches. As was typical for the artist, Renoir painted the faces of his models with controlled and precise brushwork creating a porcelain-like surface that contrasts brilliantly with the diaphanous, impressionist backdrop of river, boats, and blossoming trees just beyond the railing of the terrace. *Gloria Groom*

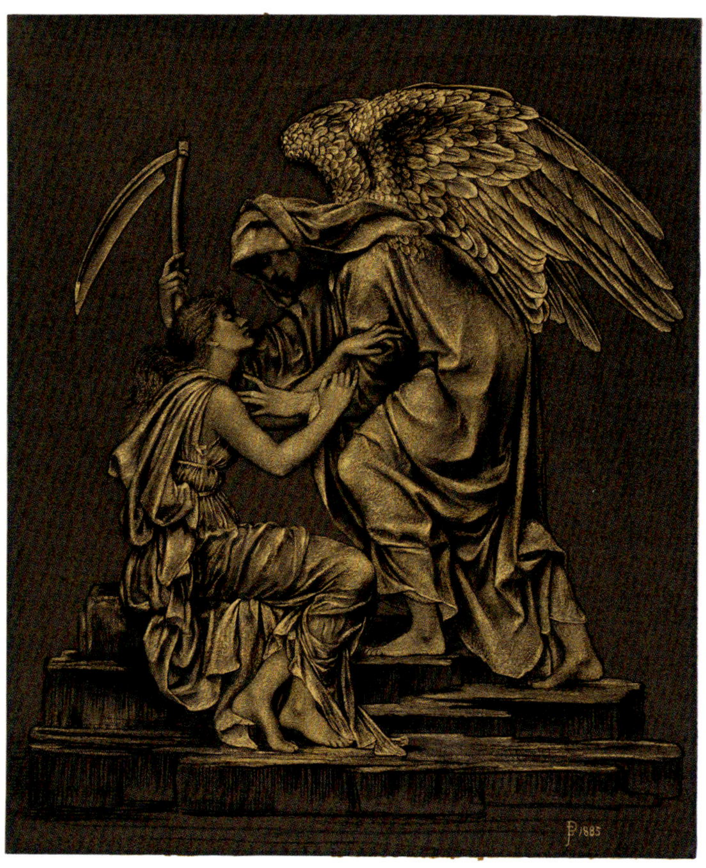

93. Evelyn De Morgan, The Angel of Death, 1885

Executed in gold-colored pastel and illusionistically rendered as if in sculptural relief, Evelyn De Morgan's *Angel of Death* vividly demonstrates the artist's consummate draftsmanship as well as her ability to render the subject of death as sublime. Although bearing death's scythe, the angel is presented as a gentle, protective figure taking the young woman's life force with the gentlest touch to her throat. De Morgan was acutely interested in Spiritualism, a Victorian quasi-religious movement, which held that our spirits survive the deaths of our bodies, and that communion with the dead is not only possible but desirable.

Even though De Morgan came from a wealthy and well-connected family, she had to overcome enormous obstacles to realize her ambitions as a painter in a stifling patriarchal culture, becoming one of a very small number of nineteenth-century female professional artists in Britain. Her style exhibits all the features of the late phase of the Pre-Raphaelite movement, with its interest in the art of the Middle Ages and Italian Renaissance and in romance, allegory, and symbolism. She was particularly attracted to the work of the fifteenth-century Florentine artist Sandro Botticelli, whose sweet, sinuous forms, limpid lines, and soft, unmodulated color strongly mark De Morgan's work. *Kevin Salatino*

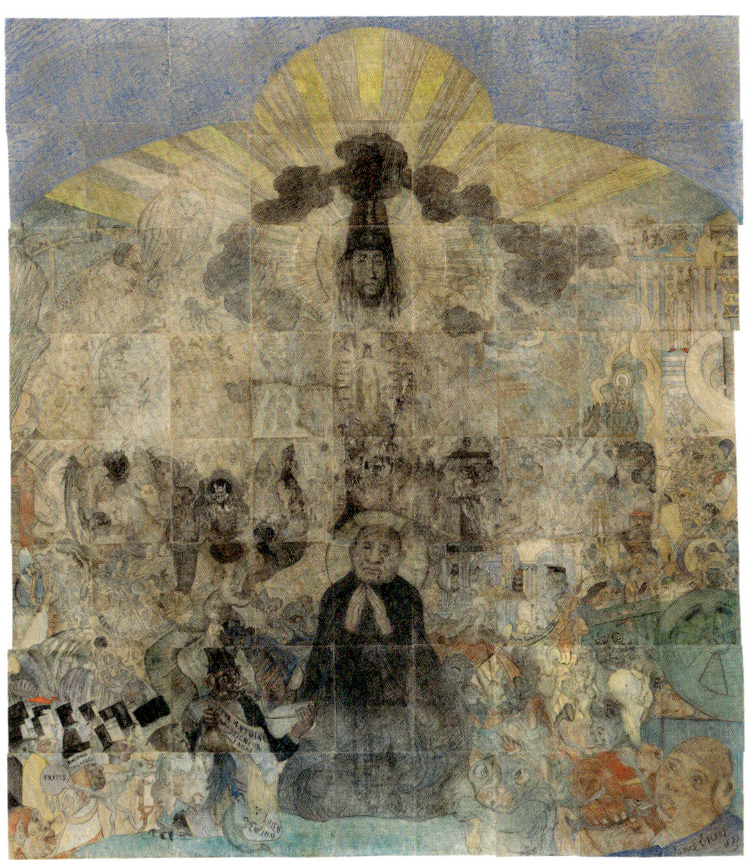

94. James Ensor, The Temptation of Saint Anthony, 1887

Depictions of Saint Anthony and his struggle in isolation against demonic temptation have a long history in art. I've often wondered if artists favor the story of Saint Anthony because it prompts sublimation. The artwork does not dictate the mores of society; rather, it empathizes with the monstrous aspects of being human by forming those aspects into exactly that: monsters. A harpy, dragons, and the Chimera and Sphinx appear alongside playful inventions such as a solider with legs inspired by scientific illustrations of dinosaur and bird skeletons. James Ensor's depiction of the story is a unique and very personal revelation. I appreciate the work for its resourcefulness, being made of humble materials—fifty-one sheets of paper that are colored and scraped with crayons, charcoal, and pencil—which bring balance to the drawing's ambitious scale. Saint Anthony and Christ offer us an anchor, for fear we drift away on the back of a deranged octopus. Dense, expansive, and immutable, Ensor's work amplifies a sound: It is a cacophony that rattles and disturbs, but it is not so disturbing that you look away. You search for yourself in the crowd and wonder who you relate to most. *Brook Hsu*

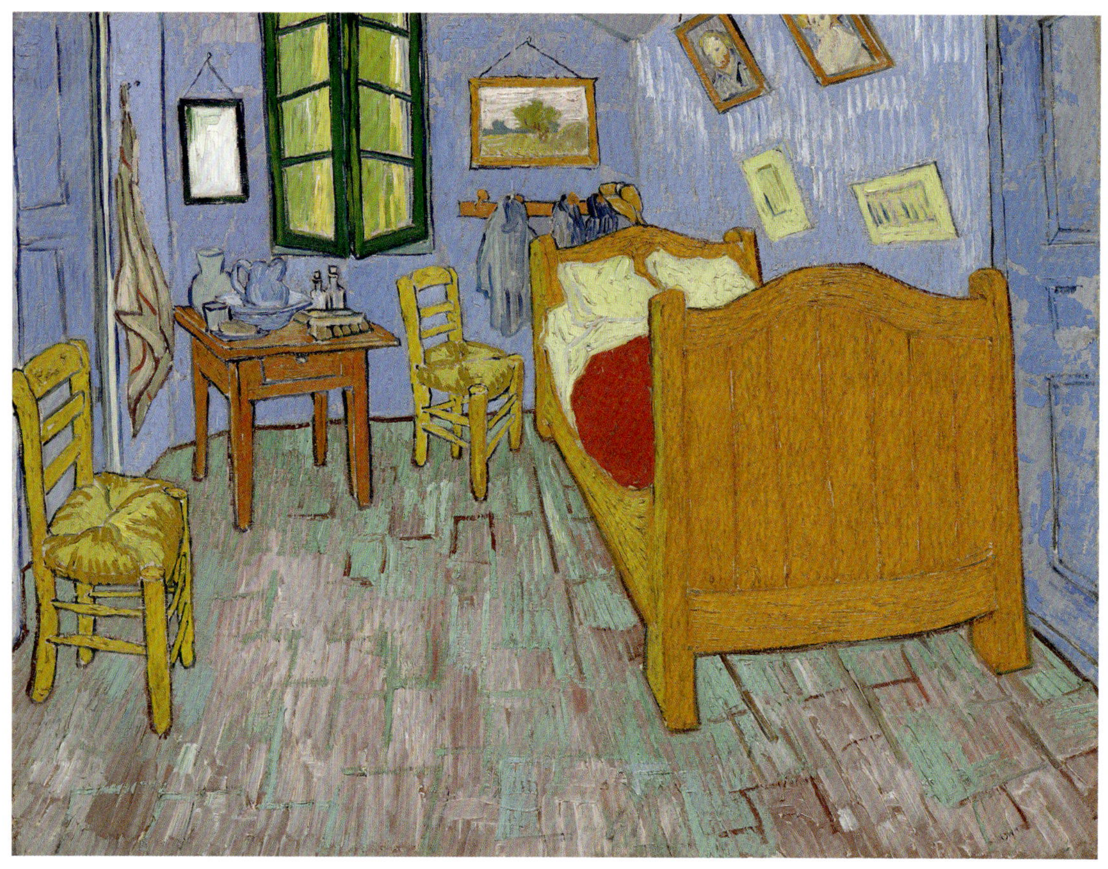

95. Vincent van Gogh, The Bedroom, 1889

Perhaps the most famous depiction of a bedroom in Western art history, this vibrant painting documents Vincent van Gogh's sleeping quarters in his beloved "Yellow House" in Arles, France. The composition exists in three versions, the first of which Van Gogh conceived in October 1888, a month after he moved into the home. In a letter to his brother Theo, he described having painted "the walls pale lilac, the floor in a broken and faded red, the chairs and the bed chrome yellow, the pillows and the sheet very pale lemon green, the bedspread blood-red, the dressing table orange, the washbasin blue, the window green." With its bold colors, thick and broken brushwork, and sharply receding lines, the picture might suggest a nervous energy. But the artist understood it as a calming and restful image.

The painting in the Art Institute's collection is Van Gogh's second version of the scene, made nearly a year after the first, in September 1889. He produced a third, smaller version at the same time as a gift for his mother and sister. *Emerson Bowyer*

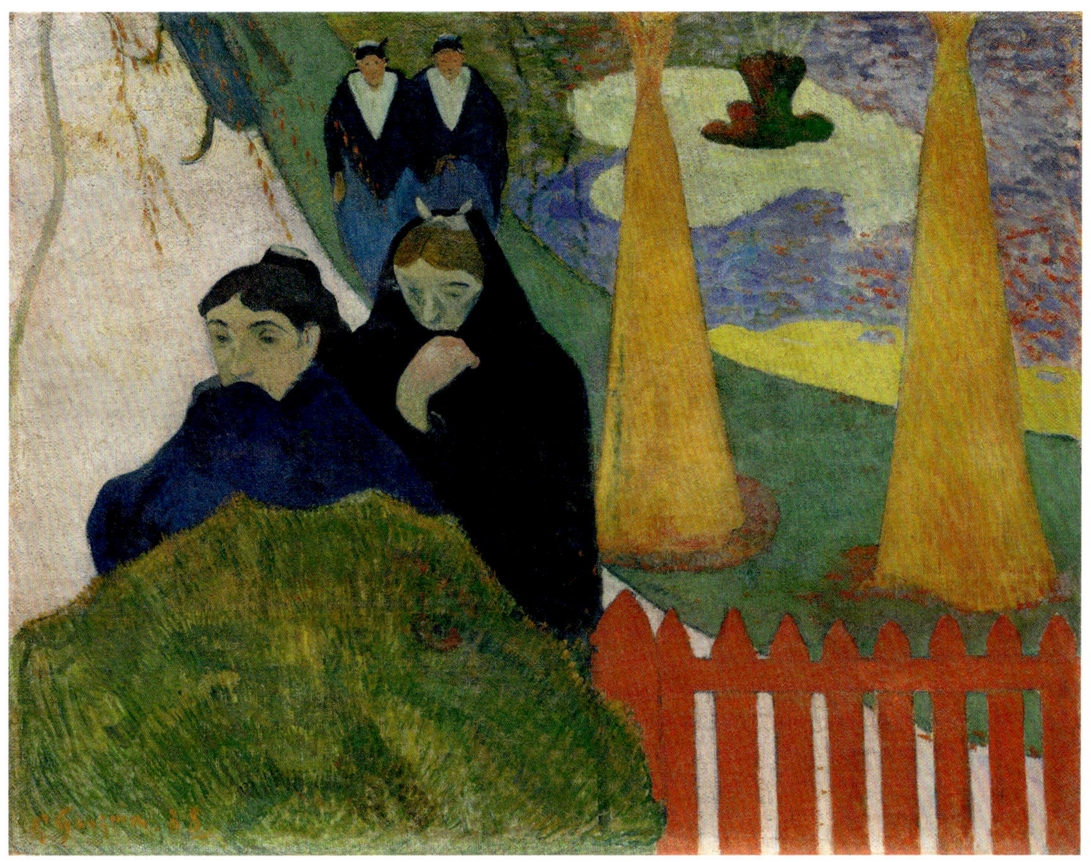

96. Paul Gauguin, Arlésiennes (Mistral), 1888

During the winter of 1888, Paul Gauguin spent a troubled two months with Vincent van Gogh in the southern French city of Arles. He painted the enigmatic *Arlésiennes (Mistral)* during this stay. The painters' time together was intended to be the beginning of an artist's colony, but their relationship grew increasingly tense, and Van Gogh's mental health deteriorated.

Set directly across the street from the house they shared, the painting depicts four women somberly processing through a public garden. The space is tilted radically upward, and complex, three-dimensional forms are reduced to simple, flat shapes. For example, twin orange-yellow cones—probably protective hay coverings to shield plants from the frost—tower at the right like abstracted human figures. Wrapped in dark shawls, the two closest women cover their mouths against the frigid air. Their gestures are withdrawn and introspective, and their passage is seemingly blocked by a bright red fence and large green bush. Perhaps the composition's oddest element is the appearance of a face within the bush. This face—an intentional inclusion by the artist—adds an uncanny, watchful presence to the scene. It exemplifies Gauguin's exploration of what he believed to be the mysteries that suffuse everyday life. *Emerson Bowyer*

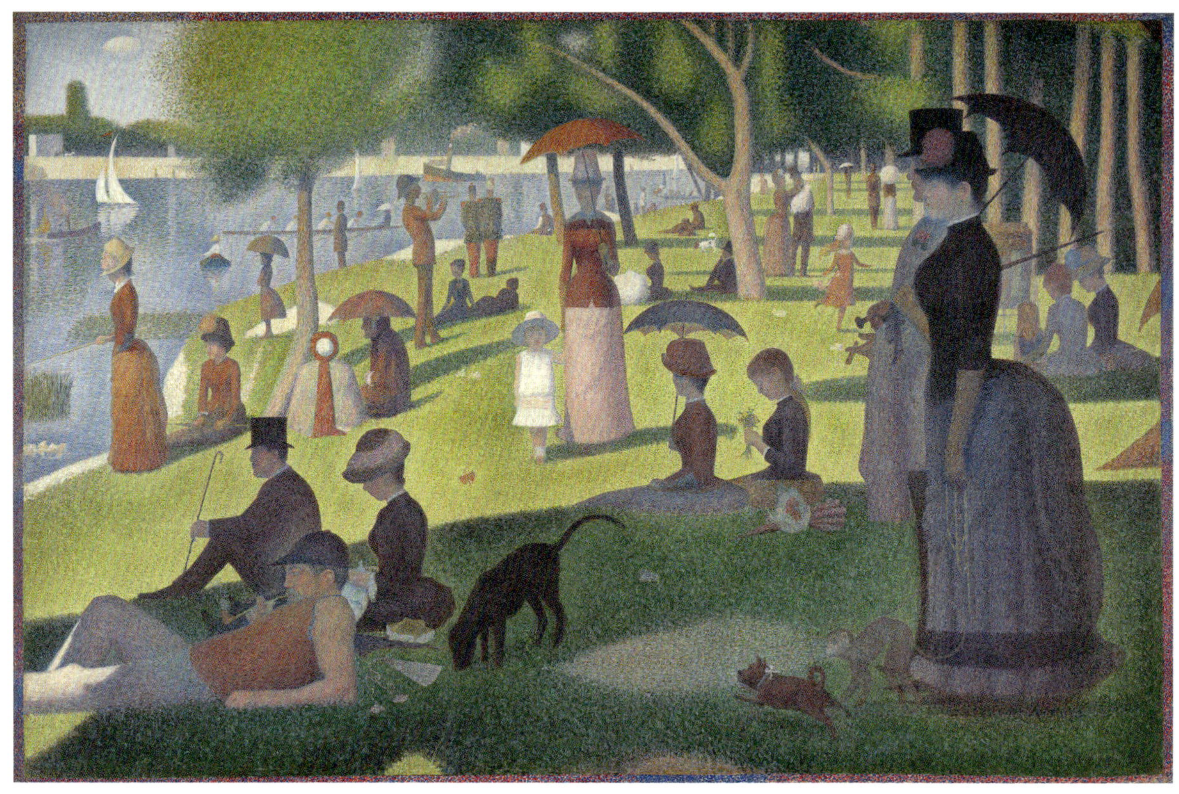

97. Georges Seurat, A Sunday on La Grande Jatte—1884, 1884–86

In *Ferris Bueller's Day Off*, Ferris's best friend Cameron Frye intensely studies this nearly ten-foot-wide painting during a scene set at the Art Institute. Featuring people of every age and social class on the banks of the River Seine, *A Sunday on La Grande Jatte—1884* has captivated visitors ever since its arrival at the museum in 1924.

If we, like Cameron, come closer to the painting, figures and forms dissolve into dots and dashes of complementary colors laid side by side, characteristic of Seurat's pointillist technique. Many smaller painted and drawn sketches and several larger canvases, in which Seurat laid out the parameters for the landscape and figures, led up to this majestically composed scene. Seurat returned to the work two years after its start date, amplifying the silhouettes of some figures and adding others. Some of these, like the monkey on the leash, seem so integral to the final composition that it is hard to imagine them as add-ons, but others, like the man carrying a rolled newspaper in the furthest distance, are barely noticeable. To the artist, however, every decision was essential to his aim of making a painting of modern life equivalent to a classical Greek frieze. *Gloria Groom*

98. Mary Cassatt, The Child's Bath, 1893

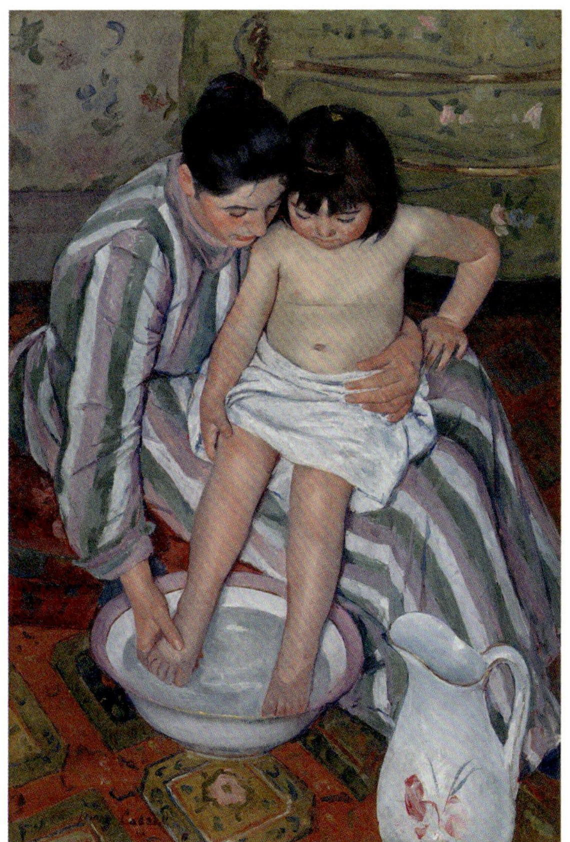

In *The Child's Bath*, prolific American painter and printmaker Mary Cassatt renders a tender scene of modern life with the dynamic brushwork associated with the French Impressionists, with whom she exhibited beginning in the late 1870s. Bold in composition and technique, the work features the elevated, flattened perspective of the Japanese prints the Impressionists favored. Amid the interplay of floral and geometric patterns, Cassatt constructed her scene as a balance of opposites: the child's legs against the skirt stripes and the edge of the chest of drawers extending upward echoed in the foreground placement of the pitcher—a later and precariously placed addition.

Using oil paint of a rich, paste-like consistency, Cassatt varied her brushwork to achieve a sculptural surface. Her nuanced strokes add a sense of roundness moving across and around the child's form, in contrast to the short, peaked strokes in the crumpled towel. Cassatt then dug the back of the brush or the metal ferrule that holds the bristles into the still-wet surface to create the soft delineation between the child's chest and rounded torso. Daring in her choice of subject matter in male-dominated Parisian art circles, Cassatt's unique point of view and sensuous surfaces continue to make her paintings come alive.
Kelly Keegan

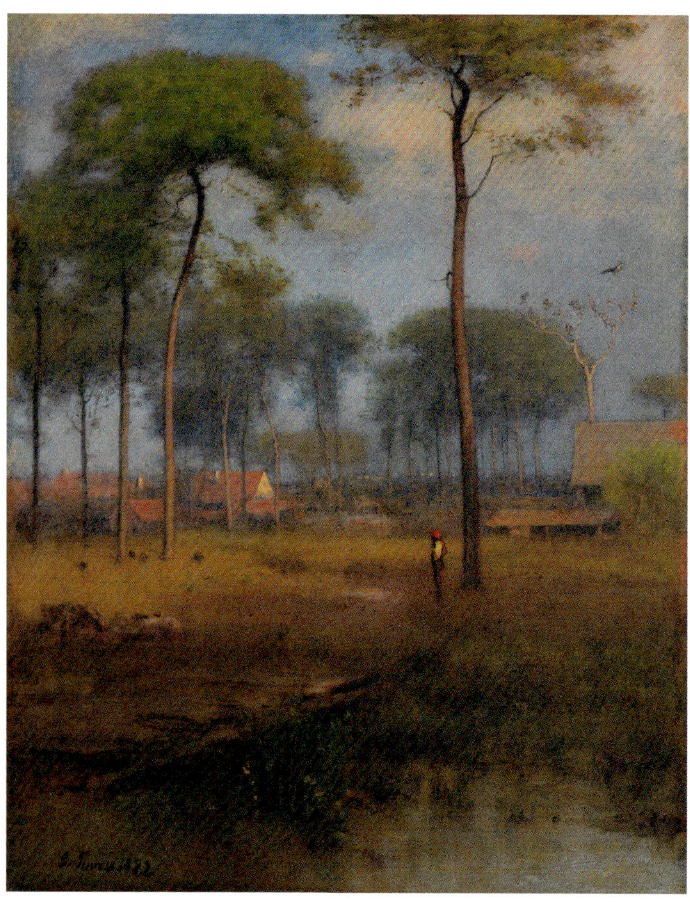

99. George Inness, **Early Morning, Tarpon Springs**, 1892

It's just before daybreak, when the world is almost—but not quite—fully formed. Soft, hazy brushstrokes outline trees, houses, and a morning sky awash in pink and yellow dawn. Even without a map on hand, it's easy to guess that we're close to the sea. It's the moisture in the air, the humid colors. The flashes of blue above the buildings on the left, too, suggest water nearby. A central figure in a red cap stands beside a towering pine, at ease in reflection.

Early Morning, Tarpon Springs is a glimpse of painter George Inness's seaside Florida home. Inness was devoted to the mystical teachings of Swedish theologian Emanuel Swedenborg. In his landscape paintings, he strove to unfold Swedenborg's understanding of the divine presence in nature through attention to color, tone, and emotional impressions.

To some, Inness's work marks a transitional period in American landscape painting, bridging the distance between the Hudson River School's grandeur and later movements toward abstraction. Fittingly, *Early Morning, Tarpon Springs* represents a liminal moment—from pink dawn to the emerging day. Inness offers us a chance to linger in fleeting beauty, to pause below the pines and feel the salt air on our skin. *Lois Taylor Biggs*

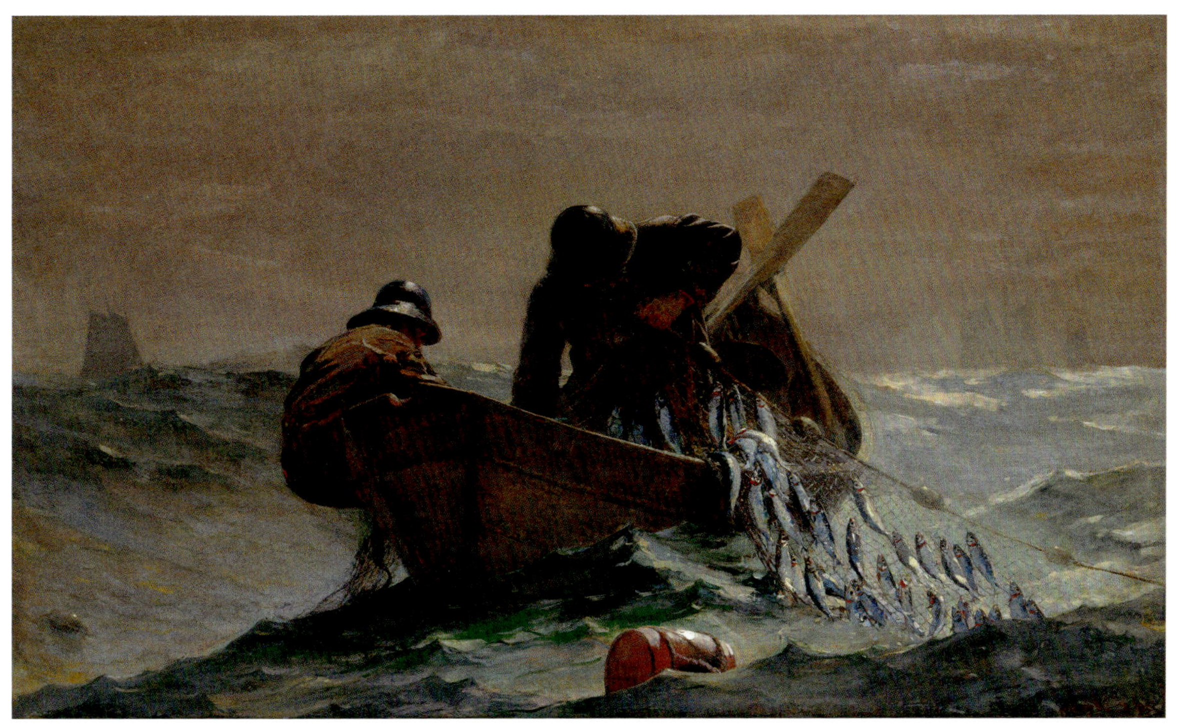

100. Winslow Homer, The Herring Net, 1885

Stare at Winslow Homer's *Herring Net* long enough and you might begin to hear the crashing of waves and feel the ocean's spray on your face. While other painters around this time favored idyllic, tranquil waterscapes, Homer chose instead to depict the unforgiving realities of life at sea. Inspired by his time in small fishing villages along the coast of Maine and in England, Homer witnessed firsthand the daily struggle of laborers against the raw power of nature. This theme—humanity versus nature—would come to define much of his later work.

Homer captured the heroic effort of fishermen as they haul in a catch of herring. The sea, with its sharp waves and relentless tides, doesn't just fill the canvas—it commands it, a central character in its own right. The painting is as much about teamwork and survival as it is about isolation. One fisherman, the primary figure, stands out in quiet solitude despite the coordinated labor. My eyes linger on the faint ships in the background—are they approaching, or drifting away? There's a tension in that ambiguity that deepens my worry for what lies ahead for these individuals. *Emily Fry*

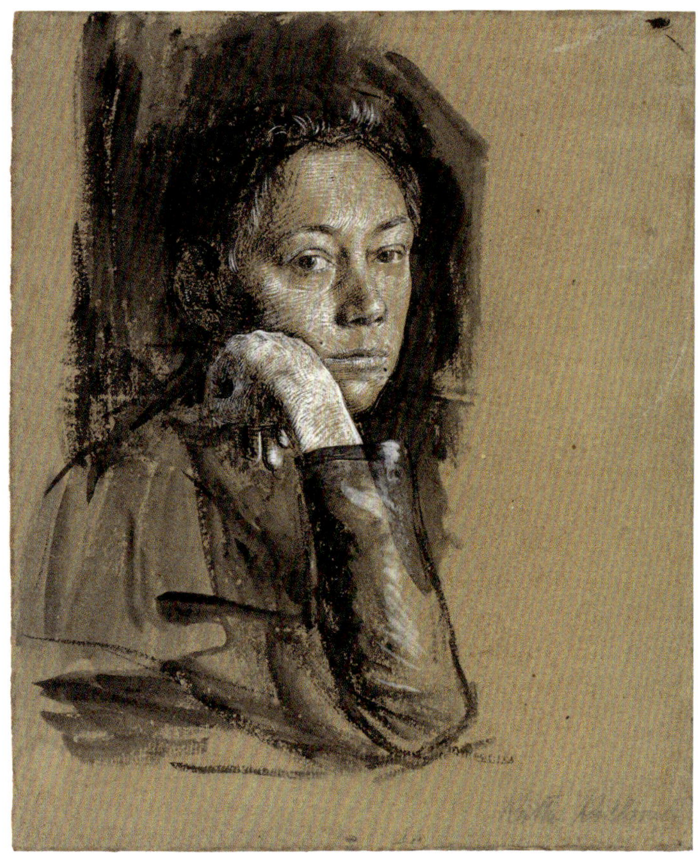

101. Käthe Kollwitz, Self-Portrait, 1891–92

The seeds of Käthe Kollwitz's conviction and compassion were planted at an early age. Her parents encouraged her artistic abilities with drawing lessons; their political views included reformist ideas about women's rights. When Kollwitz was eighteen, she attended classes at the Union of Women Artists in Berlin. At the time, the German art academies denied entrance to women.

Kollwitz often used her own face and those of models in works of social conscience, commenting on the horrors of both world wars. The intense gaze we see in this self-portrait, created when Kollwitz was around twenty-four, attests to her serious nature. Kollwitz used self-portraits as a means of self-reflection; she created over one hundred of them throughout her fifty-year career. In the Art Institute's drawing, the background and her upper body are loosely described, whereas her unsmiling eyes and hand are carefully delineated in delicate marks of ink and white gouache. This contrast reflects her lifelong propensity to focus on hands as a means of expression. The mottled brown paper acts as a third color. The power behind this self-portrait presages a later remark in her diary, "Don't hide yourself—be the person you are, and find your essence." *Jay A. Clarke*

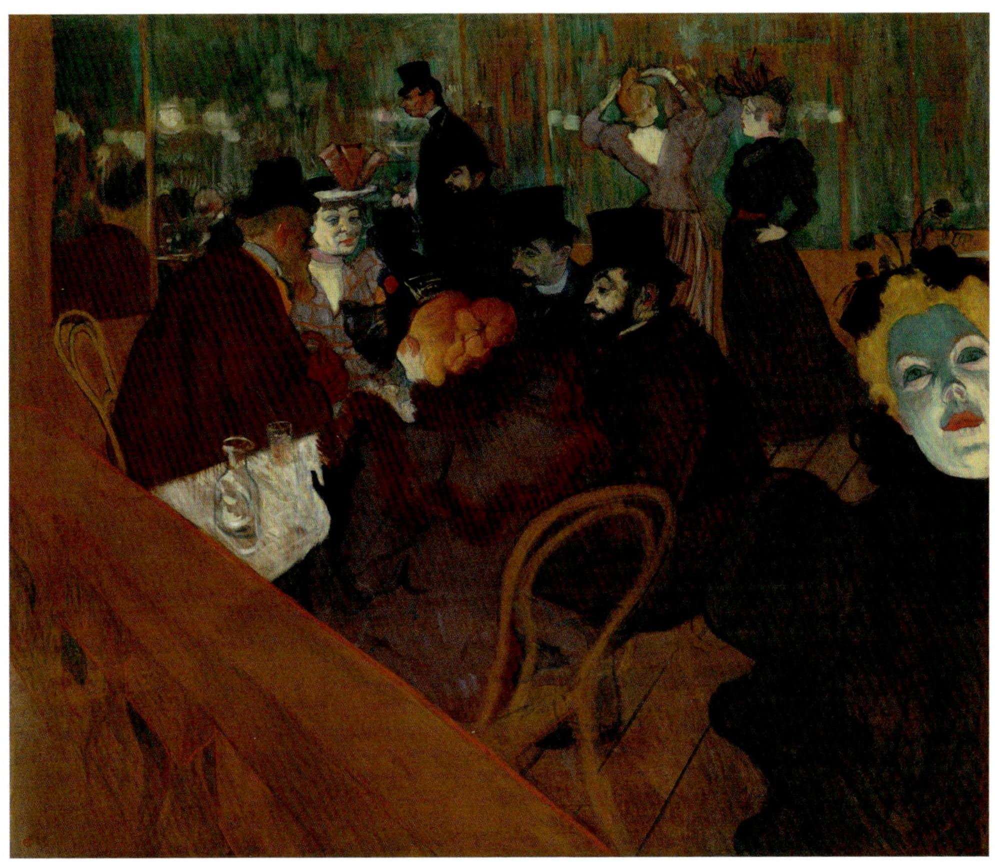

102. Henri de Toulouse-Lautrec, **At the Moulin Rouge**, 1892–95

Café-concerts were popular venues for drinking and entertainment in late nineteenth-century Paris and attracted the interest of artists such as Henri de Toulouse-Lautrec. The Moulin Rouge, which opened in 1889, was the most famous of the café-concerts, and Toulouse-Lautrec was a habitué of the establishment—he even had a permanently reserved table. His painting *Equestrienne* (1887–88), now also in the Art Institute's collection, was acquired by the owner of the nightclub as decoration for the lobby.

At the Moulin Rouge is a cleverly observed group portrait of the (in some cases) infamous customers and entertainers who formed part of the artist's circle. Standing in the background, the dancer La Goulue arranges her hair. Seated at the table are dancers La Macarona and Jane Avril, as well as photographer Paul Sescau, poet Édouard Dujardin, and vintner Maurice Guibert. Singer May Milton peers out from the right edge of the painting, her face harshly lit and a shocking acid green—the Moulin Rouge was designed to have electric lighting and Toulouse-Lautrec reveled in the artistic possibilities of artificial glare. The artist himself appears in the center background of the painting, a diminutive figure accompanied by his much taller cousin, the physician Gabriel Tapié de Céleyran. *Emerson Bowyer*

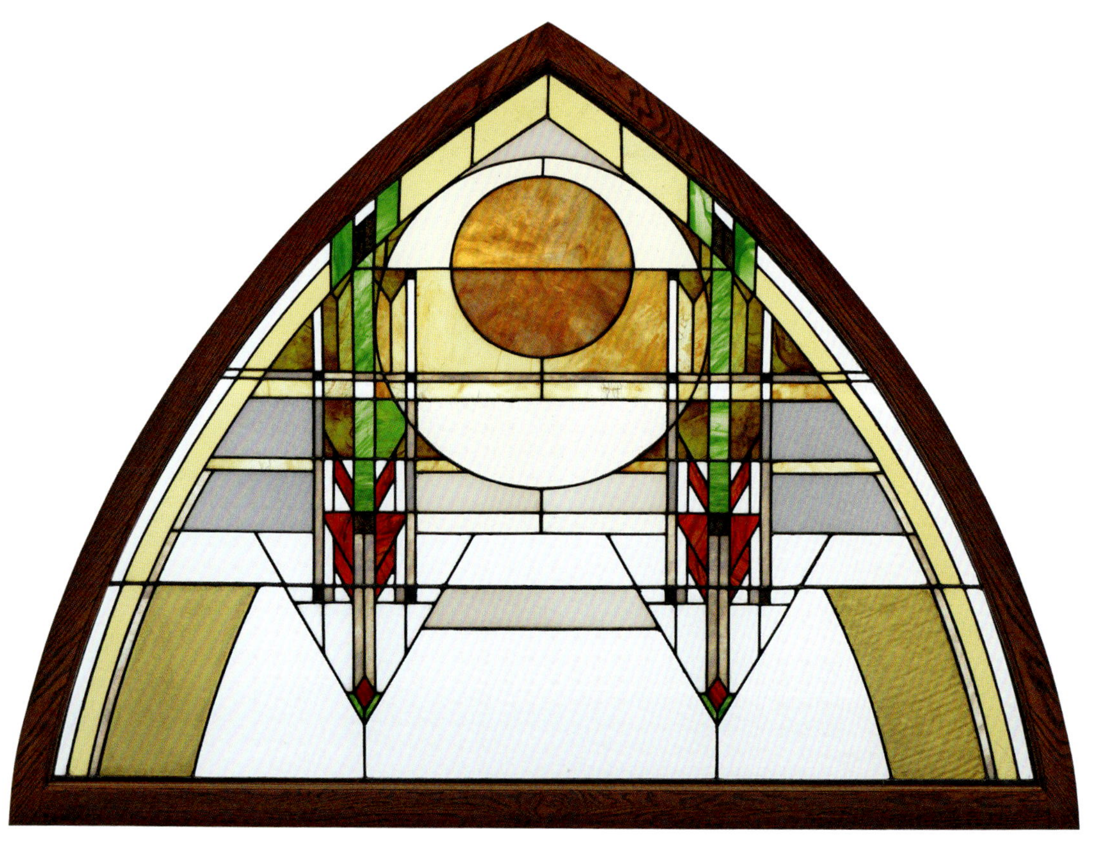

103. Marion Mahony Griffin, **Window from Church of All Souls, Evanston, Illinois**, 1903

Visitors to an intimate stone church in Evanston, Illinois, would have been greeted by this large, arched window featuring the dramatic image of the sun rising over an abstracted landscape of jewel-toned stained glass. Designed by Prairie School architect Marion Mahony Griffin, one of the first licensed women architects in the United States, the atmospheric church featured an extensive decorative program—including a figurative mural, furniture, and geometric stained-glass light fixtures and windows—that rivaled the most elaborate homes by Frank Lloyd Wright, Griffin's longtime employer.

The message of hope and renewal embodied by this modern glass work also suggests Griffin's deeper engagement with the project—her only independent built work. The commission came from Griffin's close ties to this progressive Unitarian congregation, which was known for its embrace of poetry and drama as part of religious life. Although a half a world away, this church prefigures Griffin's later work in Australia, where she and husband Walter Burley Griffin founded a community in Castlecrag that embraced theater, spiritualism, and environmental conservation. *Alison Fisher*

104. Edvard Munch, The Girl by the Window, 1893

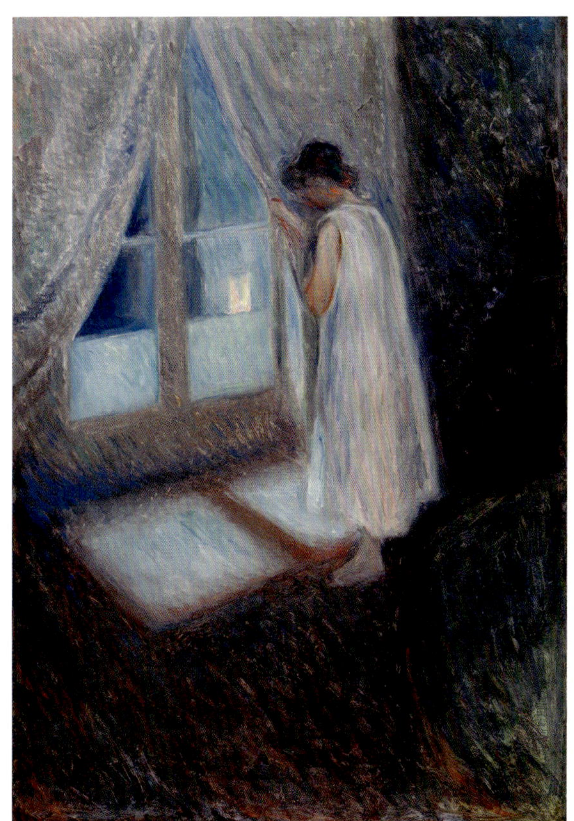

Standing before a window in the dead of night, a young girl draws back a curtain to gaze at the street from her darkened room. Deep shadows envelop the interior, obscuring all but the suggestion of a rounded piece of furniture at the lower right. The darkness, combined with the sharply tilted floor, gives a sense of precariousness and isolation to the figure. Loosely applied brown, blue, and violet tones enhance the melancholy atmosphere. The window serves as a symbolic barrier, separating the interior from the outside world, but also as a membrane, through which moonlight casts glowing rectangles upon the floor. Although the girl's actions suggest a narrative, the painting only provides mystery—we cannot see her facial expression, nor what she observes.

Girl by the Window belongs to a group of nocturnal scenes painted by Edvard Munch in the early 1890s, all characterized by moody blue tonalities. Around that time he penned a manifesto in which he declared that artists should depict "living people who breathe and feel, suffer and love." This focus on the psychological realities of human existence found its ultimate expression in Munch's iconic work *The Scream* (1893; Nasjonalmuseet, Oslo).
Emerson Bowyer

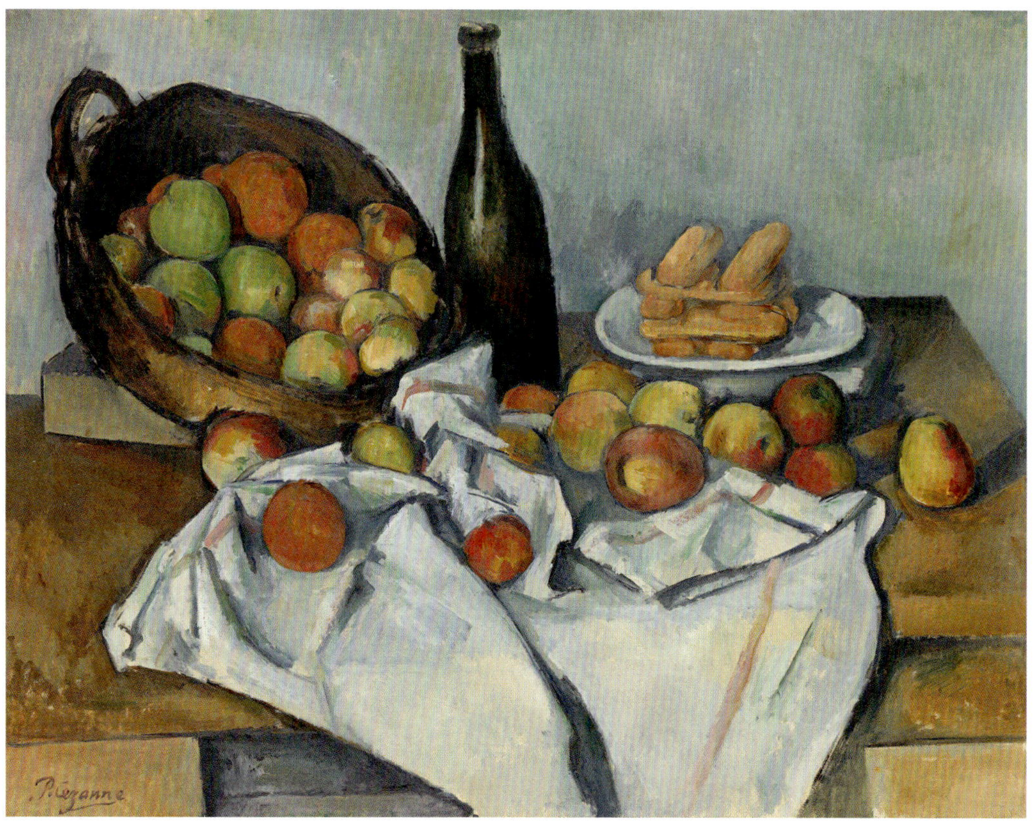

105. Paul Cezanne, The Basket of Apples, about 1893

In many ways Paul Cezanne was the odd man out among the artists branded as "Impressionists"—those who showed their works outside of France's state-sponsored Salon exhibitions. Early on, he painted landscapes, the typical Impressionist subject, but his arresting and complex still lifes changed the traditional *nature morte* (dead nature) genre and continue to puzzle and tantalize today.

At first glance, *The Basket of Apples*, the first of Cezanne's works to enter the museum's collection, appears to be a fruit-laden table setting anchored by a wine bottle. Closer looking reveals shifts in reality conveyed by the misaligned tabletop, tilted bottle, cascading apples, and the precarious tower of cookies known as *langues de chat* (cat tongues), which magically stop just short of falling out of the picture. Furthering the sense of what has been called the artist's "controlled chaos" are the shifts in brushwork from the thick strokes used to model fruits within the cloth's thick sculptural forms to the sketch-like marks used around the edges of both the table and the cloth. Cezanne rarely signed his paintings, so his signature at the bottom left suggests the importance he ascribed to this painting or to its original owner. *Gloria Groom*

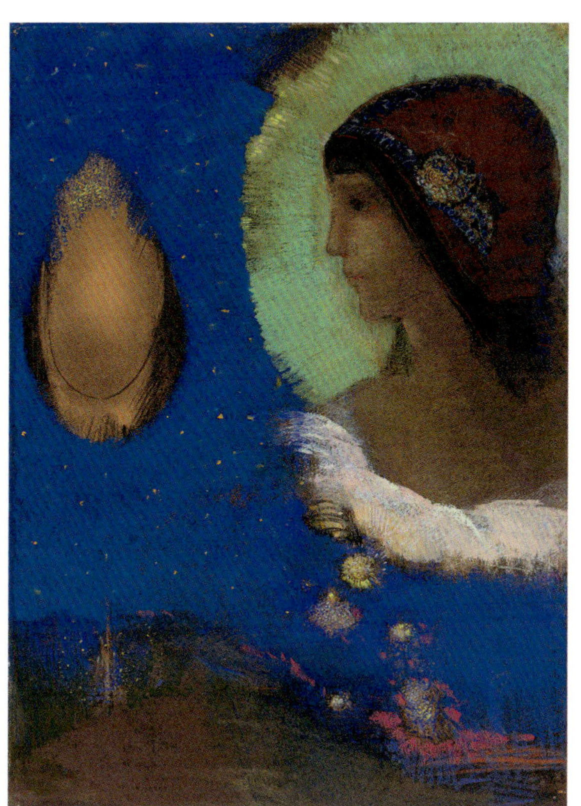

106. Odilon Redon, Sita, about 1893

Over a long career, Odilon Redon created prints, drawings, and paintings that drew on his fascination with science, religion, landscape, and his own imagination. During the first half of his working life, Redon created monochromatic prints and drawings. It was not until the 1890s that he began using brightly colored pastels. Made from ground color pigments bound together and formed into sticks for drawing, pastel enjoyed a revival during the 1890s, a wave that Redon rode to great commercial success.

Redon used two titles for this pastel—*Sita* and a more poetic description: "Her head surrounded by a golden-green radiance, against a blue sky, stardust falling, a shower of gold, under a sort of underwater mound." In the ancient Hindu text *Ramayana,* Sita is the wife of Rama and the divine incarnation of the goddess Vishnu. Sita is abducted and carried into the sky but, mid-flight, she lets her veil and jewels fall down to earth so that her husband might find them. Here, Sita's head, inside a lime-green, radiating light, stares at an egg- or cell-shaped orb, both surrounded by yellow stars amid a luminous blue sky. Rather than directly illustrating the *Ramayana* text, Redon created his own imagined world.
Jay A. Clarke

What's in a Frame?

Chris Brooks and
Charles Pietraszewski

Paintings get all the glory, but the Art Institute leads the field in framing works in period-appropriate frames. So, what makes a frame the right fit?

Beginning in the mid-1400s, the picture frame as we think of it today took shape and form: an independent structure that separates the real world from the artist's unique vision of it. For many centuries cabinetmakers, joiners, carvers, gilders, and artists have created frames to accentuate painted images. As tastes and styles changed over time, so did the frames that present and protect the paintings in them. This makes it extremely rare to find a painting in its original frame. Over the last half century, many institutions have made concerted efforts to return works to period-appropriate frames. The Art Institute, a leader in this effort, possesses an exceptional collection of period frames. Most visitors probably don't give them much thought, but for decades the Art Institute has had a conservation team devoted to restoring, adapting, and fabricating frames for the museum's vast collection. Working with paintings conservators, curators, and scholars, the frames conservators at the Art Institute strive to ensure each painting is paired with an appropriate frame.

The pairing of Andrés López Polanco's *Margaret of Austria, Queen of Spain* (fig. 1) with its frame feels incredibly intentional. Although it is not original to the painting, this frame has clearly lived a life. Its surface wear feels appropriate for something close in age to the painting. There are signs of resizing, and the near-perfect alignment supports the idea that some sections may have been carved on a ripple machine used for frames made in Northern Europe beginning in the seventeenth century. Unfortunately, our records offer little detail, and the back has been altered in a way that isn't reversible. If those additions could be removed to expose the joinery, we might be able to find out when and where it was made. As it stands, the frame carries its history visibly—much like the portrait it houses.

Every time I pass the painting in the galleries, I don't just notice the portrait itself—I'm drawn to the frame and how it embodies elements of the painting's energy. Gilded in bright gold with a high burnish, the frame still holds a luminous sheen typical of traditional water gilding, slightly softened by time. The surface isn't flat: It's rippled, fluted, and richly carved. All that texture keeps the brilliance of the gold from feeling overwhelming. Instead, it catches light in complex ways, and the shadows cast by the undulating forms create an almost theatrical effect. The fluted frieze (fig. 2) is especially eye-catching. It doesn't look like the architectural fluting you'd find on a classical column. Instead it flows like soft waves. Under gallery lighting, it creates a subtle rhythm of shadow and highlight that brings the frame to life. That movement connects to the painting itself. The queen's ruffled sleeve is a delicate system of lace and texture, echoed

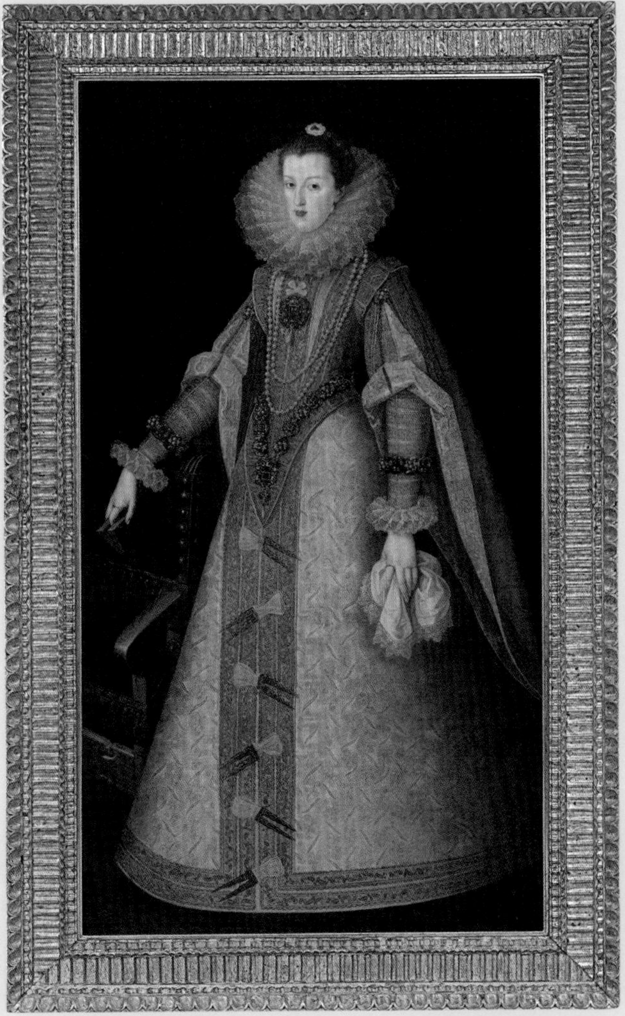

Fig. 1. Andrés López Polanco (Spanish, active 1608, died 1641). *Margaret of Austria, Queen of Spain*, about 1610. Oil on canvas; framed: 230.5 × 139.1 cm (90¾ × 54¾ in.). Gift of Mrs. Sydney Gorham and Mrs. Walter Kohler, Jr.; Mrs. James Conger, Eugene McVoy in memory of Mr. and Mrs. Eugene McVoy, 1941.975.

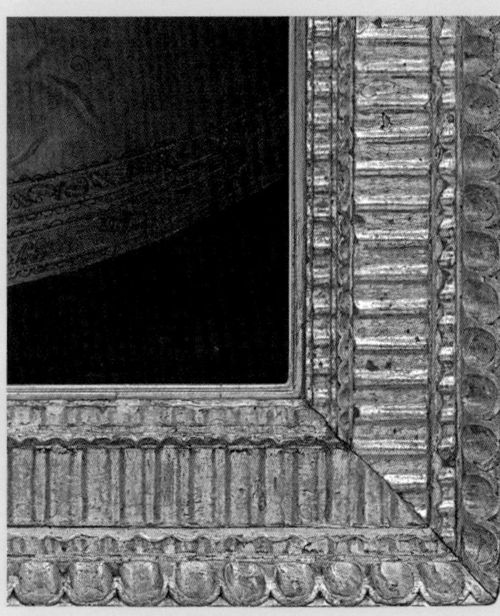

Fig. 2. Detail of the lower-right corner of *Margaret of Austria, Queen of Spain* and its frame.

by the curves and fine lines of the frame. Even the swirling patterns in the dress fabric mirror the flow of the carved wood moldings. The outer edge suggests bold seventeenth-century Spanish or Italian craftsmanship, while the rippled sight edge (the edge of the picture frame directly adjacent to the painting) feels more controlled, almost machined, like Netherlandish cabinet maker frames. The combination feels both deliberate and mysterious.

The frame on Vasily Kandinsky's *Painting with Troika* (fig. 3) is exceptional for entirely different reasons. Kandinsky painted the frame himself, and it is original to the painting. Beginning in the mid-1800s and continuing into the next century, some artists in Europe and America began to consider the concordance of picture and frame. This desire for harmony called for artist's frames—like this one—that diverged in style from the ornate, gilded frames of previous centuries.

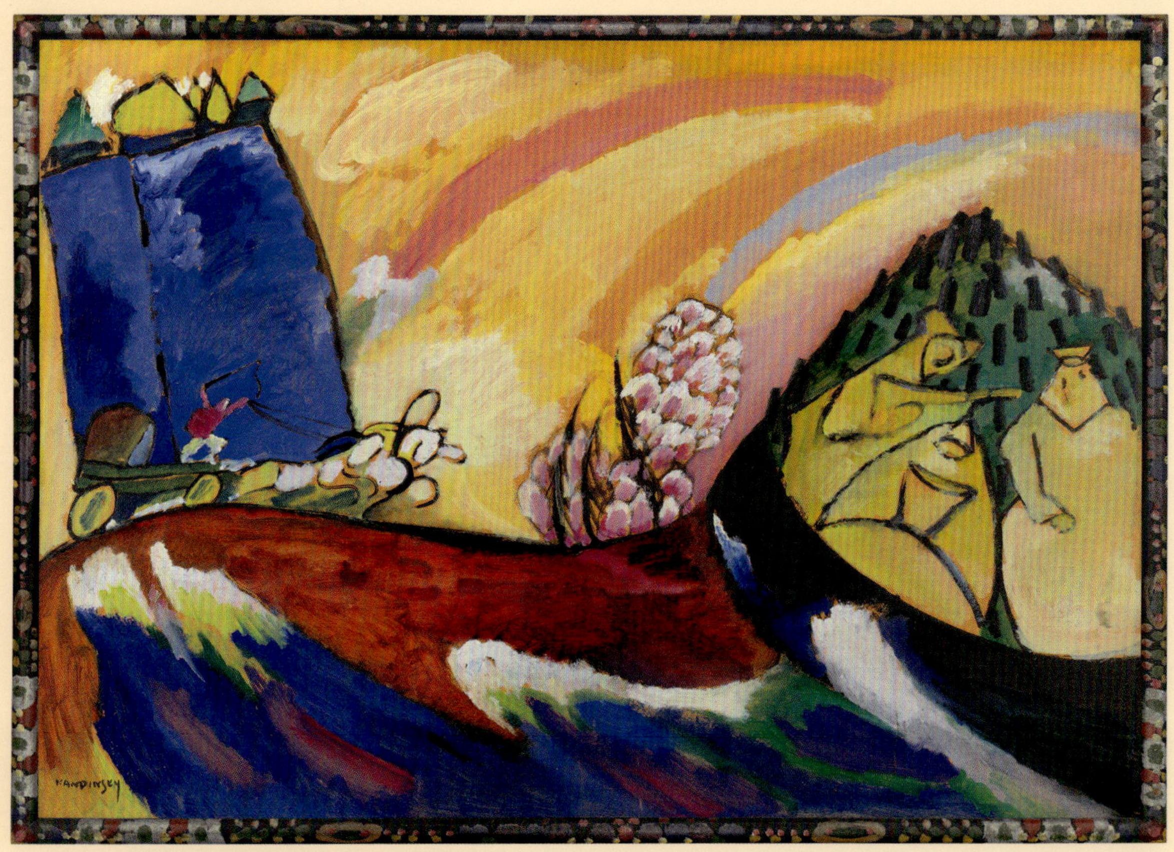

Fig. 3. Vasily Kandinsky (born Moscow [formerly Russian Empire, now Russia], 1866; died Neuilly-sur-Seine, France, 1944). *Painting with Troika*, 1911. Oil on cardboard; in artist's painted frame; 69.7 × 97.3 cm (27 3/8 × 38 5/16 in.). Arthur Jerome Eddy Collection, 1931.509.

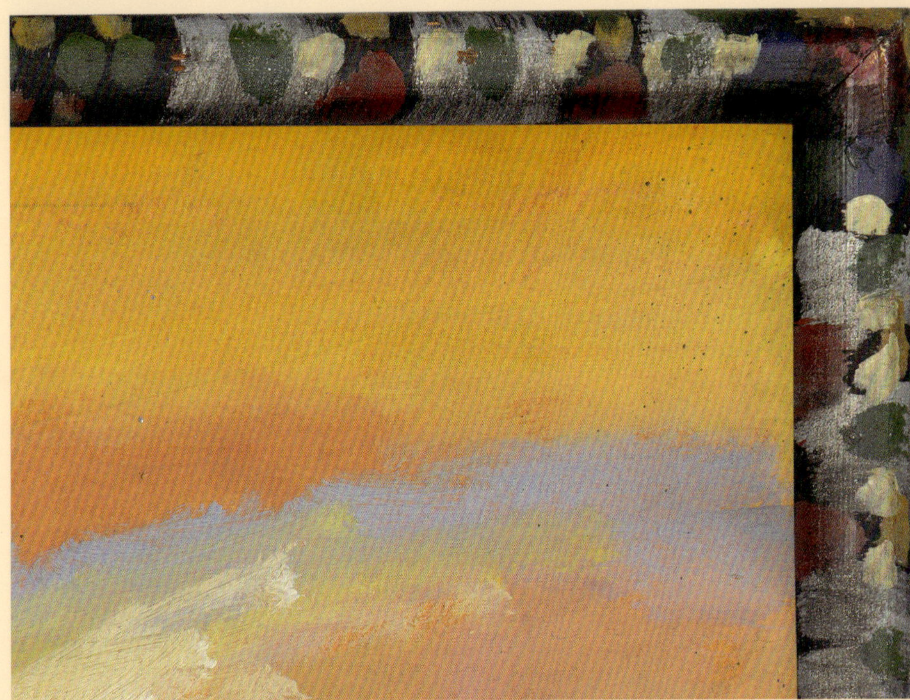

Fig. 4. Detail of the upper right corner of *Painting with Troika* in its frame.

Kandinsky's hand-painted frame reflects his ideas and illustrates changes in framing at the dawn of the twentieth century. In Germany, artists—Kandinsky among them—were interested in folk art, which they believed to have a pure and simple approach to understanding and looking at the world around them. Other frames from this period reflected this idea through the use of plain wood profiles. Many were painted black, highlighting the bold colors of the paintings. Kandinsky in particular was influenced by the Bavarian folk art tradition of *Hinterglasmalerei*, reverse paintings on glass, which had decorated borders. He also drew inspiration from Russian icon paintings, which were usually a single piece of wood with the center carved out for the painting, allowing the raised edge to act as the frame.

While Kandinsky's frame and painting are two separate pieces, there is evidence to suggest that the frame was painted while attached to the painting. Kandinsky painted the frame with blue and metallic silver, but unintentional spatters made it onto the picture itself in the lower left and upper right corners (fig. 4). Although Kandinsky was part of a new direction in frame design, this example retains elements that began centuries before. The painted corners recall sgraffito decoration prevalent on sixteenth-century Italian frames. This design element evolved and was reimagined over the centuries, as seen in many European frames with highly decorative corners. For his frame, much like his art, Kandinsky looked to the past for inspiration and from this created a uniquely modern vision.

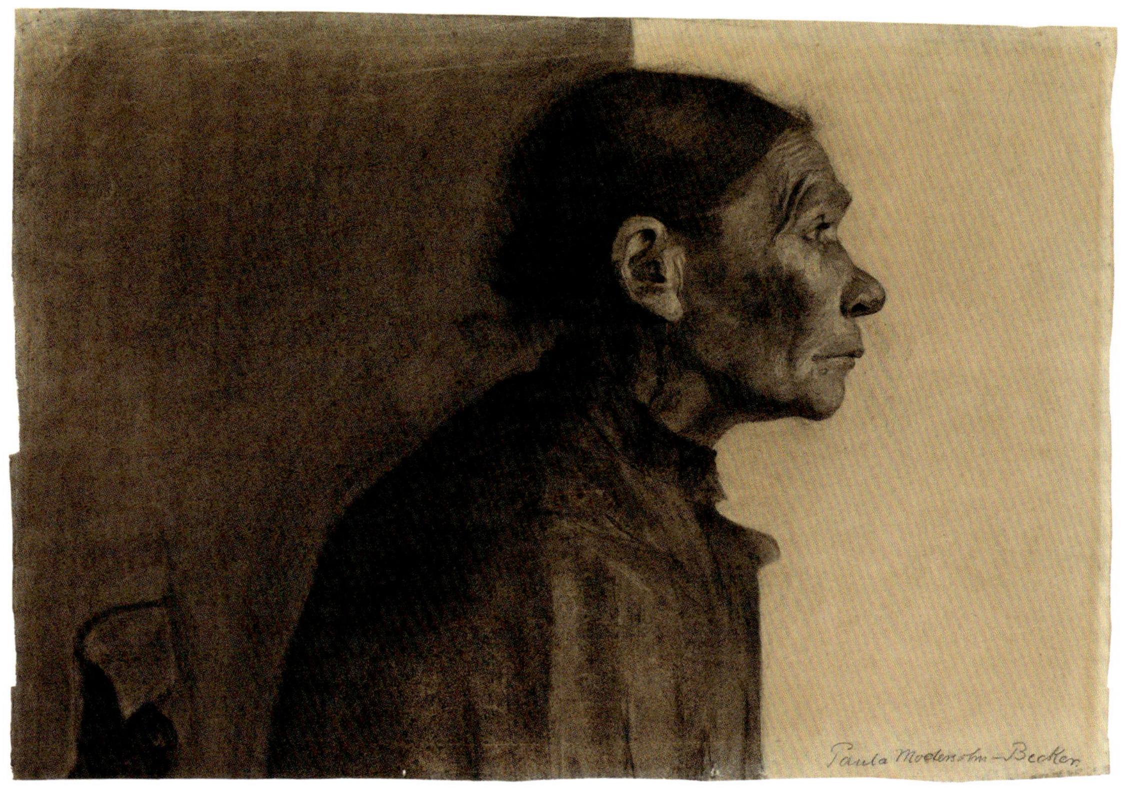

109. Paula Modersohn-Becker, Woman in Profile, Turned Right, 1898–99

Between 1898 and 1899, Paula Modersohn-Becker created a remarkable group of drawings of the inhabitants of Worpswede, a small village in northern Germany. The force of these intensely rendered drawings, mostly of women, derives not only from their superb handling but also from the way in which they capture the truth and vulnerability of their sitters.

Artists like Modersohn-Becker went to Worpswede beginning in the late 1800s in search of an "untouched" paradise, far from industrialized urban spaces and rife with picturesque imagery for their paintings and drawings. Modersohn-Becker made *Woman in Profile, Turned Right* during her first months in Worpswede, and unlike her peers, who depicted landscapes, she focused on residents of the local poorhouse. The Art Institute's drawing depicts a woman's face in sharp profile, carefully set against the warm tone of the paper, while her garment is barely described by the sharpened charcoal. The black background, comprising the left half of the sheet, is set down with broad strokes, their movement contrasting with the stillness of the model. The minimal nature of the setting only suggests the back of the chair on which the model is seated, its shape resembling a flower petal as much as a chair back. *Jay A. Clarke*

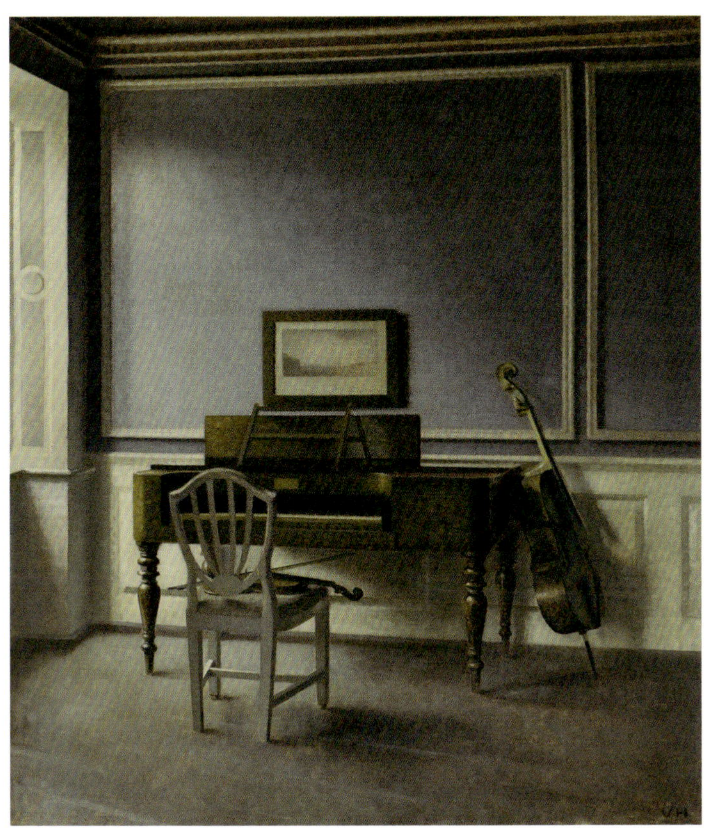

110. Vilhelm Hammershøi, **Interior. The Music Room, Strandgade 30**, 1907

On September 15, 1898, Vilhelm Hammershøi and his wife Ida moved to an apartment on the upper floor of Strandgade 30 in Copenhagen, where they remained until 1909. This stay coincided with the most productive period of the artist's career, during which he painted his best-known series of works: ever-evolving variations on the interior of his apartment. Hammershøi regularly depicted this corner of his drawing room, both with and without the figure of Ida. For the artist, the apartment was akin to a stage set, and he used furniture and household objects like props, endlessly positioning and repositioning them not according to their domestic function but rather to their aesthetic effect.

In *Interior. The Music Room, Strandgade 30*, a minimal arrangement featuring musical instruments is illuminated by soft light filtering through a window just outside the frame. But without a human presence to animate the instruments, the scene evokes only silence. Carefully painted with small, flickering brushstrokes, the picture embodies the poet Rainer Maria Rilke's observation that "Hammershøi is not one of those about whom one must speak quickly. His work is long and slow, and at whichever moment one apprehends it, it will offer plentiful reasons to speak of what is important and essential in art." *Emerson Bowyer*

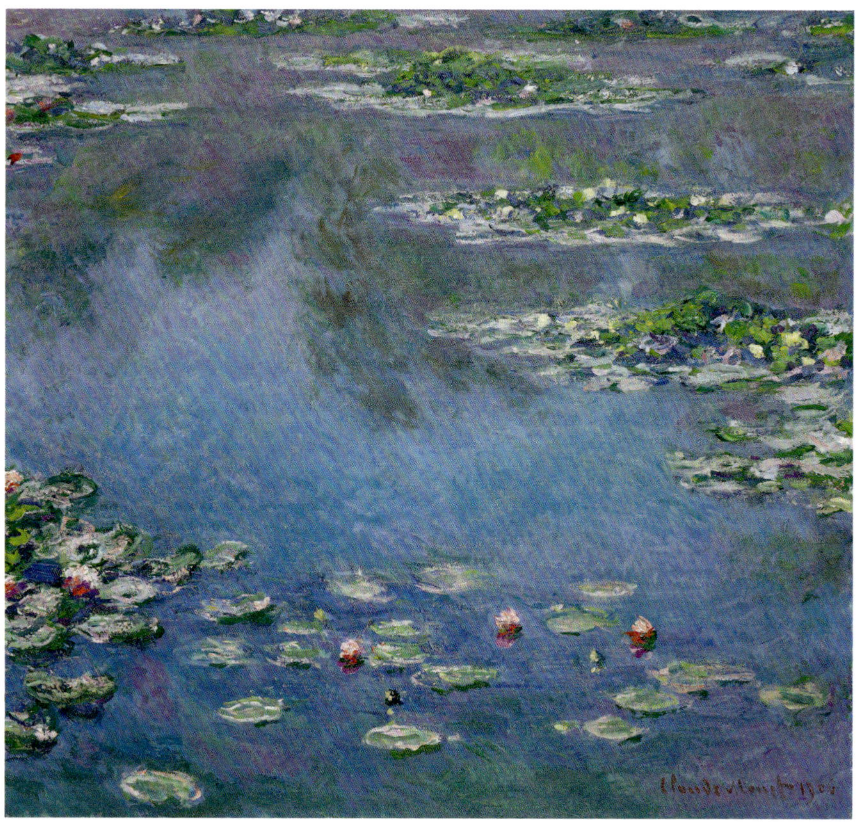

111. Claude Monet, Water Lilies, 1906

Little did Claude Monet know that the water garden he created three years after buying his Giverny, France, property in 1890 would become his primary inspiration over the next two and a half decades. These paintings, numbering around 250, mark Monet's artistic journey from more straightforward depictions of the pond spanned by the wooden Japanese bridge to the monumental and near-abstract series on the water lily theme he made in preparation for his murals at the Musée de l'Orangerie in Paris between 1914 and 1926.

Water Lilies, one of a group of paintings on the subject made between 1903 and 1908, comes at the midpoint of Monet's developing style and spatial experimentations. The nearly square format underscores his move away from painting the conventional zones of land, sky, and water to focus solely on the water's surface. Clusters of water lilies at bottom left and top right frame a watery path, while the water's surface reflects trees and clouds. Although the dreamlike quality of floating forms might seem to be a natural development for the artist, he considered these works "an obsession," a sentiment borne out by technical examinations on the Art Institute's canvas, revealing many significant changes made to the painting in progress.
Gloria Groom

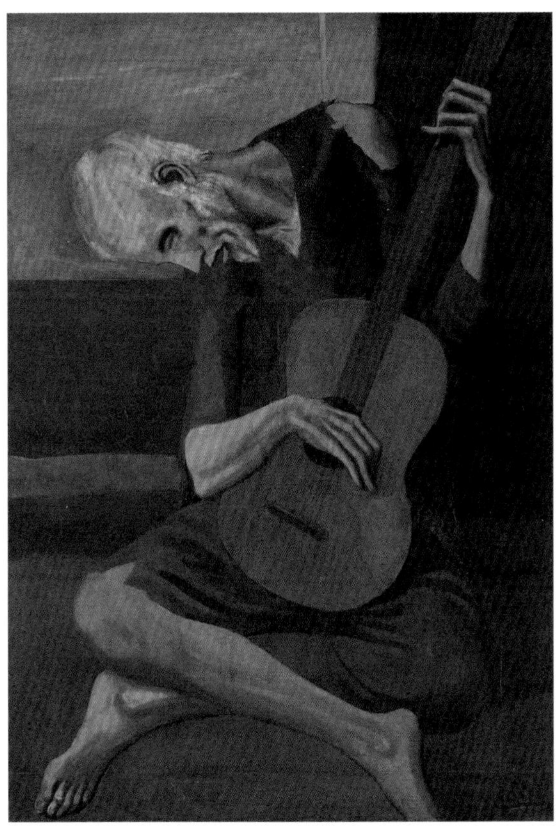

112. Pablo Picasso, **The Old Guitarist**, 1903–4

This soulful image—which Pablo Picasso painted when he was only twenty-two years old—remains among the most haunting and melancholic of his Blue Period. At this early moment in his career, Picasso was forced to live quite frugally, and his limited means are evident in the work's construction—a panel support cobbled together from several fragments and reused at least three times, with earlier paintings still partially visible underneath.

With time, Picasso would become one of the twentieth century's great pictorial experimenters, always testing the viability of bodies in space. Here the guitarist's expressive figure seems to fold over onto itself, such that if he were to stand, his gaunt body would tower over the painting. Bowing with psychological weight and strumming sorrowfully on his instrument, the guitarist's elongated form reflects Picasso's deep admiration of the Spanish Mannerist El Greco. In fact, this painting was made in Barcelona shortly before Picasso established his studio at the Bateau-Lavoir in Paris. It became the artist's first work to enter the Art Institute's collection, and it remains a cornerstone of holdings that today include more than 350 works spanning his career. *Caitlin Haskell*

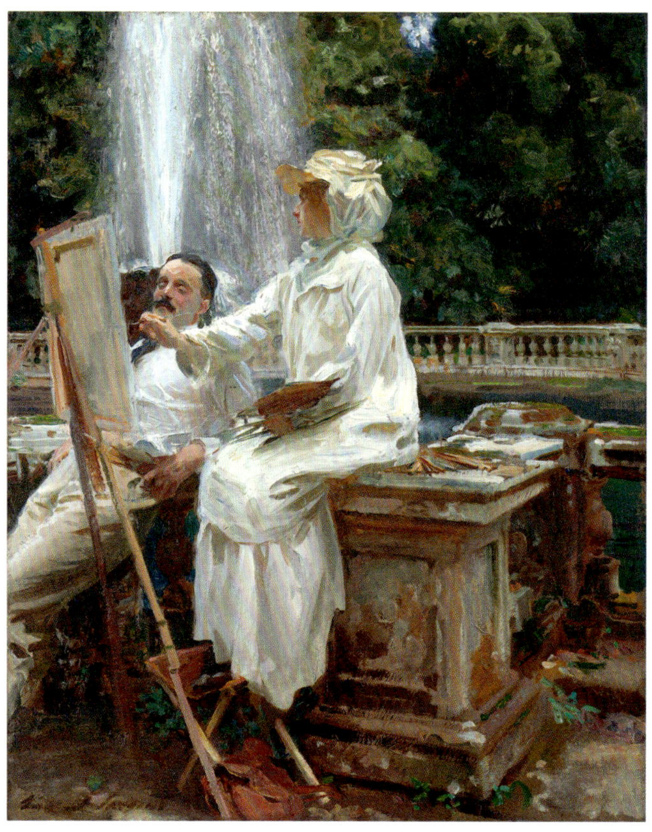

113. John Singer Sargent, **The Fountain, Villa Torlonia, Frascati, Italy**, 1907

Although best known for his portraits, John Singer Sargent was also an intrepid traveler and used his frequent trips to find artistic inspiration, as seen here. This painting showcases Sargent's skill as both a landscape painter and a portraitist as he captured his friends and frequent travel companions Wilfrid and Jane Emmet de Glehn.

But why stop at this particular villa and perch on this particular fountain? While we can only speculate, it might have had something to do with the family who owned the villa. The aristocratic Torlonia family built one of the most celebrated collections of ancient Roman sculpture in the 1800s—a collection that remains intact today. Their great wealth also meant that they were one of the largest landholding families in the Rome region, and their villa at Frascati was famed for its gardens and fountains. Sargent and his friends were following in the footsteps of many earlier artists, aristocrats, and tourists who traveled to Italy to visit archaeological sites and historic collections of ancient Roman art. But while others were entranced by the traces of the distant past, here Sargent focused on his contemporaries and the momentary effects of light and color as he painted outdoors.
Lisa Ayla Çakmak

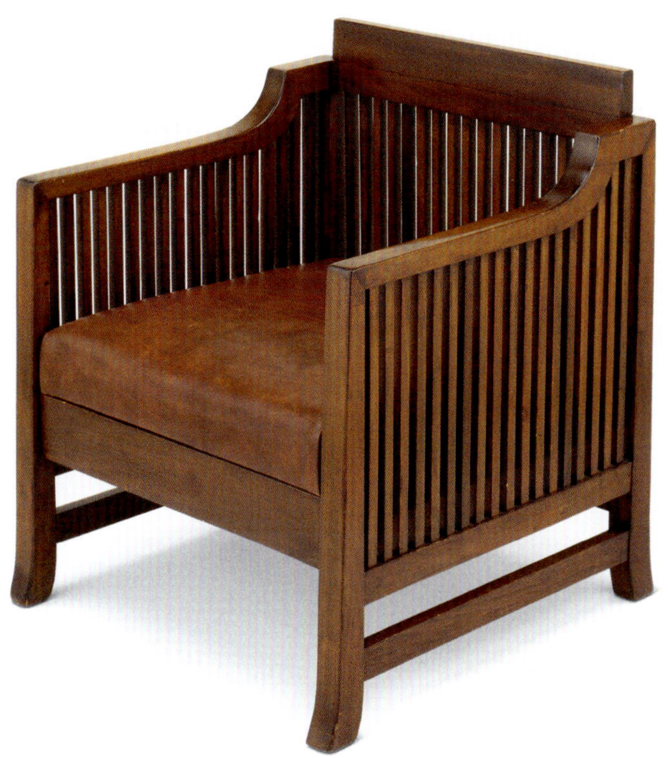

114. Frank Lloyd Wright, **Spindle Cube Chair**, 1902–6

Frank Lloyd Wright prioritized function over comfort in this chair designed for the architectural studio attached to his suburban Chicago home. Photographs from when Wright lived and worked in the space show it paired with a corresponding table designed for his growing collection of Japanese prints. Wright broke the hard geometry of the chair's cubic form to allow the armrests to gently slope under the table. When the sitter pulled it up to the table, the slatted sides and back enclosed them, requiring them to keep their body and attention focused on the artwork on the print stand. Together, the pair creates a room within a room, a pattern Wright repeated throughout his designs for his own, and other, homes.

This chair is also significant as one of Wright's early experiments using unit-based design, in which a consistent approach to form, scale, and proportion unifies interrelated objects. Wright would more fully develop these ideas in the 1930s when he began designing his Usonian homes. Wright designed these homes and their furniture with the goal of making beautiful, functional architectural designs affordable and accessible to middle-class Americans.
Sarah Holian

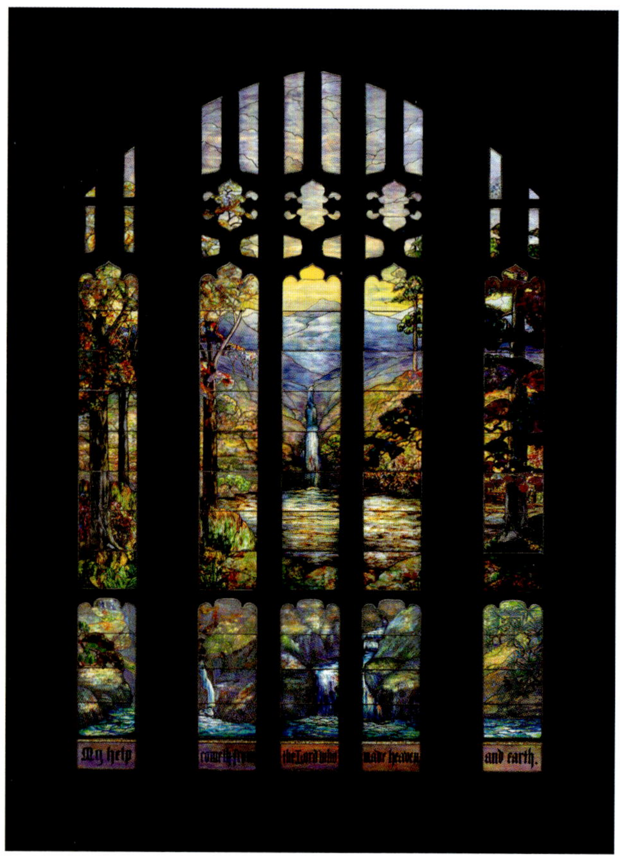

115. Tiffany Studios, design attributed to Agnes F. Northrop, Hartwell Memorial Window, 1917

This soaring vista is an idealized view of Mount Chocorua, New Hampshire, realized through a kaleidoscope of glass fragments. The window—among the most complex stained-glass landscapes produced in the US—originally adorned the Central Baptist Church (now the Community Church) in Providence. Mary Hartwell commissioned the window in honor of her late husband, Frederick. Inspired by the view from his family home, the scene captures the transitory beauty of nature—the setting sun, flowing water, and dappled light dancing through the trees—in an intricate arrangement of vibrantly colored glass.

Agnes F. Northrop designed the window at the renowned art and interior design firm Tiffany Studios, collaborating with specialists who developed glass formulas, made the glass, selected pieces for each project, cut them to fit the design, and united the pieces with strips of lead or copper soldered together. To achieve the window's highly natural effects, artists built up different types of glass anywhere from two to five layers thick across each of the window's forty-eight panels. At every stage of its creation, Tiffany Studios' team of designers and craftspeople sought innovative ways to realize this landscape in light. *Elizabeth McGoey*

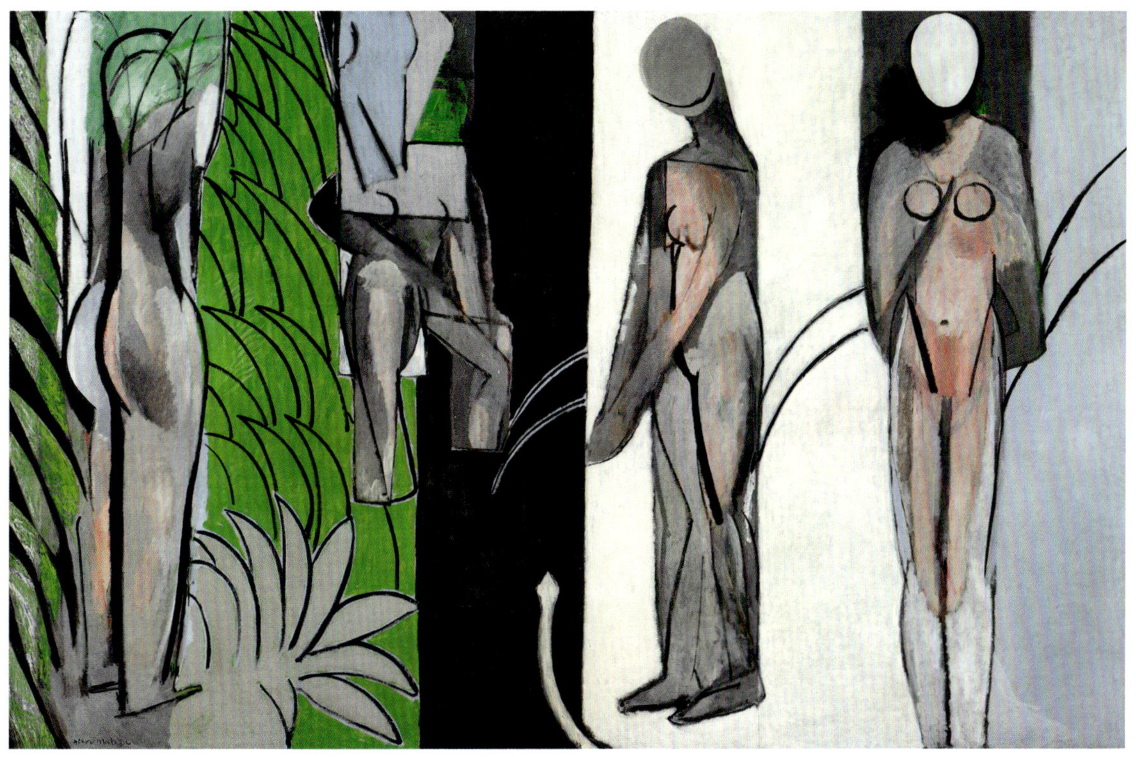

116. Henri Matisse, **Bathers by a River**, 1909–10, 1913, and 1916–17

Nearing the end of his life—and clearly gratified that *Bathers by a River* had found a permanent home at the Art Institute—Henri Matisse wrote to the museum's director and described this monumental painting as one of his five most "pivotal" works. Originally conceived as part of a pastoral mural commission for Russian collector Sergei Shchukin, the composition underwent dramatic transformation over an eight-year period, during which it remained in Matisse's studio. What began as a lyrical, idyllic landscape evolved into a stark, abstracted scene influenced by Cubism and the tensions of a world at war.

Marking a radical shift in style and mood, Matisse replaced naturalistic color with a restrained palette. He converted the formerly radiant blue river into a solid black band that dramatically divides the canvas at the center. He also overpainted the bathers with gray and simplified their forms, lending them a solemn, hieratic presence. The strong vertical divisions of color now create a dynamic rhythm with the four fragmented figures. This persistent revision reflects Matisse's evolving exploration of abstraction, especially his innovative use of black—not just as a contour, but as an expressive, structural force. *Tacy Wagner*

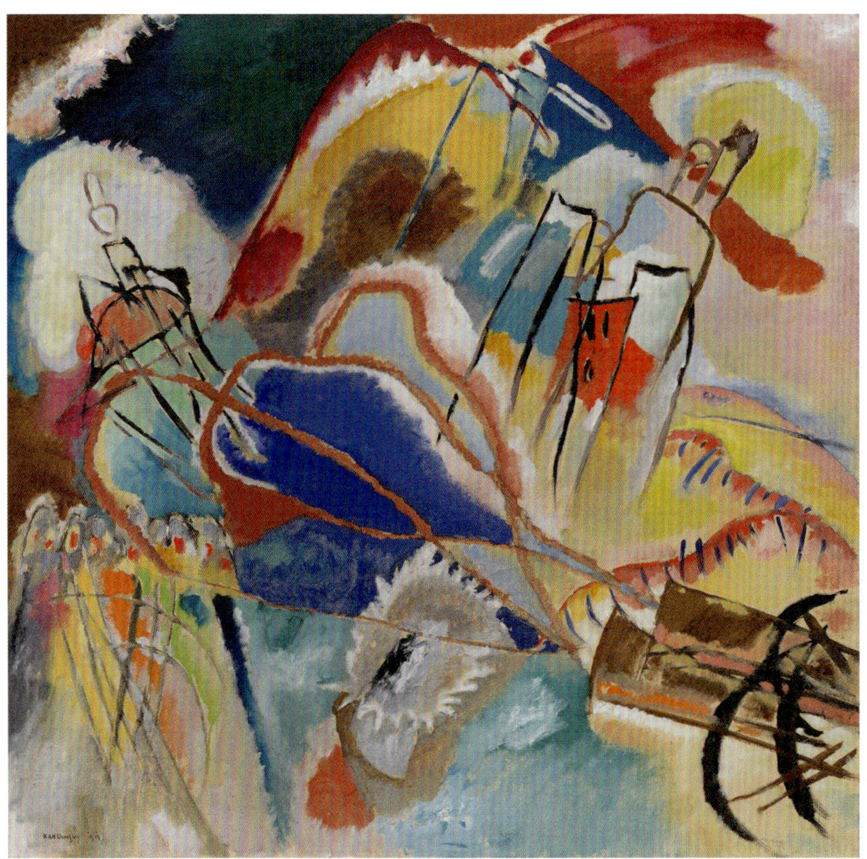

119. Vasily Kandinsky, Improvisation No. 30 (Cannons), 1913

As a Russian citizen living in Munich in the years before World War I, Vasily Kandinsky was especially sensitive to the threat of international conflict, knowing he risked internment or expulsion from Germany should war break out. This eventuality came to pass shortly after Kandinsky painted *Improvisation No. 30 (Cannons)*, a work that marks a turning point in his path toward abstraction. Material forms that correspond to emotional states dissolve into bursts of color and line, yet some references remain recognizable: smoking cannons, a huddled crowd, and towers on a hill. Capturing the tensions of the time, these elements suggest a world teetering between exhilaration and destruction.

In a letter to Chicago lawyer and collector Arthur Jerome Eddy, who purchased the work from the artist in 1913, Kandinsky wrote: "The presence of the cannons in the picture could probably be explained by the constant war talk that has been going on throughout the year. The title 'cannons' . . . is not to be conceived as indicating the picture's 'contents.' . . . Rather, the true contents are what the spectator experiences while under the effect of the forms and color combinations." *Tacy Wagner*

120. María Blanchard, Still Life with a Box of Matches, 1918

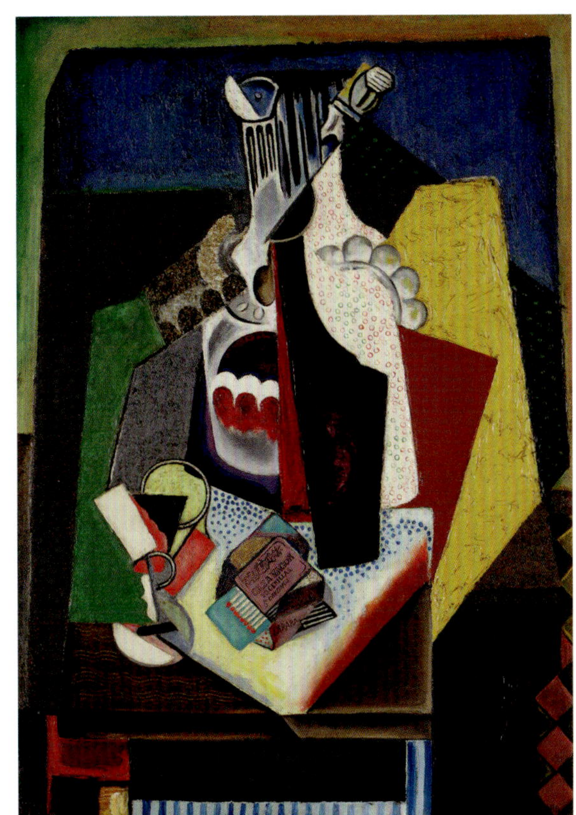

Still Life with a Box of Matches revels in visual wit. María Blanchard took a materially rich approach to Synthetic Cubism, a phase of Cubism in which artists used bright colors and simple shapes in a collage-like manner to further explore light effects, spatial relationships, and fractioning of perspective. At center right, small pink and pale green circles form the body of a soda siphon, suggesting bubbly carbonation. At lower left, Blanchard passed a comblike tool through brown paint to evoke the table's wood grain. She also used glass beads and sand to vary the texture of distinct areas surrounding the bottles, absinthe glass, and other café table accessories.

Besides creating some of the most rigorous works in the Cubist idiom, Blanchard was one of only a few women to contribute to the movement's theoretical and technical aims in the years immediately before and after World War I. In her lifetime, she had vocal champions, including artists Juan Gris and Diego Rivera, and the influential dealer Léonce Rosenberg, whose prestigious Galerie de l'Effort Moderne offered her exclusive representation the year this work was painted. Rivera once praised Blanchard as being, in his view, the best Cubist after Picasso.
Tamar Kharatishvili

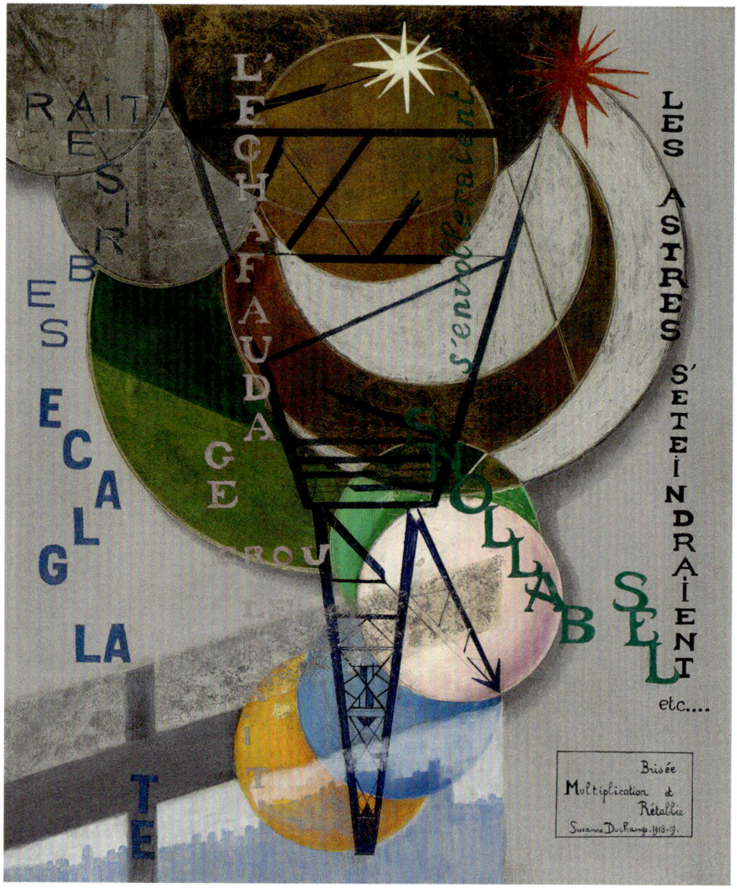

121. Suzanne Duchamp, **Broken and Restored Multiplication**, 1918–19

The letters, words, and phrases distributed across the surface of *Broken and Restored Multiplication* recall *calligrammes*—poetry in which the physical placement of letters on the page lends additional meaning to its subject matter. Here, they offer a sober commentary on the state of the world in the immediate aftermath of World War I. The work's title suggests a world out of balance and belies its careful design, laid out by the artist with the aid of mechanical instruments such as compasses and rulers.

The work conveys disorder and breakage through an array of visual and verbal strategies. Suzanne Duchamp painted a schematic Eiffel Tower, rendered upside down. In the painting's lowest horizontal register, blue brushstrokes suggest a far-off skyline, while abstract discs in pink, green, silver, and brown ascend upwards. A copper sliver represents a crescent moon, and white and red stars suggest sparks or starbursts. Duchamp painted fragmentary phrases in different typefaces and colors across the canvas, playing with collaged passages of metallic paint, to suggest disorientation: "The mirror would shatter," "the scaffolding would totter," "the balloons would fly away," "the stars would dim." *Tamar Kharatishvili*

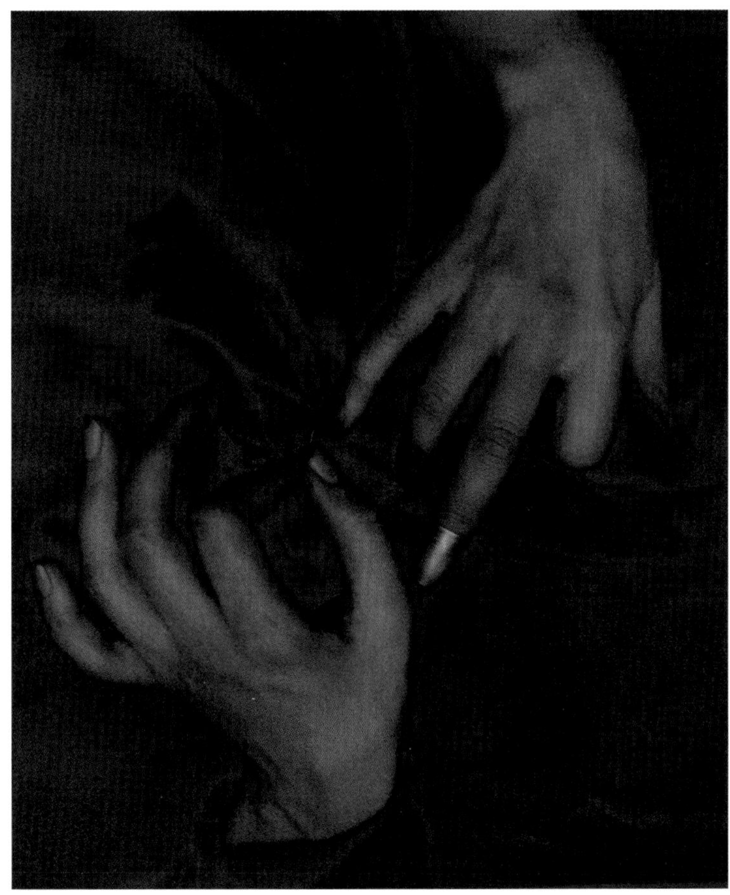

122. Alfred Stieglitz, **Georgia O'Keeffe—Hands and Thimble**, 1919

Over the course of nearly twenty years, Georgia O'Keeffe posed for some five hundred photographs by the photographer and gallerist Alfred Stieglitz. Her beauty, Stieglitz felt, could not be captured through portraits of her head and face alone; her torso, feet, and especially her hands, as seen here, were equally expressive. He called the results a "composite portrait" that, taken together, could make visible the essence of O'Keeffe's many "selves."

Throughout the first half of the twentieth century, Stieglitz worked tirelessly to change Americans' perception of new art, especially photography. He wrote essays and edited magazines advocating for photography's artistic merit and organized the first American exhibitions of artists including Pablo Picasso, Henri Matisse, and Paul Cezanne. From 1908 to 1917, he operated an influential Manhattan gallery known simply as 291. O'Keeffe held her debut exhibition at 291 in 1917, and the two began an affair shortly thereafter, eventually marrying in 1924. In 1921 Stieglitz held an exhibition of approximately forty of his pictures of O'Keeffe—including *Hands and Thimble*—at another New York gallery. *Yechen Zhao*

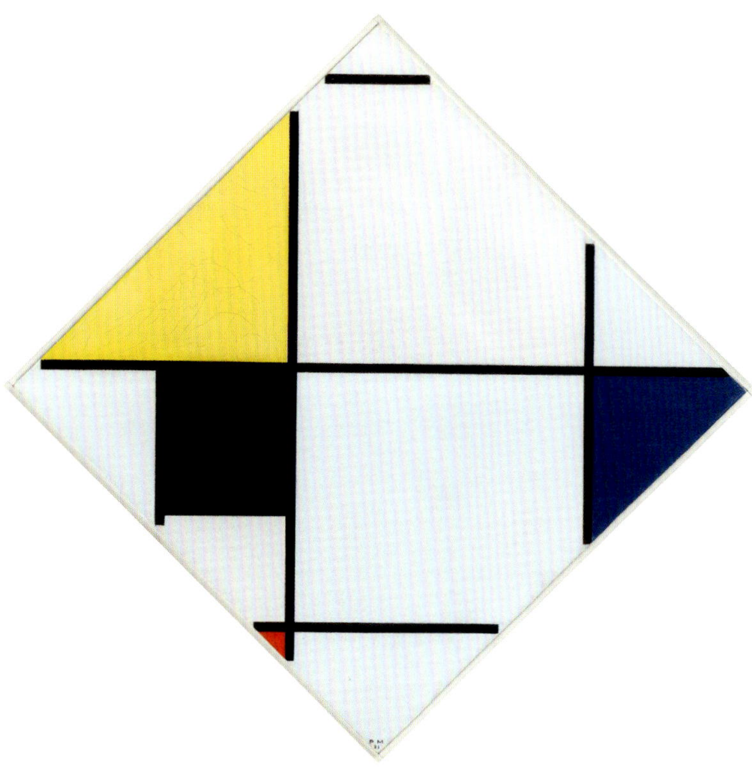

123. Piet Mondrian, **Lozenge Composition with Yellow, Black, Blue, Red, and Gray**, 1921

Lozenge Composition with Yellow, Black, Blue, Red, and Gray reflects Piet Mondrian's revolutionary vision of abstraction rooted in nature. Initially a painter of representational landscapes, Mondrian gradually reduced natural forms to vertical and horizontal lines and limited his palette to primary colors, as well as black, white, and gray, seeking to express an underlying universal harmony. This painting—one of sixteen diamond-shaped or "lozenge" works—marks a pivotal moment in that evolution.

By rotating the canvas on its axis, Mondrian introduced a dynamic tension between the painting's content and the canvas edge, probing the relationship between what is depicted and what contains it. The black grid suggests enclosure, while a single line reaching the slanted upper-right side hints at expansion beyond the canvas. This duality—combined with the artist's practice of hanging works high on the wall—invites a heightened spatial, and perhaps even spiritual, engagement.

A leading figure of the De Stijl (The Style) movement, Mondrian sought to unify art, architecture, and design through simplicity and balance. Though austere in appearance, *Lozenge Composition* is deliberately and meticulously structured—any small change would disrupt its delicate equilibrium. For Mondrian, such visual order pointed toward a more harmonious, even utopian future; he famously asserted that "the straight line tells the truth." *Tacy Wagner*

124. Constantin Brancusi, *Golden Bird*, 1919–20

The toy
become the aesthetic archetype

As if
some patient peasant God
had rubbed and rubbed
the Alpha and Omega
of Form
into a lump of metal

A naked orientation
unwinged   unplumed
        —the ultimate rhythm
has lopped the extremities
of crest and claw
from
the nucleus of flight

The absolute act
of art
conformed
to continent sculpture
—bare as the brow of Osiris—
this breast of revelation

an incandescent curve
licked by chromatic flames
in labyrinths of reflections

This gong
of polished hyperaesthesia
shrills with brass
as the aggressive light
strikes
its significance

The immaculate
conception
of the inaudible bird
occurs
in gorgeous reticence . . .

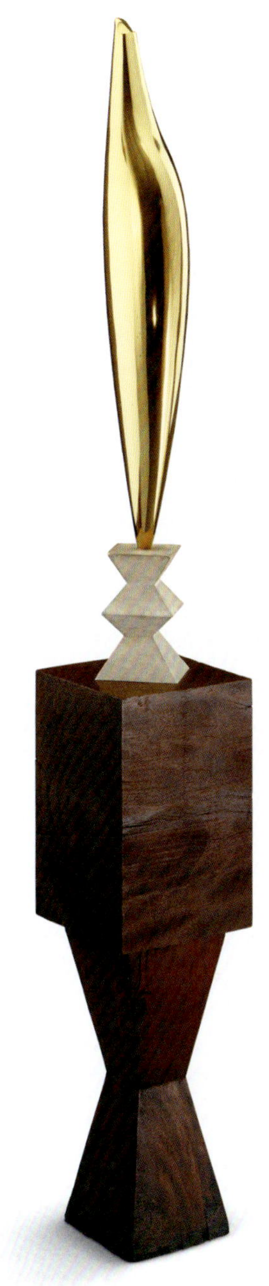

"Brancusi's Golden Bird" by Mina Loy

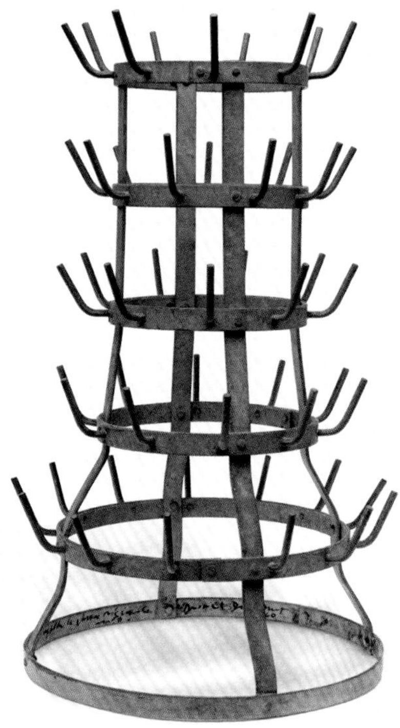

125. Marcel Duchamp, Bottle Rack, 1914 and 1959

In 1913 Marcel Duchamp fully rejected painting and asked whether one could make works that were not "art" in the conventional sense. His answer was the readymade: an ordinary object—often mass-produced—designated as art through his selection. By removing these objects from their usual contexts and signing them, Duchamp radically challenged the definition of art, undermining tradition, production, and institutional authority.

Many original readymades were lost, and Duchamp recreated or acquired replacements. This version of *Bottle Rack* (*Porte-bouteilles*) was made for the 1959 exhibition *Art and the Found Object* in New York. Duchamp, unable to locate a bottle rack in the US, enlisted fellow artist Man Ray in Paris. Man Ray found one at the same department store—Bazar de l'Hôtel de Ville—where Duchamp had purchased the original in 1914.

Among the show's participants was a young Robert Rauschenberg, who acquired the *Bottle Rack* after the exhibition tour and, in 1960, had Duchamp sign it. Duchamp inscribed: "Impossible de me rappeler la phrase originale [Impossible for me to recall the original phrase]/M.D./Marcel Duchamp/1960." This object stands as an example of one of the great art historical transgressions and of the transmission of ideas across twentieth-century art.
Giampaolo Bianconi

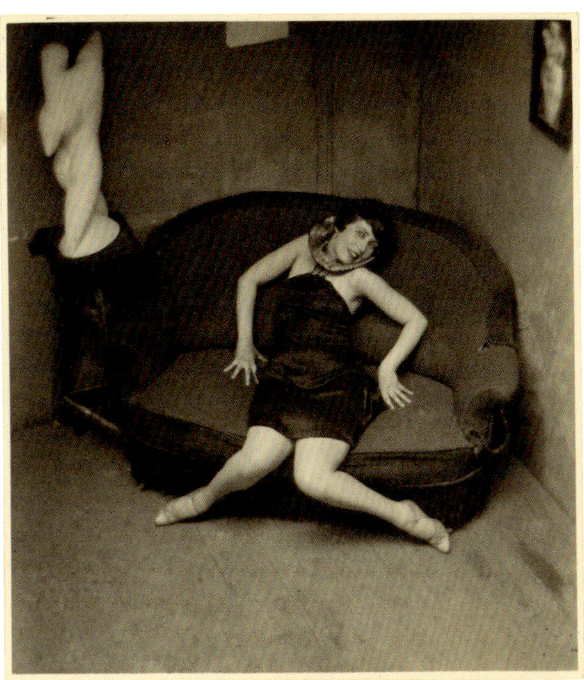

126. André Kertész, **Satiric Dancer, Paris** (variant), 1927

In 1915 André Kertész began submitting pictures to newspaper and exhibition competitions in his native Hungary. He arrived in Paris one decade later greatly attuned to the possibilities of photographs as both unique objects and mass-media images. This gorgeously printed view of the dancer Magda Förstner posing in the Montparnasse studio of sculptor Etienne (István) Beöthy (who, like the photographer and dancer, was also a Hungarian émigré) is a variant of one published by the Berlin leisure magazine *Die Dame* in 1927 to illustrate a parable of marital infidelity.

Clad in a short halter dress with a ruff around her neck, Förstner perches alluringly on a couch, her lower legs swiveled outward as if imitating a Charleston step. Beöthy was pursuing an abstracted figural language in sculpture, just as Kertész was in photography, and his statue *Direct Action*, visible in a corner next to the sofa, serves as a foil for the latter's camera work. The published photograph became an icon—and possibly gained its current title—only in the 1960s, when Kertész recovered the negative and reprinted it multiple times. The Art Institute's version, meanwhile, is believed to be unique. *Elizabeth Siegel*

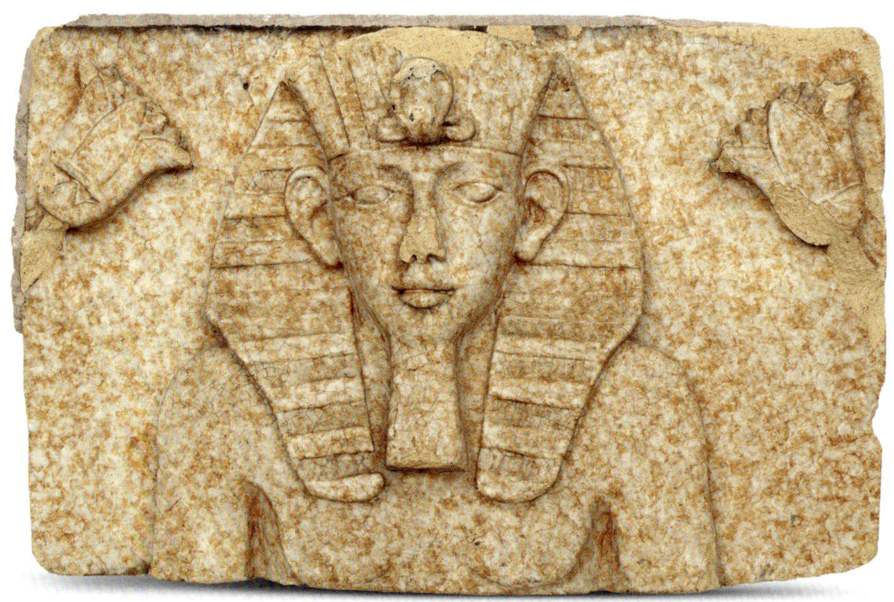

127. Walter T. Bailey, **Facade Panel from the National Pythian Temple, Chicago, Illinois**, around 1927

For those fortunate enough to have seen it, the National Pythian Temple was a spectacle. The eight-story structure was an impressive Egyptian Revival–style building clad with a yellow glazed terracotta skin featuring dazzling reliefs of pharaohs, griffins, rams—even the face of Cleopatra. Built in 1928, the temple was demolished in 1980. The site has been vacant since. Fortunately, pieces of the building's sun-kissed terracotta survived, including this panel featuring the head and shoulders of an Egyptian pharaoh flanked by lotuses.

Imagine the pride Bronzeville residents must have felt when the building was constructed. The temple was the tallest building in the Bronzeville neighborhood, built by the Knights of Pythias, a Black fraternal and benevolent organization on what was then called Chicago's Black Wall Street. It was designed by Walter Thomas Bailey, Illinois's first licensed Black architect, and was billed as the country's largest building financed, designed, and built by African Americans. The opening of King Tutankhamen's tomb in 1922 sparked a worldwide wave of Egyptian-inspired architecture—including the Pythian Temple. But the temple was also a bold and early attempt to reconnect African Americans to Africa—specifically Egypt, seen as one of the most advanced and sophisticated ancient civilizations. *Lee Bey*

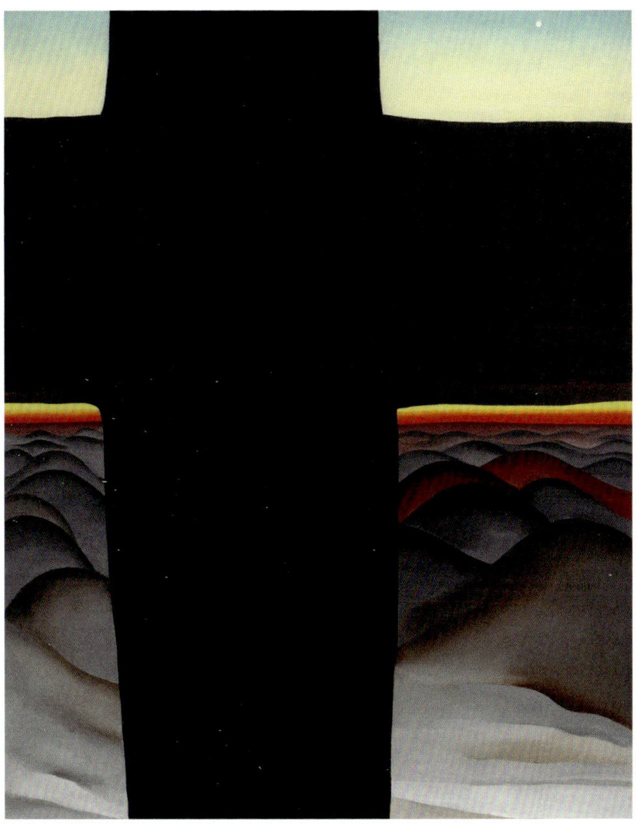

128. Georgia O'Keeffe, **Black Cross, New Mexico**, 1929

Desert hills roll below bands of red-yellow sunlight just breaking over the horizon. Above, pale blue sky surrounds a lone celestial form. A thick, dark cross stretches across the canvas, splitting the sky and landscape into four asymmetrical quadrants. It is simple compared to the rolling mountains, but close viewing reveals color variations, wooden pegs, time's rusty impacts. Perhaps on the other side, it is emblazoned with red light from the low sun.

Georgia O'Keeffe observed crosses like this one during her late-night walks through the New Mexico desert. In a 1943 Art Institute exhibition catalogue, the Catholic-raised artist recalled these outings and the objects' symbolic effect: "I saw the crosses so often—and often in unexpected places—like a thin dark veil of the Catholic church spread over the New Mexico landscape."

The painted cross may have been placed by the Penitentes, a secretive Catholic lay brotherhood likely formed by Spanish settlers and Indigenous peoples of the region. Layers of history collide in their practice: Native tradition, Spanish colonization, religious persecution, and syncretic resilience. These layers are present but unspoken in this painting, which brings us back to tangible ground—to expressions of faith in a vast, unfolding desert. *Lois Taylor Biggs*

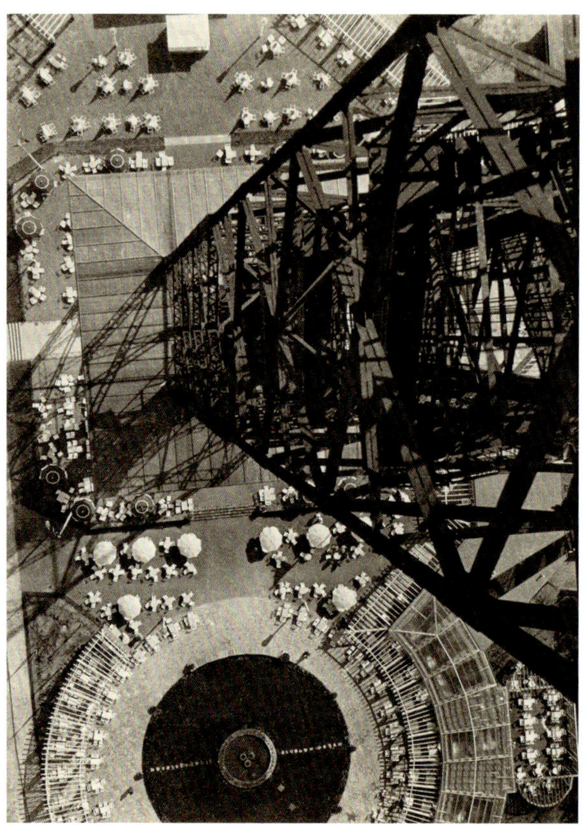

129. László Moholy-Nagy, Berlin Radio Tower, 1928

Over the winter and spring of 1927–28, Bauhaus professor László Moholy-Nagy took a series of photographs including perhaps nine views looking down from the Berlin Radio Tower, one of the most exciting new constructions in the German capital. Moholy had already photographed the Eiffel Tower in Paris from below, looking up through the tower's soaring girders. In Berlin, however, Moholy turned his camera around and pointed it straight down at the ground. This plunging perspective showed off the Radio Tower's spectacular narrowness; it was finished in 1926, rising vertiginously to a height of 450 feet from a base seven times smaller than that of its Parisian predecessor (which opened in 1889). Moholy attached exceptional importance to this bold image: He hung it just above his name in a room devoted to his work at the Berlin showing of *Film und Foto*, a mammoth traveling exhibition that he had helped prepare. Moholy also offered this view and one other to Julien Levy, the pioneering art dealer, when Levy visited him in Berlin in 1930. The following year the pictures went on view at the Levy Gallery in New York in Moholy's first solo exhibition of photographs. *Matthew S. Witkovsky*

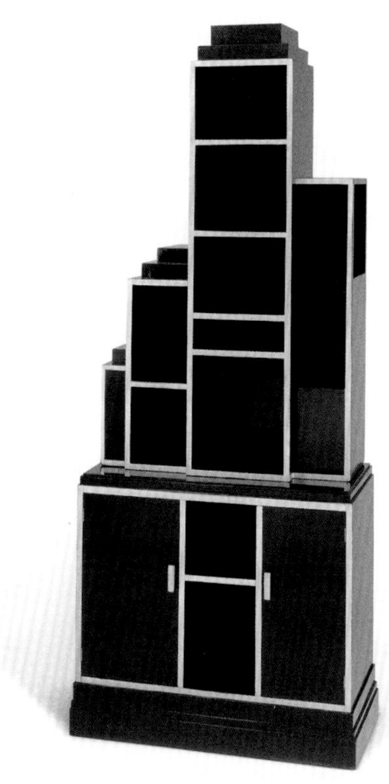

130. Paul Theodore Frankl, **Skyscraper Cabinet**, about 1927

In a 1927 *House & Garden* article, Paul Frankl wrote, "In my own creations for the modern American home, I have kept within the architectural spirit of our time . . . they call my chests of drawers, my dressing tables, my bookcases—'Skyscraper'—to which I blushingly bow." In stark contrast to the traditional, historic-revival forms that dominated the furniture trade, Frankl tapped into the spirit and the geometries of the evolving urban landscape to reshape interiors. Indeed, every detail of this cabinet reflects the architecture of America's rising cities, including its stepped form, sharp and simplistic moldings, flat surfaces, metallic finishes, and overall feeling of height and power.

Frankl's vision for modernist furniture that reflected the changing times extended beyond formal qualities into functionality. He wanted to use height to expand the possibilities for furnishing small spaces. Not even sixteen inches deep, the small footprint of this cabinet was designed to conserve space in small city apartments, while the stepped compartments and openings on the side of the cabinet allow the display of objects on three of its four sides. Frankl's innovative design translates the bold verticality and efficient design principles of America's skyscrapers into a novel, practical solution for contemporary living. *Elizabeth McGoey*

Towers on the Prairie

Alison Fisher

People come from all over the world to see Chicago's skyscrapers. Their innovative combination of technology and style reshaped the city and spread across the world.

The skyscraper was born in Chicago. In the 1940s and 1950s, scholars boldly claimed that International Style modernism had emerged from the first generation of tall buildings erected in the city. This theory made the birth and development of the skyscraper in Chicago seem natural and almost inevitable, tying the work of early masters of the tall building such as William LeBaron Jenney, Louis Sullivan, Daniel Burnham, and Holabird and Roche (see fig. 1) to that of a new generation that came to dominate after World War II led by German émigré Ludwig Mies van der Rohe and his many followers.

But what is a skyscraper? This sense of the term was first used in an 1883 article in the *Chicago Daily News* describing the "high building craze." However, tall buildings of this era were generally only around ten stories, supported by hybrid structural systems, including cast iron, wood, stone, and brick. Many of these early pioneers, such as Jenney's first Leiter Building (1879), were also set apart by their use of elevators, a new technology at the time, as economic pressures—largely in cities with high real estate costs like Boston, New York, and Chicago—stoked the drive to build ever higher.

As Chicago moved beyond the rebuilding frenzy following the Great Chicago Fire of 1871, these factors came together to produce a style or type that appeared to architectural critics as an altogether new development. Pressure to produce maximum space at minimum expense, with structures suited to Chicago's wobbly clay soils, led to the rapid adoption of all-steel framing beginning in 1889. The local reputation for prioritizing profits over tradition also played a role, encouraging more minimally ornamented terracotta facades with large plate glass windows, in contrast to early tall buildings

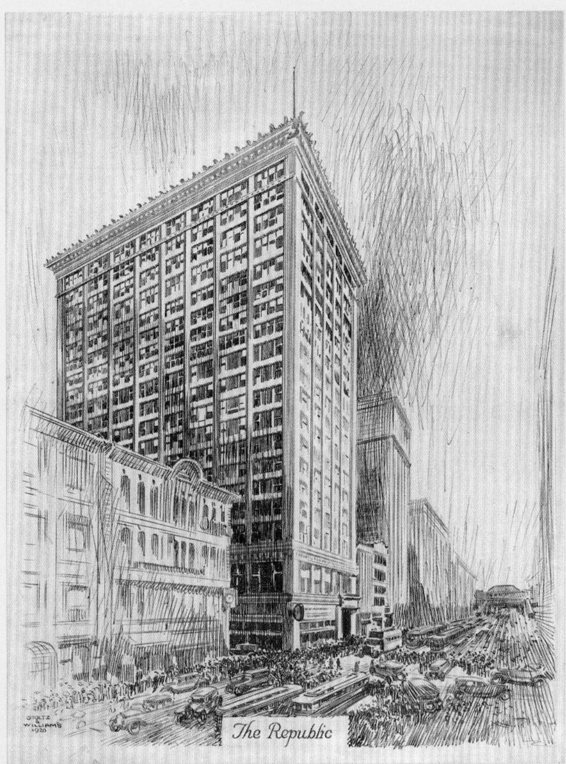

Fig. 1. Holabird and Roche (American, 1883–1927); illustrated by Stoltz and Williams (American, active 20th century). *Republic Building, Chicago, Illinois, Perspective*, 1920 [building 1902–05]. Ink on paperboard; 60.3 × 49.1 cm (23 3⁄4 × 19 5⁄16 in.). Gift of Richard Nickel, 2025.292.

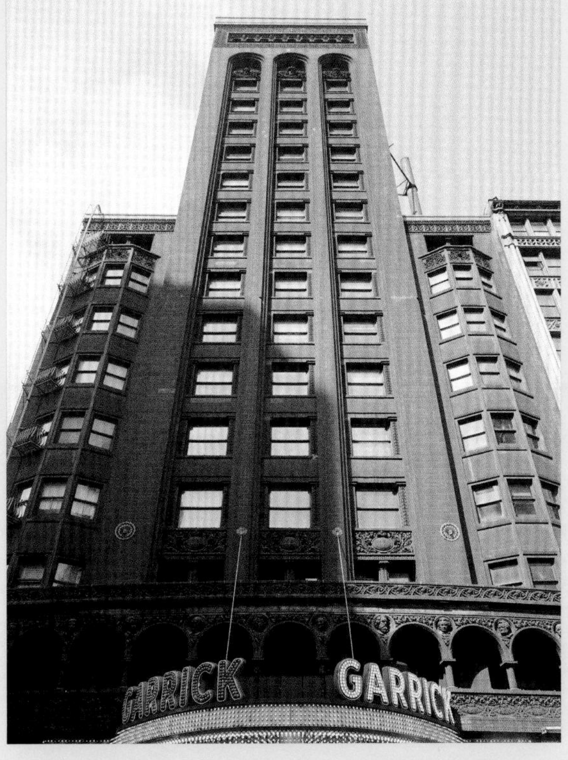

Fig. 2. Richard Nickel (American, 1928–1972). *Untitled (Exterior View of the Garrick Theater Building* [designed by Louis Sullivan]*)*, about 1955, printed 1973. Gelatin silver print; 45.4 × 35.4 cm (17 7⁄8 × 13 15⁄16 in.). Series VIII, box 138, Richard Nickel Archive, Ryerson and Burnham Art and Architecture Archives, The Art Institute of Chicago.

in New York, which were often crowned by a riot of architectural details including mansard roofs, dormers, and towers.

Ultimately, the first true definition of the skyscraper related not only to height, but to a combination of many factors that signaled broader architectural, urban, and cultural shifts. Unsurprisingly perhaps, the first person to attempt a more holistic description of these developments was Chicago architect Louis Sullivan. In his 1896 article "The Tall Office Building Artistically Considered," Sullivan called on designers to advance the next phase of development with authentic architectural expressions that celebrated, rather than masked, the skyscraper's exceptionalism: "It must be every inch a proud and soaring thing, rising in sheer exultation that from bottom to top it is a unit without a single dissenting line" (see fig. 2).

With some important exceptions, notably the 1922 competition for the Tribune Tower, which attracted diverse submissions from modern and traditional architects alike, the next giant leap forward in skyscraper design would come after World War II. Widely

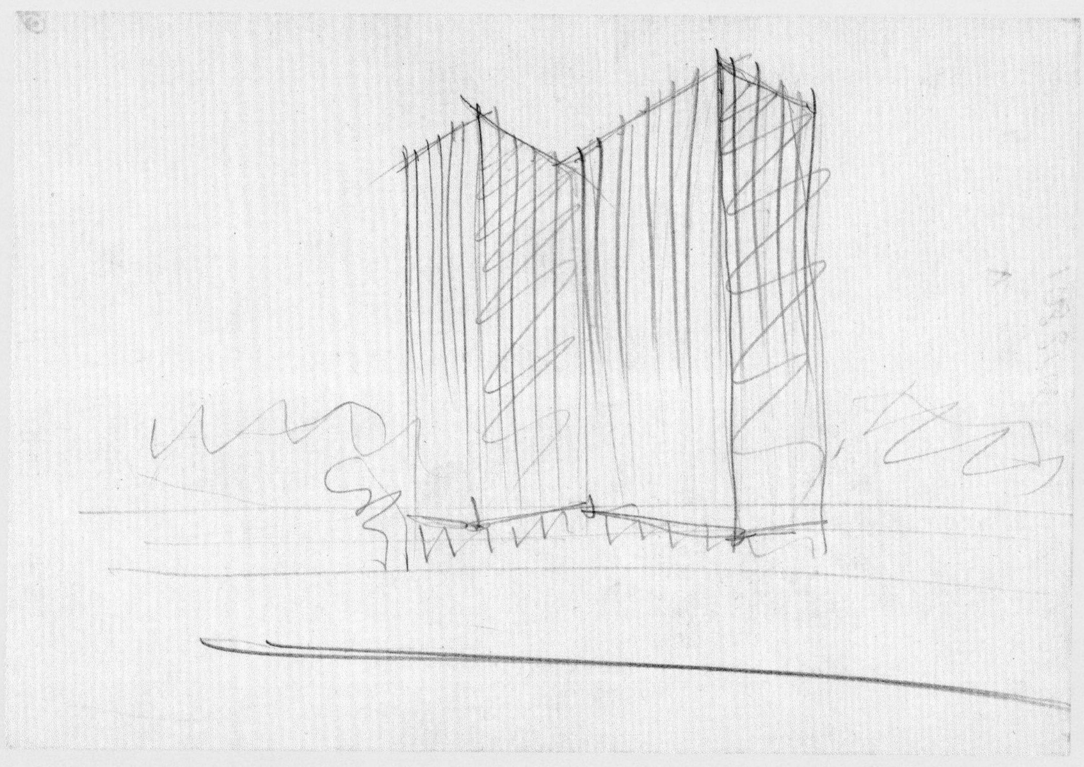

Fig. 3. Ludwig Mies van der Rohe (American, born Germany, 1886–1969). *Highrise Buildings, Chicago, Illinois, Perspective Sketches*, about 1946–48. Graphite on note paper, mounted on archival board; 15.2 × 21.7 cm (6 × 8⁹⁄₁₆ in.); including board: 25.3 × 36.1 cm (10 × 14¼ in.). Art Institute of Chicago, Purchased with funds provided by the Architecture Society and the Alexander C. and Tillie S. Speyer Foundation in Honor of John Zukowsky; through prior gift of the Three Oaks Wrecking Company and Carson, Pirie, Scott and company; Samuel P. Avery Endowment and Edward E. Ayer Endowment in memory of Charles L. Hutchinson, 1992.9.

credited with establishing a model for steel-and-glass skyscrapers that would be built throughout the US in the 1960s and 1970s, architect Ludwig Mies van der Rohe was one of many influential artists, designers, and architects who emigrated to the United States due to the rise of the Nazi party in Europe. Mies's first realized tall buildings were a series of residential towers in Chicago built in the 1940s, a decade after he moved here to lead the architecture program at the Illinois Institute of Technology. The most famous of these is 860–880 Lake Shore Drive, twin black steel–framed, curtain-wall skyscrapers, completed in 1949 (see fig. 3). While Mies went on to build iconic skyscrapers in Chicago, New York, and beyond, his most important local contribution might be his influence on the next generation. Mies's students held important roles at several local firms including Skidmore, Owings & Merrill, a firm that dominated tall building innovation for over sixty years, from their iconic Chicago office building for Inland Steel in 1950 to the world's tallest building, the Burj Khalifa in Dubai, in 2009. This firm also pioneered a new architectural language for supertall buildings, guided in part by visionary designers like Myron Goldsmith and realized through new structural systems like the bundled tube developed for the Sears (now Willis) Tower by architect Bruce Graham and engineer Fazlur Khan in 1970–74 (see fig. 4).

Postmodern architects in the 1970s and 1980s, such as Helmut Jahn, interrupted the long modernist influence in skyscraper design with exaggerated forms and eclectic references to historical architecture. Today tall buildings are less easily categorized. Towers by Chicago architect Jeanne Gang, for example, employ digital design and take inspiration from sources as wide-ranging as topographic maps (see fig. 5) and pyramids, aiming for results that blend traditional considerations, like aesthetics and performance, with new ones, such as community and sustainability. In this way, from the 1880s to today, skyscrapers have served as powerful symbols of scientific achievement, economic power, and the human capacity for imagination.

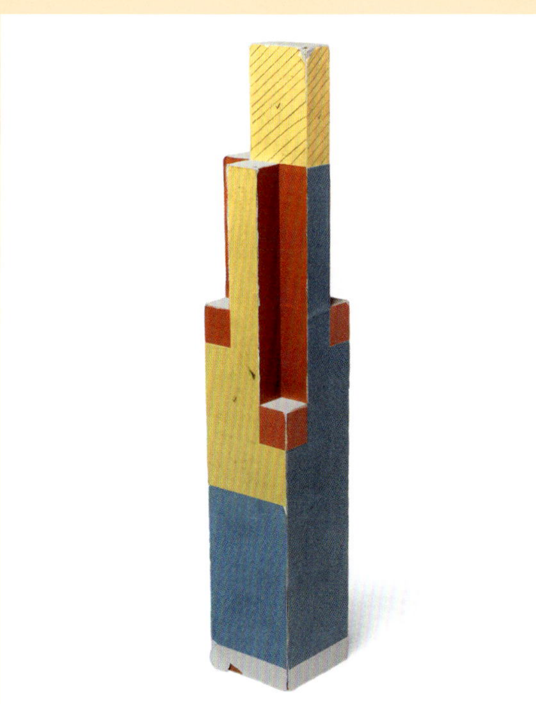

Fig. 4. Skidmore, Owings & Merrill (American, founded 1936); Bruce Graham (American, born Colombia, 1925–2010). *Sears (Willis) Tower, Chicago, Illinois, Massing Model*, about 1969. Graphite, paper, and wood; 37 × 6 × 6 cm (14 9/16 × 2 3/8 × 2 3/8 in.). Gift of Skidmore, Owings & Merrill LLP, 2018.544.28.

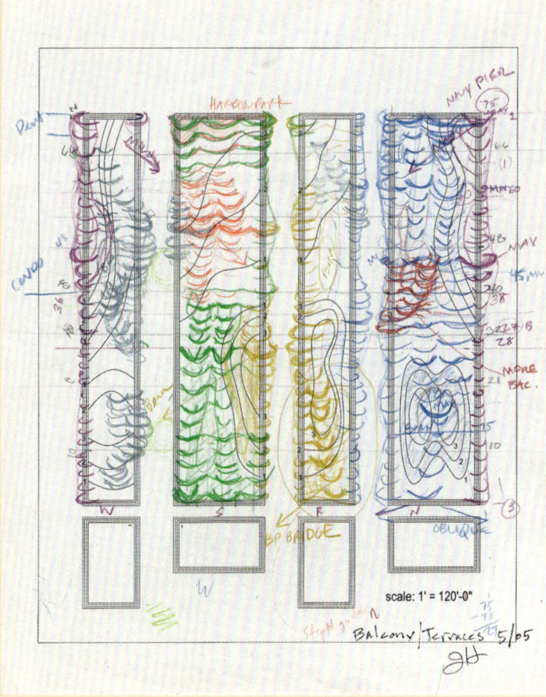

Fig. 5. Studio Gang (American, founded 1997); Jeanne Gang (American, born 1964). *Aqua Tower, Chicago, Illinois, Elevation Study*, 2005. Colored pencil, pen, digital print on paper; 28 × 21.6 cm (11 × 8½ in.). Architecture and Design Curatorial Discretionary Fund, 2023.3024.

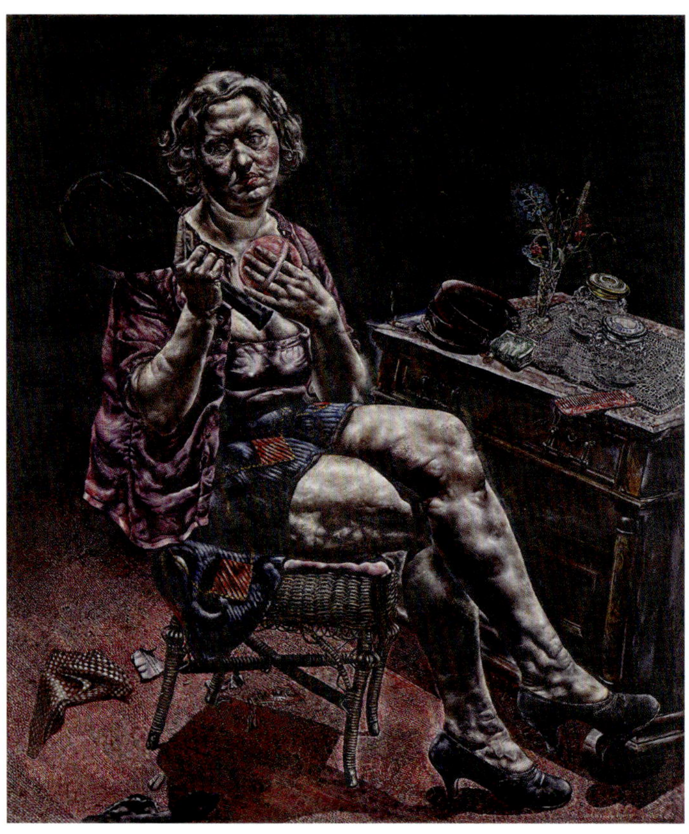

131. Ivan Albright, **Into the World There Came a Soul Called Ida**, 1929–30

It's tempting to read Ivan Albright's meticulous and unforgiving rendering of his subject's flesh, replete with wrinkles, dimples, and discolorations, as a form of violence against women. After all, Ida Rogers was only nineteen when the artist hired her to pose for this painting. Like a sorcerer, Albright transformed Ida from a radiant and self-possessed adolescent into a sagging and self-scrutinizing middle-aged woman. She gazes forlornly into a mirror, powder puff strapped like a shield across her fingers. Her blue-toned skin ripples beneath the surface, evoking both life and death.

What compelled Albright to paint such a picture, a metaphorical tossing of Ida's body to the dogs of society with its unrealistic beauty standards and rampant misogyny? As a young man, Albright worked as a medical illustrator, sketching the injuries of American soldiers during World War I. The influence of this experience on his art is perhaps best captured in a poem about this painting by the contemporary American poet Rita Dove: "He kept to his task, applying paint / like a bandage to the open wound." These lines invite us to read Albright's grotesque detailing of Ida's body not as an act of violence but as an act of care.
Molly Bryson

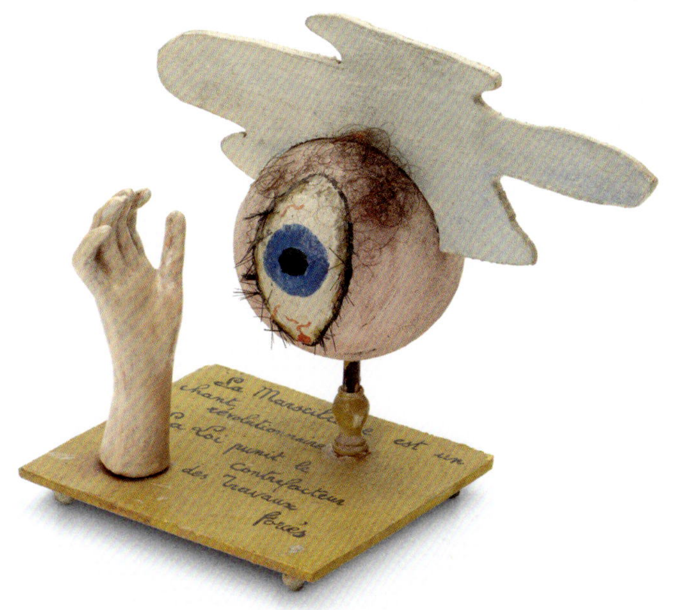

132. Claude Cahun, Object, 1936

Claude Cahun created *Object*, originally exhibited without a title, for the 1936 *Exhibition of Surrealist Objects* at Galerie Charles Ratton in Paris, a landmark show that established object-making as a practice integral to Surrealist art. Incorporating found objects and encouraging subconscious, poetic associations, the work combines two classic Surrealist motifs—the eye and the hand—in an incongruous manner. The eyeball, turned on its side and mounted as if a specimen, bisects a cloud shape, with a toy doll's hand rising from a card-like base. The work's French inscription draws from disparate sources, a strategy common in Surrealism. The first, "The Marseillaise is a revolutionary song," is a well-known slogan associated with the French Popular Front, and the second, "The law punishes counterfeiters with forced labor," is a line taken from Belgian currency.

Born Lucy Schwob, Cahun adopted her masculine alias Claude around 1919, and frequently collaborated with her partner, Marcel Moore (the chosen name of Suzanne Malherbe), to produce a body of written and visual work that consistently confronted traditional notions of gender and identity. Working primarily in photography, collage, and photomontage, Cahun usually designed her assemblages to be photographed and then discarded, making *Object* an incredibly rare extant example of her three-dimensional work. *Tamar Kharatishvili*

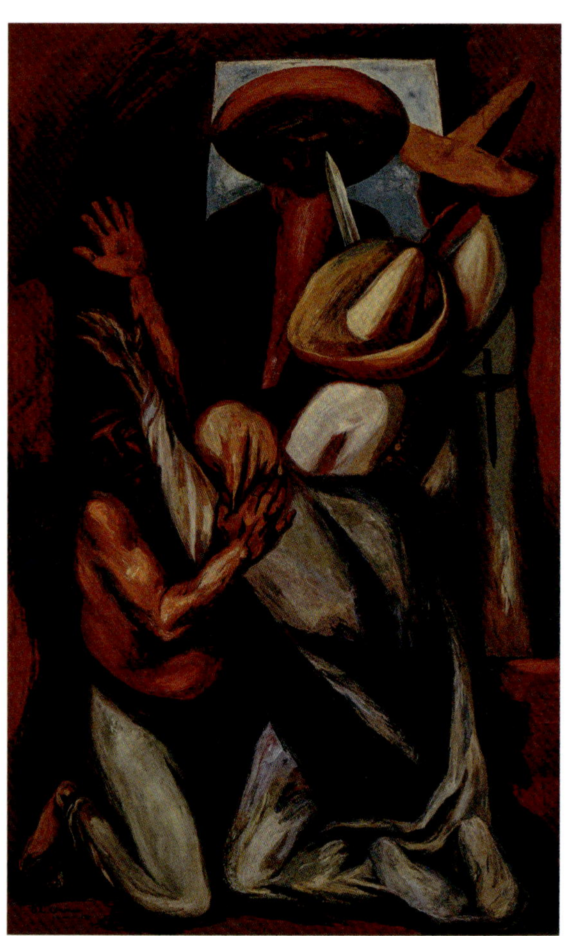

133. José Clemente Orozco, Zapata, 1930

Framed by blue skies, Emiliano Zapata towers in the doorway of this dark space; a sword points at his eye. Crowded in front of him stand two soldiers wearing bandoliers of bullets. In the foreground, two kneeling figures hold each other, one with arms outstretched.

As a museum educator, I encourage asking questions of works of art: What is the relationship between these figures? What do you think happened right before this moment? What might happen next?

Zapata was a leader of the Mexican Revolution who fought for land reform and the rights of agrarian workers and Indigenous people. To many, Zapata's cause was noble, and his efforts earned him the title of hero. Yet José Clemente Orozco's depiction of Zapata, with his looming presence and use of expressive dark browns and reds, disrupts this idealized narrative. Orozco supported the goals of the Revolution, but he was disturbed by its brutality and Zapata's role in the bloodshed. "People grew used to killing," he mused.

The painting prompts us to ask: What role does violence play in revolution? And how can we reconcile Zapata's simultaneous heroism and harm? *Kloie Rush-Spratt*

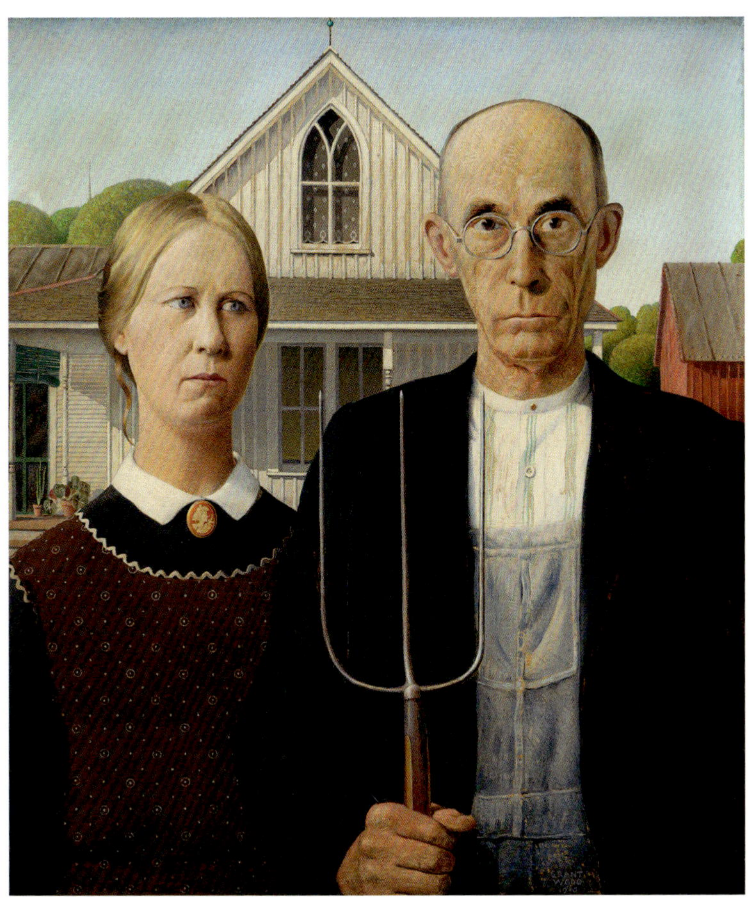

134. Grant Wood, American Gothic, 1930

Even when Grant Wood painted *American Gothic*, the stern farmer and his adult daughter looked old-fashioned. They stand in front of a wood-framed farmhouse with a gothic-style window that struck the artist as wildly out of place when he spotted it in Eldon, Iowa. After making an oil sketch of the house, Wood posed his sister Nan and dentist B. H. McKeeby as people who might live in such a home. For inspiration, he looked to "tintypes from my old family albums," imagining his models as inhabitants of the 1880s, surrounded by symbols of their vocation and virtue. The sturdy pitchfork, thriving potted plants, and church steeple barely visible behind the trees: These tell us who these people are and how they spend their lives.

American Gothic achieved near-instant fame upon its exhibition at the Art Institute in 1930. In retrospect, we can see Wood's iconic work as part of an interwar effort to define a distinctly American aesthetic as unpretentious and enduring as the rickrack on the woman's apron. This honest, hardworking, God-fearing pair stands in for a simpler and better time. But as with all nostalgic visions of times gone by, they prompt a question: Did the past we yearn for ever truly exist? *Ginia Shubik Sweeney*

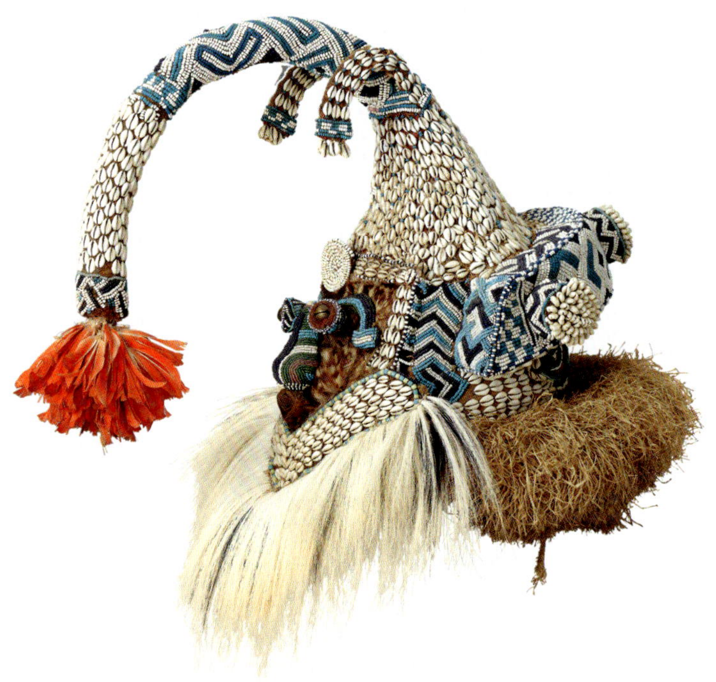

135. Helmet Mask (Mukenga), possibly late 1800s to mid-1900s, Congo Free State or Belgian Congo

The striking projection from the top of this helmet mask (Mukenga) imitates an elephant's trunk flanked by tusks. The Kuba kingdom participated in the lucrative ivory trade with European powers from the late 1800s onwards, and association with elephants signaled community members of high status. The tuft of red parrot feathers on this mask shows that its owner was an eagle-feathered chief known as *kum aphoong*, one of many titles in the kingdom's hierarchy. Other signs of Mukenga's prominence are its complex decoration with cowries and glass beads, the spotted fur from a civet cat that marks its face, and its beard of white monkey hair.

Worn exclusively by the kum aphoong, this mask dances on the day of his installation and on the occasion of the funeral rites for Kuba aristocrats. Its most important appearance, however, is for the eagle-feathered chief's own funeral. During the three days before the chief is buried, the mask is displayed on a mannequin wearing a costume similar to that of the mask dancer. In the past, Mukenga would always be buried with its owner, which explains its rarity in Western collections. *Constantine Petridis*

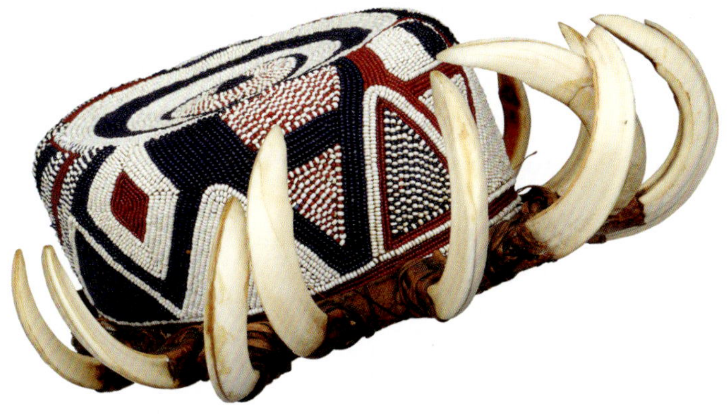

136. Tusk Hat (*Ogut Tigo*), early 1900s, British East Africa or Tanganyika

The attribution of this hat to the Luo people of what is now Kenya and Tanzania, and its identification as an *ogut tigo*, is based on comparison with a strikingly similar example photographed in Kenya's Nyanza region in 1936 by the renowned British anthropologist Sir Edward E. Evans-Pritchard. Expensive and difficult-to-acquire materials, such as glass beads imported from Europe in the late 1800s or early 1900s, signal the elevated rank of those who owned headgear like this tusk hat. Adding to its status connotations are the series of outwardly projecting warthog tusks that form a sort of fringe around the head of the wearer. The unidentified man in Evans-Pritchard's photo wears his prestige hat along with other insignia, including beaded earrings, a necklace of ostrich egg shells, and metal bracelets and finger rings. He also holds a walking stick over his shoulder, while a sheathed dagger hangs from a bandolier across his body. An interesting side note: One of the most famous Luo descendants in the United States is Barack Obama, the forty-fourth president of the United States, and one of Chicago's sons. *Constantine Petridis*

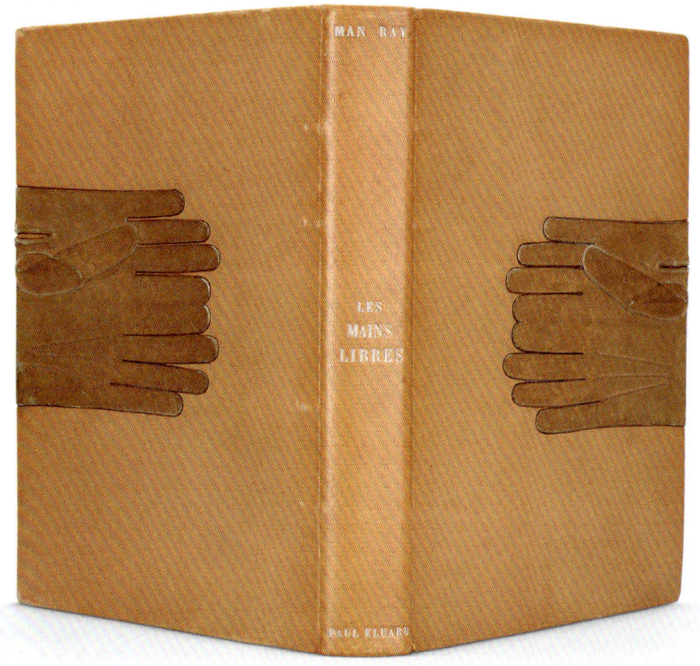

137. Mary Reynolds, Free Hands, 1937–42

The inventive bookbinder Mary Reynolds lived as an American expatriate in Paris for thirty years. There, she befriended prominent avant-garde artists and writers, and crafted custom, handmade bookbindings for many Surrealist publications. The one-of-a-kind bindings express a personal response to the work of Reynolds's many friends and creative collaborators. The binding of Man Ray and Paul Éluard's illustrated book of poems, *Les mains libres*, features collaged elements and found objects: Two bisected women's gloves reveal Reynolds's deft leatherworking skills and express Surrealist visual play and eroticism.

During World War II, Reynolds remained in Paris even after the Nazi occupation of France and stayed to aid the French Resistance after many of her friends had fled. After a perilous escape in 1942, she lived in New York with her lover Marcel Duchamp until the war subsided. Reynolds then returned to her home and studio in Paris where she lived until her death in 1950. In her honor, Duchamp, along with Reynolds's brother Frank B. Hubachek, worked to preserve her library of Dada and Surrealist literature and seventy-one of her original handmade bindings, ultimately entrusting the collection, along with archival photographs and correspondence, to the Art Institute. *Castor Santee*

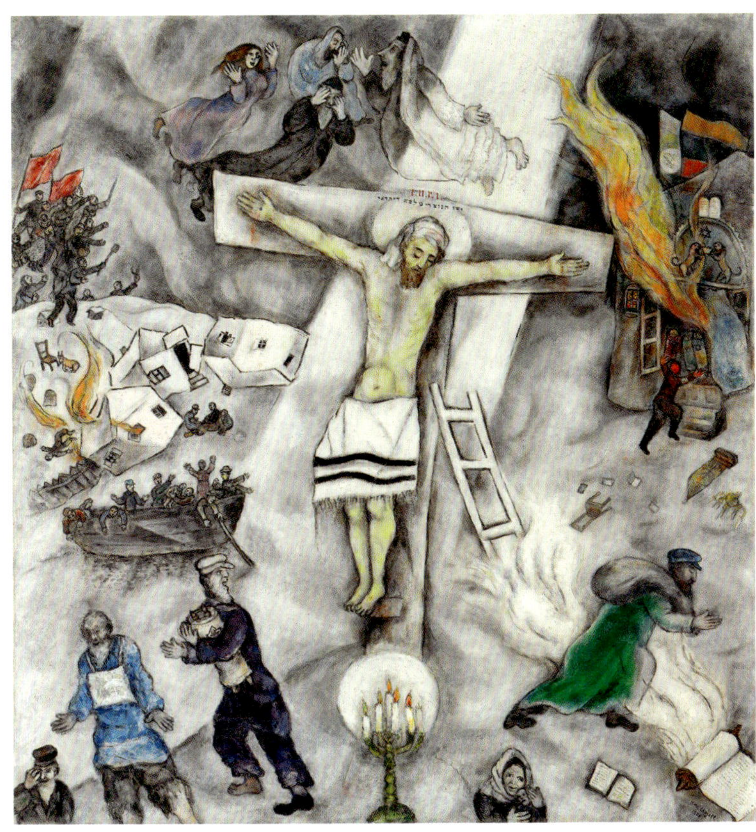

138. Marc Chagall, White Crucifixion, 1938

White Crucifixion is one of Marc Chagall's most poignant political canvases. The artist presents the crucified Christ as a martyr, clad in a traditional Jewish prayer shawl. Chagall's characteristic compositional strategy dislodges the central subject from the landscape. Here, the tone is alarming, showing a synagogue on fire, a ransacked village overtaken by soldiers, a burning Torah, and a boat of refugees amid other scenes of persecution. Painted during the rise of National Socialism in the 1930s, these vignettes unequivocally condemn Nazi violence and persecution.

Sometime between January and May of 1940, Chagall made changes to the painting, reworking its most explicit and incendiary references to fascism. These modifications included painting over two swastikas—one on the armband of the soldier in front of the burning synagogue, and one originally present in the lighter-colored flag above it. He also removed an inscription from the sign around the bearded man's neck at lower left, which read, in German, *Ich bin Jude* (I am a Jew). Chagall may have feared for the work's safety as he shipped it out of war-torn Europe in 1941. Within a year of World War II's conclusion, Chagall worked closely with Daniel Catton Rich, then the Art Institute's director, to ensure that the painting entered the museum's collection. *Tamar Kharatishvili*

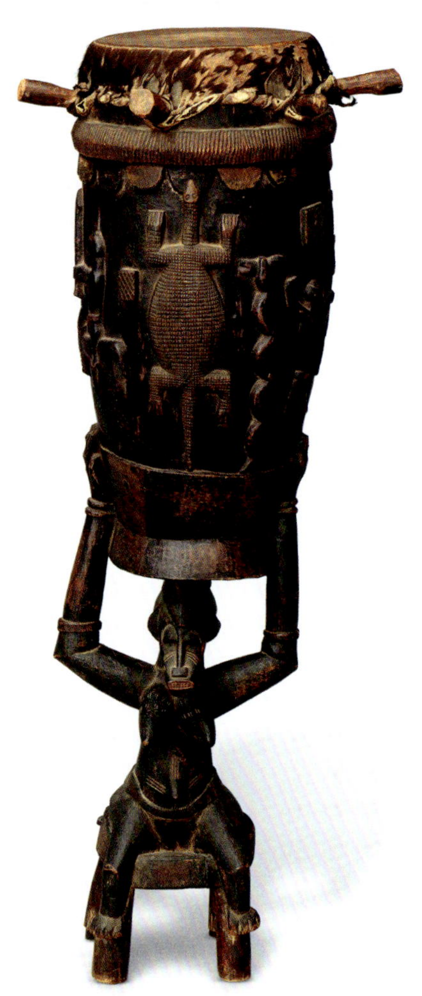

139. Female Caryatid Drum (*Pinge*), about 1930–50, Côte d'Ivoire

Membrane drums like this one, known as *pinge*, were once used in the context of military activities, but in more recent times they are primarily sounded during initiations and funerals. According to research by art historian Anita Glaze, this densely decorated example was made in the 1930s or 1940s in a workshop of specialized wood carvers in northern Côte d'Ivoire. The rare female caryatid suggests that it likely functioned in the context of funerals for important women of Tyekpa, a woman's organization responsible for maintaining social order and group cohesion. To this day, Tyekpa performances comprise songs in a secret language that criticize and ridicule male behavior. The load-bearing seated figure, which Glaze described as "a female Atlas who balances with composure the world on her head," symbolizes the key role women play in Senufo society as family founders and spirit intermediaries. The complex bas-relief decoration around the drum includes humans in war scenes and animals that refer to Senufo religious beliefs and philosophical concepts. This pinge was featured in the now defunct Museum of Primitive Art's landmark exhibition on Senufo art, which traveled to Chicago in 1964. *Constantine Petridis*

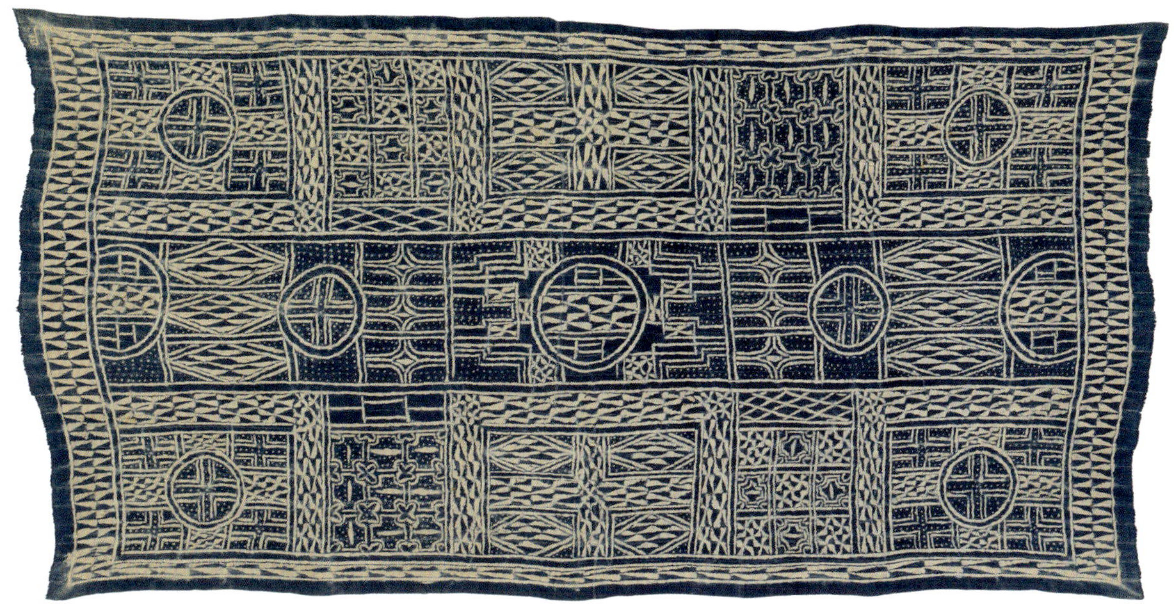

140. Display Cloth (*Ndop*), 1910–37, Cameroon Grassfields

In the Grassfields region of west-central Africa, rulers have displayed this type of patterned, indigo-dyed cloth as a ceremonial backdrop for over a century. Commonly known as *ndop*, it signifies prestige, tradition, and exclusivity. Ndop's enduring value lies in the complex process that defined its earliest creation, where each stage of production took place in a different location throughout what is today Nigeria and Cameroon. Royal emissaries carried the components across vast distances to reach individual expert artisans; one cloth traveled over 2400 kilometers and took months to complete. Thus, historically only the *fon* (king) could afford it.

Sultan Ibrahim Njoya of the Bamum kingdom (ruled 1886–1933) spurred a shift in production: He harnessed the processes entirely within his capital city of Foumban. The change resulted in a unique style with symbols that refer to rulers, palace architecture, treasury stores, and protective devices. By the 1930s Foumban was the renowned center of an evolving art market directed at expatriates. The signature in one corner of this example suggests that a skilled craftsperson made it within that context. It was purchased in Foumban by Clara Gebauer, a graduate of the School of the Art Institute of Chicago, who lived in Cameroon as part of the German Baptist Mission. *Janet Marion Purdy*

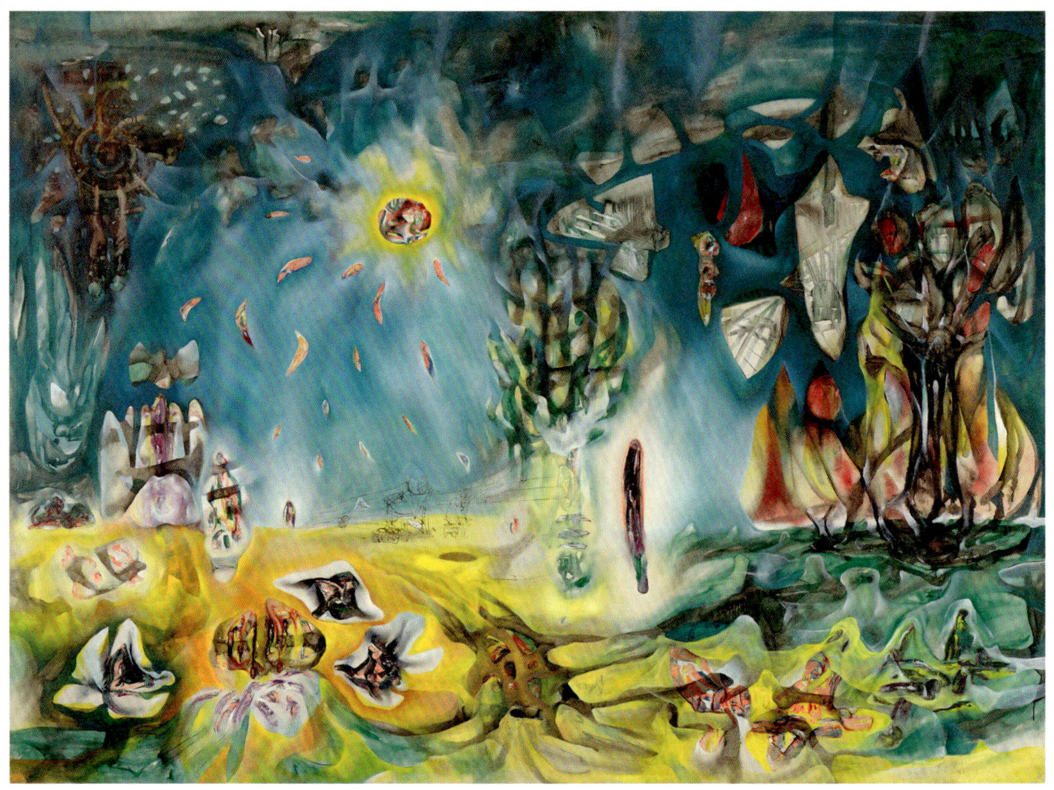

141. Roberto Matta, The Earth Is a Man, 1942

The striking title of this painting honors poet Federico García Lorca, who was assassinated in 1936 by Spanish Nationalist forces opposed to his homosexuality and his liberal views. Lorca's death inspired Roberto Matta to create a painting and a screenplay, both titled *The Earth Is a Man* and each featuring apocalyptic imagery and shifting perspectives. Through vaporous oil washes and biomorphic forms, Matta evokes destruction and renewal, reflecting his humanist belief in transformation and the role of art in society.

The Earth Is a Man is the culmination of Matta's "psychological morphologies," or what he sometimes called "inscapes," blending the terminology of landscapes with interior visions. Matta depicted both the unconscious mind and humanity's place in a universe shaken by violence during World War II. Drawing from Surrealist automatic painting, occult beliefs in a "fourth dimension," and personal experiences—including a volcanic eruption he witnessed in Mexico in 1941—the painting visualizes a molten dreamscape that blends cosmic energy with inner psychic turmoil.

Exhibited in New York in 1942, this mural-size canvas became a key example of automatic painting and influenced emerging American artists who would later be known as Abstract Expressionists. It stands as a visionary meditation on the relationship between the individual psyche, society, and the universe. *Tacy Wagner*

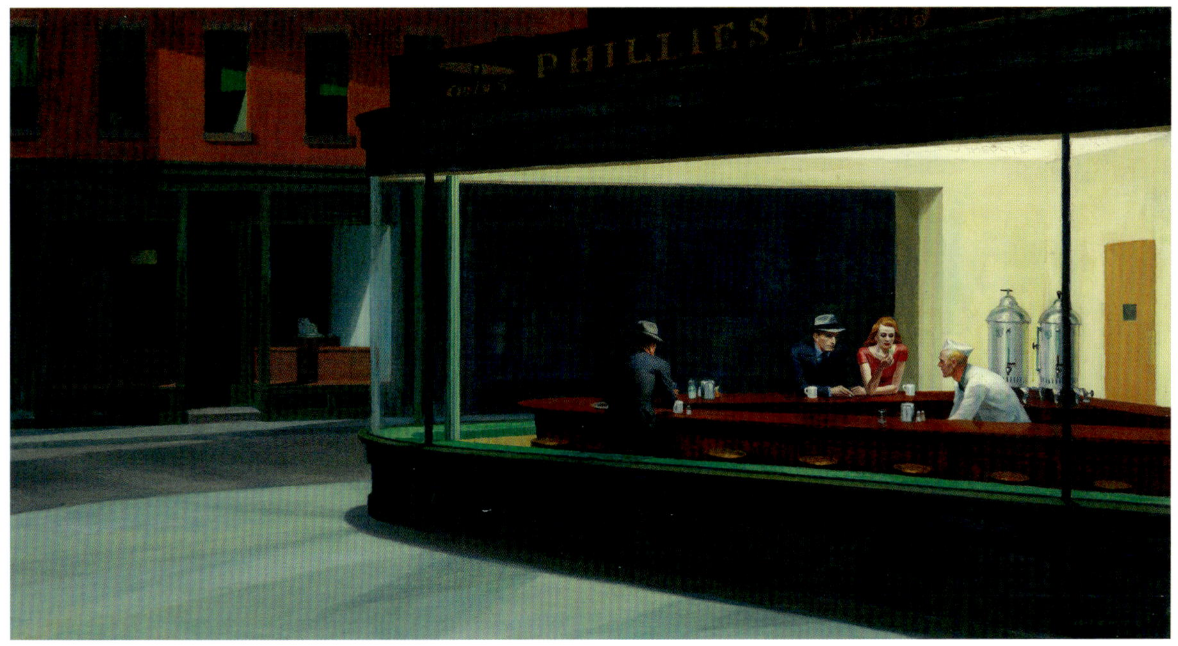

142. Edward Hopper, **Nighthawks**, 1942

Shortly after the bombing of Pearl Harbor and the United States' subsequent entrance into World War II, Edward Hopper conceived of *Nighthawks*. Afraid of aerial attack by the Nazis, New York City dimmed streetlights and required citizens to observe nightly blackout drills. Yet Hopper showcased a brilliantly lit diner with four figures inside—the "nighthawks" who inhabit this nocturnal world. After completing the work in January 1942, he exhibited it at the Art Institute, which immediately acquired it.

The painting has intrigued and beguiled ever since. Viewers are positioned outside the diner, with no door to offer a way in. The four figures are together yet separate, their relationships and interactions unclear. Their presence evokes the nature of urban existence: One experiences a constantly changing panorama of humanity but can never fully understand the everyday dramas seen only in glimpses. And although the figures take center stage, architecture and light play equally commanding roles, creating a balanced, quiet composition with few details to distract from Hopper's crystalline vision.

Nighthawks has, over time, become associated with ideas of alienation and isolation. Hopper always denied that this was his intention, although he did concede that "unconsciously, probably, I was painting the loneliness of a large city." *Sarah Kelly Oehler*

Surrealism, Chicago-Style

Caitlin Haskell

Chicago's intrepid collectors, galleries, and museums embraced the young Surrealist movement and helped launch it worldwide.

When André Breton published the first Surrealist Manifesto in October 1924, it may have seemed that he was providing a definition of the quintessential Surrealist artwork: "psychic automatism in its pure state." But at this early moment, when Surrealism in all media was still speculative and nascent, Breton's manifesto was not so much a dictum as it was an invitation to commence a search. Discoveries were needed, and young poets, painters, and photographers—Max Ernst (see fig. 1), Man Ray, Yves Tanguy—were among the first to answer the call. Applying themselves as daring aesthetic researchers, they developed techniques to suspend their conscious minds. In their search for epiphany, they closed their eyes to how paintings had

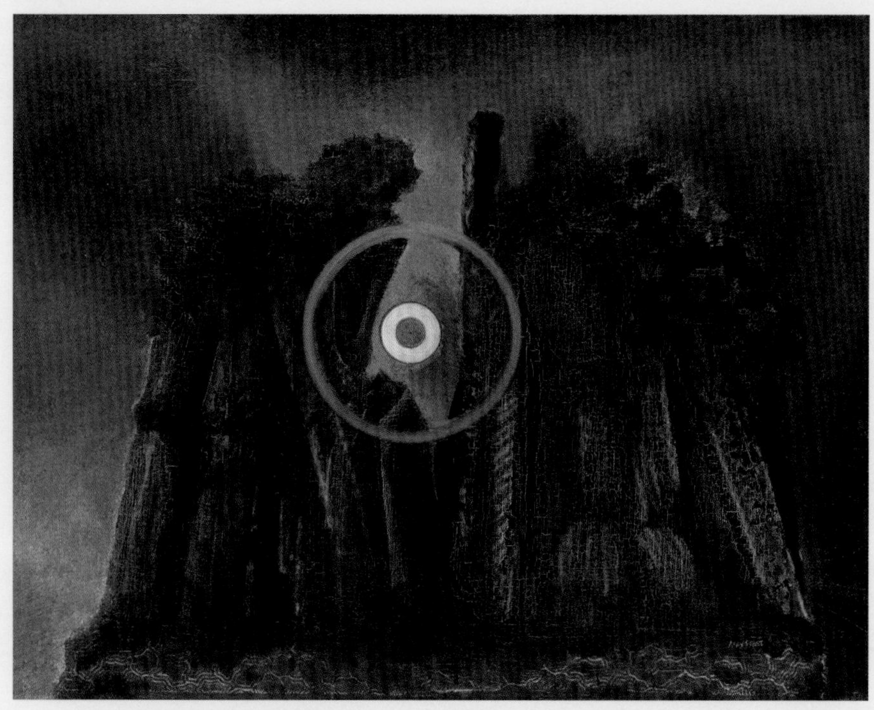

Fig. 1. Max Ernst (French, born Germany, 1891–1976). *Forest and Sun*, 1927. Oil on canvas; 66 × 82.5 cm (26 × 31½ in.). Bequest of Richard S. Zeisler, 2007.276.

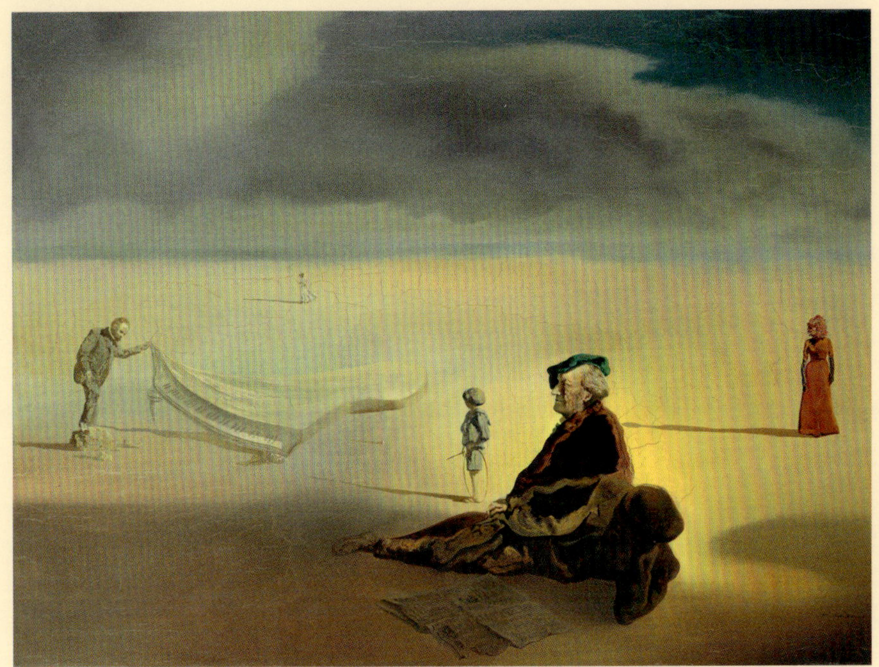

Fig. 2. Salvador Dalí (Spanish, 1904–1989). *A Chemist Lifting with Extreme Precaution the Cuticle of a Grand Piano*, 1936. Oil on canvas; 48.3 × 64.1 cm (19 × 25 ¼ in.). Gift of Mr. and Mrs. Joseph R. Shapiro, 1996.390.

been made before and produced images with a radical closeness to unmediated thought.

No twentieth-century movement had a more profound effect on Chicago than Surrealism. Indeed the zeal with which the city's collectors, gallerists, and curators responded to Surrealist art helped launch the movement globally. By 1933, audiences here had already been introduced to the incorrigible Catalan, Salvador Dalí—a twenty-nine-year-old painter with a miniaturist's precision and a mood-altering command of color. By the time Dalí's face appeared on the cover of *Time* magazine in 1936, Ruth Page, a Chicago-based dancer and choreographer, had already purchased one of his most tantalizing "apparitions," *A Chemist Lifting with Extreme Precaution a Cuticle of a Grand Piano* (fig. 2). It was soon joined by the apocalyptic *Inventions of the Monsters* (1937), purchased by the Art Institute for the prestigious Joseph Winterbotham Collection in 1943. This passionate commitment to Surrealist production, sustained by both museums and savvy private collectors, made Chicago one of the movement's most vital sites of development.

Consider, for example, Lindy and Edwin Bergman, preternaturally astute collectors of Surrealism, who developed close relationships with artists and acquired works with a regularity that approached compulsion. By the 1970s, they had amassed such a stunningly comprehensive collection of works by Joseph Cornell that the reclusive artist reportedly forbade them to purchase more. Today 116 works from the Bergman Collection are on permanent view in the Art Institute's galleries, with Cornell (see fig. 3) represented by more than thirty extraordinary collages and glass-fronted "boxes," each a self-contained journey for the imagination. Installed densely, the works are always exhibited together and provide the gravitational center of the Surrealism galleries, which feature works by

Surrealists active in Europe before World War II (Hans Bellmer, René Magritte, and Joan Miró) alongside works of the 1940s and after by Leonora Carrington, Arshile Gorky, Wifredo Lam, and Roberto Matta. Joined by the aforementioned Winterbotham Collection and works given by other consummate collectors, such as Joseph and Jory Shapiro and the artist Mary Reynolds, this enormously rich collection is unsurpassed in any American museum.

Rightly considered a collection *of* collections, the Art Institute's Surrealism holdings allow us to see how the movement shifted over time in its geography and theoretical commitments. For instance, during and after World War II, Mexico became an especially vital site for Surrealism's continuing invention. Shortly after her work was selected for the 1940 *International Exhibition of Surrealism* in Mexico City, the Spanish-born painter Remedios Varo took refuge in Mexico and made it her permanent home, finding profound inspiration in its culture past and present. Varo's major breakthrough arose in the 1950s, when she joined her painterly precision (learned in Madrid alongside Dalí) to an almost alchemical exploration of techniques that stretched from decalcomania (an automatic transfer technique) to rubbing her works with quartz crystals. Compositions such as *Still Life Reviving* (fig. 4)—Varo's largest work on canvas and her final painting—are suffused not only with psychological drama, but also with the sense of poetry and material enchantment so often associated with Cornell, who, like Varo, continued his practice well into the postwar period.

None of these singularly accomplished artists—Cornell, Dalí, Ernst, Varo—were a perfect fit with Surrealism as it was formulated in 1924. Dalí, who had initially

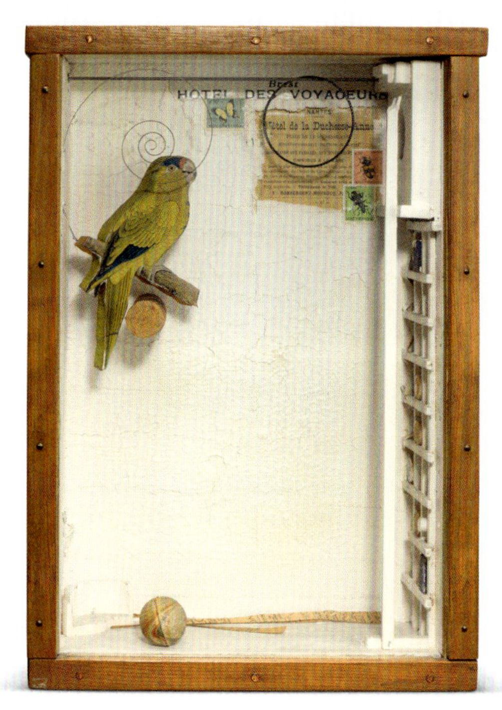

Fig. 3. Joseph Cornell (American, 1903–1972). *Untitled (Hôtel de la Duchesse-Anne)*, 1957. Box construction; 44.8 × 31.2 × 11.3 cm (17 5/8 × 12 1/4 × 4 7/16 in.). Lindy and Edwin Bergman Joseph Cornell Collection, 1982.1868.

held such promise in Breton's eyes, was ultimately shunned by the movement for his untenable politics and commercial aims. Cornell, shy and solitary, stood apart from Surrealism's tendency for social action, while Ernst decamped to the deserts of Sedona. Varo reached her heights belatedly, after she had dropped affiliation with any movement. Yet even Surrealism's early architects recognized that their vision could not be bound to an established credo but rather required continual reinvention by those who committed themselves to the movement's radical point of view. Chicago's artists, collectors, and museums shaped what Surrealism would be by ceaselessly seeking out its newest manifestations. The force of their efforts and the clarity of their conviction are on display in the Art Institute's galleries every day.

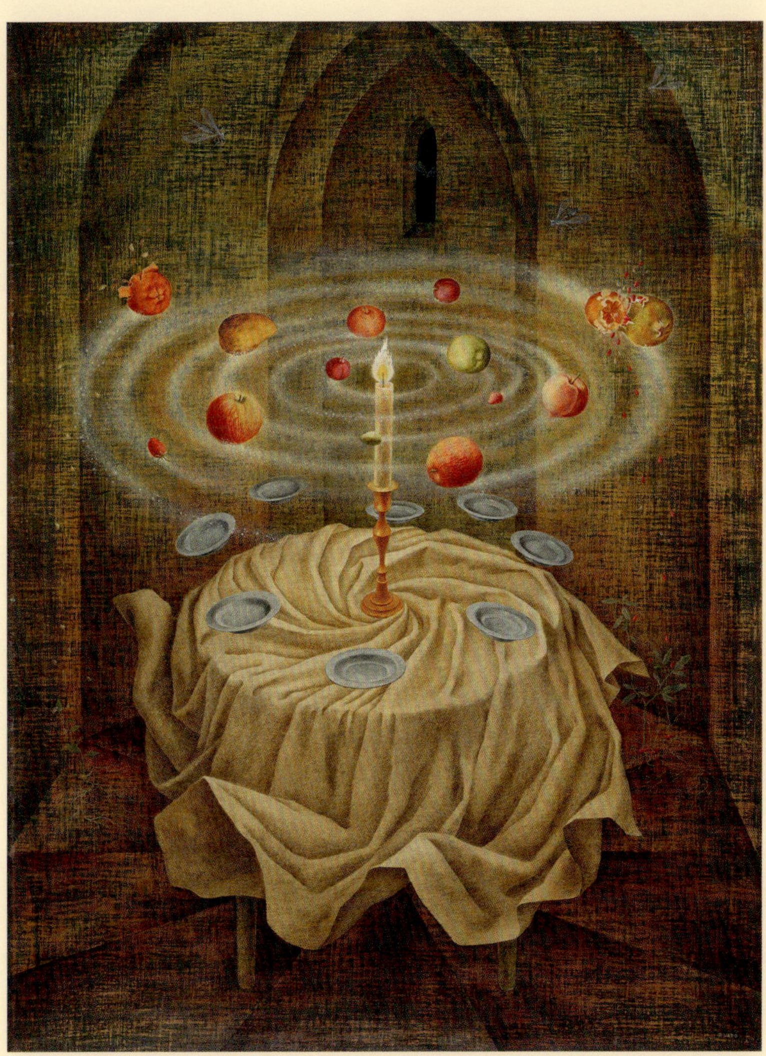

Fig. 4. Remedios Varo (Spanish, active Mexico, 1908–1963). *Still Life Reviving* (*Naturaleza muerta resucitando*), 1963. Oil on canvas; 109.9 × 80.1 cm (43 ¼ × 31 ½ in.). Joseph Winterbotham Collection, 2024.87.

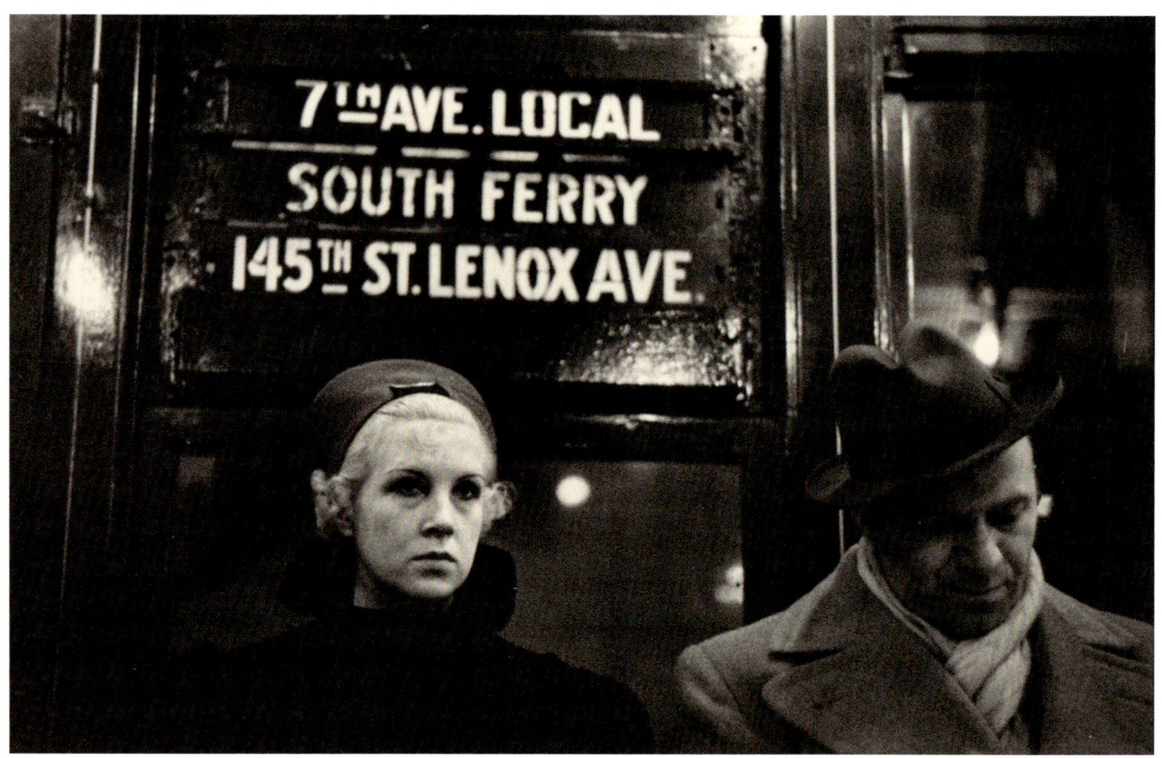

143. Walker Evans, **Untitled (Subway Portrait)**, 1938–41

A progenitor of documentary photography, Walker Evans influenced generations of photographers with his crystal-clear pictures of vernacular American culture and small-town life. After spending two years photographing rural communities for the Farm Security Administration during the Great Depression, Evans returned to New York, where, over three winters, he surreptitiously photographed subway riders in the city. Using a 35mm camera strapped to his chest, its lens poking out between coat buttons, Evans produced more than six hundred portraits that capture people unguarded, often lost in their own thoughts. He wrote of the project, which sought to avoid the vanity and artifice of conventional studio photography: "People's faces are in naked repose down in the subway." Evans only published these photographs two decades later, editing them into the 1966 book *Many Are Called*. This particular image is the very first in the book; however, the published version crops out the man on the right and focuses on the woman's blank stare. *Yechen Zhao*

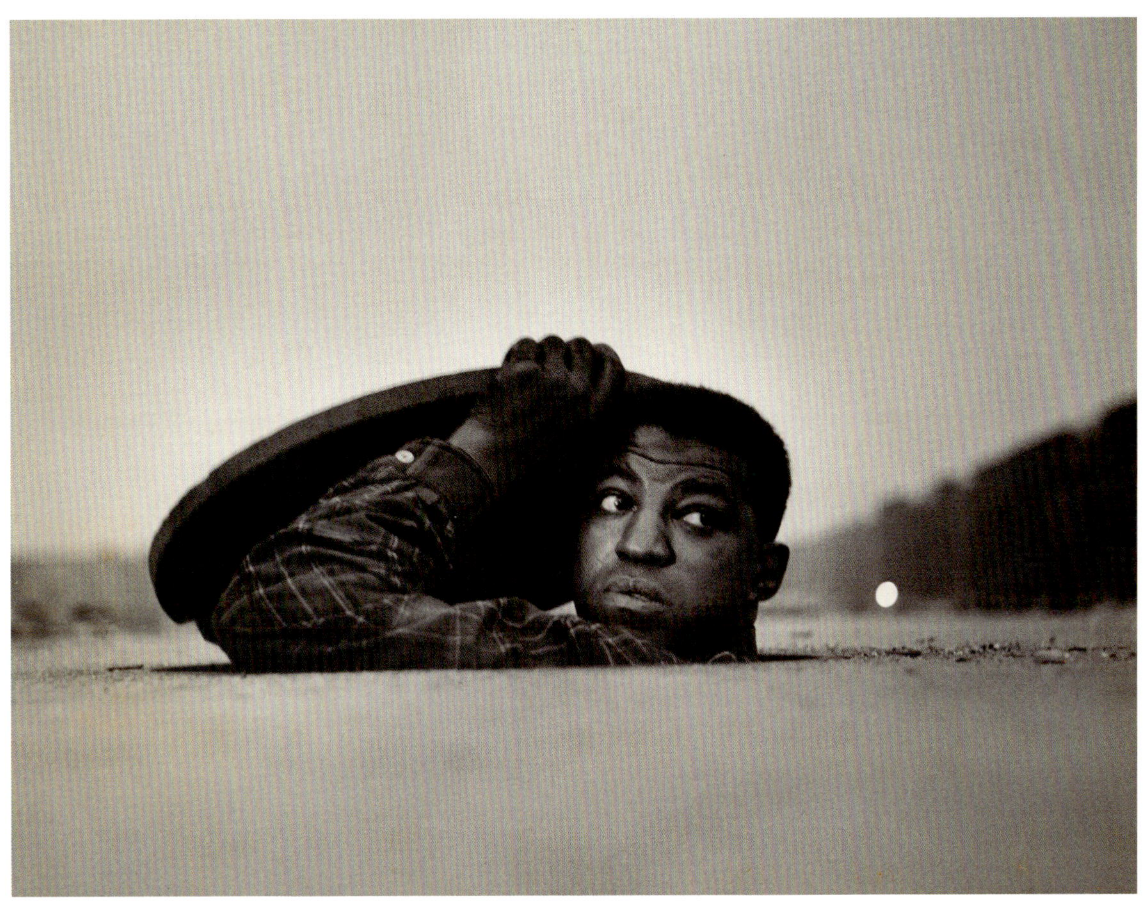

144. Gordon Parks, The Invisible Man (Harlem, New York), 1952

Beginning in the 1940s, the self-taught photographer Gordon Parks documented over six decades of American life and culture, focusing on race relations, poverty, civil rights, and urban life. Four years after joining *Life* magazine as its first Black staff photographer, Parks collaborated with writer Ralph Ellison on the photographic series *A Man Becomes Invisible*, which appeared in the magazine on August 25, 1952. Earlier that year, Ellison had published his groundbreaking novel *Invisible Man*, which traces the journey of an unnamed Black protagonist through the brutal realities of racism in postwar America. Parks staged photographs that dramatize scenes from Ellison's novel: Here, he imagines the closing moments of the book, when the narrator—portrayed in the picture by Ellison's friend John Bates—ends his hibernation and emerges above ground. This iconic image, which zooms in on Bates's wary expression as he pops out of a manhole, became the opening image for the article in *Life*.
Alexandra Kader Herrera

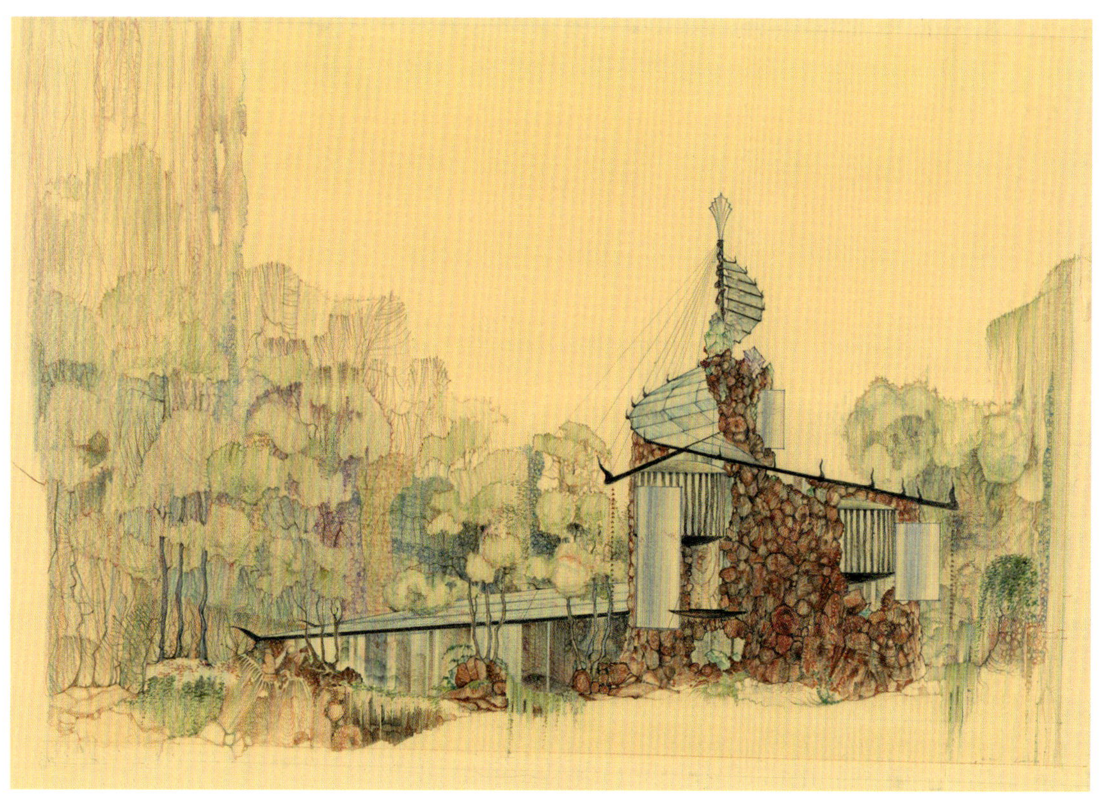

145. Bruce Goff and Herb Greene, **Eugene and Nancy Bavinger House, Norman, Oklahoma, Elevation**, 1950

On their wooded plot outside Norman, Oklahoma, artists Eugene and Nancy Bavinger wanted a house that would match their creative sensibilities, accommodate their tropical plant collection, and become a family home. They did not have to go far to find an architect—they commissioned Bruce Goff, then chair of the School of Architecture at the University of Oklahoma. Goff, a self-taught architect who began as a teenage apprentice in Tulsa, embraced individuality and independence, resulting in daring, unconventional designs.

For the Bavingers, Goff delivered a stone confection: a craggy, 180-foot-long rock wall that rose nearly sixty feet and coiled in a logarithmic spiral. In this presentation drawing, Herb Greene, a student studying and working with Goff, rendered fantastical vegetation inspired by Surrealist paintings. The roof—translucent corrugated plastic panels held in place by cables tethered to the central spire—would bathe the interior in light, a continuous space filled with plants, shallow pools, and suspended pods for living and sleeping areas. Using over two hundred tons of local red sandstone interspersed with Goff's signature blue-green glass cullet chunks, the Bavingers spent five years finishing the construction with help from university students. Although demolished in 2016, the Bavinger house remains an achievement in organic design and American architecture. *Craig Lee*

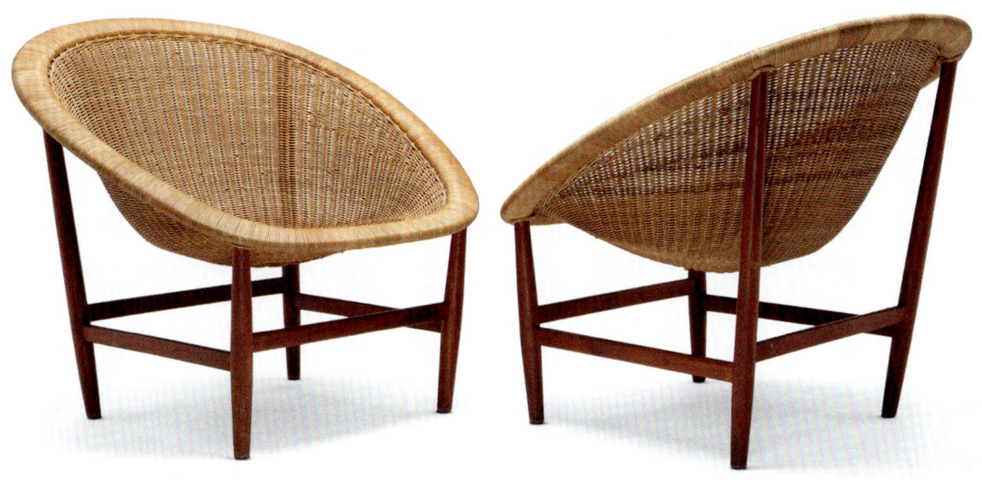

146. Nanna and Jorgen Ditzel, Basket Chairs, about 1950

At twenty-seven (Nanna) and twenty-nine (Jorgen), the Ditzels were recently married and fresh out of school when they designed their Basket Chair in 1950. In addition to studying cabinetmaking, they had been students of Kaare Klint, the so-called grandfather of Danish modern design. The chair's woven rattan seat appears to float atop the teak frame, showing its technical sophistication and craftsmanship. During the 1950s, these material and formal features would emerge on the international stage as hallmarks of Danish design. But before this now iconic chair won a silver medal at the 1951 Milan Triennale, one critic compared it to a laundry basket and described it as so bold it was almost funny.

What about this chair was so bold? The Ditzels' 1952 design for upholstered floor cushions to furnish a boardroom offers insight. They were serious in their suggestion that workplace meetings be conducted in a relaxed environment where people lounged on the ground instead of gathering around a table. The Basket Chair springs from a similar philosophy: Neither rigid and upright like a dining or desk chair, nor upholstered and reclining like a conventional lounger, it proposes casual seating for a modern domestic interior in which formality is superseded by relaxation. *Maggie Taft*

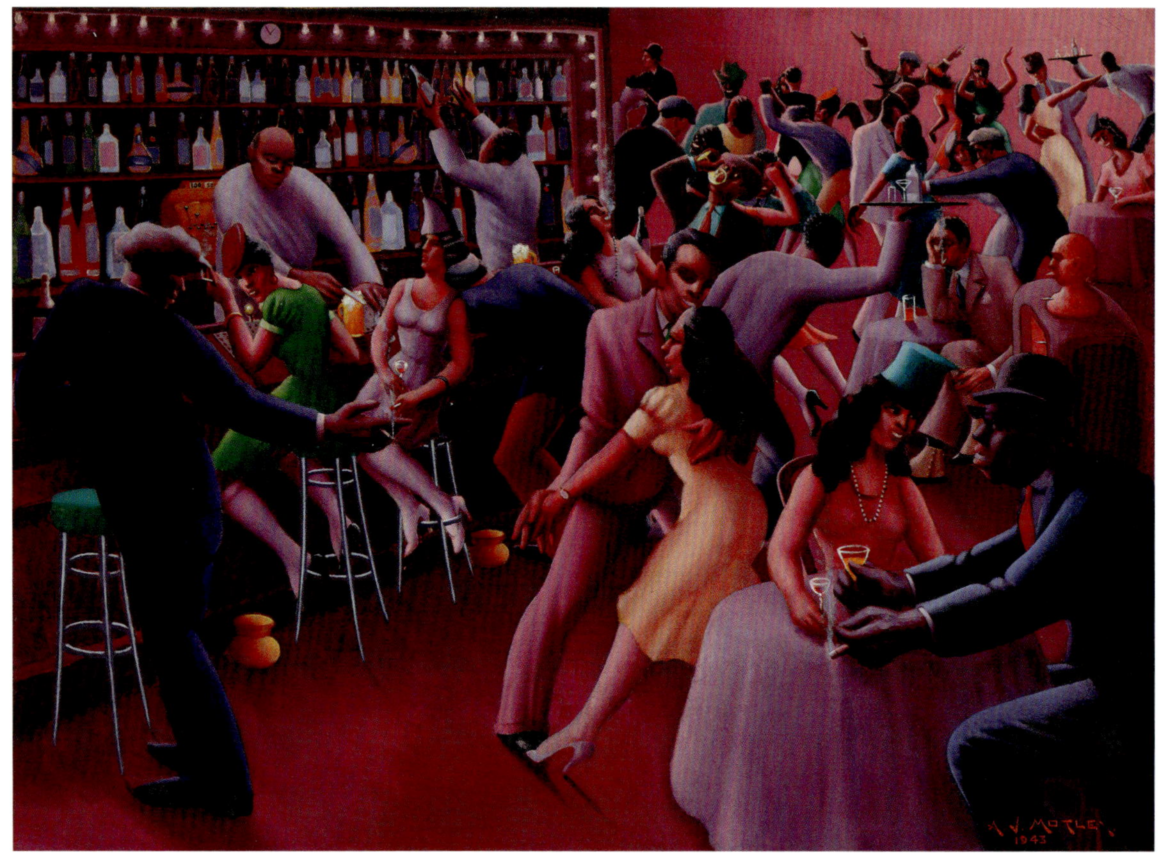

147. Archibald John Motley Jr., Nightlife, 1943

This painting sounds loud—music playing from the jukebox, glasses clinking, feet on the floor. This painting feels hot and sweaty—bodies crowded together, moving together. This painting smells strongly—cigarette smoke, cologne, and perfume swirling in the air. Some people might find a setting like this overwhelming, but to me, it looks like a good time. Black people fill the composition, dancing, drinking, and shooting the breeze. They wear jewel-toned dresses and suits and distinctive hats that catch the eye. Warm purple light washes over the late-night scene, making the gray uniforms of the workers and the white stockings of the women appear almost lavender.

This nightclub was part of the Bronzeville Stroll, a twelve-block strip that was the center of Black life on the South Side of Chicago from the 1920s to the 1950s. Though Black people were subject to racial violence in a strictly segregated Chicago, and many worked long hours at grueling factory jobs, they still found time for joy.

Archibald Motley Jr. tried to honestly represent Black people in his art to counter the racist caricatures he saw all around him. Here, he brings a thriving community to life. *Loren Wright*

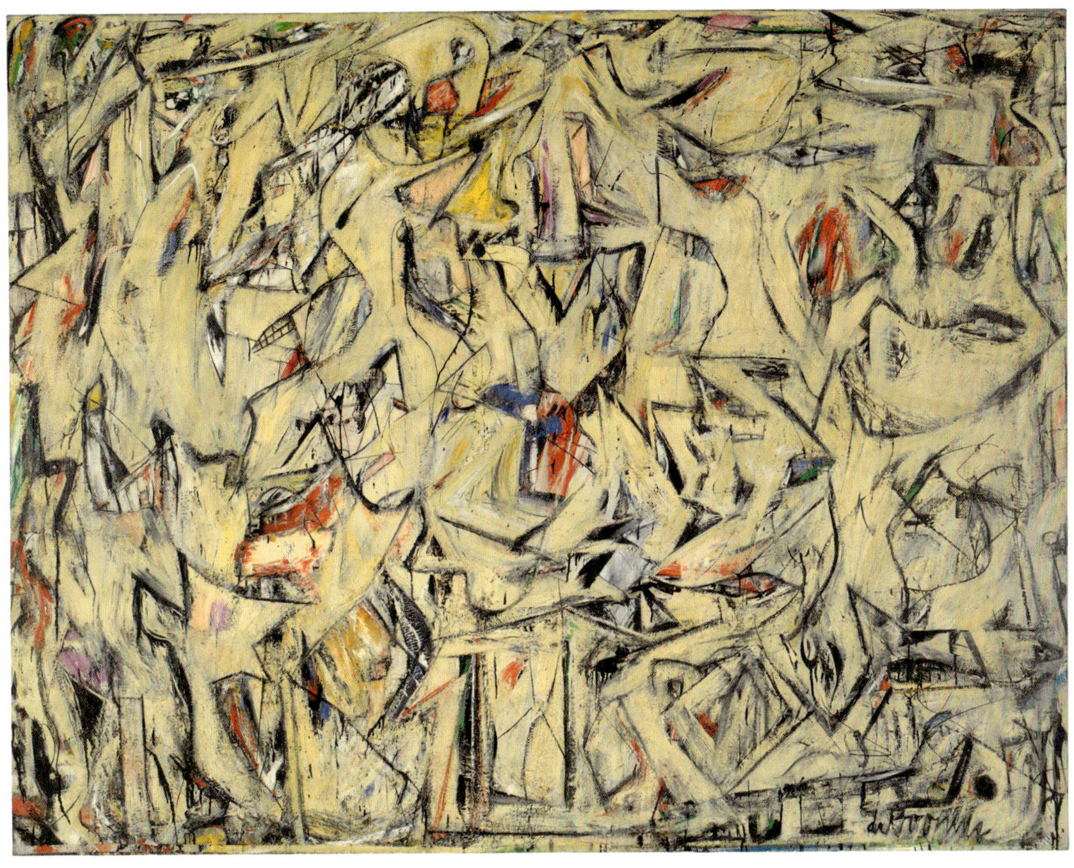

148. Willem de Kooning, Excavation, 1950

For several months at the beginning of 1950, Willem de Kooning labored over *Excavation*, the largest easel painting he would ever create. This monumental picture is characterized by an allover composition that teems with interlocking forms built up with layers of oil paint and delineated with black enamel lines. Within this compact, two-dimensional arrangement of flat shapes, one finds cartoonish anatomical or architectural fragments including eyes, grinning mouths, windows, and a door (at lower center). Like much of de Kooning's production, *Excavation* therefore defies the traditional distinctions between representation and abstraction, figure and ground, foreground and background, and drawing and painting. An easily overlooked detail may be a clue to the picture's title, possibly inspired by excavation sites the artist saw around New York City: De Kooning likely produced the narrow band along the bottom edge by applying masking tape to the canvas early in the painting process and then removing it later, a technique he employed in other works to achieve crisp boundaries. Like the splashes of vibrant color that peek through the brushy swathes of yellowish paint and fluid black contours, this thin strip exposes a lower stratum of the painted structure, thereby "excavating" the layered, heavily worked surface. *Charlotte Healy*

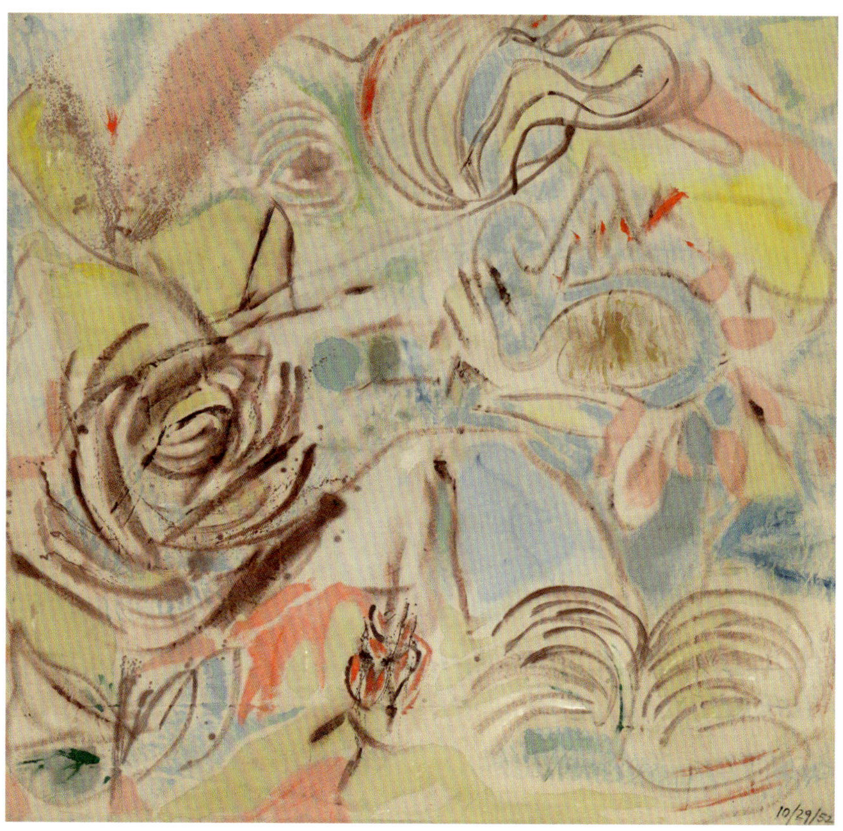

149. Helen Frankenthaler, 10/29/52, 1952

Helen Frankenthaler made her first soak-stain painting—which became her signature—just three days before she made *10/29/52*. Working directly on unprimed canvases (often stapled to the floor of her studio), she blended pigments with commercial oil paint, house paint, enamel, turpentine, and kerosene until the concoction could spill freely from the coffee cans she used for mixing and pouring. The diluted paint would absorb into the canvas and dry with the translucent appearance of watercolors. Frankenthaler's soak-stain technique redefined abstract painting by collapsing the distinction between medium (thinned oil paint) and support (raw canvas). Her endless investigations into the material properties of paint played a critical role in the transition from the active gestures of Jackson Pollock's dripped skeins to the flat expanses of color in Color Field painting.

Known by its date, this landmark painting is infused with color and overlaid with rhythmic, gestural lines and quasi-representational forms that suggest a continued meditation on the coastal landscapes of Nova Scotia, where Frankenthaler traveled in the summer of 1952. *10/29/52* is an exemplar of Frankenthaler's technical ingenuity and her ability to imbue abstractions with references to figuration and landscape in highly personal ways. *Makayla Bava*

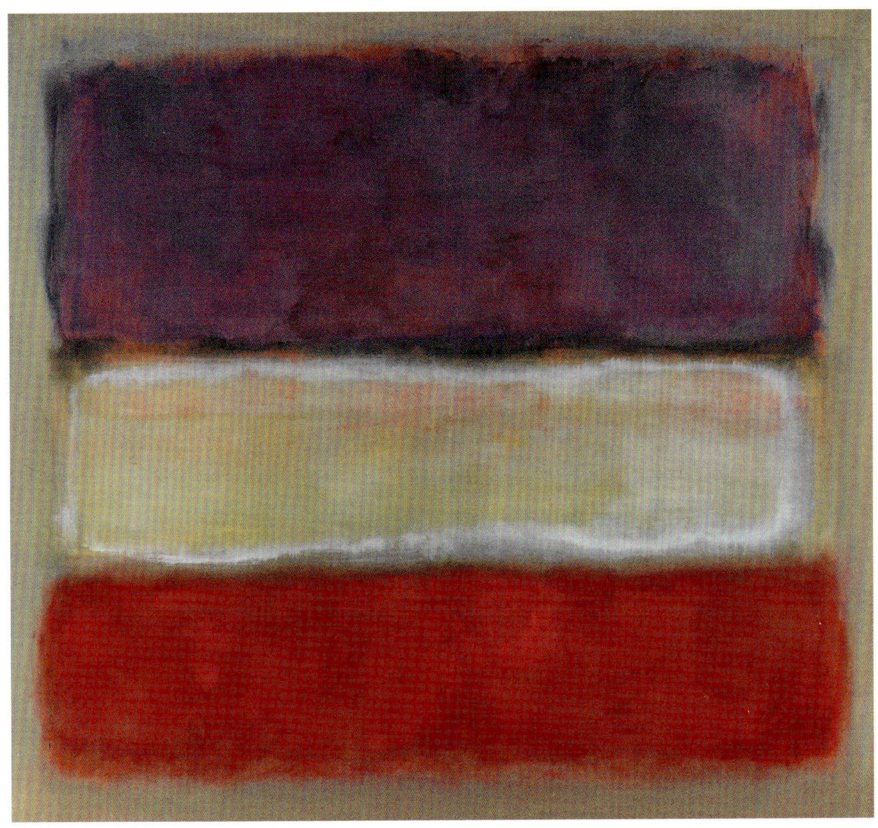

150. Mark Rothko, Untitled (Purple, White, and Red), 1953

At first glance, this painting appears simple: Three rectangles—deep purple at the top, luminous white in the center, and vivid red below—hover against a murky ground. Yet these blocks are far from static; edges bleed and colors blur into one another. The forms shift forward, recede, and dissolve. *Untitled (Purple, White, and Red)* is a defining example of Mark Rothko's mature style. He believed that only paint could evoke powerful emotion and allow one to transcend the boundaries of the body. "It should be breathed onto the canvas," he said—applied not as labor, but as presence, as atmosphere. With thin washes and translucent layers, colors soak into the canvas and feather at the edges. Rothko even rotated the painting while working, letting white pigment drip into the other fields, breaking the geometry and creating a sense of movement. The result is a composition that seems to glow from within, rejecting concrete materiality in favor of an elusive, almost spiritual presence. For Rothko, painting was a way to move beyond representation, to create a space where viewers might feel something profound: grief, wonder, stillness, or connection. He believed painting could offer a moment of transcendence—something both deeply human and sublime. *Annika Bohanec*

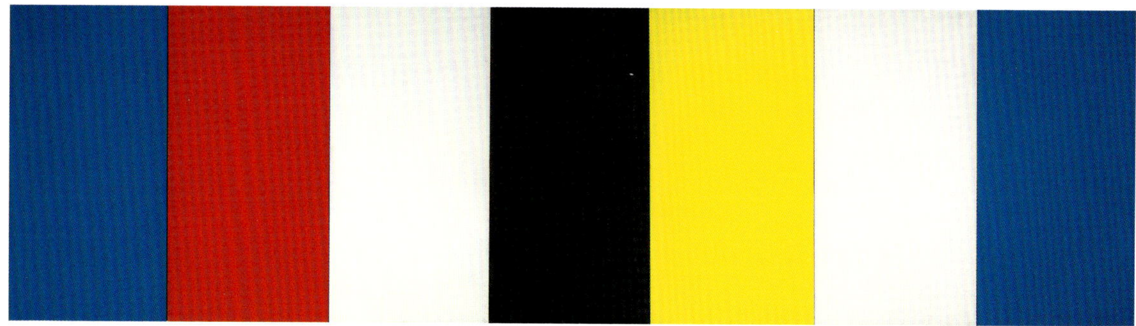

151. Ellsworth Kelly, **Red Yellow Blue White and Black II**, 1953

Among the Art Institute's significant holdings of Ellsworth Kelly's work across media, *Red Yellow Blue White and Black II*'s striking clarity sets it apart. After serving in World War II, Kelly returned to Europe in 1948, living and working in France. This painting was created at the exact moment he began to eschew direct observation of his subject matter in favor of pure abstraction. He began experimenting with the nearly infinite possibilities of the color spectrum, chance ordering, and multipanel composition. This seven-panel painting is the largest in a series of works Kelly made while in Paris. Emphasizing color, shape, and sequence, the black panel both divides and joins the three panels on either side of it; the white panels simultaneously separate and pair colors together; and the blue panels at either end close and unify the multipart composition.

Ellsworth Kelly's art expanded the vocabulary of abstraction through formally spare but conceptually rich work. The impact of *Red Yellow Blue White and Black II* on the development of Minimalism, hard-edge painting, and post-painterly abstraction reverberates throughout late twentieth-century art. *Thea Liberty Nichols*

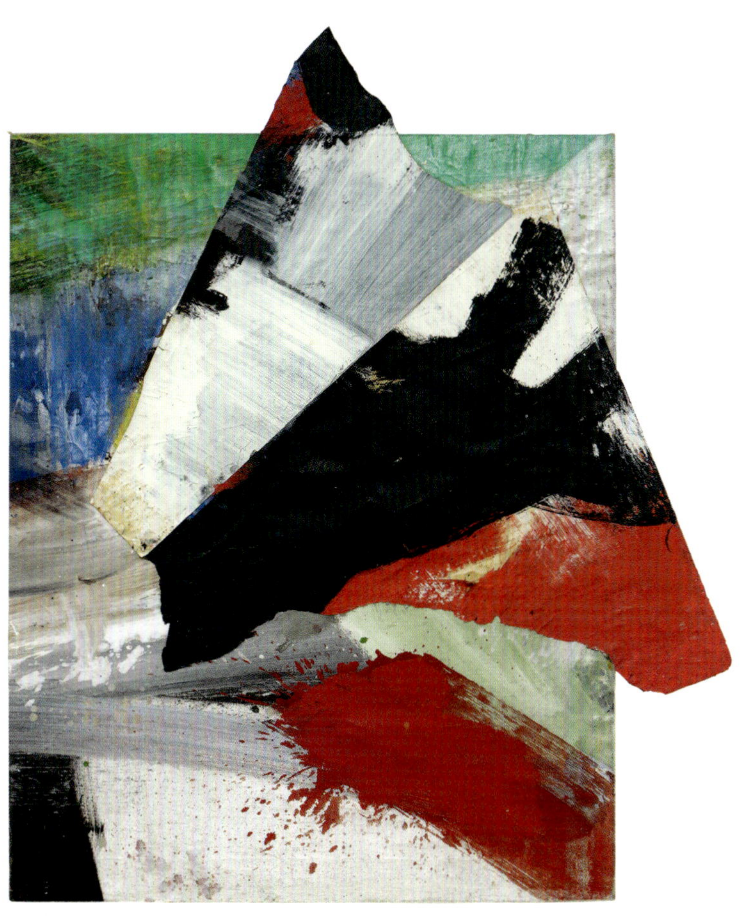

152. Ed Clark, **Untitled**, 1957

One of the principal innovators of postwar American abstraction, Ed Clark is best known for making paintings with such tools as push brooms and rags and for abandoning the rectilinear canvas in favor of altogether irregular geometries. Through these radical experiments, Clark's confident and expansive brushstrokes became the primary compositional element of his paintings, revealing his deep interest in color and in the material qualities of the medium. This work is an early example of Clark's shaped paintings. Here, his gestural brushwork extends beyond the perimeter of the canvas with protrusions made of painted paper supported by wooden stretcher bars.

Clark was born in New Orleans and raised primarily in Chicago. After serving in the Air Force during World War II, he attended the School of the Art Institute of Chicago and L'Académie de la Grande Chaumière in Paris on the G.I. Bill. He spent the majority of his life living and working in New York and Paris in artist circles that included other second-generation abstract painters including Beauford Delaney, Sam Francis, Joan Mitchell, and Jack Whitten. *Makayla Bava*

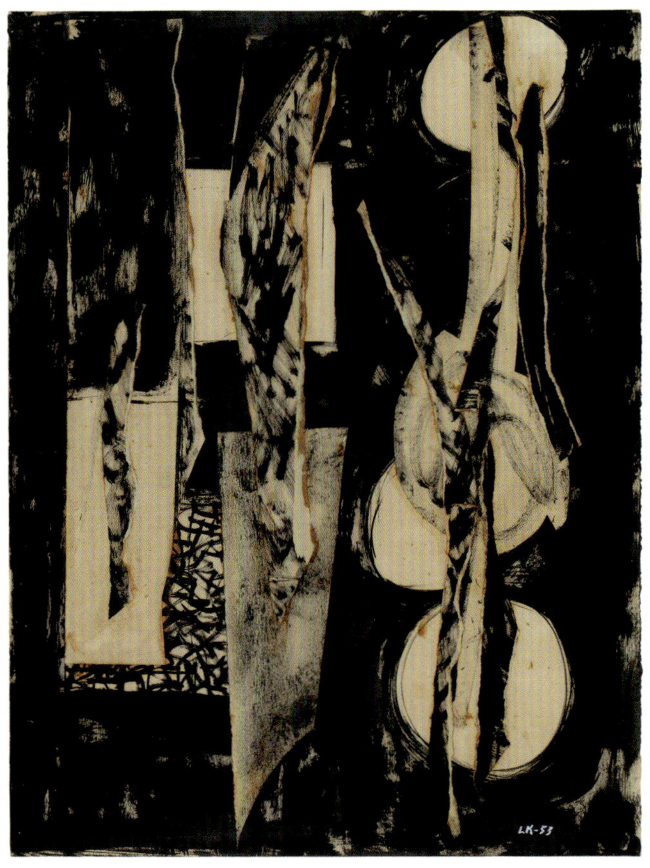

153. Lee Krasner, Black and White, 1953

In 1953 Lee Krasner hung her drawings from floor to ceiling on her studio walls. Later she walked in and hated it all. She tore up the drawings and threw the pieces on the floor. Weeks later, those pieces sparked her interest, and she started collaging.

As a painter, I know this place well. Whether editing, ripping, tearing, pouring, or cutting—in the wake of destruction lies a change of heart that embraces risk, uncertainty, rebuilding, and a fresh start.

Looking at *Black and White*, one of Krasner's early collages, that fresh start is fully present in her construction, animation, and abstract invention. This artwork comes out of Krasner's years of studying and internalizing cubist space. Working with ten pieces of paper chosen from that pile of torn drawings—each with its own particular shape, character, and brush marks in tones of black, white, and gray—Krasner cleverly played with contrasts between light and dark, organic and geometric, and the ambiguity between what is collaged and what is directly painted onto the surface. To my eye, these choices are brilliant and moving, and they justify her reputation as one of the foremost first-generation women Abstract Expressionists. *Judith Geichman*

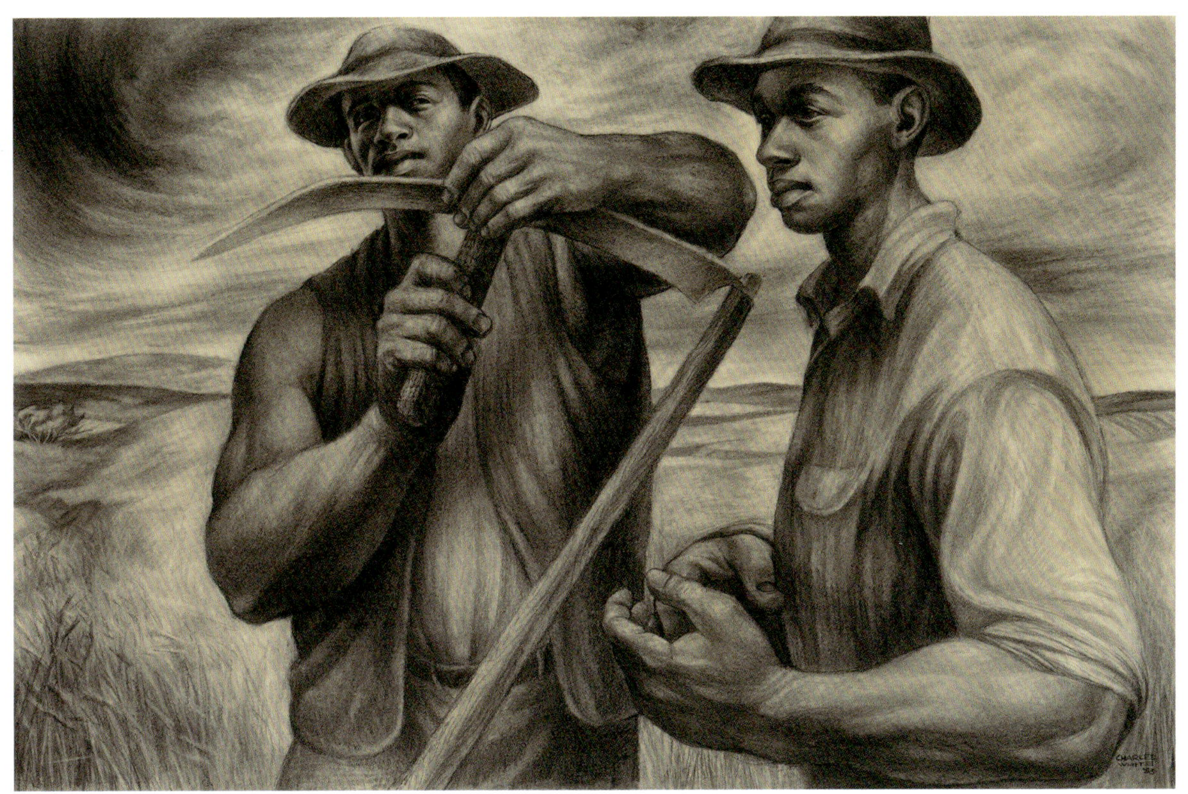

154. Charles White, Harvest Talk, 1953

Chicago-born Charles White described his art as a "broad universal statement about the search for dignity." He participated in the Civil Rights Movement and supported Socialist causes, affirming his commitment to portraying the struggles of Black and working-class communities.

His heroic drawing of two rural workers, *Harvest Talk*, reflects these interests as well as a broader network of international influences. In 1946 White studied printmaking with the collective Taller de Gráfica Popular (Popular Graphic Art Workshop) in Mexico City, where he also found inspiration in mural painting. Deepening his engagement with Socialist ideals, he traveled to the Soviet Union in 1951. The drawing nods to these experiences, particularly through the large scythe—similar to a sickle, a symbol for farmers in the flag of the USSR—at center. Following his call to make art accessible to all sectors of society, White included this work in a portfolio of lithographs offered by *Masses and Mainstream* magazine.

Harvest Talk was first owned by Max Gordon, founder of the Village Vanguard, a legendary New York jazz club that White frequented. This provenance underscores his influence within cultural circles beyond the fine arts, where he formed close relationships with other prominent Black figures such as singer Harry Belafonte, poet Langston Hughes, and actor Sidney Poitier.
Felipe Villada Ruiz

The School in a Museum

Thea Liberty Nichols

The grassroots beginnings of the Art Institute's school and museum reflect the enduring influence of artists on Chicago.

You can trace the origins of Chicago's artist-built institutions all the way back to thirty-five local artists in 1866. Artistic imagination and investment gave birth to the School of the Art Institute of Chicago (SAIC) in 1866 and to the museum in 1879; they are now the last remaining pair of its kind in the country. SAIC began by offering artist-taught classes in studio art, and the museum's early collection of plaster casts supported this curriculum. Today, the connection between the Art Institute and SAIC remains strong: The museum's world-renowned collection supports student scholarship in a broad and interdisciplinary scope of practices, and SAIC graduates have gone on to a wide range of creative professions including teaching, museum work, and art making, on display within the Art Institute's collection.

In the past, the museum itself also offered art classes, and several SAIC graduates actually got their start in them—including Karl Wirsum (BFA 1961), who enrolled at age six. Wirsum's later exposure to Coast Salish (Kwakwa̱ka̱'wakw) carved wood, Peruvian drinking vessels, and Navajo (Diné) woven blankets within the museum's collection is evident in the near symmetry, contour lines, and encapsulated forms found in *Screamin' Jay Hawkins* (fig. 1). The sights as well as the sounds of Chicago were also a central source of inspiration for Wirsum, especially the live, improvised blues music he regularly heard performed at Maxwell Street Market on the Near West Side. Acquired by the museum the year after it was made, Wirsum's painting was also selected by its subject, the singer Jalacy "Screamin' Jay" Hawkins, for his 1970 album cover.

Christina Ramberg (BFA 1968, MFA 1972) also scoured Maxwell Street Market together with friends, classmates, and her SAIC painting instructor Ray Yoshida (BFA 1953).

Fig. 1. Karl Wirsum (American, 1939–2021). *Screamin' Jay Hawkins*, 1968. Acrylic on canvas; 121.9 × 91.4 cm (48 × 36 in.). Mr. and Mrs. Frank G. Logan Purchase Prize Fund, 1969.248.

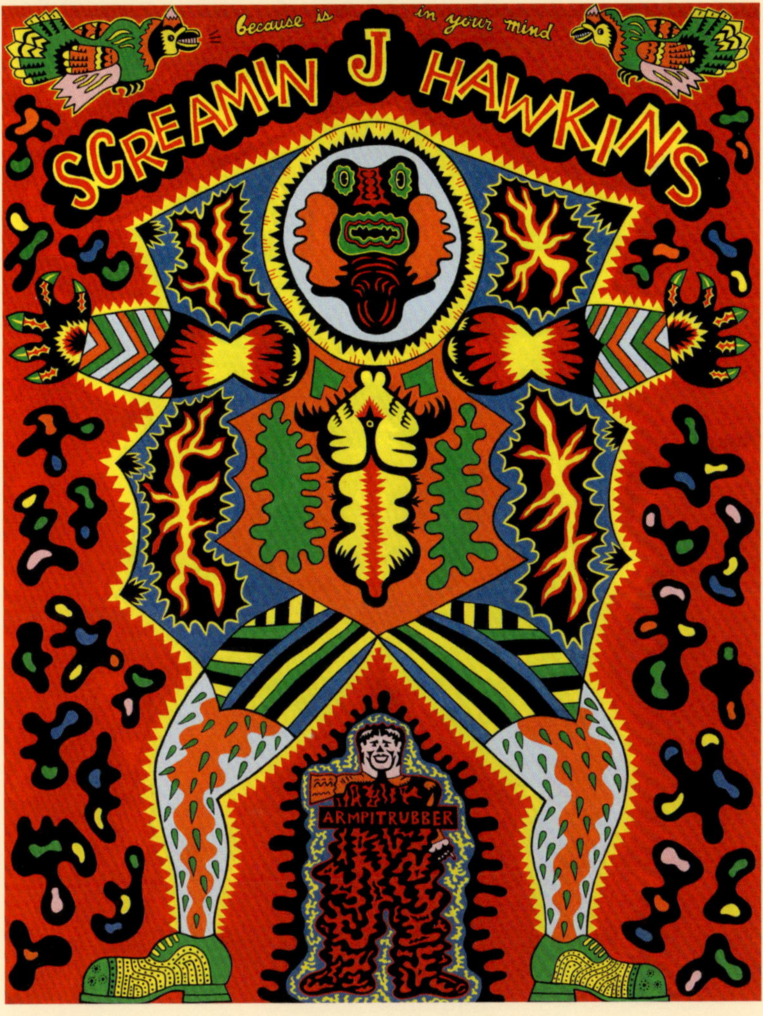

Ramberg's hunt for "trash treasure"—a term underlining the value ascribed to the castoffs she collected—yielded dolls, buttons, women's fashion advertising, and romance comics. The fragmented female figure in *Loose Beauty* (fig. 2) is an iconic example of the ways these sources infiltrated her provocative, noirish work. The subject's anonymity and lack of agency emphasize the act of looking above all else, underscoring the centrality of voyeurism to Ramberg's collecting activities as well as her artwork.

Richard Hunt (BAE 1957) also searched Chicago streets and junkyards, scavenging car parts, old pipes, and other scrap metal to create his sculptures. Since Hunt earned a degree in art education from SAIC, he taught himself how to solder and weld. Using a torch like a paintbrush, his art is marked by a sense of transformation and motion. These materials and techniques are epitomized by *Hero Construction* (fig. 3), a figure that blends man with machine.

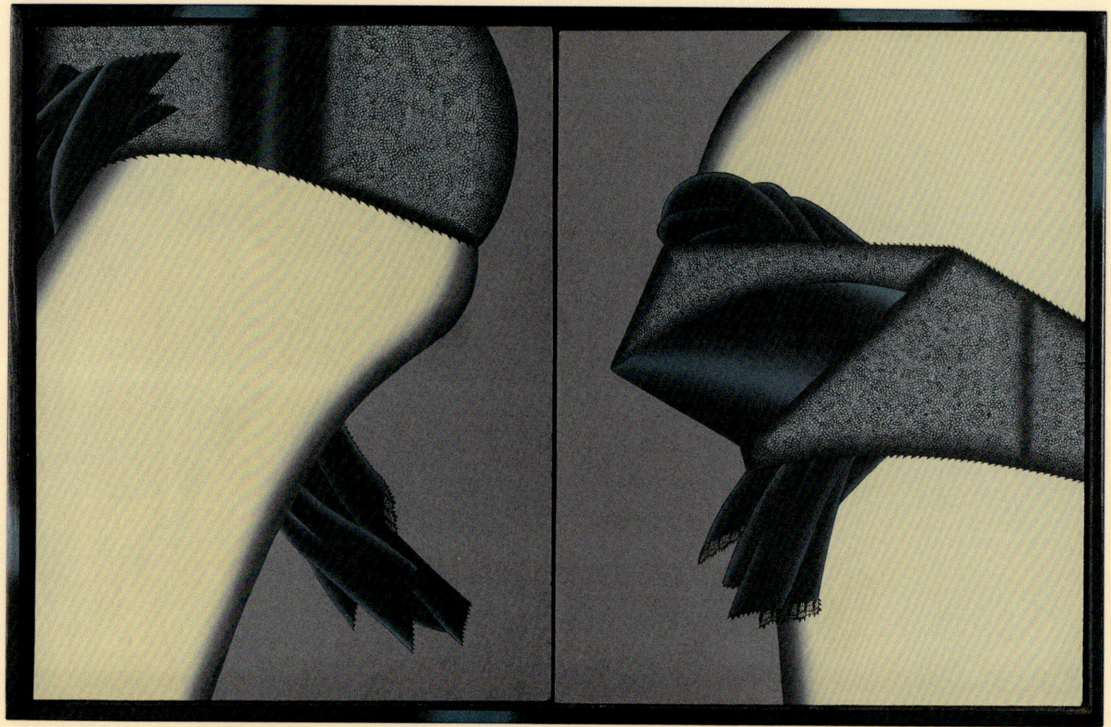

Fig. 2. Christina Ramberg (American, 1946–1995). *Loose Beauty*, 1973. Acrylic on Masonite; diptych, each panel: 48.3 × 37.5 cm (19 × 14¾ in.); framed: 51.5 × 78.2 cm (20¼ × 30¾ in.). Twentieth-Century Purchase Fund, 1973.336.

Like Wirsum, Hunt also took children's art courses at the museum, but prior to that, his innate love of art was nurtured at Bronzeville's South Side Community Art Center (SSCAC). Like SAIC, it was founded by a group of local artists, including Dr. Margaret Burroughs (BA 1942, MA 1948, HON 1987), in 1941. In continuous operation ever since, the SSCAC has mounted exhibitions and offered classes by such luminaries as Elizabeth Catlett, Eldzier Cortor, and Charles White, the last two of whom also studied at SAIC in the late 1930s.

A prodigious polymath, Burroughs was an artist, author, educator, and activist. A student of Kathleen Blackshear at SAIC, she benefited from inclusive instruction featuring art made throughout history and across the globe. Blackshear also encouraged Burroughs in her pursuit of visual art as well as her study of African and African American heritage. This led to Burroughs helping found and direct the DuSable Black History Museum in 1961. Originally built from Burroughs's own art collection displayed in her living room, it was the nation's first museum to promote and celebrate Black culture.

Like the artist-founders of SAIC, Burroughs was an institution builder in her own right, and Hunt was the fortunate beneficiary of her efforts, which helped launch his celebrated career as one of the most prolific sculptors of public art in America. Throughout its history, SAIC has also been an incubator of educators, as well as artists, who were oftentimes one and the same—including Wirsum and Ramberg, who both taught for decades at their alma mater. As this select cross-section of artists illustrates, SAIC and the Art Institute share an artist-centered, academic core that helps make a plurality of creative pursuits possible.

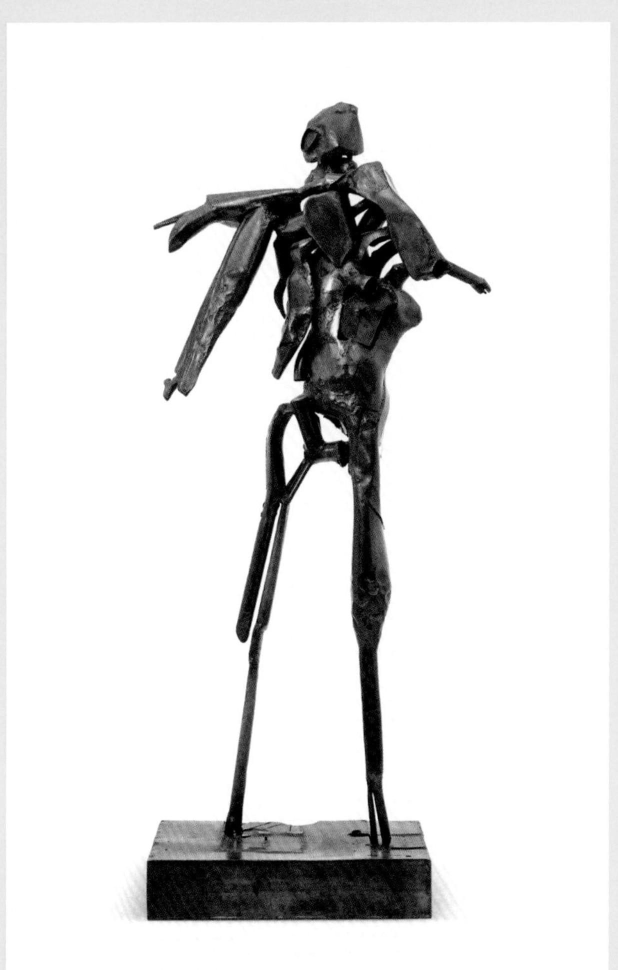

Fig. 3. Richard Hunt (American, 1935–2023). *Hero Construction*, 1958. Steel; without base: 162.6 × 73.7 cm (64 × 29 in.); approx. base: h.: 12.7 cm (5 in.). Gift of Mr. and Mrs. Arnold H. Maremont, 1958.528.

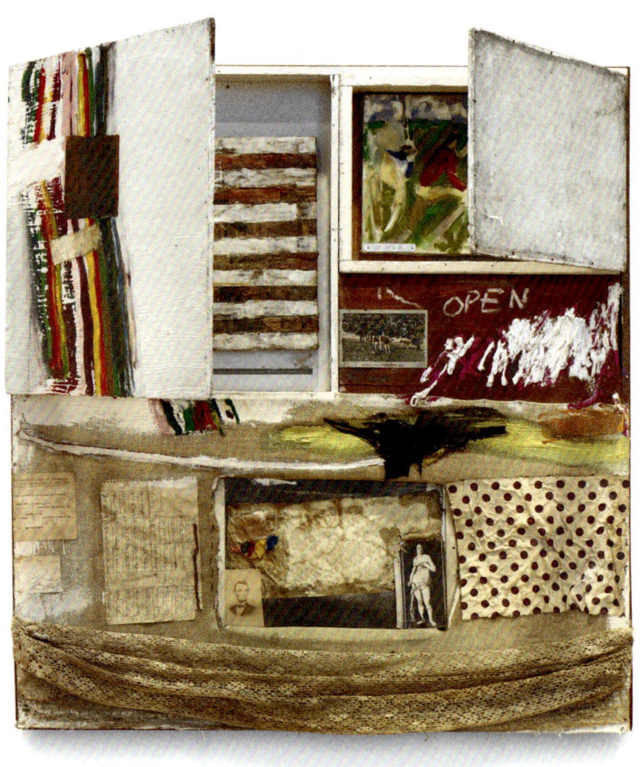

155. Robert Rauschenberg, **Short Circuit**, 1955

Short Circuit is among the most personal of Robert Rauschenberg's *Combines*—hybrid works that merge painting, sculpture, and things from everyday life. In the mid-1950s, Rauschenberg began incorporating domestic objects such as windows, doors, and fabric into his hybrid sculpture-paintings. *Short Circuit* includes a curtain-like netting, a Judy Garland autograph, a John Cage–David Tudor program, a portrait of Abraham Lincoln, and images of Renaissance and modern American figures. Together, these fragments suggest both personal memory and a shared American experience.

The work also includes contributions from two of Rauschenberg's close companions: a painting by Susan Weil and, originally, a *Flag* painting by Jasper Johns—both hidden behind hinged cabinet doors. The Johns flag was stolen in 1965 and later replaced at Rauschenberg's invitation by the artist Elaine Sturtevant, who was known for replicating iconic artworks to explore authorship and originality. Her *Flag* here is not a copy but a conceptual artwork in its own right. Through this layered history, *Short Circuit* becomes a meditation on collaboration, memory, and the often unclear distinction between original and copy—central concerns for Rauschenberg. *Giampaolo Bianconi*

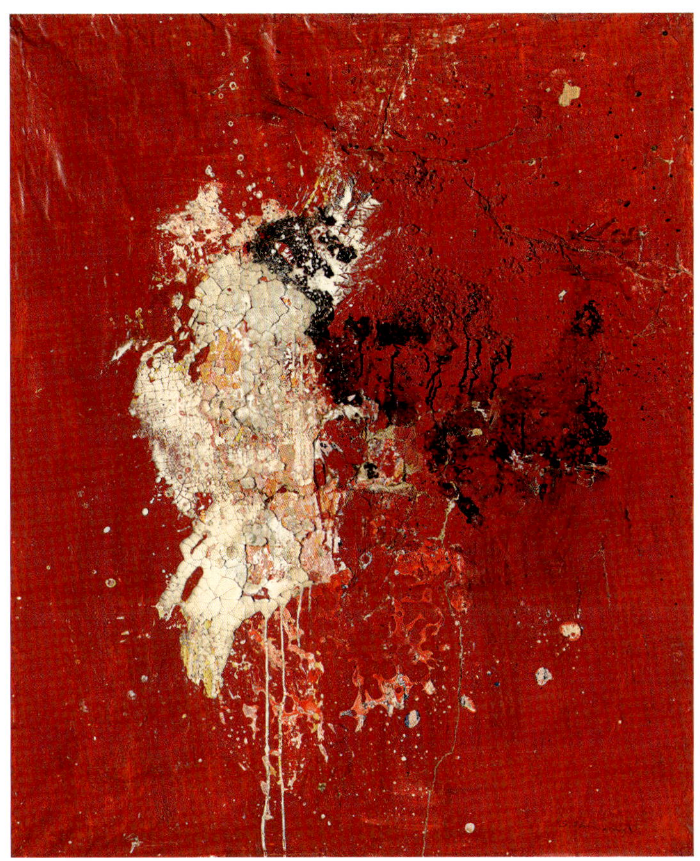

156. Shozo Shimamoto, **Untitled**, 1957

Shozo Shimamoto was a cofounder of the Gutai Art Association, postwar Japan's most significant avant-garde collective. In fact, Shimamoto gave the collective its name—*gutai* means "embodiment" or "concreteness." The group formed in 1954, advocating for an exuberant and ethically invested freedom of expression. For Gutai artists, process was paramount; each member sought out new ways of wielding materials, often for public performances that could result in finished works. "I believe," Shimamoto wrote, "that the first thing we should do is to set paint free from the paintbrush."

Accordingly, he developed methods for shooting bags of paint from a cannon and throwing glass bottles of paint against expanses of unstretched cloth. In this untitled work, two aqueous white and black passages (possibly created by paint-cannon) seem to stain the stark red ground. The artist painted on newspaper, which has dried unevenly, rippling and warping the field as a whole. Pebble-like chunks of dried media build up the surface, while holes, splits, and lifted regions of paint disrupt it. The tension between destruction and creation—or the capacity to transform a destructive act into a constructive one—is clearly key to Shimamoto's art.
Kate Nesin

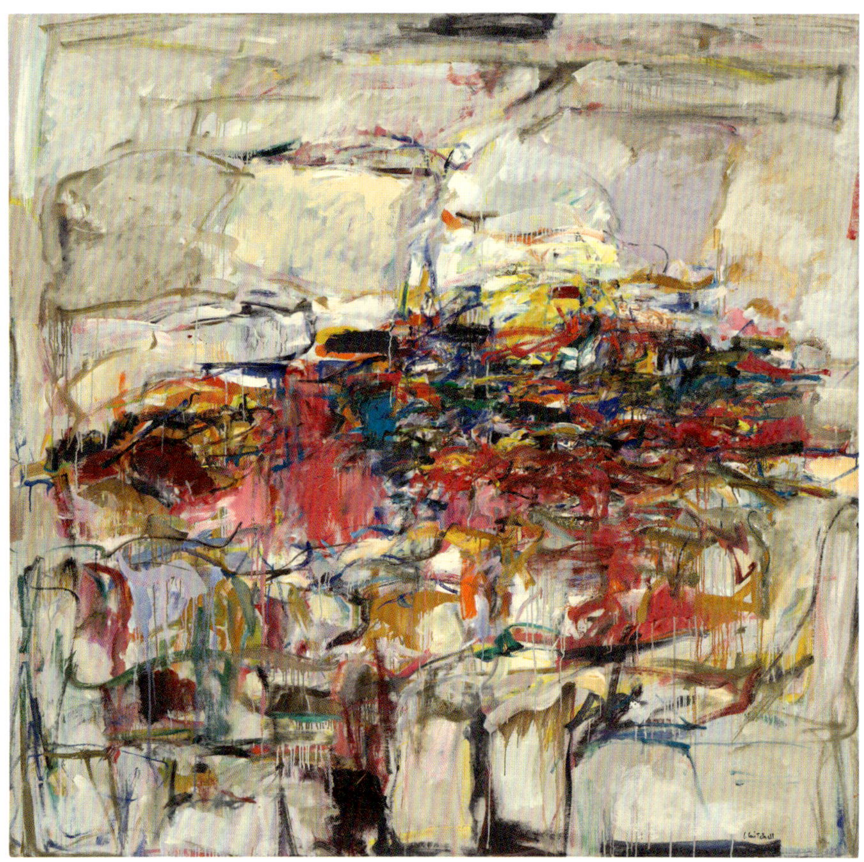

157. Joan Mitchell, City Landscape, 1955

Joan Mitchell's vibrant abstractions are anchored in the particularities of place. Or, to quote poet Eileen Myles, they are "an inventory of the feeling of a place." Mitchell carried her landscapes around with her throughout an itinerant life that took her from Chicago to New York to Paris and into the French countryside of Vétheuil, where she ultimately made her home in 1968.

Mitchell fell in love with painting in the Art Institute's galleries of French Impressionism. She came to the museum with her family as a young girl in the 1930s and 1940s, and she learned these works by heart as a student at the School of the Art Institute of Chicago. In *City Landscape*, a spectacular tangle of pale pink, scarlet, mustard, sienna, and black, Mitchell transports the feeling of Impressionism—its emotional range, achieved through color, light, and sensitivity to mark—into her own moment of postwar American abstraction. Some have wondered if this mass of coagulating strokes and small cascades is a reference to Chicago, with liquid reflections of the city against Lake Michigan, or the swirling nerve center of New York, where the work was made. Yes, it was built from the feelings of both of these places, and it helps you feel where you are too. *Caitlin Haskell*

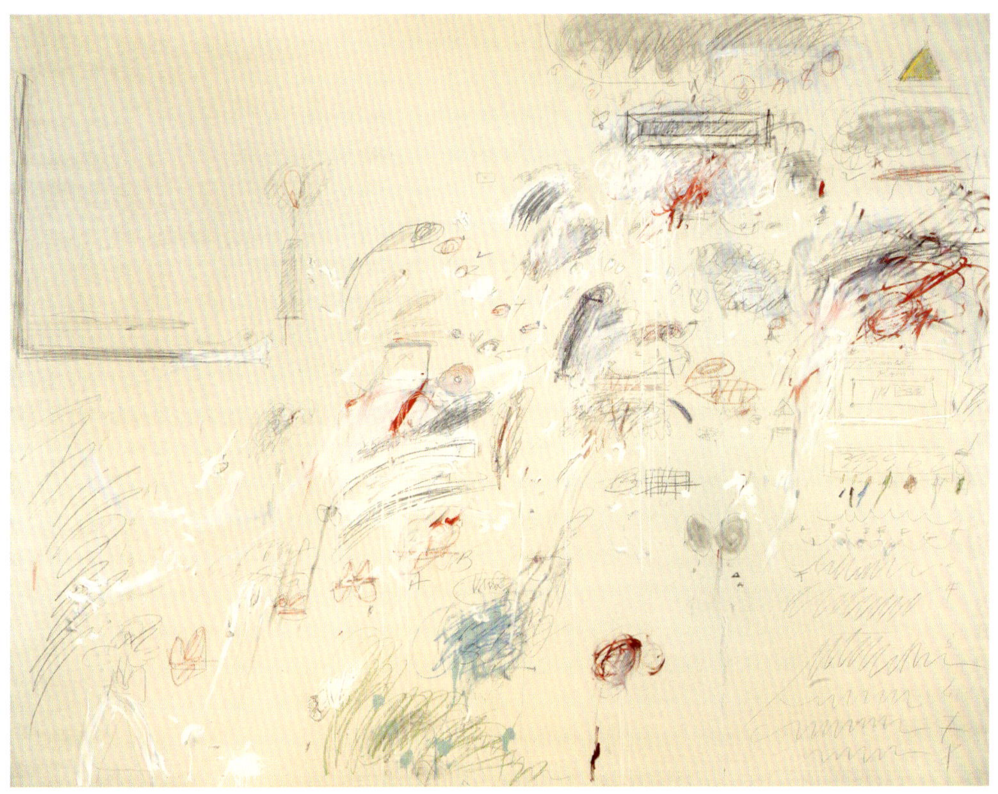

158. Cy Twombly, The First Part of the Return from Parnassus, 1961

How do we reconcile unreadable marks with florid literary references or casual scribbles with impassioned ones? Cy Twombly's work compels and confounds in equal measure. An American artist transfixed by ancient histories, Twombly moved in 1959 to Rome, where his painting flourished during the early 1960s. *The First Part of the Return from Parnassus* comprises all the elements for which he would gain renown. From visceral smudges of pigment to intimate pencil notations, some marks seem emphatic, others more atmospheric, partially erased. Twombly's name and the place and year of making appear legibly within nested boxes, centered along the right edge; in the lower right corner, by contrast, he scrawled lines of what he called "pseudo-writing." These works transgress whatever boundaries typically separate reading from looking, writing from drawing and painting. Twombly's title is suitably layered and obscure too. In Greek mythology, Mount Parnassus was home of the Muses, sacred to Apollo, but he borrowed his full title from a trio of anonymous English plays, written around 1600, in which university graduates fail to make a living despite their scholarly training. Twombly painted a companion canvas, *The Second Part of the Return from Parnassus*, also in the Art Institute's collection. *Kate Nesin*

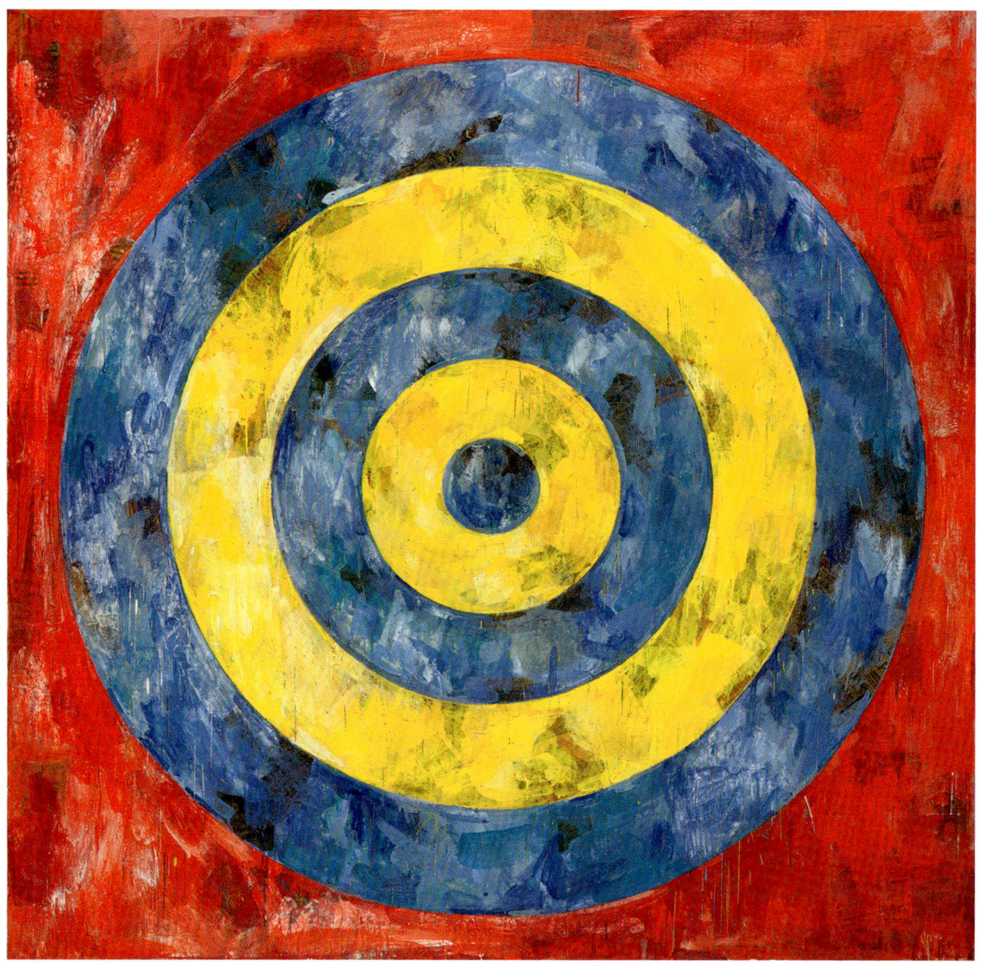

159. Jasper Johns, Target, 1961

Jasper Johns populated his work with a set of instantly recognizable "found" motifs: numbers, letters, maps of the United States, and the American flag, as well as targets. These controlled, cool, and cerebral paintings contrast with those of the previous generation's Abstract Expressionism while retaining the material emphasis of their marks.

For *Target*—the largest and last of this series begun in 1955—Johns employed a palette of primary colors as limited and colloquial as the image itself. He emphasized his gestural paint handling in the work by using oil and encaustic (a quick-drying medium of pigment mixed with hot wax), which recorded each stroke and drip of his paintbrush almost with the three-dimensionality of a sculpture. This technique yielded not just a painting but a painted object. By highlighting the subtle nuances between form and material, Johns layered physical considerations with representational (a target) and abstract (the geometry of concentric circles) considerations. *Thea Liberty Nichols*

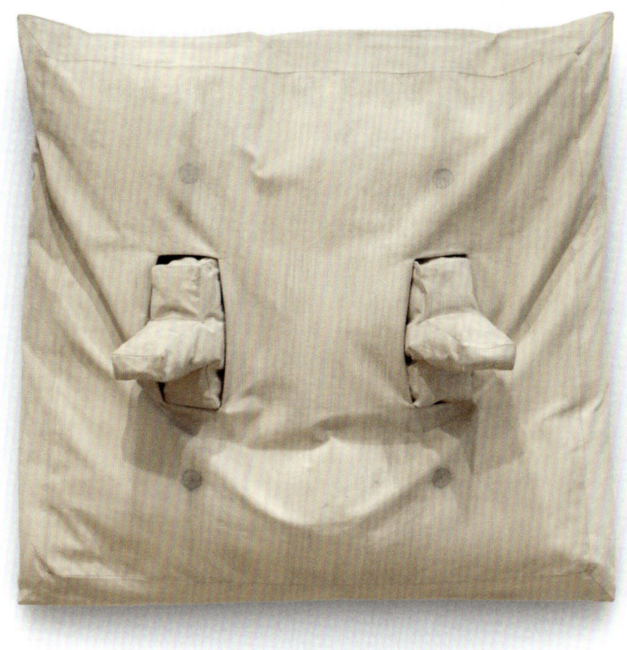

160. Claes Oldenburg, Soft Light Switches—"Ghost Version" II, 1964–71

Hamburgers and housedresses, vacuum cleaners and tubes of lipstick—for seventy years, Claes Oldenburg used unremarkable, everyday things as the subject matter for his sculptures. Variously soft, hard, large, and small, they take the stuff of life and transform it in humorous and disturbing ways, often both at the same time. Oldenburg began his career in the late 1950s, during a period of economic prosperity in the US. Mass production flooded the market with commodities while the burgeoning advertising industry transformed these goods into objects of desire. Oldenburg's play with materials, form, and scale cannily comments on the absurdity of modern life.

Ridiculously oversize, *Soft Light Switches—"Ghost Version" II*, along with its counterpart *Light Switches—Hard Version Replica (Brown)* (1964–69), demonstrates the radicalness of Oldenburg's seemingly simple maneuvers. To make his "soft sculptures," Oldenburg, assisted by his then-wife, artist Patty Mucha, relied on conventional dressmaking techniques. He used a pattern cut from stiff material to cut a fabric prototype before creating the "final" iteration (often made from vinyl). The first pattern became the "hard" version of the *Light Switch*, the completely white prototype the "ghost" version. Typical of Oldenburg's work, the soft, droopy ghost light switch evokes a simultaneously grotesque and sexualized human form. *Paulina Pobocha*

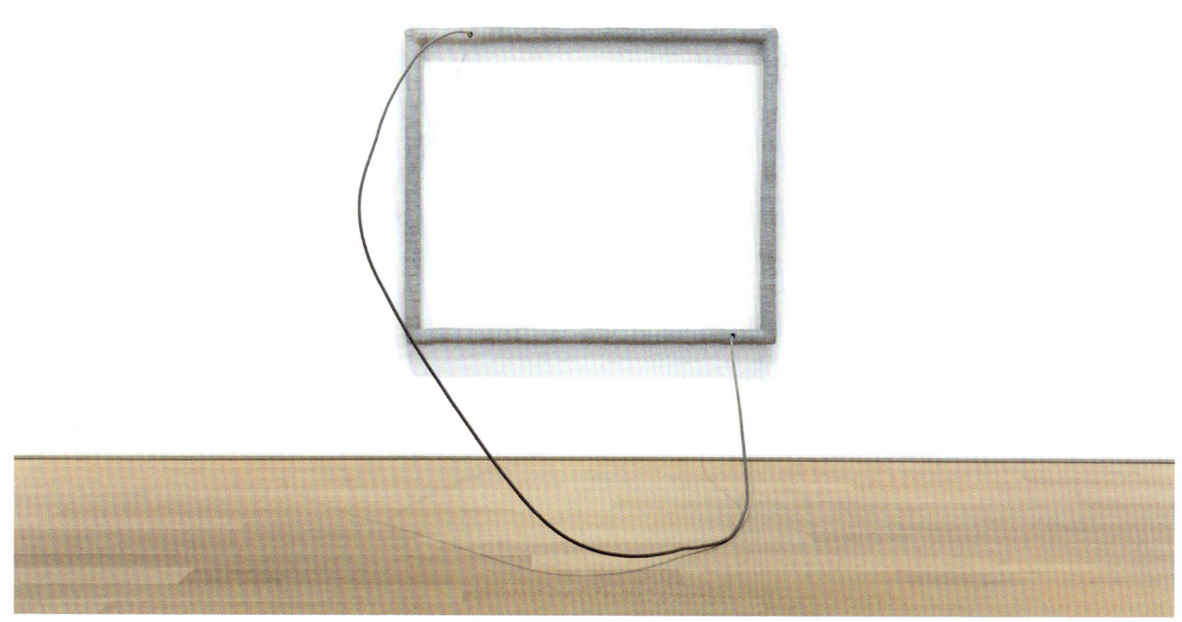

161. Eva Hesse, Hang Up, 1966

Eva Hesse's career was short, but her influence remains outsized. She studied painting in the late 1950s before turning to sculpture, exploring that medium through the eccentric behaviors and expressive capacities of her chosen materials. In fact, Hesse considered *Hang Up* the first work to achieve the "absurdity or extreme feeling" she always sought.

Its structuring device is a wooden rectangle, like the outline of a painting but framing only blank wall. This rectilinear contour is wrapped in strips of cloth and sensitively painted with an ombré effect, shading from pearly gray at the upper left corner to ash gray at bottom right. An unruly hanging wire emerges from, and connects, these same two corners: Hesse contradicts her sturdy, geometric frame by means of an organic loop of industrial tubing, which projects awkwardly into the gallery space, then sags to touch the floor with unexpected tenderness. *Hang Up* plays with the formal conventions of both painting and sculpture (flat versus in the round, on the wall versus on the ground), and its title is playful, too—an instruction for installing the work, and a phrase that describes an emotional preoccupation or inhibition.
Kate Nesin

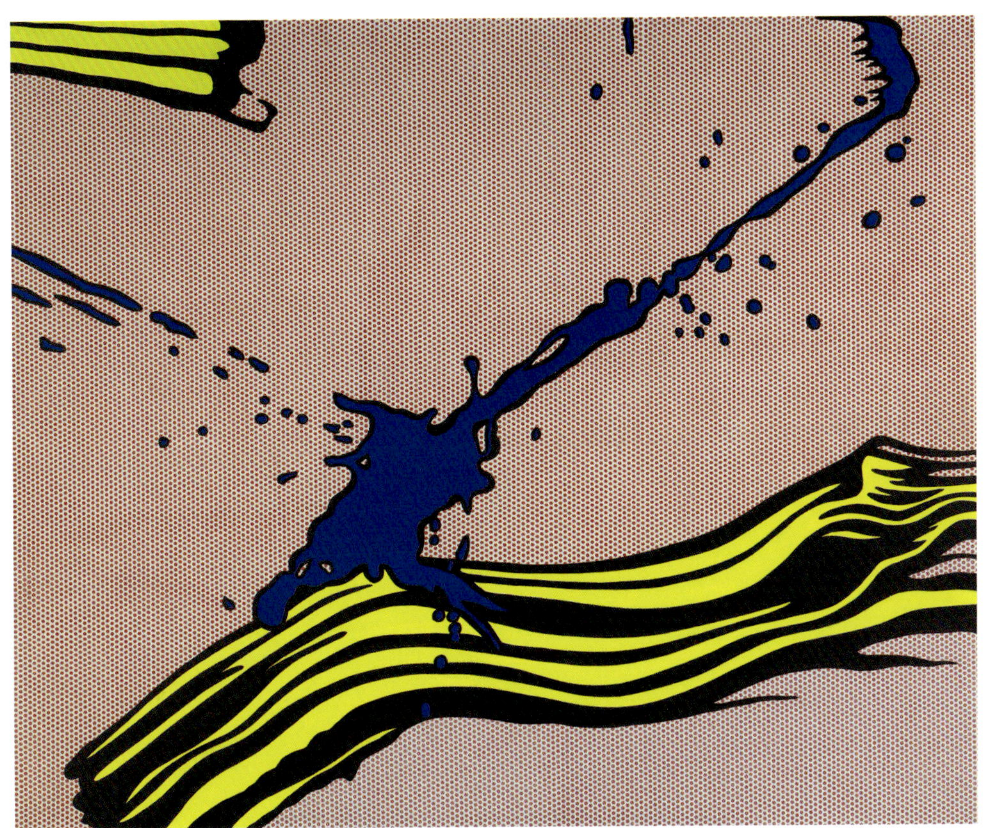

162. Roy Lichtenstein, **Brushstroke with Spatter, 1966**

In 1949 *Life* magazine published an article about Jackson Pollock carrying the famous subhead "Is he the greatest living painter in the United States?" Fifteen years later *Life*'s article on Roy Lichtenstein promoted the provocation to the title itself: "Is He the Worst Artist in the US?"

Lichtenstein's *Brushstroke with Spatter* is a picture of a picture, and all pictures and paintings are markers of time. Lichtenstein flattened the deep space of the gestural paintings of the Abstract Expressionists to whom his practice had been rhetorically, uncharitably compared. In *Brushstroke with Spatter*, we see the act of painting now mediated through a halftone printing process and stylized graphic quotations of Willem de Kooning's squeegee-like streaks and Pollock's splatters. The action that signaled passion, decisiveness, and soul in American postwar painting is here tamed, framed, remembered—somehow both frozen and dilated. If the Abstract Expressionists accounted for the painter painting in real time, Lichtenstein humbly inquires, how then do we account for time after it has been mediated by a screen or an eye? *Alex Da Corte*

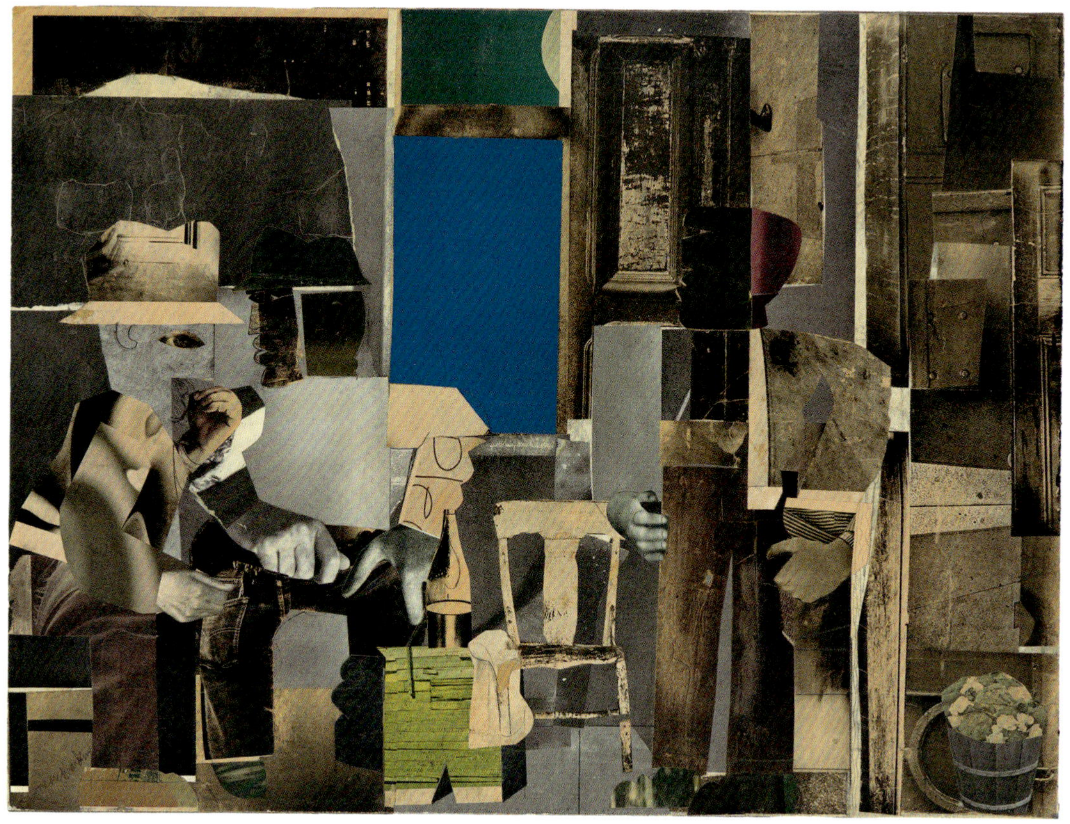

163. Romare Bearden, Gray Interior (aka Gray Morning), 1969

Figure and ground coalesce in Romare Bearden's *Gray Interior* due to the similarity in color and texture of the papers used. Two men sit in intense conversation; their eyes, though in profile, stare out at us. Another, sturdy figure is a mass of Photostat scraps: a wooden door, a gray sky, a gum-covered sidewalk. At center, a chair sits next to a green crate set with a bottle and pitcher, but this is no invitation. The scene is overcast and aloof, save for the cerulean pane that draws the eye.

Though most famous for his collages, Bearden only began them in 1964 at age fifty-three; he had previously created political cartoons and social realist and Cubist canvases. His work melds boyhood memories of agrarian Charlotte, North Carolina; Harlem Renaissance extravagance; and the grueling labor of Pittsburgh steelworkers. Bearden's family was prosperous during Reconstruction, but that wealth quickly eroded as Jim Crow violence threatened Black aspiration. Still, despite America, Bearden found joy in representing Black interior life after forebears like Giotto, Pieter de Hooch, and Edgar Degas. The result, as in *Gray Interior*, can be bristling but resonant. As the poet Derek Walcott wrote of Bearden's work, "Dawn bleeds without a sound." *Alex Jen*

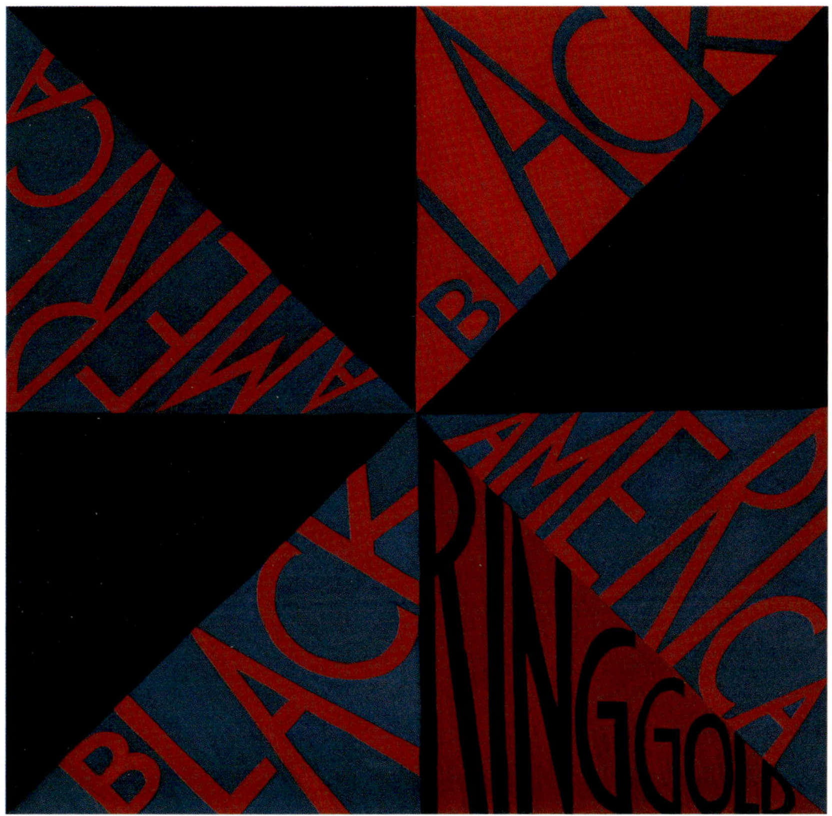

164. Faith Ringgold, **Black Light Series #7: Ego Painting**, 1969

Part of Faith Ringgold's *Black Light* series (1967–70), *Ego Painting* reflects her commitment to challenging historical narratives. The artist used the letters of her name as both form and content—fragmenting identity while asserting presence. She also substituted the conventional base pigment of white gesso with black, subverting dominant conventions within Western oil painting traditions. With nuanced shades of black, *Ego Painting* draws attention to the complexity within darkness. As Ringgold wrote, "dark colors must be placed next to other equally dark colors in order to see their true surface quality, color value, and depth of contrast."

This multicolored square made up of eight triangles borrows its compositional format from Kuba textile designs of the Democratic Republic of the Congo. This design motif creates layered word associations—the work simultaneously reading "BLACK AMERICA," "BLACK RINGGOLD," "RINGGOLD AMERICA," and "AMERICA BLACK." *Ego Painting* is as responsive to the cultural landscape of the 1960s and 1970s as it is relevant to our present—posing questions about visibility, representation, and whose contributions are preserved in the art historical record. Ringgold's work insists on inclusion, embedding Black identity and history within the language and lineage of painting. *Annika Bohanec*

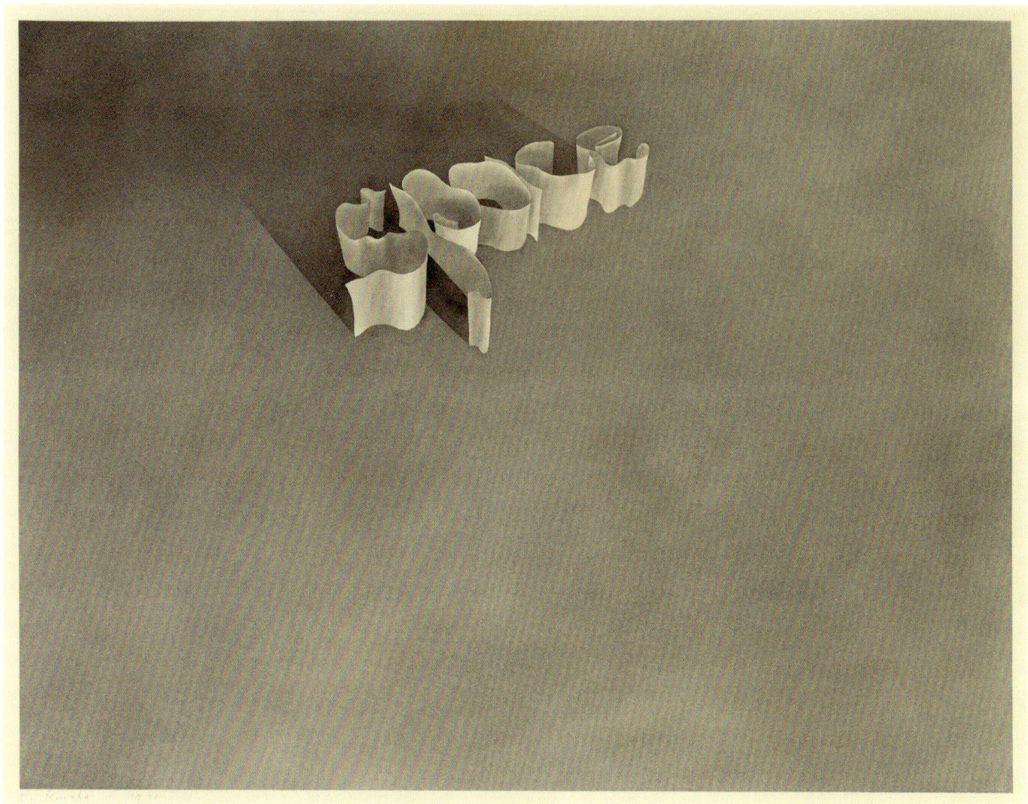

165. Ed Ruscha, Space, 1971

When I first saw *Space*, I was astonished—was it drawn or airbrushed? Known for his innovative use of words, Ed Ruscha toyed with the paradoxical in *Space*. Curled strips of paper rest on an invisible surface; a single light source casts a shadow, generating three dimensions out of thin air. In defiance of the word's meaning, there are no spaces between the letters. The inclusion of pastel is almost imperceptible; I finally spotted a yellow halo above the letter *c*, like a sunrise viewed from outer space. Ruscha's use of gunpowder, which he chose for its tonality and ability to easily correct and conceal, adds to the illusion. He soaked the gunpowder pellets in water to neutralize them and was left with a fine mixture of sulfur and charcoal. When rubbed on paper with a rag, it produced a flawless surface. With a microscope I could see more of Ruscha's magic: deep grooves from an X-Acto blade and tape residue hugging the letters that were once cut and masked with an adhesive stencil. Dark ridges of gunpowder accumulated along the tape, which left behind a white surface on which Ruscha could outline the letters inside the smoky gray. Ruscha wasn't just drawing—he was making space. *Mel Becker Solomon*

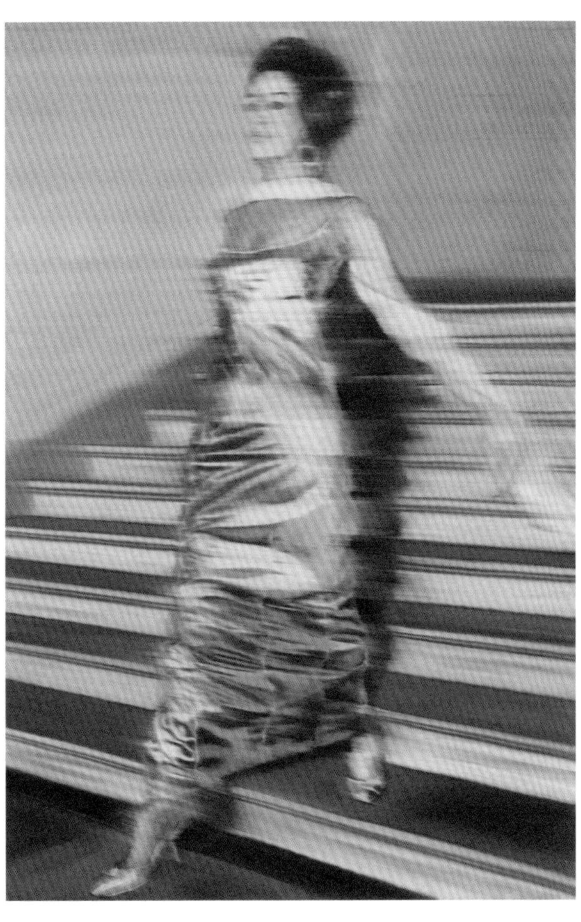

166. Gerhard Richter, Woman Descending the Staircase, 1965

Gerhard Richter deliberately blurred this rendering of a photograph (taken from a magazine or newspaper, in a manner related to Pop Art) to evoke abstraction, movement, or instability. I find this juxtaposition compelling: As a student I was told that art shouldn't (or couldn't) do more than one thing at a time. Richter capaciously laid out multiple forms and possibilities for art. In his book *The Daily Practice of Painting*, he wondered why and how painting was useful—or even possible—in the modern world. His persistence, painting in the face of doubt and exploring the future of painting, indicates a certain productive willfulness.

I am intrigued by the way Richter's strategies resisted and complicated Marcel Duchamp's *Nude Descending a Staircase* (1912; Philadelphia Museum of Art), a work deploying a machinelike, cubist visualization of movement and time. For Richter, the goal was not to copy but to differ, to transform or renew painting after Duchamp signaled its end (a declaration made many times over the last century plus). Richter proposed that no absolute truth can be located in a singular artistic genre or style. Painting allows the artist to suspend, postpone, blur, or exceed any single genre or reference. *Tony Cokes*

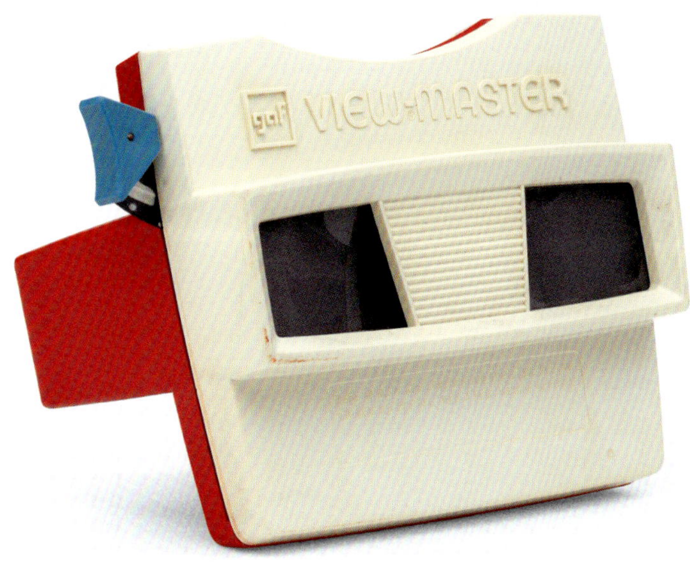

167. Charles Harrison, **View-Master** (**Model G**), about 1976

As a young designer working freelance jobs in Chicago, Charles Harrison created the View-Master's now iconic modern design in 1958. He replaced the boxy, dark-brown Bakelite housing of this stereoscopic viewer with a lightweight body in colorful, injection-molded plastic, one of many revivals of the product after its debut at the 1939 World's Fair.

Harrison first moved to Chicago to attend the School of the Art Institute of Chicago, one of the few US institutions offering degrees in design, a relatively new field at the time. Despite his great talent and strong education, Harrison, a Black man, struggled to find work after graduation due to racial discrimination. Perseverance and classes at the legendary Institute of Design led to his eventual hiring by one of his freelance clients, the behemoth retailer Sears, Roebuck. He was soon promoted to head the company's design group and became one of the few Black executives in Chicago. Harrison designed over six hundred products for Sears, including many innovative bestsellers, guided by his lifelong respect for the role objects play in daily life and the importance of creating things of beauty, value, and utility. *Alison Fisher*

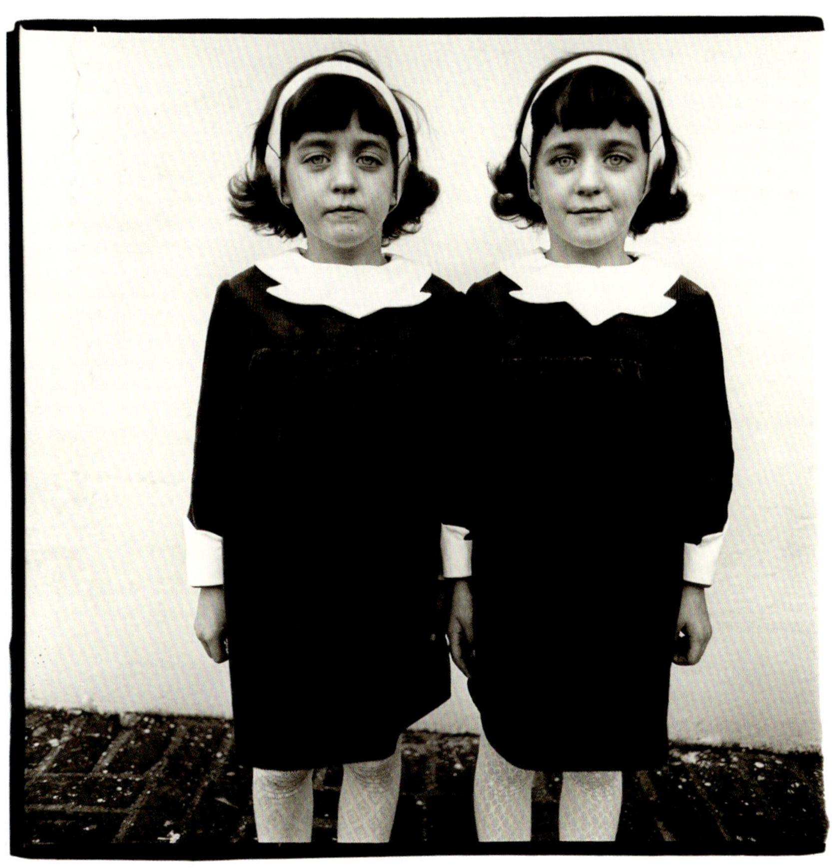

168. Diane Arbus, **Identical twins, Roselle, N.J. 1966**, 1966

Two years before she received her first camera, in a high school essay on Chaucer, Diane Arbus wrote: "There are and have been and will be an infinite number of things on Earth. Individuals all different, all wanting different things, all knowing different things, all loving different things, all looking different. . . . That is what I love: the differentness."

Arbus's appreciation for the unusual, eccentric, and extraordinary led her to photograph a range of subjects over the thirty years of her career—cross-dressers, people with gigantism, art philanthropists, nudists, and, as here, identical twins. No one knows how Arbus learned about a 1966 small-town Christmas party being held for local twins and triplets, but it is in keeping with her interest in how people are who they are. Isolating these seven-year-old girls against the wall of the Knights of Columbus hall in Roselle, New Jersey, and photographing them in her typically straightforward manner, Arbus underscored the details: matching homemade dresses (which were green but appear black), lace stockings bunched below the knees, and a barely discernible difference in each girl's camera "manner." Such details alternately belie and reinforce the uncanny suggestion of two thoroughly identical individuals. *Elizabeth Siegel*

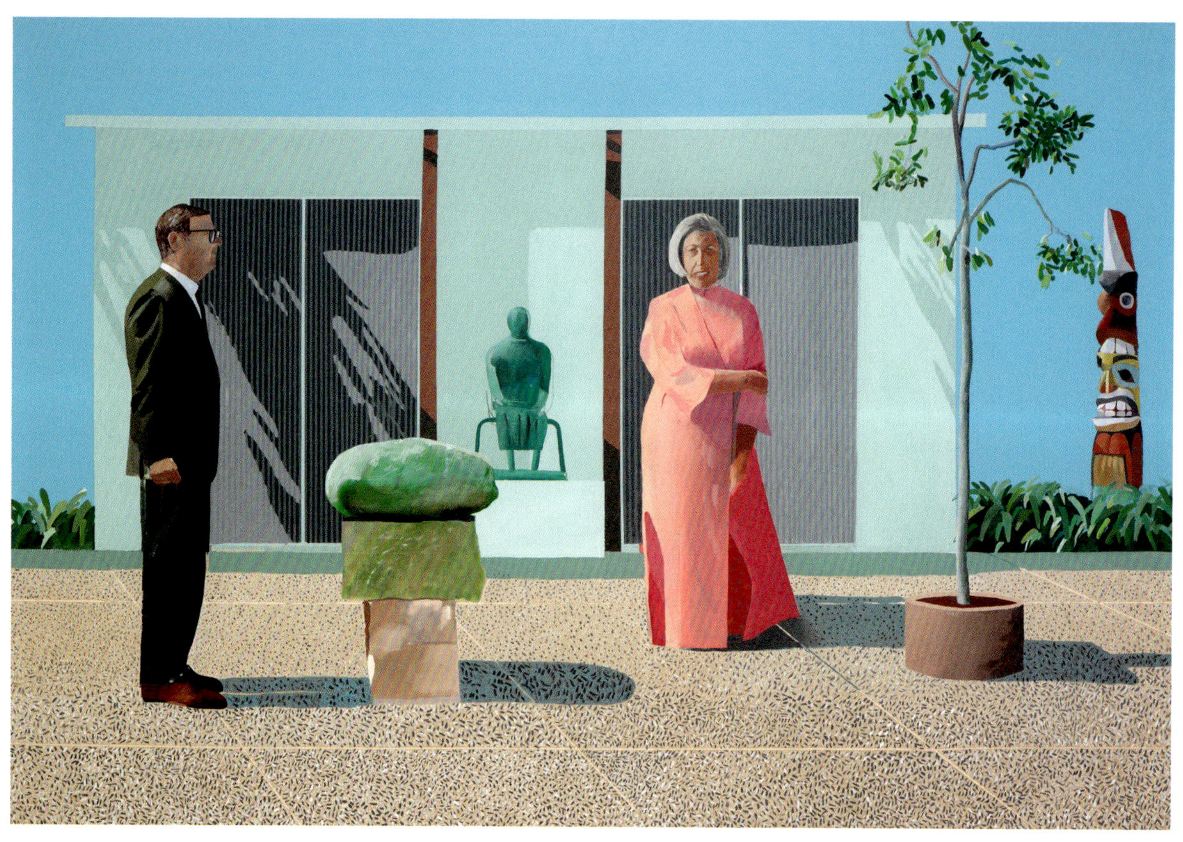

169. David Hockney, American Collectors (Fred and Marcia Weisman), 1968

One of several double portraits that preoccupied David Hockney in the late 1960s and early 1970s, *American Collectors (Fred and Marcia Weisman)* is an iconic homage to Los Angeles—a formative setting for Hockney's artistic evolution—and a meditation on the human condition. There is both joy and a searing honesty in the way Hockney depicted Mr. and Mrs. Weisman. The prominent Los Angeles collectors stand within the domestic space of their shared home and garden, yet they seem to exist in their own worlds, independent of each other and lost in thought. Hockney refused to formally distinguish the work's protagonists from their surroundings. Positioned among their art collection, they could just as well be a part of it—a point emphatically obvious in how Marcia Weisman mirrors the pose of William Turnbull's sculpture found near the center of the composition. Graphic, flat, and candy-colored, *American Collectors* borrows stylistic tropes from Pop Art but deploys them to explore the psychological complexities of human connection. *Annika Bohanec*

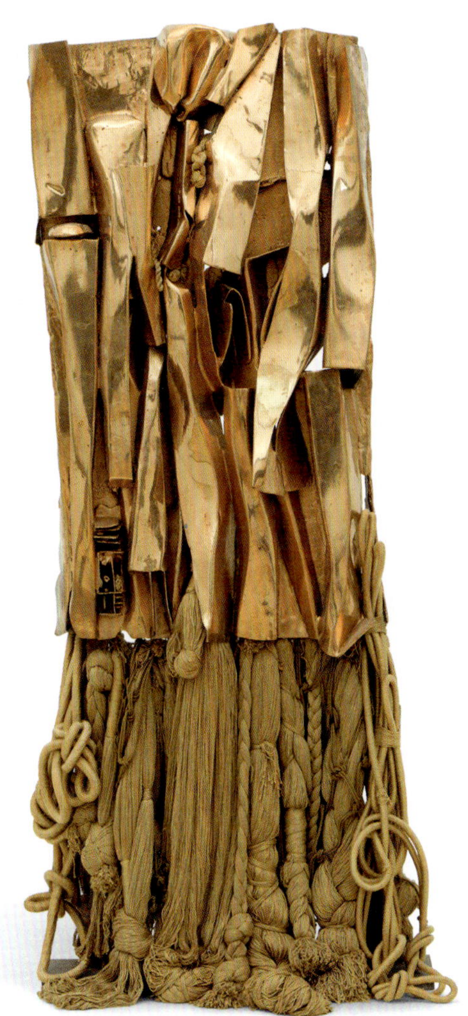

170. Barbara Chase-Riboud, **Zanzibar / Gold #2**, 1977

Undermining its apparent material properties, silk fiber appears to support hefty metal in Barbara Chase-Riboud's *Zanzibar / Gold #2*. This inversion is, in the artist's words, a revolt against "the tyranny of the base." In addition to her work in sculpture, Chase-Riboud is also a poet and novelist. This is one of six works named after her poem "Why did we leave Zanzibar?", a reflection on the history of enslavement and forced migration from East Africa; "We could have stayed on the beach / Clinging to the rocks like bats," she wrote. In this light, the meaning of the sculpture's materials becomes clear: The silk no longer reads as adornment, but as net, chain, or shroud. The golden bronze above does not gleam with triumph; it overwhelms the fibers beneath with the weight of history.

Across all media, Chase-Riboud imbues abstract symbols and images with historical and political references. *Zanzibar / Gold #2* is an example of the artist working at the height of her talents to make a work whose significance is palpable, from its title to its physicality. *Giampaolo Bianconi*

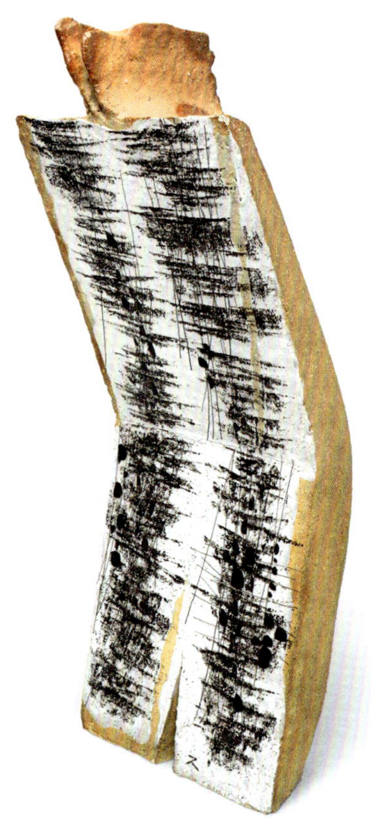

171. Suzuki Osamu, Clay Figure (*Dogū*), 1965

While technically a vessel, this two-foot-tall ceramic work looks more like a figure bowing at the waist. The artist, Suzuki Osamu, likely intended this; he titled this piece *Dogū*, the name for ancient Japanese terracotta figures. In addition, the peach-colored Shigaraki clay used here is similar in color to prehistoric wares. On top of the clay body, Suzuki "drew" with a dry black glaze upon white slip. The work is signed in black glaze with the character *su*.

The avant-garde Sōdeisha movement was founded by three young artists from Kyoto, the youngest of whom was Suzuki. All three were sons of traditional potters. Instead of relying on traditional ceramics for inspiration, these artists tapped into the modernist ideas of their contemporaries throughout the world and used clay to create abstract works of sculpture. Sōdeisha is a distinctly Japanese avant-garde movement that negated the conventional ideas of clay (form, decoration, use) codified over centuries. *Janice Katz*

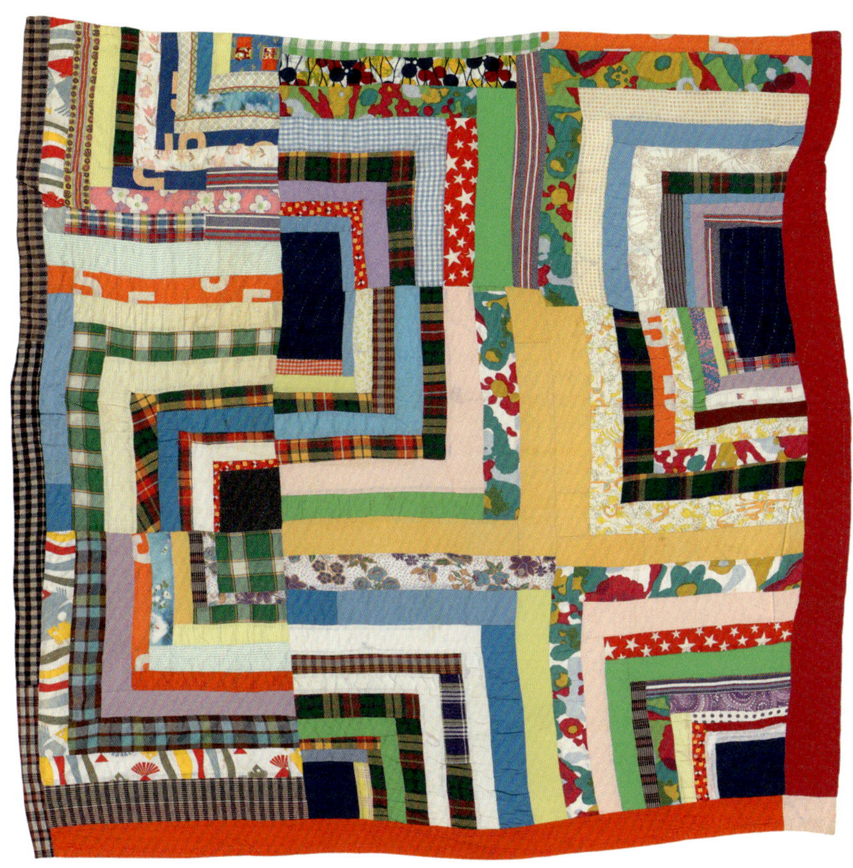

172. Jessie T. Pettway, **Housetop Half–Log Cabin Quilt**, about 1975

Gee's Bend, Alabama, has been a center for Black American quiltmaking for over a century, but the larger quilting community—and the art world—only began to recognize the singular artistry of these makers in the late 1960s. Gee's Bend quiltmakers uniquely interpreted well-known pieced quilt patterns and used bolder colors and a wider range of fabrics than other American quilters. For the most part, they were making quilts out of necessity and recycling fabrics from worn clothing. Here, Jessie Pettway has created a large-scale variation of the typical Log Cabin quilt pattern, splitting concentric squares in half and rearranging them to interrupt and enliven the expected symmetry.

Pettway is one of almost fifty Gee's Bend quilters with the same surname, an inheritance forced on them by plantation owner Mark H. Pettway, who enslaved the ancestors of many Gee's Bend residents in the 1800s. Gee's Bend quilts are at the center of a dialogue about categorizing work variously labeled as folk art, vernacular, self-taught, craft, and outsider art. But in the words of scholar Alvia Wardlaw, Pettway and her Gee's Bend community "have created a body of art so rich in its content and so remarkable in its execution that it now enhances dramatically the American cultural landscape." *Melinda Watt*

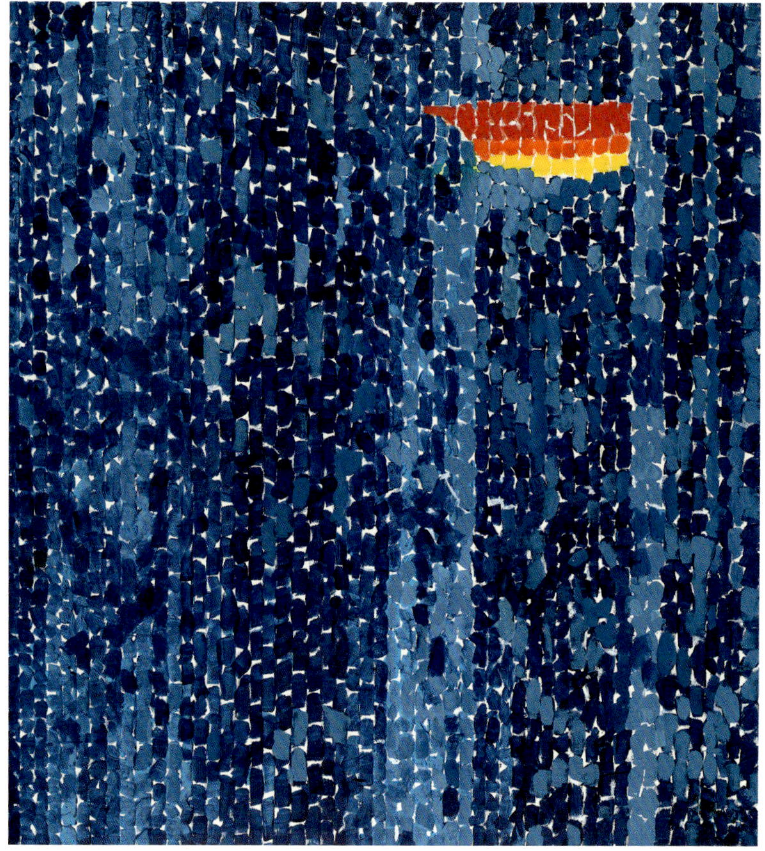

173. Alma Thomas, **Starry Night and the Astronauts**, 1972

Starry Night and the Astronauts is the final painting in Alma Thomas's space series, showing her fascination with America's Apollo missions, which began in the late 1960s. She represented the night sky as a rich range of vertically stacked, mosaiclike dabs of blue paint, which came to be known as the Alma Stripe. The streaks of red, orange, and yellow in the upper right capture the feeling of movement Thomas imagined astronauts might experience in space. Both rhythmic and arresting, *Starry Night and the Astronauts* evokes the exploration and invention that marked Thomas's lifetime and her artistic practice.

Born in 1891, Thomas witnessed vast technological advancements over the course of her life, from color television to air and space travel, which found their way into her work. Her widely acclaimed abstractions—painted after decades of representational work—combine her interests in the environment and technology. She strove to capture the vibrant spectrum of colors and shimmering light of the natural world in her art. *Thea Liberty Nichols*

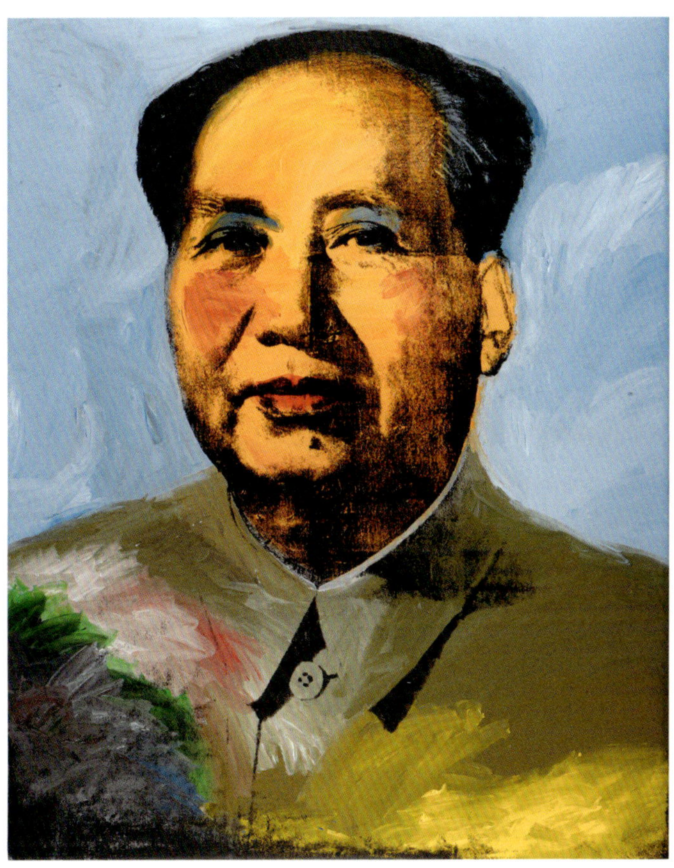

174. Andy Warhol, Mao, 1972

I have to say this isn't my favorite Andy Warhol subject; I'm a bigger fan of his death and disaster paintings. But this painting is huge. Monumental. It mimics the scale of propaganda images of Mao Zedong you see in historical photos from China. It's interesting for a painting to take on propaganda. Warhol made painting do things it had never been asked to do before.

This painting is as old as I am. Mao died when I was four years old, and as an American, I don't have a complex understanding of China and its history or culture. Most of what I know is probably also propaganda. Wikipedia says that in 1972 Nixon was traveling to China to open diplomatic and trade relations; this photograph of Mao was all over the press. Warhol, of course, enjoying his worldwide fame, took this image and made a silkscreen. He gave Mao a makeover, using paint as makeup.

Warhol was compulsive; Google says he made 209 paintings of Mao. That seems like a lot, but is it? It's hard to compare the power of repetition as it was understood in 1972 to what we understand today. Warhol was obviously prescient about how repetition increases the power of an image—but also drains it. *Wade Guyton*

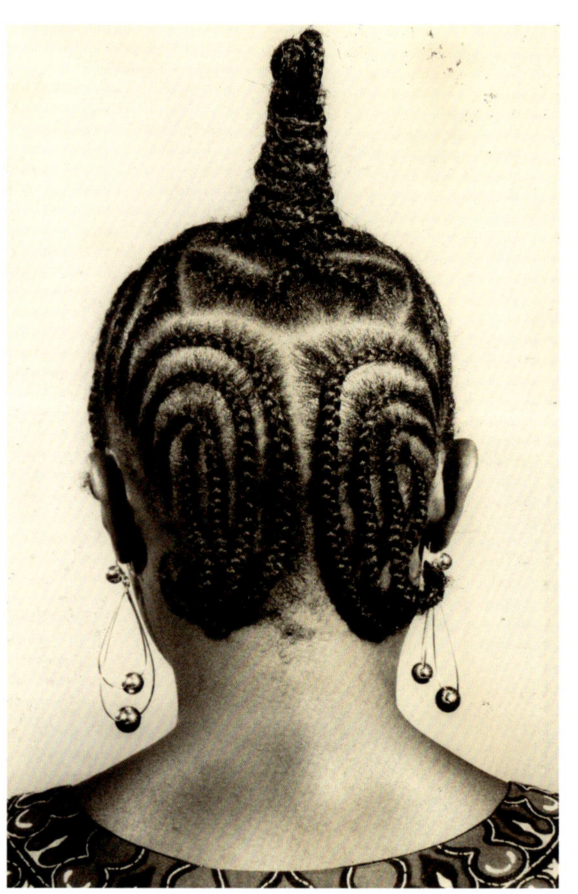

175. J.D. 'Okhai Ojeikere, *Ife Bronze*, 1972

Born in Ovbiomu-Emai, a rural town in southern Nigeria, J.D. 'Okhai Ojeikere began making photographs in the 1950s, working as a press photographer before opening his own portrait studio. After Nigeria gained independence from Great Britain in 1960, Ojeikere increasingly came into contact with Nigeria's literary and artistic communities in Ibadan and Lagos, and he eventually joined the Nigerian Arts Council. At a 1968 cultural festival organized by the council, Ojeikere photographed the traditional hairstyles of participants, some remarkably elaborate—the more intricate designs could take up to a week to complete. He soon began systematically photographing hairstyles and ultimately devoted decades to the project, traveling across Nigeria and producing an archive of more than one thousand images. Using neutral backgrounds, Ojeikere typically photographed his sitters' hair designs from behind or in profile, emphasizing the fine detail and sculptural quality of the styles rather than the individual's likeness. These elaborate constructions were usually produced for celebratory occasions and often given names rich with cultural significance. The name of this hairstyle (and the photograph's title) refers to a group of cast bronze heads from the twelfth-century Ife kingdom unearthed in Nigeria in 1938.
Antawan I. Byrd

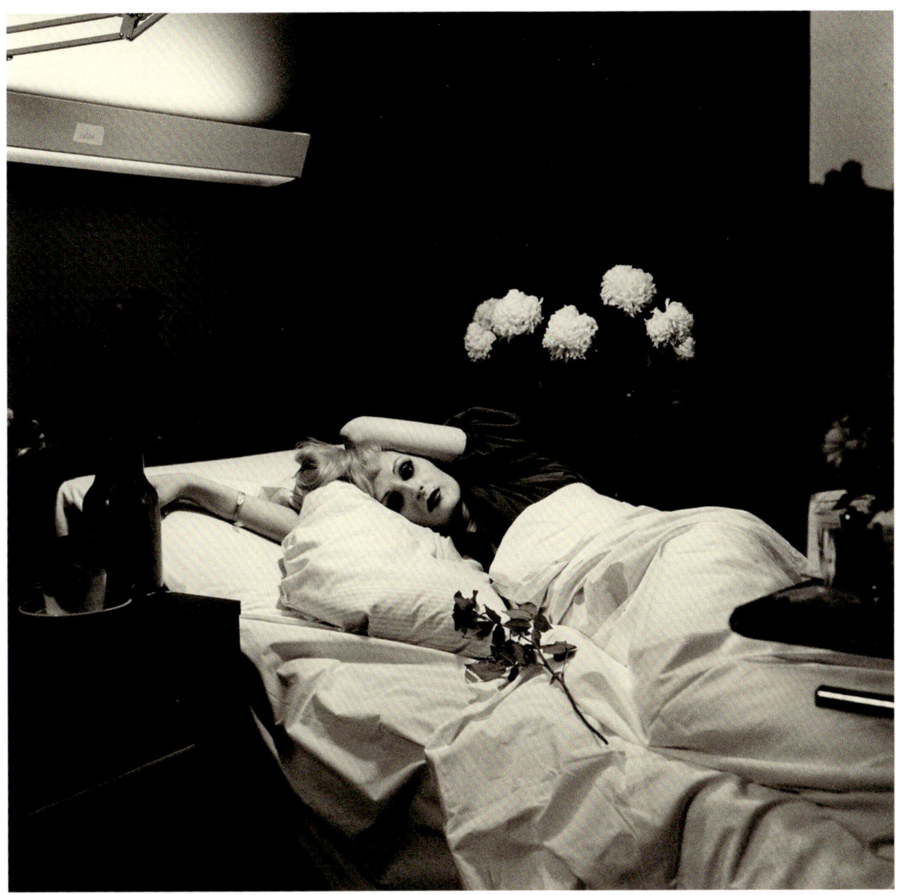

176. Peter Hujar, Candy Darling on Her Deathbed, 1973

Peter Hujar joined two of his key interests in this iconic picture: the specter of death and the juxtaposition of glamour and reality. Hujar made this portrait of Candy Darling, a transgender performer who appeared in Andy Warhol's experimental films, several months before her death from leukemia at the age of twenty-nine. Here, Darling poses in a hospital bed with a full face of makeup, carefully framed by flowers. A single red rose lies next to her as she looks directly at the camera. Her hospital bracelet could easily be mistaken for a gold bangle. Much about the image transcends the functional anonymity of a hospital room—the overhead lighting appears more like a diffuse spotlight than a harsh fluorescent tube.

In a farewell letter to friends, Darling wrote, "Unfortunately before my death I had no desire left for life. Even with all my friends and my career on the upswing I felt too empty to go on in this unreal existence. I am just so bored by everything. You might say bored to death." This final letter reflects much of what Hujar captured in his photograph: the tension between drama and despair and Darling's affectation of stoic resolve in the face of existential hardship. *Grace Deveney*

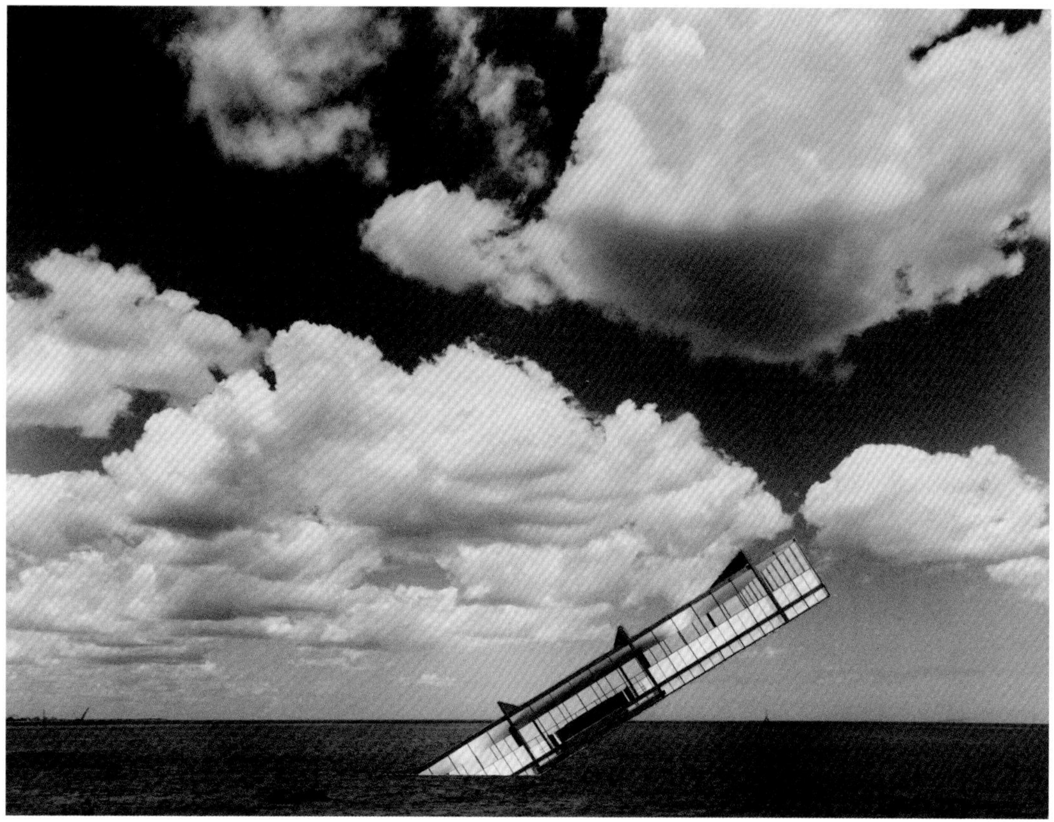

177. Stanley Tigerman, The Titanic, 1978

Despite its catastrophic tone, this photomontage—an analog image that splices photographs together—was designed to inspire authenticity. A well-proportioned building sinks into a placid Lake Michigan, recalling the sinking of the *Titanic* into the ocean.

The year was 1978, and the architect of the sinking building, Ludwig Mies van der Rohe, had been dead for nine years. The creator of this work, architect Stanley Tigerman, remained bereft but fed up. For thirty years, Mies van der Rohe's mute structures, such as S. R. Crown Hall or the 860–880 Lake Shore Drive apartments, ignited the Second Chicago School with their sedate palettes of industrial materials and methods. Like most architects, Tigerman adored Mies's singularity. Yet Tigerman lamented that the zealotry of Mies's acolytes had led to the supercharged commercialization of his legacy, or a lot of bad corporate copies. Is the only way to end a flawed descendancy to sink it?

The image is not meant to task the viewer with envisaging the death of Modernism but rather to challenge the very nature of indoctrination. Tigerman's own work and legacy would aim to do just that, with an irreverent wink to his colleagues. *Thomas Kelley*

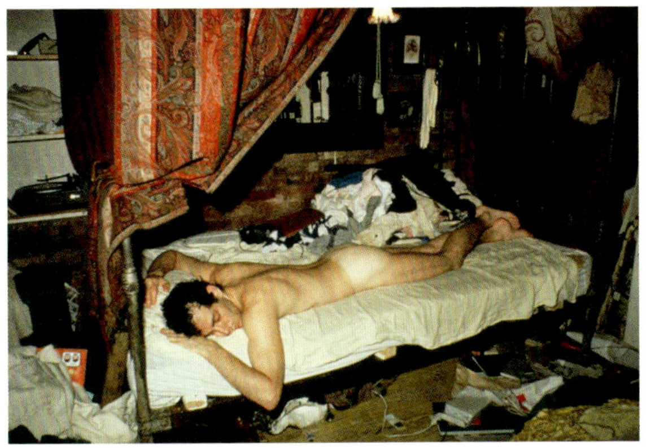

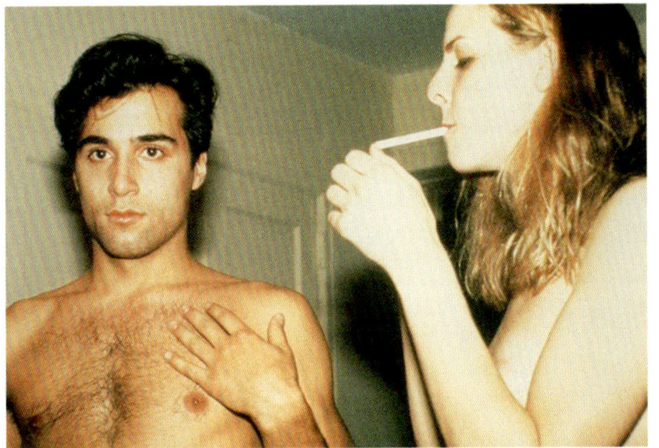

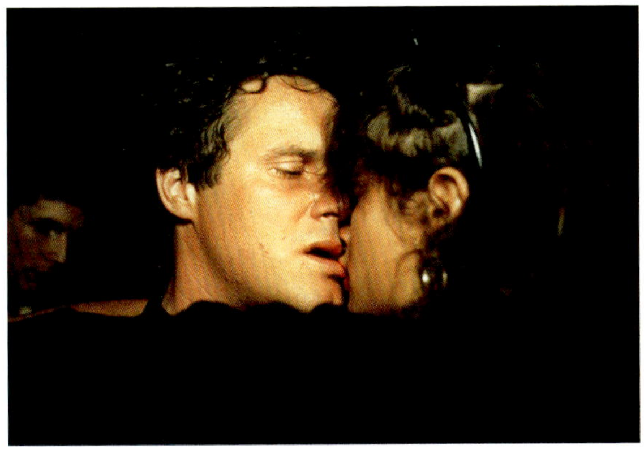

178. Nan Goldin, The Ballad of Sexual Dependency, 1979–2001

For thirty-five years Nan Goldin has obsessively recorded her life experiences, and her slide installation *The Ballad of Sexual Dependency* represents the zenith of this endeavor. A hybrid of photography, film, and installation art, the work projects hundreds of Goldin's photographs in a unique sequence accompanied by a specified soundtrack. Images representing couples, gender roles, dependency, and alienation are paired with evocative songs such as Dean Martin's "Memories Are Made of This." It is appropriate that images of her subjects' fantasies and sorrows should be realized as short-lived projections. Many artists adopted the slide projector as an artistic vehicle in the 1960s and 1970s for performance-based work, and *The Ballad* codifies live presentations by the artist that amounted to performances held for fellow artists in the clubs and cinemas of 1980s New York.

Goldin's pictures, like images of family vacations or holidays, embrace photography's potential for immediacy, emotion, and anecdote. Unlike such snapshots, however, they capture Goldin, her friends, and her family in moments of intimacy—addiction, hospitalization, lovemaking, violence—and depict the rollercoaster of human emotions that accompanies such moments. In this way, *The Ballad* offers a more exposed, and potentially more honest, version of the traditional domestic slideshow. *Michal Raz-Russo*

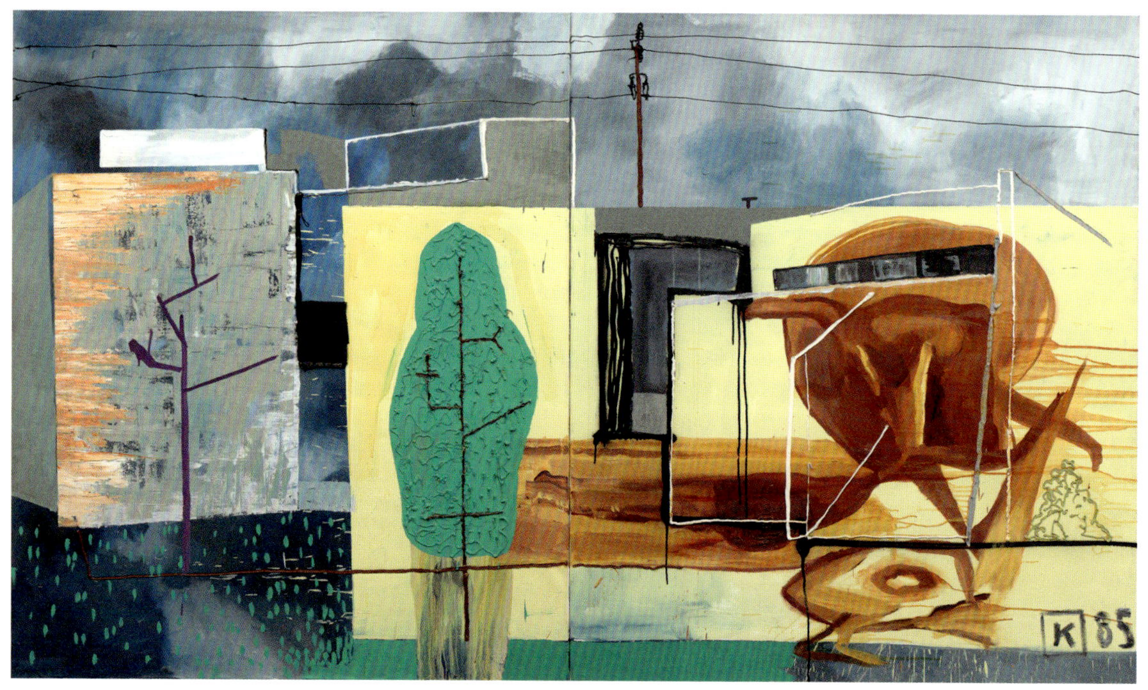

179. Martin Kippenberger, Betty Ford Clinic, 1985

In *Betty Ford Clinic* (*Betty Ford Klinik*), Martin Kippenberger used long, horizontal drips, gestural washes, and impasto sketches of trees and telephone wires to construct a chaotic composition that carries a sense of dread and anxiety. Kippenberger based this image on a newspaper photograph of the then-new California rehabilitation center for substance use disorders. In the mid-1980s Kippenberger painted a series of architectural sites of the twentieth century, including the Guggenheim Museum and the United Nations building in New York as well as a Lake Constance sanatorium and the infamous Stuttgart Stammheim prison in Germany.

In this painting, Kippenberger presented the built environment as a repository for psychic, social, and historical weight. *Betty Ford Clinic* becomes an image whose meaning deepens through association with addiction, retreat, performance, and recovery. Of his promiscuous use of images from every corner of contemporary life, Kippenberger famously once said, "Every picture I see belongs to me the instant I understand it." It's impossible not to feel that here.
Giampaolo Bianconi

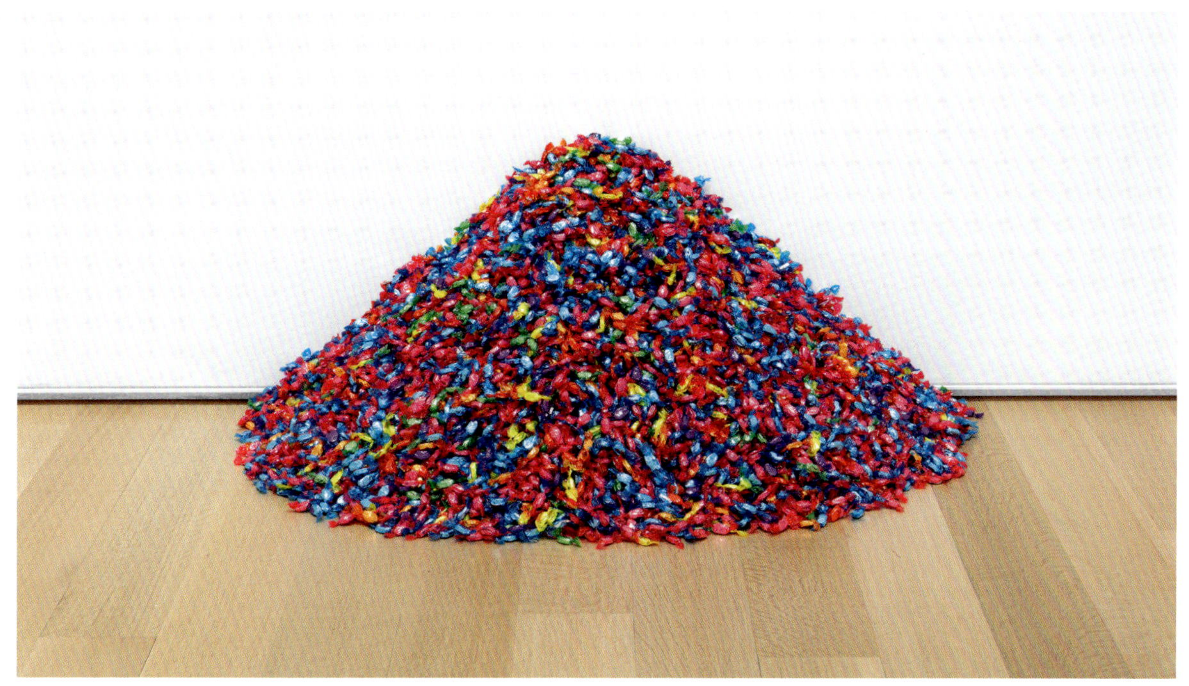

180. Felix Gonzalez-Torres, "Untitled" (Portrait of Ross in L.A.), 1991

Felix Gonzalez-Torres made powerful, poetic, and often mutable work from commonplace materials, expanding the parameters of conceptual and minimal art. He transformed clocks, candy, mirrors, stacks of paper, and strings of lights into open-ended artworks, which shift in form and scale with each installation according to decisions made by their owners, exhibitors, and audience. In this way, Gonzalez-Torres's work embraces contradiction and complexity.

Composed of commercially available candies in shiny, multicolored wrappers, *"Untitled" (Portrait of Ross in L.A.)* has an ideal weight of 175 pounds, and per the artist's parameters, the work can be installed in various configurations, such as piled in a corner or center of a room or spread out across the floor. The work's ideal weight could be a reference to the average body weight of an adult male, or perhaps the weight of Ross Laycock, the artist's partner referred to in the title, who died of complications from AIDS in 1991 (as did Gonzalez-Torres in 1996). Viewers may take candy, thus depleting the supply while literalizing abstract feelings such as pleasure and grief. The work's caption lists "endless supply," suggesting cycles of both regeneration and repetition. *Thea Liberty Nichols*

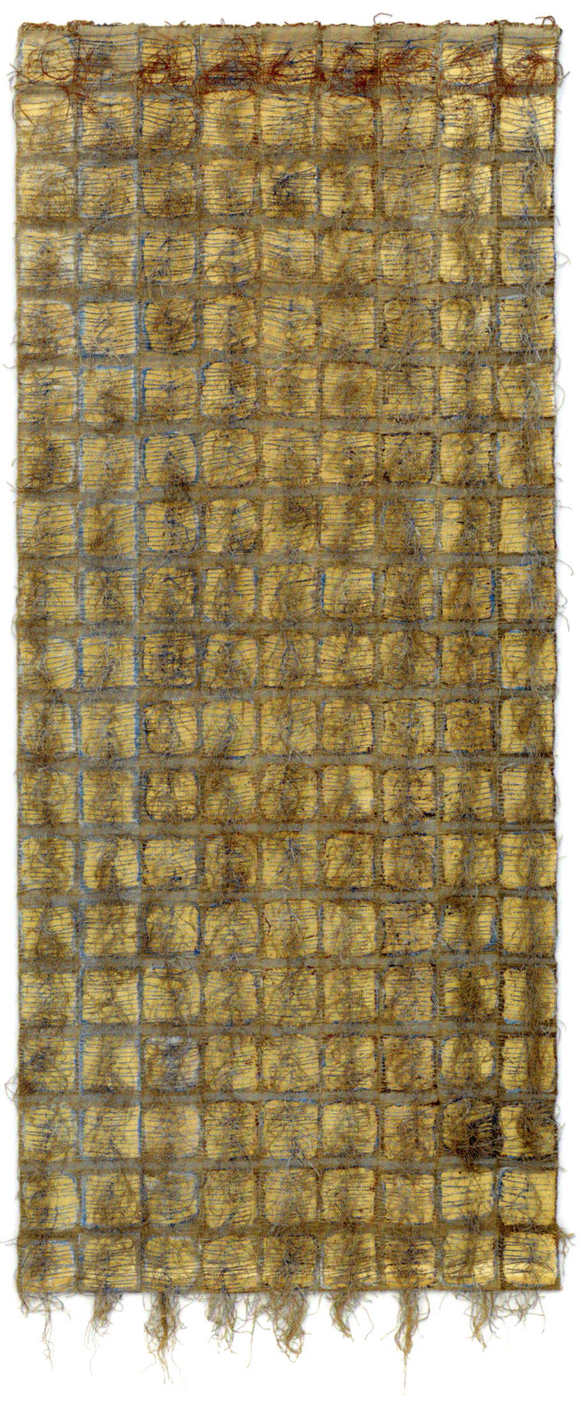

181. Olga de Amaral, Alchemy III, 1983

Alchemy III (*Alquimia III*) comes from Olga de Amaral's largest series: more than forty works that refer to protoscientific attempts to transform cheap metal into pure gold, or more broadly, to purify or perfect elements. In Amaral's hands, simple materials—in this case, linen, cotton, and pigment—are transformed into something of greater cultural value by artistry and the application of gold leaf. In addition to this transformation of materials and value, the Japanese practice of *kintsugi* inspired her. In kintsugi, artisans decorate repaired ceramic objects by highlighting the breaks with gold, thus celebrating imperfections.

Amaral is part of the foundational generation of artists who, in the 1960s, developed non-functional, sculptural textiles that led to the moniker Fiber Art. Trained in architectural drafting, and introduced to weaving at Cranbrook Academy of Art in Michigan in the 1950s, Amaral has created work in fiber characterized by her experimentation in materials and traditional loom-based structures. She has challenged textile conventions by using fibers to create something outside the tradition of "textile."
Melinda Watt

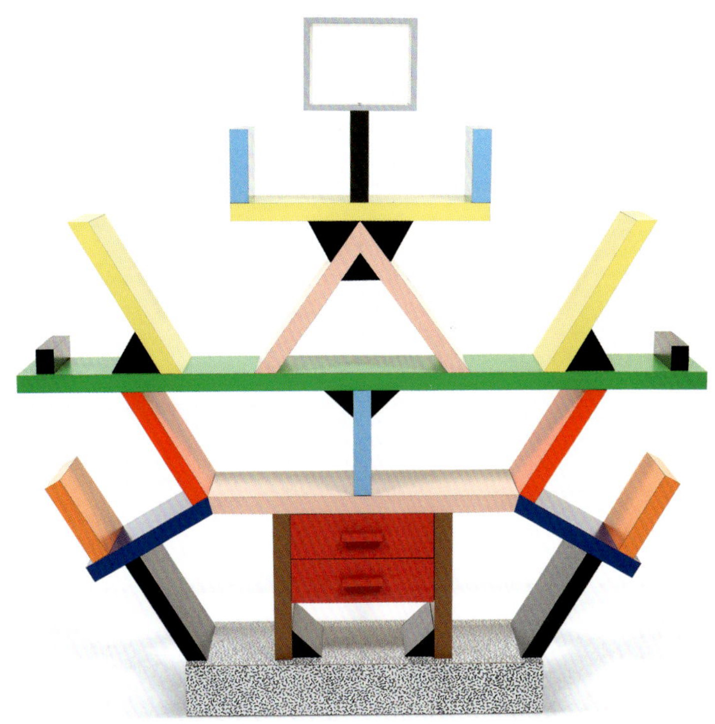

182. Ettore Sottsass Jr., **Carlton Room Divider**, 1981

With its geometric shapes, unconventional angles, and bright colors, the totemic Carlton Room Divider, designed by Italian architect Ettore Sottsass, exemplifies a new, more playful, vision of design that developed in the second half of the twentieth century. Sottsass founded the Memphis Group, a design collective that desired to break free from the perceived self-seriousness of design's past—particularly modernism—with an irreverent and unorthodox spirit. Members produced fashion, product design, and architecture that embraced bold colors, historical references, broken or irregular forms, and rich ornamentation. They deliberately challenged the minimalist principles of modernist design.

A Memphis icon, the Carlton Room Divider features a dynamic arrangement of squares, rectangles, and triangles stacked in a complex system of real or implied equilateral angles. Combining the functions of a room divider, shelving unit, and storage chest, it offers a fresh take on conventional furniture design, acting as both a useful object and an avant-garde sculpture. The divider's slanted shelves, which appear impractical, are designed to prevent books from toppling over. Sottsass conceived the work to be sold at the market's higher end, but he chose materials considered cheap and accessible. Made with medium-density fiberboard and plastic laminate, it highlights Memphis's rebellious and playful approach to design.
Anna Burckhardt Pérez

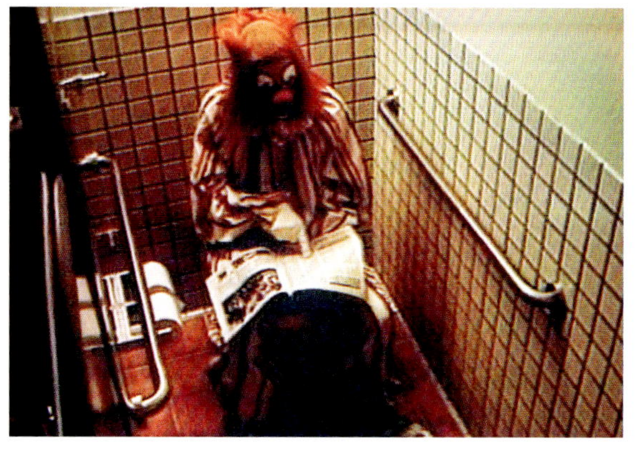

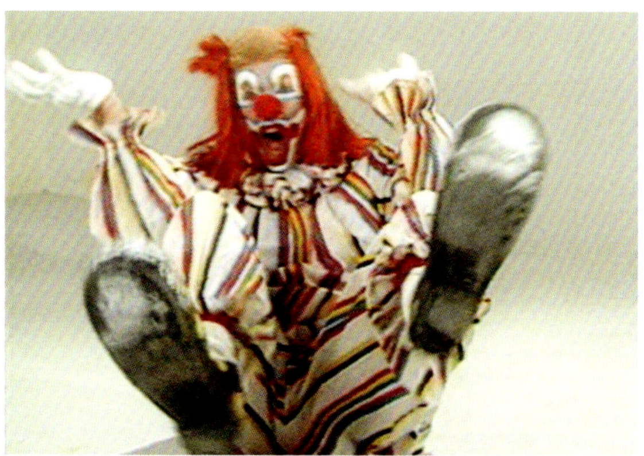

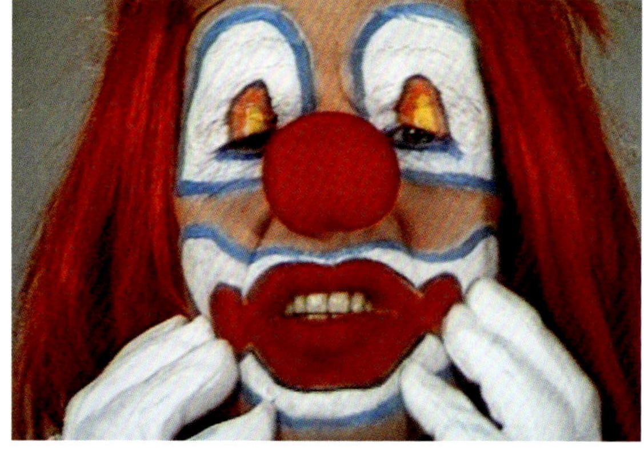

183. Bruce Nauman, Clown Torture, 1987

The compact title *Clown Torture*—hilarity and horror pressed side by side—signals both the emotional range and the sense of collapse or collision at the core of Bruce Nauman's work. The artist prioritized intensity and disorientation over audience comfort. Nauman once vividly explained that from early on, he has tried to "make art . . . that was just there all at once. Like getting hit in the face with a baseball bat."

Indeed, this work's structural complexity also yields sheer cacophony. Two pedestals each support a pair of stacked monitors, two of which are upright, a third installed upside down, the fourth installed on its side. Two projections fill facing walls, and sound from all six fills the gallery space. Actor Walter Stevens takes on multiple clown characters across these screens, doomed to repeat every gag on an endless loop: from unsuccessful attempts to balance a goldfish bowl on the tip of a broom handle to opening a door booby-trapped to douse him with water. In the sole joke-free sequence, the clown is captured off-duty as well, sitting on a toilet but surveilled by a security camera, as if unable to escape the mandate to perform, even in his most private moments. *Kate Nesin*

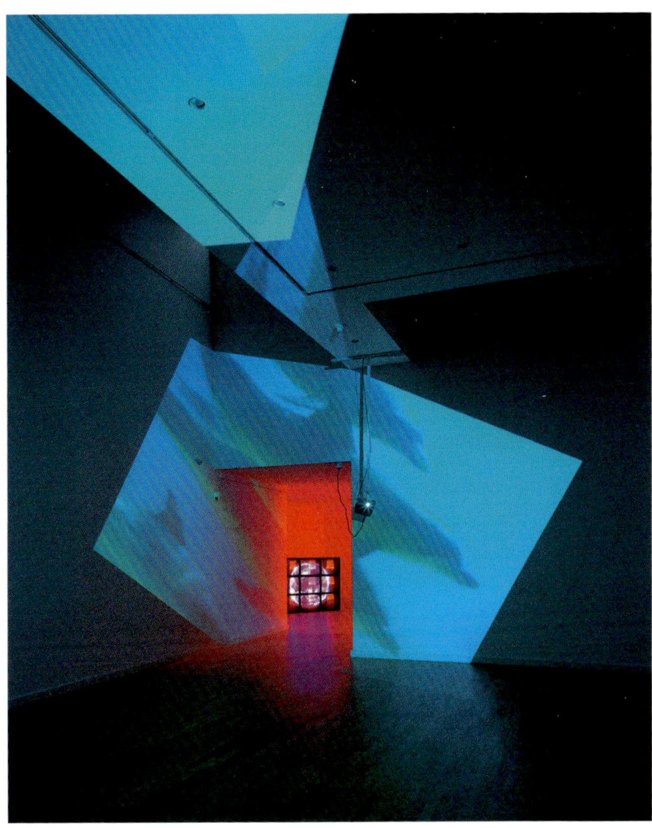

184. Diana Thater, **Delphine**, 1999

California-based artist Diana Thater once observed, "Nature is a screen where we project ourselves. Nature is the ultimate other." In her 1999 video installation *Delphine*, dolphins swim freely—boundless, untrained, and untethered by the expectations of performance engendered in captivity. Thater mirrors this sense of fluidity in how she projects her videos. They spill across architecture, bending and refracting light and distorting the images she has filmed—her work cannot be contained. By rejecting traditional rectangular screens, she creates an experience that defies static observation and draws the viewer into a shifting, multidimensional environment.

Thater sees installation art as a dialogue between sculpture and architecture. Projected at a large scale—onto entire ceilings, walls, and floors—her work dissolves the distance between the artwork and the viewer. *Delphine* compels us to confront our own enclosures: architectural, psychological, cultural. While the dolphins roam freely, we become acutely aware of the human-made structures we inhabit. With *Delphine,* Thater levels hierarchies between species as she disorders conventional ways of seeing. In so doing, she powerfully fosters an empathic way of understanding the world around us. *Annika Bohanec*

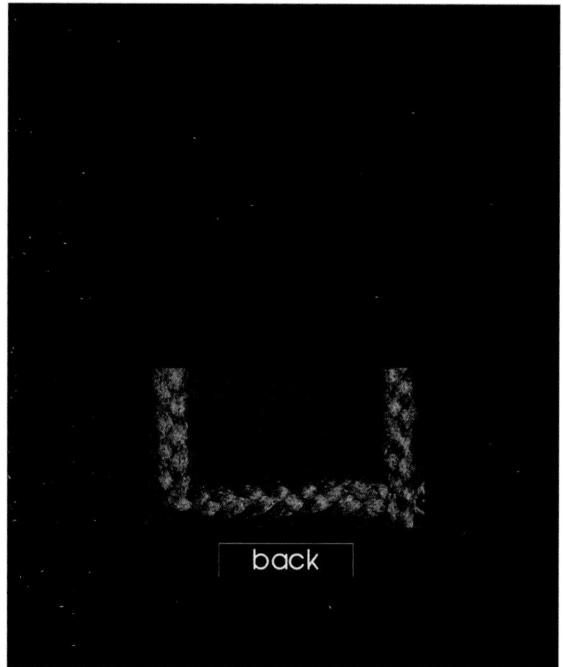

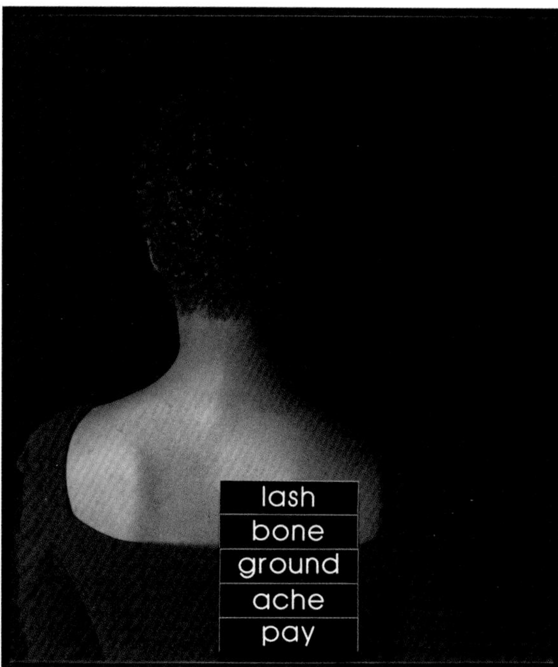

185. Lorna Simpson, Outline, 1990

"What I've tried to do with the photo work is create contradictions—an edge between the subject and the interpretation," said Lorna Simpson. In early works such as *Outline*, Simpson paired large, multipanel photographs with evocative words or phrases that took the place of conventional captions or descriptive statements.

In this work two photographs hang side by side: a braid of hair partially covered by a wooden panel and a Black woman's back emerging from shadow. The words do not describe the images but rather tag them with additional, premonitory imagery. A single word, "back," placed under the hair in the image at left, can readily be joined with those listed under the actual image of a back at right to create a set of compound words: "Lash" becomes "backlash," and so on through "bone," "ground," "ache," and "pay." In this way a subject is shown to be constructed, or pieced together, and seemingly innocent descriptive terms can be composited to conjure a narrative of violence, resistance, suffering, denial, or disillusionment. No such stories, however, are present in the images themselves. By affixing language to photographs, *Outline* distinguishes between the meanings made of text and image and leaves the viewer responsible for refashioning the terms they offer. *Grant Williams-Yackel*

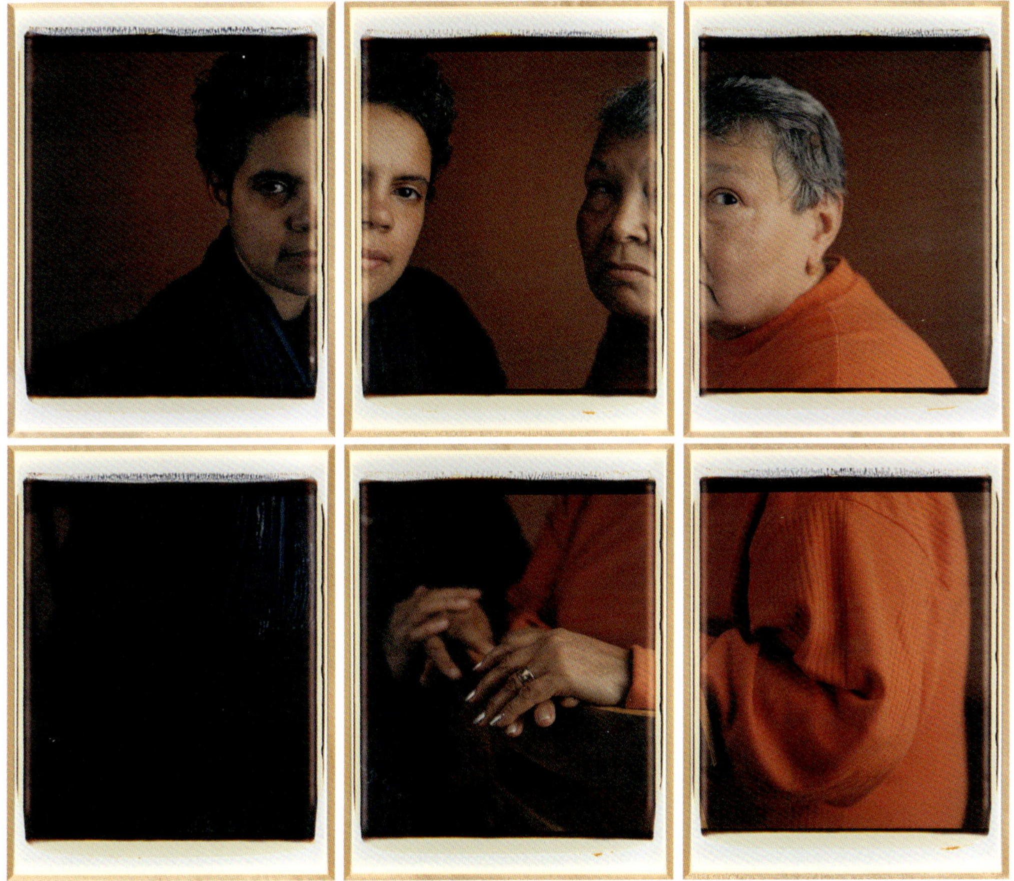

186. Dawoud Bey, Candida and Her Mother, Celia, II, 1994

After seeking out striking strangers to photograph on the street since the mid-1970s, Dawoud Bey brought his practice into the studio in 1991. He looked for lasting relationships with his subjects, and wished to answer a difficult question: "How can one represent time and multiple psychological dispositions in the photograph?"

Candida and Her Mother, Celia, II, epitomizes Bey's new approach. He created this work using a studio and large-scale equipment offered to him by Polaroid, a company that specialized in instant color photography. He lit the two women from one side and centered their hands. Bey then moved the camera lens ever so slightly between frames while the subjects stayed in place. As self-developing images, each photograph became visible nearly immediately, but because of Bey's compositional choices, each print shows only part of his planned picture. The final grid, which Bey constructed after the session, contains six photographs of the mother-daughter pair that compose a fractured whole. Their posture reflects the easy intimacy often found within families while their expressions imply that there is more below the surface of this calm depiction. *Grace Deveney*

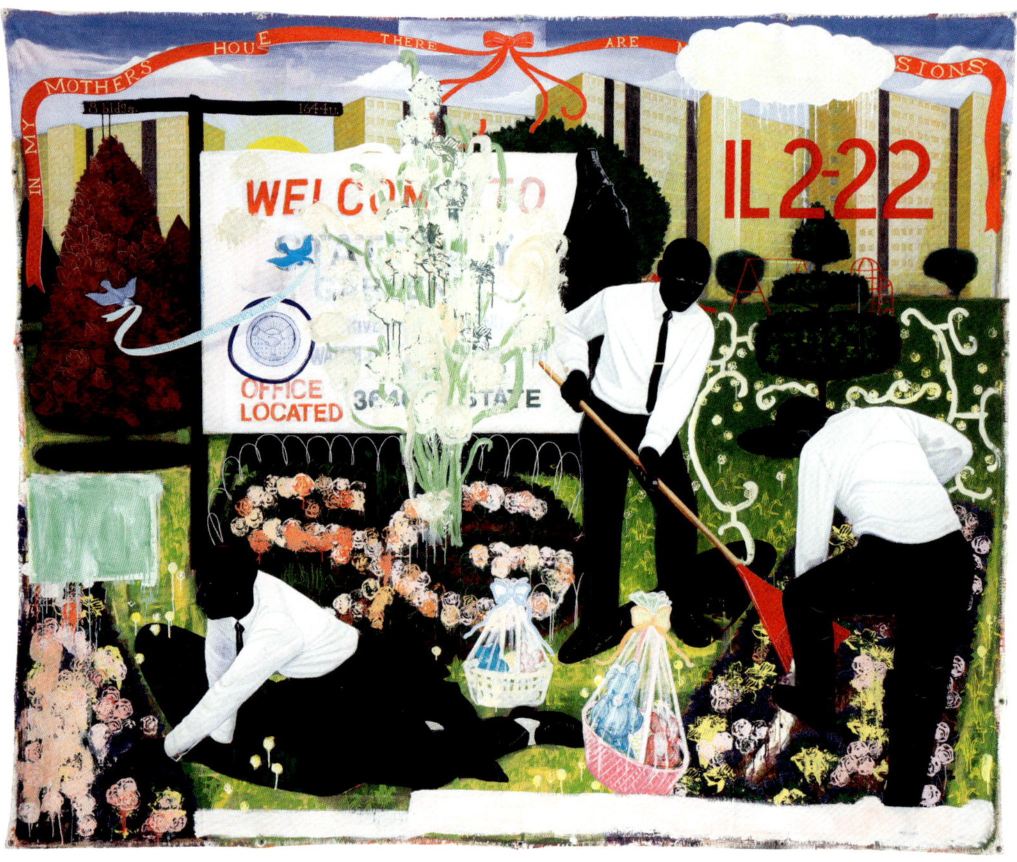

187. Kerry James Marshall, Many Mansions, 1994

The layered canvases of Kerry James Marshall's *Garden Project* series hang unstretched on the wall like tapestries, each featuring a different, idealistically named public housing complex in Chicago or Los Angeles. Chicago's Stateway Gardens—high-rises completed in 1958 and demolished in 2007—form the backdrop for *Many Mansions*, a scene of gardening labor that is also a dazzling array of painterly marks.

This garden is lush, as is Marshall's handling of his materials, from meticulously contoured leaves to caked and dripping blossoms. Three men tend the exuberant growth in immaculate white shirts, their jet-black dresswear matching the color of their skin. Marshall grew up in public housing, and what he calls the "overabundance" of *Many Mansions*—the sky almost bluer than blue—was intentional: "I wanted to evoke some of the hope that the projects started with, but also to demonstrate a little bit of the despair," as utopian ideals gave way to systemic decay. A red ribbon inscribed with the words "In my mother's house there are many mansions" tops the composition, a feminist revision of a well-known biblical line (John 14:2). But notably, Marshall obscures the two words of his title beneath a cartoonishly fluffy cloud, weeping paint.
Kate Nesin

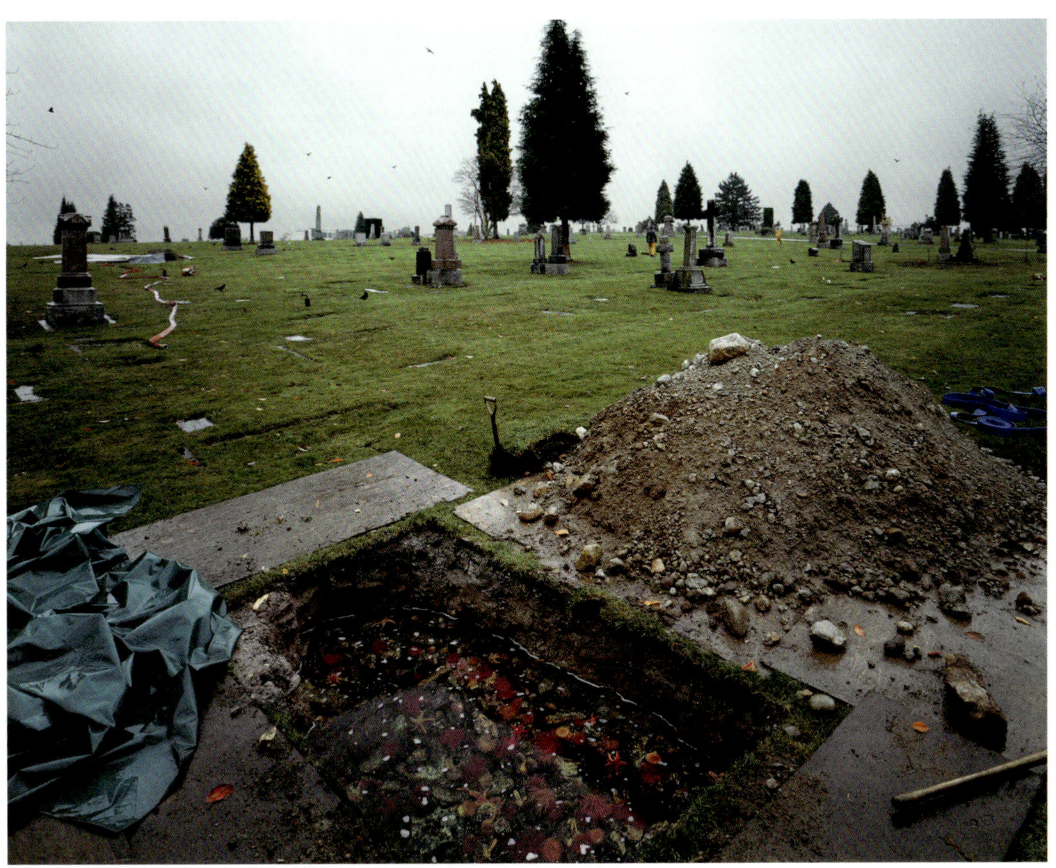

188. Jeff Wall, The Flooded Grave, 1998–2000

The day is gray. The rain will surely start again and interrupt your accustomed ramble. You pause to peer into a freshly excavated grave (a downpour must have sent the diggers for cover?). The hole is flooded, but instead of mud, you see the ocean floor, teeming with aquatic life. You rub your eyes in disbelief.

Measuring some seven by nine feet, Jeff Wall's hallucinatory image owes as much to the art of painting as it does to the technology of photography. The picture's power trades on our expectation that a photograph records a real-life instant, but here the "decisive moment" is wholly constructed, the product of daunting artifice. Twenty-four months in the making, *The Flooded Grave* was shot at two Vancouver cemeteries and required the creation of a made-to-measure ocean floor. Wall took a cast of the slippery grave and then created a tidal ecosystem in the studio, photographed it, and digitally fitted the result to the two-cemetery composite.

The ocean, like the grave, is a metaphor for "the depths," for the subterranean eddies that overdetermine our everyday. The conceit would be a cliché, as the artist has noted, if the stacked metaphors did not compel an utterly riveting picture, a picture that demands we understand it as an allegory of art itself. *Jack Bankowsky*

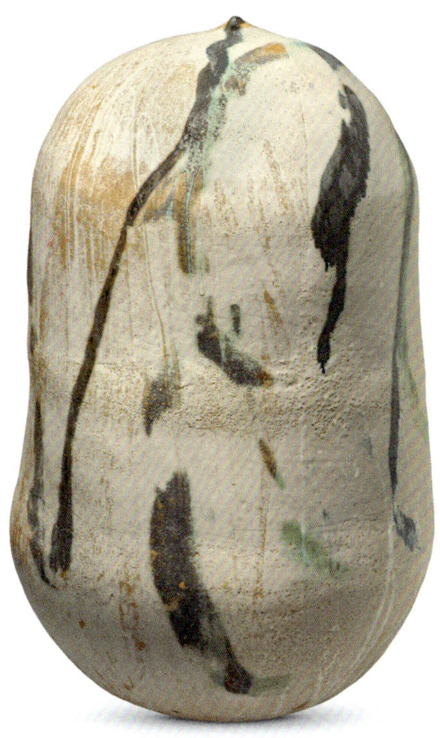

189. Toshiko Takaezu, Dancing Brush, 1990

Dancing Brush shows Toshiko Takaezu's mastery in uniting form and surface into a single, expressive vessel. This hand-built "closed form" serves as both sculpture and canvas, showcasing her belief that glaze and form must become "one total and complete piece." Takaezu applied glaze with the rhythm and spontaneity of a dancer, rotating the vessel in her hands as she brushed sweeping strokes across its surface. In *Dancing Brush*, she layered glazes in fluid, gestural movements, allowing each application to interact uniquely with those beneath it.

To construct *Dancing Brush*, one of her monumental works, Takaezu shaped the base using molds. As she built the piece upward, she "force-dried" the interior using burning newspaper or a handheld torch, a technique that ensured structural stability while allowing her to work at scale with remarkable fluidity and height.

Because glaze colors only reveal themselves after firing, she relied on her intuition and deep understanding of material and chemistry to realize the final form. Unlike other abstract expressionists, Takaezu had to embrace unpredictability, which brought a sense of anticipation to each finished piece, where glazes might fuse, contrast, or shift in tone during the kiln firing.
Darlene Fukuji

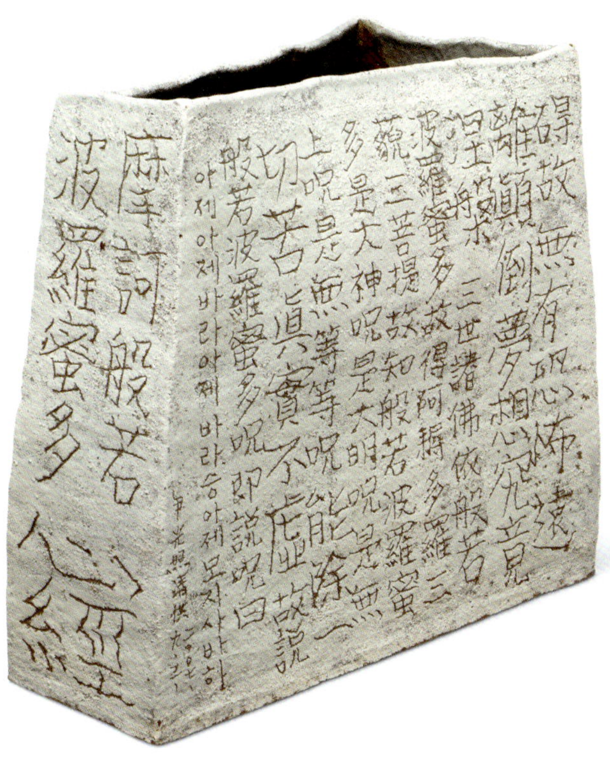

190. Yoon Kwang-cho, Heart Sutra, 2007

Korea's enduring ceramic tradition continues to inspire and be reimagined by contemporary artists. This work by Yoon Kwang-cho was inspired by *buncheong* ware, a grayish-green stoneware decorated with white slip that flourished in the early Joseon dynasty (1392–1897) due to its bold forms and free-spirited decorative modes. After studying at Hongik University in Seoul, Yoon spent a year working in the Karatsu kiln in Saga Prefecture, Japan. During his tenure, he rediscovered the beauty and depth of buncheong ware and became a leading figure in the modern revival of this genre.

Breaking away from the use of the potter's wheel, Yoon pioneered a new approach by hand-building angular vessels through stacking and paddling clay coils. His distinctive sculptural method has opened a new chapter in buncheong ware, revitalizing its expressive, spontaneous nature with a modern sensibility. Yoon's works, though rugged and rustic in appearance, are appreciated for their understated elegance and quiet beauty, often described as "humble yet refined." Engraved on the surface of this work is the Heart Sutra, a revered Buddhist scripture. Each character was carefully inscribed by hand—a contemplative process that Yoon embraced as a form of spiritual practice and personal reflection. *Yeonsoo Chee*

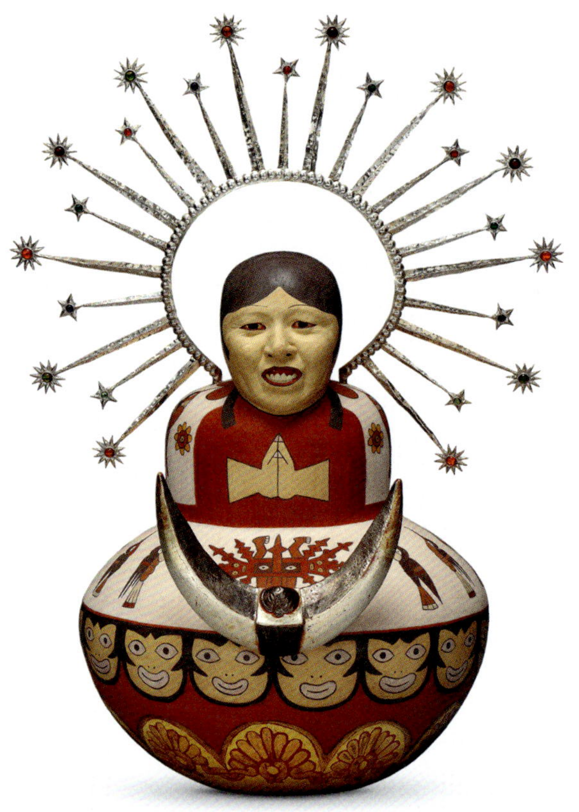

191. Kukuli Velarde, La Linda Nasca, 2011

After the Spanish conquest of the Inca Empire in the 1500s, many Andean people began believing that Indigenous deities were the true identities of Christian figures. Santiago, or Saint James, was believed to be Illapa, the Inca god of thunder and lightning. Santiago rode a white horse, and horses were previously unknown in the Americas. The sparks that sometimes flew from horseshoes when they struck rocks were reminiscent of lightning.

Inspired by this history, artist Kukuli Velarde reveals the famous statue of the Virgin of the Immaculate Conception in Cuzco's cathedral, called La Linda, to be an ancient goddess of Nasca peoples, who lived on the south coast of what is now Peru from around 100 to 600. The figure manifests the Virgin's halo and crescent moon and an array of Nasca iconography including hummingbirds, flowers, and a band of women's faces. While its overall form takes the shape of a Nasca effigy vessel, the sculpture's lifelike face suggests how these syncretic beliefs are alive in the present day. Ultimately, the work explores the dual identities that many modern Andean people may embrace—and in so doing, celebrates Indigenous survivance. *Andrew James Hamilton*

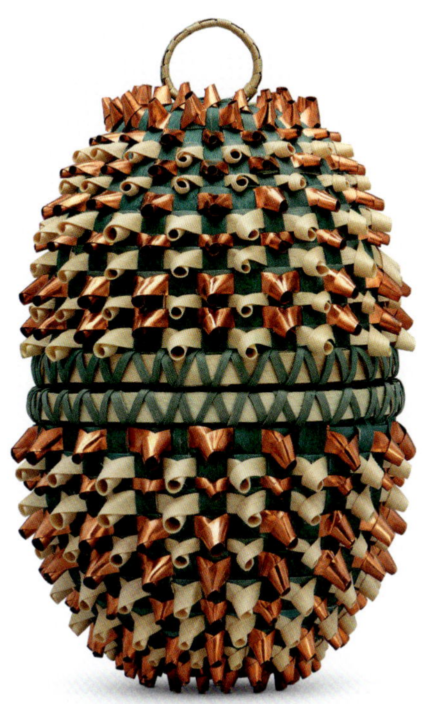

192. Kelly Church, **Sustaining Traditions—Digital Teachings**, 2018

Each spring, fifth-generation black ash basket maker Kelly Church (Match-e-be-nash-she-wish Pottawatomi/Ottawa) sets out to harvest trees in Michigan forests. Due to damage caused by the invasive emerald ash borer (EAB) insect, it is increasingly difficult to find healthy wood suitable for basket making. As an artist, teacher, and Anishinaabe culture keeper, Church is committed to the survival of her millennia-old practice. She embeds black ash teachings within her works, including *Sustaining Traditions—Digital Teachings*.

This small basket delights with its rich green hues, delicate curls, and striking shocks of orange copper. It also protects and restores. Copper holds sacred power in Anishinaabe life, and the curls lining the basket recall jingle dress cones worn for healing dances. These adornments surround unseen contents: a medicine pouch, an EAB specimen, and a USB drive containing Anishinaabe language instructions for making black ash baskets. Church intends them to be resources for her community, a way to carry black ash basketry forward despite existential threats. In *Sustaining Traditions—Digital Teachings*, Church created a sense of continuity through Anishinaabe language, medicine, and material. Her vessel creates space for tradition in the imagined future, woven as much from memory as from black ash or copper. *Lois Taylor Biggs*

Plains Art in the City

Andrew James Hamilton
and Rhonda Holy Bear

The Art Institute began collecting Native American art over a century ago, and these works continue to inspire Native artists and visitors today.

The Art Institute has stewarded works of Indigenous art nearly since its founding. In 1889 James Ellsworth made a gift of Ancestral Puebloan ceramics to the ten-year-old museum. But following the Chicago World's Fair in 1893, Native American material culture came to be collected by the newly formed Field Museum of Natural History. The Art Institute only resumed collecting Indigenous art in the 1950s with the acquisition of the Gaffron and Cummings collections of ancient Andean art.

Beginning in the late 1970s, Father Peter Powell had an outsize impact promoting Native American art within the museum. For forty-five years, Powell lent his personal collection of Plains items to the Art Institute—works such as a Teton Lakota muslin painted with a Sun Dance scene (fig. 1)—single-handedly enabling the museum to represent these important artistic traditions. Powell was an Anglican priest and an adopted member of the Northern Cheyenne who lived in Chicago. "He was a pillar of the Native community," recalls artist Rhonda Holy Bear (Cheyenne River Lakota).

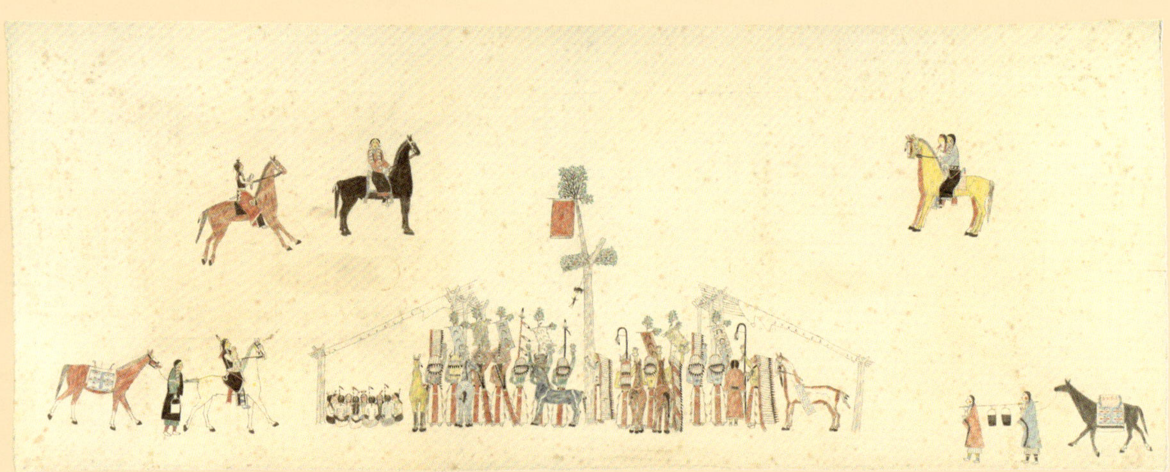

Fig. 1. *Sun Dance Scene*, c. 1885. Teton Lakota, Central Plains or Northern Plains, Wyoming, United States. Pigment and graphite on plain-weave cotton; 91.5 × 232.5 cm (36 × 91½ in.). Gift of the Powell Family in memory of their parents Father Peter Powell and Virginia Raisch Powell, 2023.1391.

Holy Bear first met Powell as a teenager. He became her mentor and lifelong friend as she developed her career, eventually becoming a renowned Native beadworker and sculptor. She wrote:

> *I left the reservation when I was fourteen and came to Chicago. I was first introduced to beading at home on the reservation. I used to watch my grandfather's sister tan hides and do beadwork, and I wanted to be just like her. In Chicago, at the powwows, everyone had beautiful beadwork, but the only way to get beadwork like that was to make it yourself. Louis T. Delgado asked me if I wanted to go to an Indian school in Uptown in the afternoons. There, I could be as creative as I wanted to be, and they had books about art. I would pore over them at home, and those pictures started having an influence on me.*
>
> *I went on a school field trip to the Field Museum, and that's where we saw the old stuff. The outfits were powerful, and it reminded me of the same kind of power I felt at home on the reservation. I just wanted to touch one of those beads, you know, if I could just get behind the glass! In my early twenties, Father Powell talked to them, and I got to go into storage with my camera. After that, I went home and started trying to make little figures with powerful faces, like those of my grandparents, dressed in beaded garments.*

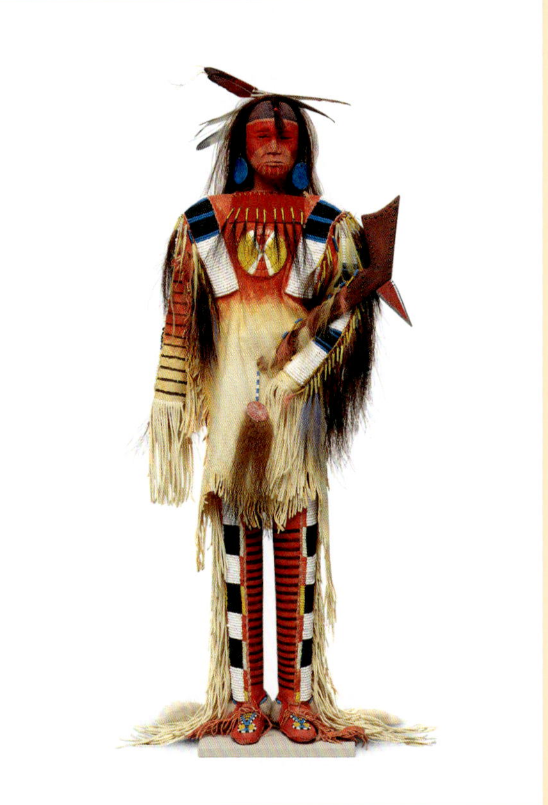

Fig. 2. Rhonda Holy Bear, Wakah Wayuphika Win, Making with Exceptional Skills Woman (Cheyenne River Lakota, born 1959). *Assiniboine Scalp Shirt Wearer*, about 1986. Wood, hide, hair, beads, feathers, and pigment; 46.4 × 22.9 × 12 cm (18 5/16 × 9 1/16 × 4 3/4 in.). Gift of the Foundation for the Preservation of American Indian Art and Culture, 2023.1396.

Father Powell acquired one of Holy Bear's early sculptures, the *Assiniboine Scalp Shirt Wearer* (fig. 2), after she completed it in 1986. The sculpture was based on watercolor portraits of Assiniboine men painted by Swiss artist Karl Bodmer in the 1830s. Powell loaned the piece to the Art Institute, where it was for many years one of the few contemporary works by a Native artist on view.

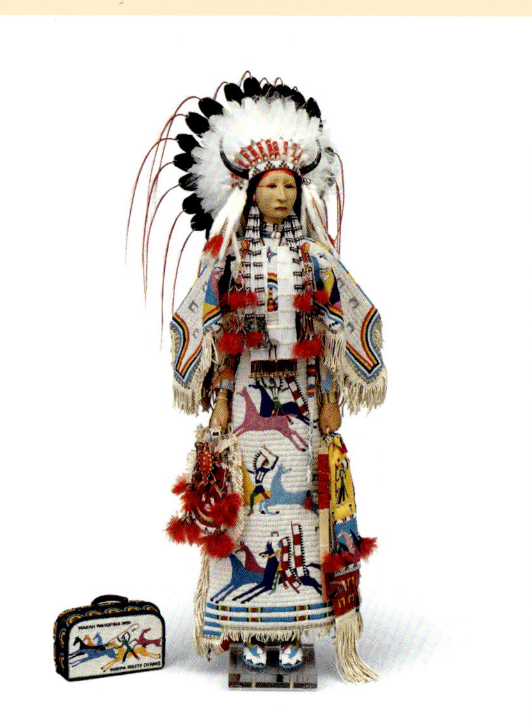

Fig. 3. Rhonda Holy Bear, Wakah Wayuphika Win, Making with Exceptional Skills Woman (Cheyenne River Lakota, born 1959). *Lakota Honor – Sees The Horses Woman – SuWakan Ayutan Win*, 2011–23. Wood, antique micro-seed beads, micro-porcupine quills, metal sequins, catlinite, shell, brass, metal, chicken feathers, hair, paint, cotton, wool, fabric, deer skin, antler, horn, and bells; 67 × 33.2 × 33.4 cm ($26\frac{7}{16} \times 13\frac{1}{8} \times 13\frac{3}{16}$ in.). Rhoades Family and Mrs. Leonard S. Florsheim Jr. funds; purchased with funds provided by Allen Turner in memory of Father Peter J. Powell, 2023.1378a–c.

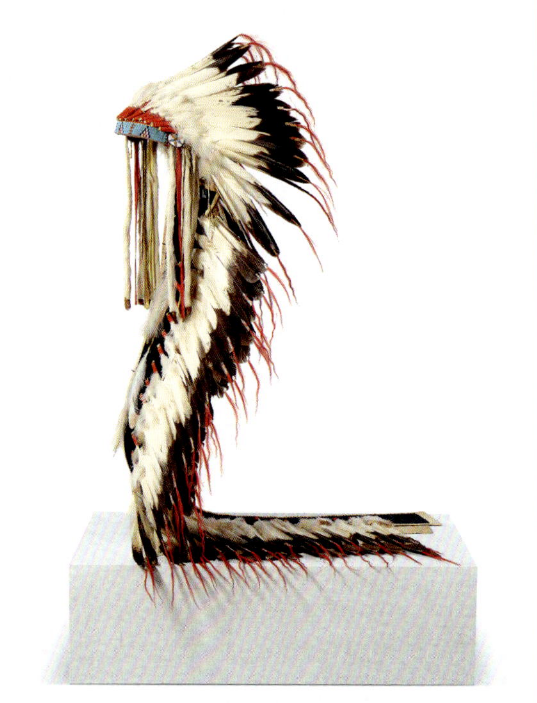

Fig. 4. *War Bonnet*, about 1890. Cheyenne, Tsistsistas, Great Plains, United States. Eagle feathers, wool, ermine tails, glass beads, and silk; h.: 294.2 cm ($115\frac{7}{8}$ in.). Gift of the Powell Family in memory of their parents Father Peter Powell and Virginia Raisch Powell, 2023.1382.

Over the course of her career, Holy Bear has continued to learn from Plains items in museum collections across the United States, teaching herself how to replicate intricate techniques like beading, quillwork, leatherworking, and carving. In 2011 Holy Bear began a very special sculpture, *Lakota Honor – Sees The Horses Woman* (fig. 3), which she modeled on her paternal grandmother, Josephine Sees The Horses Woman. Josephine, born in 1872, had a male relative killed in the Battle of the Little Bighorn. The sculpture wears a war bonnet—like the one in the Powell collection (fig. 4)—that would have belonged to her fallen kin. Holy Bear carefully made the reduced-scale regalia by hand-trimming and painting chicken feathers. She also intricately beaded the dress with images of horses, similar to those on the Powell tipi curtain (fig. 5). It took her over a decade to complete this magnum opus, which she invested with some thirty-two different techniques, all deftly executed in miniature.

When Powell passed away in 2022, his children generously gave his collection to the Art Institute, upholding his legacy of supporting Native art. The museum also acquired Holy Bear's exceptional *Lakota Honor*, with funds in part provided in Father Powell's memory.

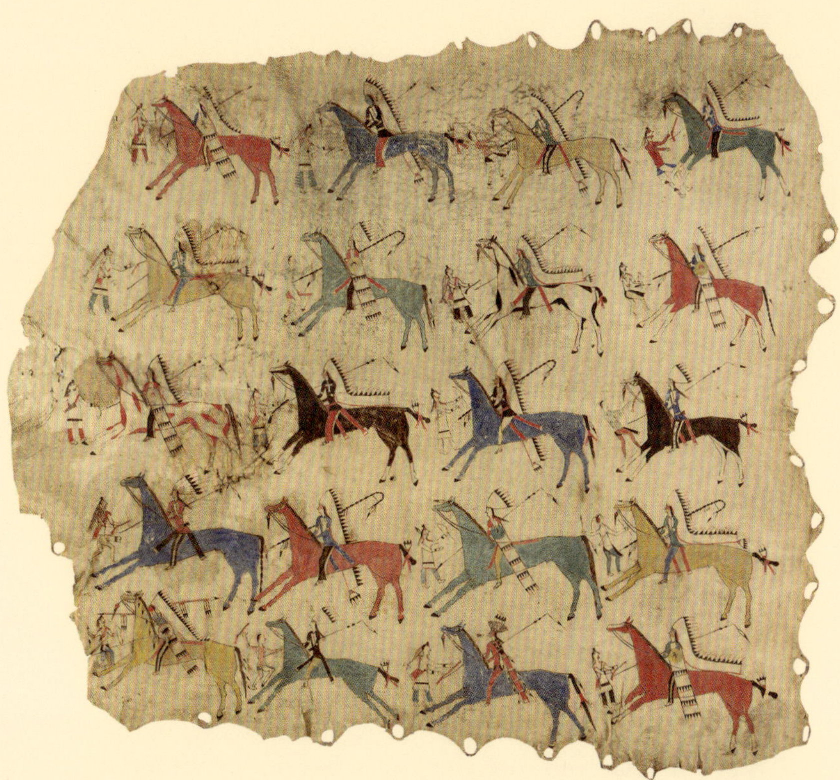

Fig. 5. *Painted Tipi Curtain: Victory Record of the Elkhorn Scraper Warrior Society*, about 1870. Cheyenne, Tsistsistas, Montana or Wyoming, Great Plains, United States. Bison hide, pigment, and stitching; approx.: 221 × 236.3 cm (87 × 93 in.). Gift of the Foundation for the Preservation of American Indian Art and Culture, 2023.1397.

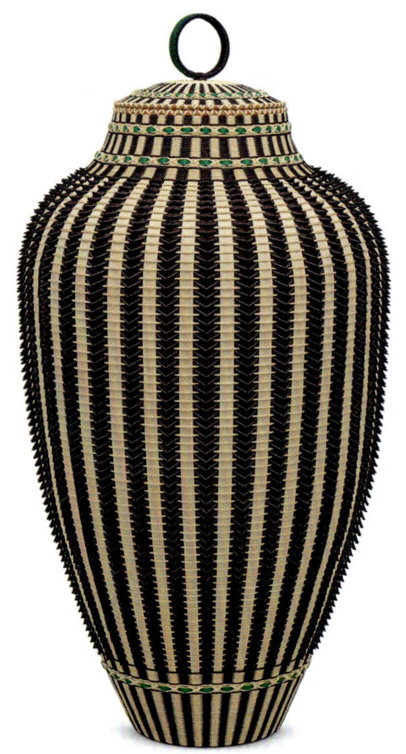

193. Jeremy Frey, Nearly Monochrome, 2022

This basket by Passamaquoddy artist Jeremy Frey is a marvel of technical innovations. For one, in the over two-hundred-year record of Maine Indian basketry in museums, no other artist has ever braided finely gauged (cut) ash wood. Although the technique is a historic Passamaquoddy weave—the braid weaving in and out and crisscrossing with the green bands—artists traditionally used braided sweetgrass rather than ash. The intergenerational transfer of Indigenous knowledge is reflected in the traditional ecological knowledge necessary to complete this masterpiece.

The form, design, and scale of this piece are technically far beyond what Frey's and my ancestors wove. When I first met Frey, the elderly basketmakers who were teaching the new generation of weavers (including his mother, who taught him) were still weaving their grandparents' baskets—styles that dated back well into the 1800s. Jeremy's grandfather wove the ancient pack basket form, woven to fit on a Passamaquoddy hunter's back and in the bow of a birch-bark canoe. Frey innovates from other traditions as well: The finial ring on this basket is from Native Hawai'ian weavers he met at Indigenous basketmakers' convenings.
Theresa Secord

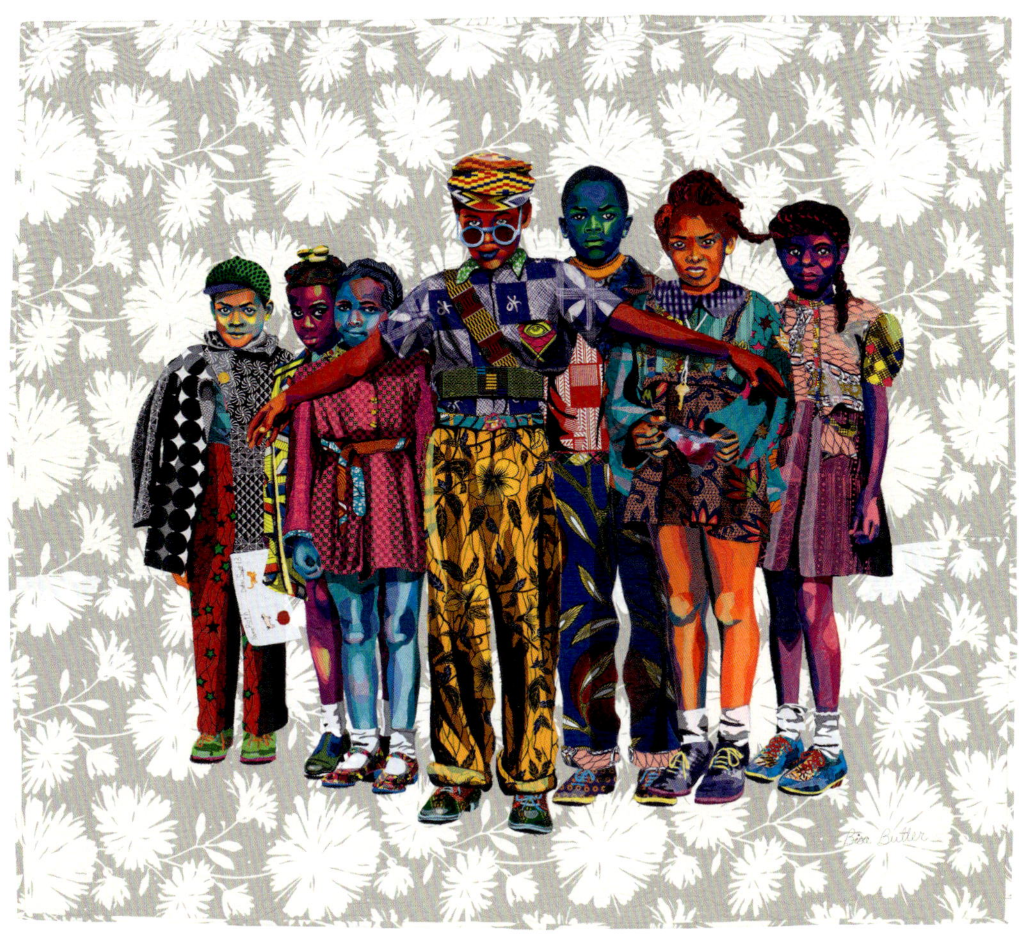

194. Bisa Butler, The Safety Patrol, 2018

As I watched the news of seventeen-year-old Trayvon Martin's murder with my father in 2012, I was stunned that the killer was not even charged with a crime. I was disillusioned, and I said, "What is this world we are living in; how will my children survive this world?" My father said, "Don't worry, Bisa, because the world that is coming will be their world. It is not mine or yours, and they will know how to live in it." This gave me a tremendous sense of calm: There are things too horrific for us to imagine, but our children will be stronger than we are; they will survive.

The Safety Patrol embodies that sentiment: The world that is coming belongs to the young. The safety patrol officer wears a kente cloth sash from my ancestral homeland of Ghana. Kente was originally worn only by royalty on special occasions. He also wears a Nigerian batik-print shirt that says "ok," reinforcing that the children will be safe. The eye on his shirt pocket represents the eye of a god watching over humanity. The children in my safety patrol are not afraid; their youthful enthusiasm for the world is protected by one of their own. *Bisa Butler*

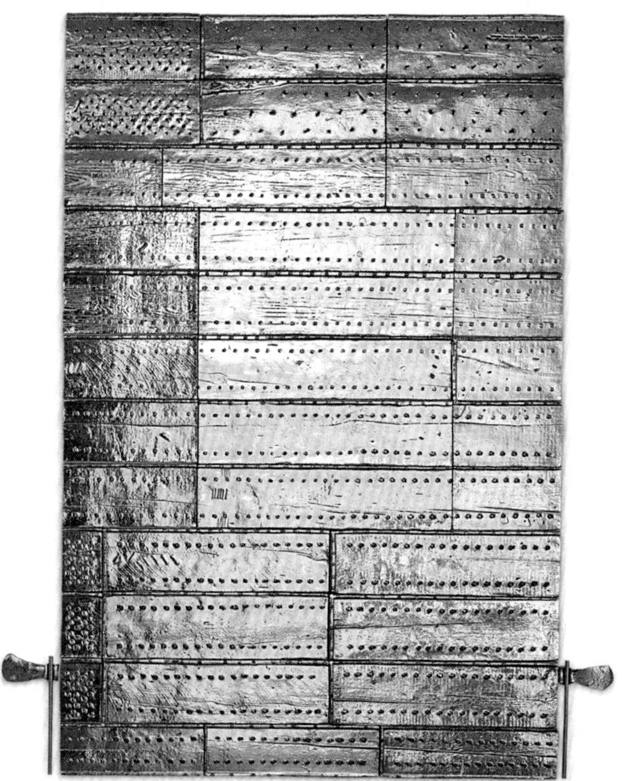

195. Rosemarie Trockel, **Grater 2**, 2006

In *Grater 2*, Rosemarie Trockel transformed the mundane kitchen gadget. She exchanged its handheld scale and metal body for a monumental array of thirty-six ceramic panels. Here, the sturdy becomes brittle, the functional unusable, the domestic assertive—even sinister—and the original object's true nature becomes uncertain. Rows of spikes and seams create a hypnotic rhythm that wavers as spacing and alignment shift. Trockel's handiwork becomes tactile in the glimmering surface, which is marred by the wood-grain texture of timber molds and clawlike scrapes of carving tools. By contrast, the two diminutive axes flanking the composition—tools of masculine trades like logging or carpentry—appear entirely absurd. The threat of their blades is undercut; they hang like the useless arms of an oversize dinosaur.

Trockel rose to prominence in the 1980s in a cultural sphere where women artists were virtually absent. She is known for her omnivorous adoption of materials and techniques associated with "women's work" to unravel gendered assumptions about artistic value, authorship, and labor. Subversion on subversion, *Grater 2* obscures the binaries that define traditional notions of gender, all the while playfully implicating the grater—not simply a tool, but a weapon of sorts, wielded in homes around the world. *Isabel Waring*

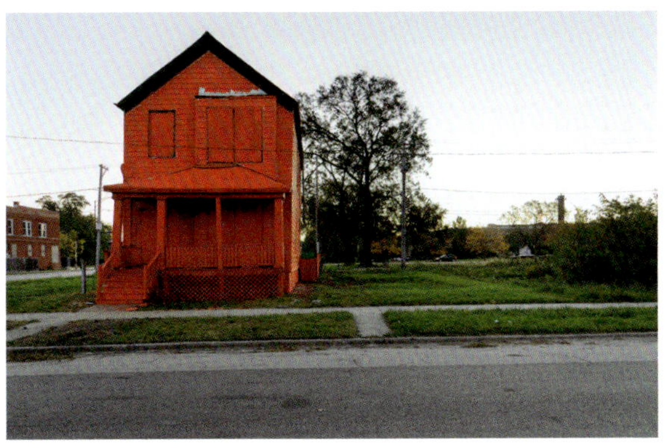

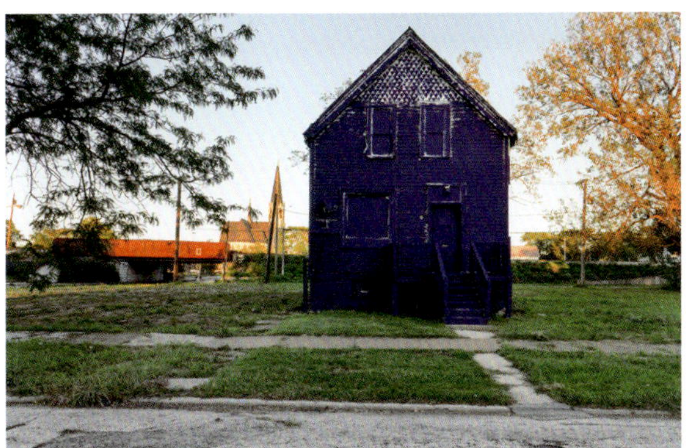

196. Amanda Williams, **Color(ed) Theory: Flamin' Red Hots** and **Crown Royal Bag**, 2014–15

For *Color(ed) Theory*, Amanda Williams painted seven condemned houses in the Englewood neighborhood of Chicago using a color palette inspired by products and services popular in Black communities. Williams painted each house monochromatically—covering doors, windows, and porches—in colors named *Crown Royal Bag*, *Currency Exchange + Safe Passage*, *Flamin' Red Hots*, *Harold's Chicken Shack*, *Loose Squares/Newport 100s*, *Pink Oil Moisturizer*, and *Ultrasheen*. Condemned houses are common on the south and west sides of Chicago, reflecting a long history of under-investment and racist urban policies in African American neighborhoods. A simple coat of paint momentarily transformed them into sites of collective memory and identity. They were ephemeral monuments.

Williams photographed each house before its demolition; these images are the only remaining evidence of her architectural interventions. They are, I think, much more than documentary images: They allow us to imagine Williams at a distinct moment in her artistic process, standing before each large-scale, chromatic object and assessing how it holds space within and against an urban field—vibrant points of resilience amidst blight. The framing of the photographs, which the artist took from the street, also shows how she imagines passersby might encounter each house, stopped in their tracks by a bold stroke of color. *Irene Sunwoo*

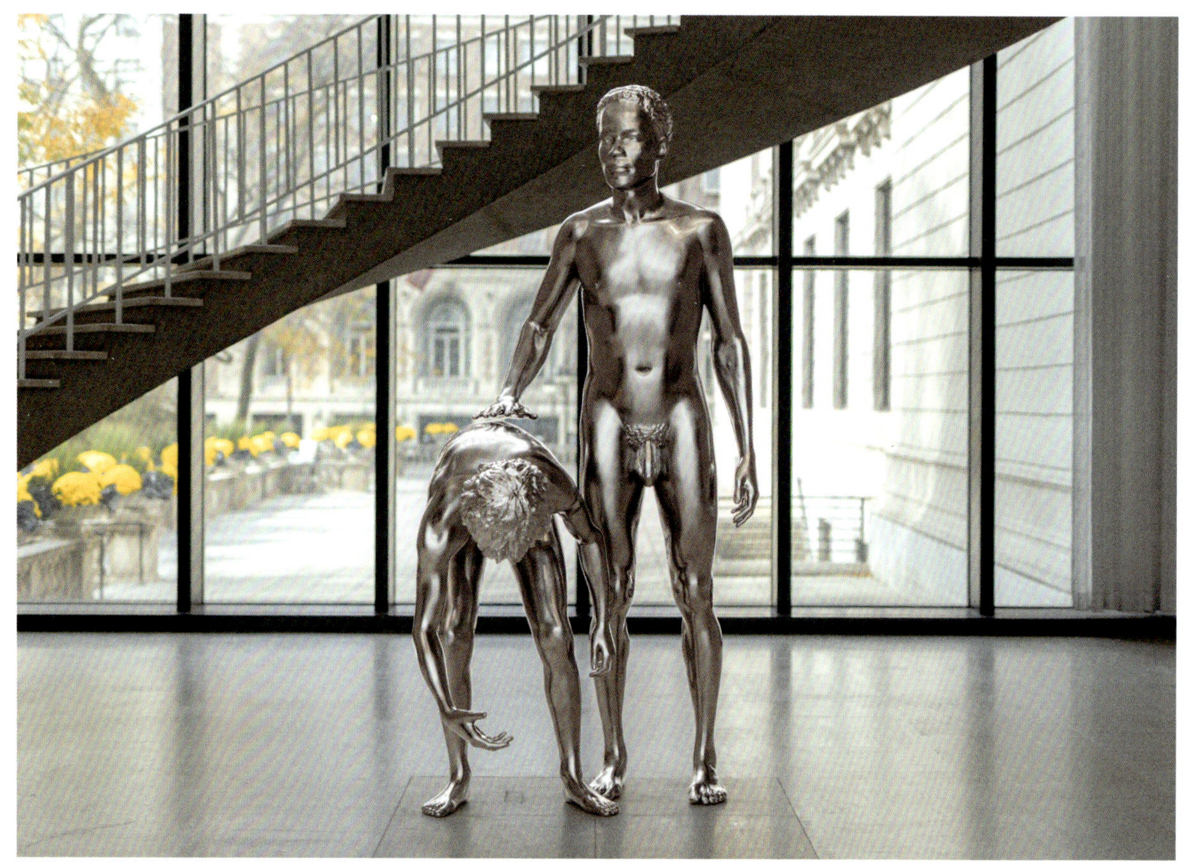

197. Charles Ray, **Huck and Jim**, 2014

By playing with expected scale, material, and subject matter, Chicago-born and Los Angeles–based artist Charles Ray has expanded the field of contemporary sculpture. His monumental work *Huck and Jim* brings the main characters from *The Adventures of Huckleberry Finn*, Mark Twain's 1884 novel about pre–Civil War America, into our present era. In the book, Huck, a white teenage boy, and Jim, an enslaved Black man, travel southward on the Mississippi River in pursuit of freedom—a contradictory journey toward states where slavery was most entrenched. For Ray, the complexity of Huck and Jim's relationship is inherently American, just as the American experiment is defined by, and undermined by, the institution of slavery.

A scene in the novel inspired Ray's sculpture. At the river's edge, Huck and Jim muse about the origins of the universe. Huck compares the number of stars in the night sky with frog spawn in the river's water. Here, Huck grabs at the imagined frog eggs. His hand is empty but full with the eggs Ray imagines. Jim reaches to touch Huck's back, but a gap remains. These moments of absence and negative space are both imaginary and real, as are the figures themselves. *Makayla Bava*

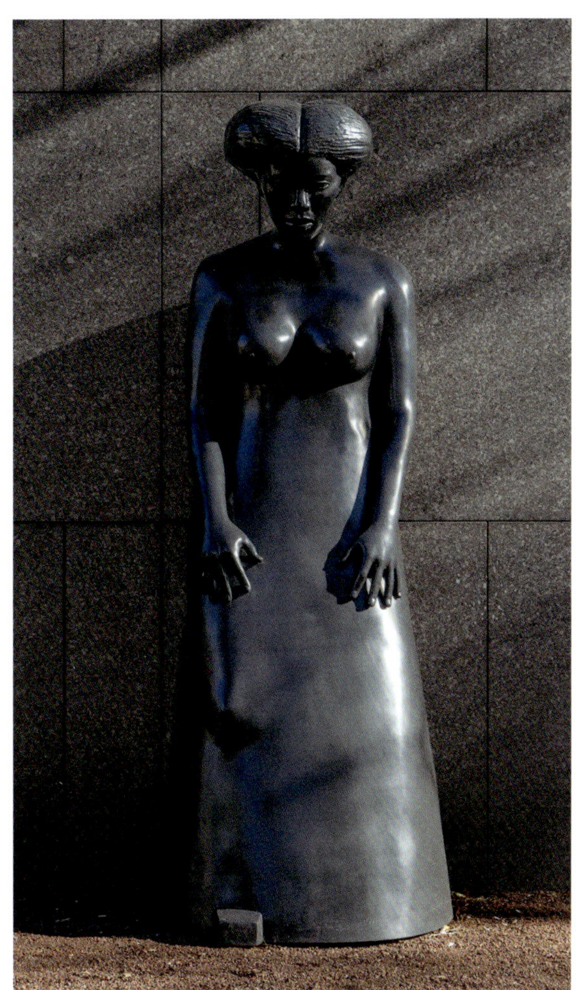

198. Simone Leigh, **Sharifa**, 2022

"Sharifa was just leaning against the wall, thinking, and that was the start of this sculpture. I knew exactly what was going on when I saw this. She was inward gazing." Simone Leigh's work depicts women, abstracted and filtered through the lens of history. *Sharifa* pictures her lifelong friend and collaborator Sharifa Rhodes-Pitts considering a woman's experience of childbirth at Leigh's prompting. Made of bronze and measuring more than nine feet tall, *Sharifa* captures the incongruities of womanhood—only immutable strength enables the vulnerability of introspection.

Leigh considers *Sharifa* her first portrait. While the sculpture carries the physical likeness of its subject, it also communicates the formidability and gravity of Rhodes-Pitts: a historian, a mother, and the author of *Harlem Is Nowhere: A Journey to the Mecca of Black America*. *Sharifa* is an amalgam of gentle curves and straight edges; her presence is architectural, her bearing is intimate. The work also engages the long history of art, most obviously in the way Leigh has positioned the figure's right foot, peeking out from beneath her gown. A feature common to ancient figurative Egyptian sculpture, and later Greek kouroi, the visibility of the right foot counters the literal stasis of sculpture, suggesting forward motion, if only in the imagination.
Annika Bohanec

List of Works

A History of the Art Institute of Chicago (in order of appearance)

Moon Flask (*Bianhu*) with Lotus Scroll and Central Floret, Ruyi Mushrooms and Plantain Leaves, Qing dynasty (1644–1911), 1736–95. China. Porcelain painted in underglaze blue; 49.3 × 37.2 × 20.3 cm (19 7⁄16 × 14 5⁄8 × 8 1⁄2 in.). Gift of Mr. and Mrs. Samuel M. Nickerson, 1900.1353.

Katsushika Hokusai (Japanese, 1760–1849). *Shower Below the Summit* (*Sanka hakuu*), from the series *Thirty-Six Views of Mount Fuji* (*Fugaku sanjurokkei*), about 1830–33. Color woodblock print, ōban; 25.7 × 37.6 cm (10 1⁄8 × 14 9⁄16 in.). Clarence Buckingham Collection, 1925.3244.

Hale Woodruff (American, 1900–1980). *Twilight*, about 1926. Oil on pressed paperboard; 71.8 × 85.1 cm (28 1⁄4 × 33 1⁄2 in.). Through prior bequest of Marguerita S. Ritman, 1993.125.

Achira Root Vessel, 200–450 CE. Nasca (present-day Peru South Coast). Earthenware and slip; 17.5 × 15.2 × 15.2 cm (6 7⁄8 × 6 × 6 in.). Kate S. Buckingham Endowment, 1955.2083.

Marc Chagall (born Vitebsk [formerly Russian Empire, now Belarus], 1887; died Saint-Paul, France, 1985). *America Windows*, 1977. Stained glass; 244 × 978 cm (96 × 385 in). A gift of Marc Chagall, the City of Chicago, and the Auxiliary Board of The Art Institute of Chicago, commemorating the American Bicentennial in memory of Mayor Richard J. Daley, 1977.938.

Andy Warhol (American, 1928–1987). *Self-Portrait*, 1964. Acrylic, silver paint, and silkscreen ink on linen; 50.8 × 40.6 cm (20 × 16 in.). Gift of Edlis Neeson Collection, 2015.126.

Norman Rockwell (American, 1894–1978). *The Dugout*, 1948. Oil and gouache on canvas; 111.8 × 109.3 cm (44 × 43 in.). Gift of The Honorable Bruce V. Rauner and Diana M. Rauner, 2025.608.

Works

1. Statuette of a Female Figure, Early Bronze Age, 2600–2400 BCE. Cycladic; probably island of Keros. Marble; 39.9 × 11.6 × 4.9 cm (15 11⁄16 × 4 9⁄16 × 1 15⁄16 in.). Katherine K. Adler Memorial Fund, 1978.115.

2. Stela of Amenemhat and Hemet, Middle Kingdom, early Dynasty 12, about 1956–1877 BCE. Probably Thebes (now Luxor), Egypt. Limestone and pigment; 31.1 × 41.7 × 6.7 cm (12 1⁄4 × 16 3⁄8 × 2 5⁄8 in.). Museum Purchase Fund, 1920.262.

3. Canopic Jars of Amenhotep, New Kingdom, Dynasty 18, reign of Amenhotep II (about 1427–1400 BCE). Tomb A7, Dra Abu el-Naga, Thebes (now Luxor), Egypt. Ceramic and pigment; each jar approx. 41.5 × 19 × 19 cm (16 3⁄8 × 7 1⁄2 × 7 1⁄2 in.). Purchased with funds provided by Henry H. Getty and Charles L. Hutchinson, 1892.36–39a–b.

4. Bird-Shaped Container (*Zun*), Late Shang dynasty (13th century–1046 BC). China. Bronze; 15.9 × 13.3 × 5.7 cm (6 1⁄4 × 5 1⁄4 × 2 1⁄4 in.). Lucy Maud Buckingham Collection, 1936.139.

5. Coffin and Mummy of Paankhaenamun, Third Intermediate Period, Dynasty 22, reign of Osorkon I (about 924–889 BCE). Thebes (now Luxor), Egypt. Cartonnage, gold leaf, pigment, and mummified human remains; 170.2 × 43.2 × 31.7 cm (67 × 17 × 12 1⁄2 in.). W. Moses Willner Fund, 1910.238.

6. Attributed to the Varrese Painter. Container for Bathwater (*Loutrophoros*), 350–340 BCE. Greek; Apulia, Italy. Terracotta, red-figure; 88 × 37.5 × 26 cm (34 3⁄4 × 14 3⁄4 × 10 1⁄4 in.). Katherine K. Adler Memorial Fund, 1984.9.

7. Architectural Relief Depicting the Gigantomachy (Battle Between Gods and Giants), 3rd–2nd century BCE. Etruscan. Terracotta and pigment including Egyptian blue; 45.8 × 46 × 21.9 cm (18 1⁄16 × 18 1⁄8 × 8 5⁄8 in.). Katherine K. Adler Memorial Fund, 1984.2.

8. Sheath with Bird and Feline or Dragon, Warring States period to early Western Han dynasty, 3rd–2nd century BCE. China. Jade; 10.6 × 5.7 × 0.5 cm (9 3⁄8 × 2 1⁄4 × 1⁄8 in.). Through prior gifts of Mrs. Chauncey B. Borland, Lucy Maud Buckingham Collection, Emily Crane Chadbourne, Mary Hooker Dole, Edith B. Farnsworth, Mrs. Mary A. B. MacKenzie, Mr. and Mrs. Chauncey B. McCormick, Fowler McCormick, Mrs. Gordon Palmer, Grace Brown Palmer, Chester D. Tripp, Russell Tyson, H. R. Warner, Joseph Winterbotham, Mr. and Mrs. Edward Ziff, 1987.141.

9. Attributed to the Chicago Painter. Mixing Jar (*Stamnos*), about 450 BCE. Greek; Athens. Terracotta, red-figure; h.: 37 cm (14 5⁄8 in.); diam.: 26 cm (10 1⁄4 in.). Gift of Philip D. Armour and Charles L. Hutchinson, 1889.22a–b.

10. Cameo Portraying Emperor Claudius as Jupiter, cameo: mid-first century, Roman; mount: late 16th century, Italian. Cameo: sardonyx; mount: gold, pearls, and enamel; 7.6 × 5.7 × 0.8 cm (3 × 2 1⁄4 × 11 in.). Gift of Marilynn B. Alsdorf, 1991.375.

11. Portrait Head of Antinous, about 130–138. Roman; Italy. Marble; 31.7 × 31 × 17 cm (12 1⁄2 × 12 × 6 1⁄2 in.). Gift of Mrs. Charles L. Hutchinson, 1924.979.

12. Portrait Vessel, 600–700. Unknown ceramist (Moche); Southern Moche region, North Coast, Peru. Earthenware with mineral slips; 35.6 × 24.1 cm (14 × 9 1⁄2 in.). Kate S. Buckingham Endowment, 1955.2338.

13. Ana De Orbegoso (Peruvian, born 1964). *Neo-Huaco #3*, from the series

¿Y qué hacemos con nuestra historia? (So What Do We Do with Our History?), 2017. Resin and gold plate; 35.6 × 24.1 cm (14 × 9½ in.). Arts of Africa and the Americas Curatorial Discretionary Fund, 2019.1194.

14. (a) Mosaic Floor Panel Depicting a Bound Rooster, 2nd century. Roman. Stone and mortar; 28.6 × 37.5 × 6.4 cm (11¼ × 14¾ × 2½ in.). Gift of Lynn Hauser and Neil Ross, 2024.1011. (b) Mosaic Floor Panel Depicting an Almond Cake, 2nd century. Roman. Stone and mortar. 27 × 27 × 6.4 cm (10⅝ × 10⅝ × 2½ in.). Gift of Lynn Hauser and Neil Ross, 2024.1012. (c) Mosaic Floor Panel Depicting a Fish on a Platter, 2nd century. Roman. Stone, glass, and mortar; 28.9 × 36.8 × 6 cm (11⅜ × 14½ × 2⅜ in.). Gift of Lynn Hauser and Neil Ross, 2024.1010. (d) Mosaic Floor Panel Depicting a Personification of a Season, 2nd century. Roman. Stone, glass, and mortar. 28.9 × 28.9 × 7 cm (11⅜ × 11⅜ × 2¾ in.). Gift of Lynn Hauser and Neil Ross, 2024.1016.

15. Relief of a Falling Warrior, 2nd century. Roman; Piraeus, Greece. Marble; 53.3 × 81 × 17.5 cm (21 × 31 15⁄16 × 6⅞ in.). Gift of Alfred E. Hamill, 1928.257.

16. Curtain, 6th century. Byzantine; Egypt. Linen and wool; plain and tapestry weaves with supplementary wefts; 192.5 × 142.3 cm (75¾ × 56 in.). Belle M. Borland and Christa C. Mayer Thurman Textile endowment funds; Textiles Discretionary Fund, 2022.1833.

17. Bodhisattva, Tang dynasty (618–907), about 725–50. China. Limestone with traces of polychromy; 157.5 × 78.1 cm (62 × 30¾ in.); Diam.: 78.1 cm (30¾ in.). Lucy Maud Buckingham Collection, 1930.84a.

18. Coin (Solidus) of Empress Irene, 797–802. Byzantine; minted in Constantinople. Gold; diam.: 2.2 cm (⅞ in.). Gift of the Classical Art Society, 2014.9.

19. Tunic, 600–800. Wari; Atarco, Nazca valley, South Coast, Peru. Cotton and wool (camelid), single interlocking tapestry weave; neck and armholes finished in wool (camelid); seams joined with wool (camelid) in darning stitches; 109.9 × 119.7 cm (43¼ × 47⅛ in.). Kate S. Buckingham Endowment, 1955.1784.

20. Aj Maxam (Maya; Vicinity of Naranjo, Petén region, Guatemala). Vessel with Dancing Maize Gods, 780–810. Earthenware and pigment; 24 × 15.8 cm (9½ × 6¼ in.). Ethel T. Scarborough Fund, 1986.1081.

21. Plum Vase (*Maebyeong*), Goryeo dynasty (918–1392), late 12th century. Korea. Stoneware with red and white slip and celadon glaze; 33 × 19.7 cm (13 × 7¾ in.). Gift of Mr. Russell Tyson, 1950.1626.

22. Duck-Shaped Ewer with Daoist Priest, Goryeo dynasty (918–1392), 12th century. Korea. Stoneware with celadon glaze; 21.4 × 17.7 × 13.2 cm (8½ × 7 × 5½ in.). Bequest of Russell Tyson, 1964.1213.

23. Standing Buddha, Pagan period (11th–13th centuries), about 12th century. Pagan, Burma (now Bagan, Myanmar). Bronze inlaid with silver; 47.4 × 21.5 × 10.1 cm (18 11⁄16 × 8½ × 4 in.). Gift of Marilynn B. Alsdorf, 2016.106.

24. Reliquary Casket of Saints Adrian and Natalia, 1100–50. Léon, Spain. Silver and oak core; 15.9 × 25.4 × 14.5 cm (6¼ × 10 × 5¾ in.). Kate S. Buckingham Endowment, 1943.65.

25. Head of an Apostle, about 1210. French; Paris. Limestone; h.: 43 cm (17 in.). Kate S. Buckingham Endowment, 1944.413.

26. Bishamon, 11th century. Japan. Wood with traces of polychromy; h. approx. 135 cm (52¾ in.). Robert Allerton Endowment, 1968.145.

27. Buddha Shakyamuni Seated in Meditation (*Dhyanamudra*), Chola period (about 855–1279), about 12th century. Nagapattinam, Tamil Nadu, India. Granite; 160 × 120.2 × 56.3 cm (63 × 47 5⁄16 × 22 3⁄16 in.). Restricted gift of Mr. and Mrs. Robert Andrew Brown, 1964.556.

28. Painted Banner (*Thangka*) of the Medicine Buddha (Bhaishajyaguru), 1300s. Central Tibet. Pigment and gold on cotton; 104 × 82.7 cm (41 × 32½ in.). Kate S. Buckingham Fund, 1996.29.

29. Moon Flask (*Bianhu*), Ming dynasty (1368–1644), Yongle period (1403–24). Porcelain painted with underglaze blue; 28.9 × 23.8 × 14 cm (11⅜ × 9⅜ × 5⅜ in.). Through prior gifts of Mr. and Mrs. Samuel M. Nickerson and other generous supporters, 2021.30.

30. Altarpiece of the Virgin and Child, 1460–70. Spain, El Burgo de Osma. Linen plain weave ground appliquéd with linen and silk plain weaves and silk velvet; embroidered with silk floss and creped threads, gilt- and-silvered-metal-strip-wrapped silk threads, seed pearls and metal spangles; retable (a): 167 × 203.5 cm (65¾ × 80⅛ in.); altar frontal (b): 89.2 × 211.8 cm (35⅛ × 83⅜ in.). Gift of Mrs. Chauncey McCormick and Mrs. Richard Ely Danielson, 1927.1779a–b.

31. Bernat Martorell (Spanish, active from 1427–died 1452). *Saint George and the Dragon*, 1434–35. Tempera on panel; 155.6 × 98.1 cm (61¼ × 38⅝ in.). Gift of Mrs. Richard E. Danielson and Mrs. Chauncey McCormick, 1933.786.

32. Niclaus Gerhaert (Netherlandish, active in Germany, 1462–1473) and Workshop. Reliquary Bust of Saint Margaret of Antioch, about 1470. Wood with traces of 19th-century polychromy; 50.8 × 45.5 × 29.6 cm (20 × 18 × 11⅝ in.). Kate S. Buckingham Endowment, 1943.1001.

33. Giovanni di Paolo (Italian, 1398–1482). *The Beheading of Saint John the Baptist*, 1455–60. Tempera on panel; 68.6 × 39.1 cm (27 × 15 3/8 in.). Mr. and Mrs. Martin A. Ryerson Collection, 1933.1014.

34. *Man of Sorrows*, 1465–70. Germany. Woodcut hand-colored with brush and watercolor on cream laid paper, edge-mounted to vellum, laid down on wooden book cover covered in hand-tooled leather with tooled metal hinges; 40.5 × 26.9 cm (16 × 10 5/8 in.). Waller Fund; gifts of Mrs. Tiffany Blake, Thomas E. Donnelley, Emil Eitel, Carolyn Morse Ely, Alfred E. Hamill, Frank B. Hubachek, Monarch Leather, and Mrs. Potter Palmer, 1947.731.

35. Jean Hey (Master of Moulins) (Netherlandish, about 1480–about 1504). *The Annunciation*, 1490–95. Oil on panel; 72.5 × 50.1 cm (28 1/2 × 19 11/16 in.). Mr. and Mrs. Martin A. Ryerson Collection, 1933.1062.

36. Medallion, probably Margaret of Lorraine (front); the Virgin Seated on a Throne Before Two Widows (back), about 1530–40. Attributed to Léonard Limosin (born France, about 1505–about 1577). Painted enamel on copper; diam.: 8.8 cm (3 7/16 in.) The Helmuth Bartsch and Neville and John H. Bryan endowment funds, 2019.1181.

37. Correggio (Antonio Allegri; Italian, 1489–1534). *Virgin and Child with the Young Saint John the Baptist*, about 1515. Oil on panel; 64.2 × 50.2 cm (25 1/4 × 19 3/4 in.). Clyde M. Carr Fund, 1965.688.

38. *Coronation Stone of Moctezuma Xocoyotzin*, about 1503. Mexica (Aztec), probably Tenochtitlan (present-day Mexico City). Basalt; 67.4 × 57.8 × 22.9 cm (26 1/2 × 22 3/4 × 9 in.). Major Acquisitions Fund, 1990.21.

39. Casket, about 1595. Venice, Italy. Rock crystal, ebony, rosewood, walnut, silver gilt, paint, varnish, and glass; 30 × 41 × 31.1 cm (11 3/4 × 16 1/8 × 12 1/4 in.). Kate S. Buckingham Endowment Fund; Paul H. Leffmann and Chester D. Tripp Major Acquisition funds; Mary Waller Langhorne and Harry and Maribel G. Blum endowment funds; Irish Gala and Harry A. Root and Curtis Chapin Palmer European Decorative Arts purchase funds; Gladys N. Anderson Endowment Fund; Richard T. Crane Memorial Fund; Mary Swissler Oldberg Endowment Fund; Decorative Arts Purchase Fund; European Decorative Arts General, Ivan and Jean Plaut, Charles R. Feldstein, General Acquisition, Bessie Bennett, and Mr. and Mrs. Joseph Varley endowment funds; Wendel Fentress Ott Fund, 2019.186.

40. El Greco (Doménikos Theotokópoulos; Greek, active in Spain, 1541–1614). *The Assumption of the Virgin*, 1577–79. Oil on canvas; 403.2 × 211.8 cm (158 3/4 × 83 7/16 in.). Gift of Nancy Atwood Sprague in memory of Albert Arnold Sprague, 1906.99.

41. *The Ascent of the Prophet to Heaven*, page from the *Khamsa* of Nizami, Safavid dynasty (1501–1722), about 1600. Iran. Opaque watercolor, gold, and ink on paper; image: 26.7 × 18.4 cm (10 1/2 × 7 1/4 in.); paper: 35.4 × 24 cm (14 × 9 7/16 in.). Lucy Maud Buckingham Collection, 1934.116.

42. Giuseppe Cesari, called Il Cavaliere d'Arpino (Italian, 1568–1640). *An Angel in Flight*, about 1599–1600. Black chalk with red chalk on cream laid paper; 39.7 × 35.5 cm (15 11/16 × 14 in.). The Harry B. and Bessie K. Braude Memorial Endowment Fund, 2021.414.

43. Tankard (*Hanap*) with Tulips, Hyacinths, Roses, and Carnations, Ottoman dynasty (1299–1923), late 1500s. Iznik, Turkey. Iznik ware, fritware with underglaze painting in blue, turquoise, red, and black; 19.6 × 15 × 10.5 cm (7 3/4 × 5 7/8 × 4 1/8 in.). Mary Jane Gunsaulus Collection, 1913.342.

44. Peter Paul Rubens (Flemish, 1577–1640). *The Holy Family with Saints Elizabeth and John the Baptist*, about 1615. Oil on panel; 114.5 × 91.5 cm (45 1/8 × 36 in.). Major Acquisitions Fund, 1967.229.

45. Giovanni Benedetto Castiglione (Italian, 1609–1664). *The Creation of Adam*, about 1645–50. Monotype in black ink on ivory laid paper; 30.3 × 20.3 cm (11 15/16 × 8 in.). Gift of an anonymous donor; purchased with funds provided by Dr. William D. and Sara R. Shorey, and Mr. and Mrs. George B. Young, 1985.1113.

46. Francesco Mochi (Italian, 1580–1654). *Bust of a Youth (Saint John the Baptist)*, 1630–40. Marble on variegated black marble socle; 40.5 × 33 × 29 cm (15 7/8 × 13 × 11 3/8 in.). From the collection of the estate of Federico Gentili di Giuseppe; purchased with funds provided by Mrs. Harold T. Martin through the Antiquarian Society; Major Acquisitions Centennial Endowment; through prior gift of Arthur Rubloff; European Decorative Arts Purchase Fund, 1989.1.

47. Cup in the Form of a Horse and Rider, 1630. Hans Ludwig Kienle (born Ulm, Germany, 1591–1653). Silver and gilded silver; 30.5 × 28.9 × 14.3 cm (12 × 11 3/8 × 5 5/8 in.). Eloise W. Martin fund; through prior acquisition of the George F. Harding Collection; Henry Horner Strauss, Pauline S. Armstrong, Harry and Maribel G. Blum, Tillie C. Cohn, Richard T. Crane Jr. Memorial, Stanford Marks, Michael A. Bradshaw and Kenneth S. Harris, Mrs. Edgar J. Uihlein Art Purchase, European Decorative Arts Capital Campaign funds; through prior acquisition from Albert D. Lasker; European Decorative Arts General, and Mr. and Mrs. Joseph Varley funds; through prior acquisition of the Kate S. Buckingham Gothic fund; Mary Swissler Oldberg fund; through prior acquisitions of the Howard V. Shaw Memorial and Kate S. Buckingham funds, 2003.114.

48. *Prince Visiting an Ascetic During a Hunt*, Mughal dynasty (1526–1857), about 1625–50. Kashmir, India. Opaque watercolor, gold, and ink on paper; image: 26.5 × 15.2 cm (10 3/8 × 6 in.); border: 29.3 × 18 cm (11 1/2 × 7 1/8 in.); paper: 40.8 × 26.5 cm (16 1/16 × 10 3/8 in.). Kate S. Buckingham Endowment, 1995.267.

49. Rembrandt van Rijn (Dutch, 1606–1669). *Old Man with a Gold Chain*, 1631. Oil on panel; 83.1 × 75.7 cm (32 3/4 × 29 3/4 in.). Mr. and Mrs. W. W. Kimball Collection, 1922.4467.

50. Jacques de Gheyn II (Dutch, 1565–1629). *Two Studies of a Roma Woman and a Roma Boy in a Large Hat*, about 1605. Pen and black iron gall ink on tan laid paper; 23 × 26 cm (9 1/16 × 10 1/4 in.). Gift of Tiffany and Margaret Blake, 1959.2.

51. Nicolas Poussin (French, 1594–1665). *Landscape with Saint John on Patmos*, 1640. Oil on canvas; 100.3 × 136.4 cm (39½ × 53⅝ in.). A. A. Munger Collection, 1930.500.

52. María Josefa Sánchez (Spanish, active 1639–1649). *Crucifixion*, 1646. Oil on panel; 63 × 39 cm (24 13⁄16 × 15⅜ in.). C. Harker and Mae Svoboda Rhodes Acquisition Fund, 2018.52.

53. Edwaert Collier (Dutch, 1642–1708). *A Vanitas Still Life with a Flag, Candlestick, Musical Instruments, Books, Writing Paraphernalia, Globes, and Hourglass*, 1662. Oil on canvas; 98 × 129.7 cm (38½ × 51 in.). Through prior bequest of Joseph Winterbotham; Rhoades Foundation and Julius Lewis Acquisition Endowment Fund; European Painting Discretionary Fund, 2020.317.

54. Jar (*Tibor*), 1700–1750. Unknown ceramist (Spanish or Criollo); Puebla de los Ángeles, Viceroyalty of New Spain (present-day Mexico). Tin-glazed earthenware with cobalt glaze; 62.5 × 40.2 × 40.2 cm (24⅝ × 15⅞ × 15⅞ in.). Gift of Eva Lewis in memory of her husband, Herbert Pickering Lewis, 1923.1443.

55. Attributed to the Stipple Master (active India, about 1692–about 1715). *A Monumental Portrait of a Monkey*, about 1705–10. Opaque watercolor and gold on paper; outermost border: 48.5 × 58.7 cm (19 × 23 in.); image: 45 × 56 cm (17¾ × 22 in.). Lacy Armour Fund, James and Marilynn Alsdorf Acquisition Fund, 2011.248.

56. Jar with Narcissus, Nandina Berries, Lingzhi Mushrooms, and Rocks, Qing dynasty (1644–1911), Yongzheng reign mark and period (1723–35). China. Porcelain painted with underglaze blue and overglaze doucai enamels; 13 × 12.2 cm (5⅛ × 4 13⁄16 in.); diam.: 12.2 cm (4 13⁄16 in.). Gift of Emily Crane Chadbourne, 1926.1322.

57. King Vulture, 1734. Meissen Porcelain Manufactory (Saxony, Germany, 1710–present); modeled by Johann Joachim Kändler (born Saxony, Germany, 1706–1775). Hard-paste porcelain and polychrome enamels; 58 × 43 cm (22 13⁄16 × 16 15⁄16 in.). Harry and Maribel G. Blum Endowment Fund, Purchased with funds provided by the Antiquarian Society, Kate S. Buckingham Fund, Charles H. and Mary F. S. Worcester Collection Fund, Auction Sales Proceeds Fund, Centennial Major Acquisitions Income Fund, Robert Allerton Trust, The Mary and Leigh Block Endowment Fund, Ada Turnbull Hertle Fund, Purchased with funds provided by Harry A. Root, Wirt D. Walker Trust, Gladys N. Anderson Fund, Pauline Seipp Armstrong Fund, Edward E. Ayer Fund in Memory of Charles L. Hutchinson, Kay and Frederick Krehbiel Fund, Purchased with funds provided by Mr. and Mrs. Stanford Marks, Helen A. Regenstein Endowment, Samuel A. Marx Purchase Fund for Major Acquisitions, Laura T. Magnuson Acquisition Fund, The Marian and Samuel Klasstorner Fund, Maurice D. Galleher Endowment, Robert Allerton Purchase Fund, Bessie Bennett Fund, European Decorative Arts General fund, Edward Johnson Fund, Elizabeth R. Vaughn Fund, Annette Mathby Chapin Fund, Wentworth Greene Field Memorial Fund, Director's Fund, Purchased with funds provided by the Edward Byron Smith, Jr. Family Foundation, Samuel P. Avery Fund, Hugh Leander and Mary Trumbull Adams Memorial Endowment, Purchased with funds provided by the G-Bar Charitable Foundation, Betty Bell Spooner Fund, Purchased with funds provided by Elizabeth Souder Louis, Irving and June Seaman Endowment Fund, Charles U. Harris Endowed Acquisition Fund, S. DeWitt Clough Fund, Purchased with funds provided by the Woman's Board of the Alliance Française of Chicago, Grant J. Pick Purchase Fund, Purchased with funds provided by Ghenete Zelleke, 2007.105.

58. *The Emperor Sailing*, from *The Story of the Emperor of China*, 1716–22. After a design by Guy-Louis Vernansal (French, 1648–1729) and others; Woven at the Manufacture Royale de Beauvais under the direction of Pierre and Etienne Filleul (codirectors, 1711–22). Wool, silk, and silvered-and-gilt-metal-strip-wrapped silk, slit and double interlocking tapestry weave with some areas of 2:2 plain interlacings of silvered-and-gilt-metal wefts; 385.8 × 355 cm (151¾ × 139¾ in.). Mr. and Mrs. Charles H. Worcester Fund, 2007.22.

59. Giovanni Battista Tiepolo (Italian, 1696–1770). *Armida Encounters the Sleeping Rinaldo*, about 1742–45. Oil on canvas; 187.5 × 216.8 cm (73 13⁄16 × 85⅜ in.). Bequest of James Deering, 1925.700.

60. François Boucher (French, 1703–1770). *Academic Study of a Reclining Male Nude*, about 1750. Black chalk, with stumping and touches of red chalk, heightened with white chalk, on cream laid paper, laid down on cream laid paper; 35.6 × 44.8 cm (14 1⁄16 × 17 11⁄16 in.). Regenstein Endowment Fund, 2009.42.

61. Soga Shōhaku 曾我蕭白 (Japanese, 1730–1781), *Mount Fuji and the Miho Pine Forest*, 1761–62. Pair of 6-panel screens; ink and light colors on paper; each: 157.5 × 362 cm (62 1⁄16 × 142 9⁄16 in.). Through prior gift of Mr. and Mrs. Samuel M. Nickerson, 2023.3068.1–2.

62. Uchikake, Edo period (1615–1868), 1775–1800. Japan. Silk, 4:1 satin damask weave; resist and tie-dyed; embroidered with silk and gold-leaf-over-lacquered-paper-strip-wrapped cotton in satin stitches; laidwork and couching; lining: silk, plain weave; sleeve edge and fuki padded with silk; 184 × 128.2 cm (72 × 50½ in.). Gift of Mary V. and Ralph E. Hays, 1999.633.

63. Artist unknown (American, active 19th century). Peacock Weather Vane, 1800–60. Pennsylvania. Iron; 131.8 × 71.1 × 2.5 cm (51⅞ × 28 × 1 in.). Elizabeth R. Vaughan Fund, 1952.549.

64. Joshua Johnson (American, about 1763–after 1825). *Mrs. Elizabeth Grant Bankson Beatty and Her Daughter Susan*, about 1805. Oil on canvas; 82.9 × 72.8 cm (32⅝ × 28⅝ in.). Purchased with funds provided by Robin and Tim Reynolds and Jill Burnside Zeno; Bulley and Andrews, Edna Graham, Love Galleries, Mrs. Eric Oldberg, Ratcliffe Foundation, and Quinn E. Delaney funds; Walter Aitken, Dr. Julian Archie, Mr. and Mrs. Perry Herst, Jay W. McGreevy, Mr. and Mrs. John W. Puth, Stone Foundation, and Mr. and Mrs. Frederick G. Wacker Jr. endowment funds; through prior acquisitions of the George F. Harding Collection and Ruth Helgeson, 1998.315.

65. Emperor's Semiformal Court Robe (*Jifu*), Qing dynasty (1644–1911), 1790–1820. Manchu; China. Silk and gold-leaf-over-lacquered-paper-strip-wrapped silk, slit tapestry weave with interlaced outlining wefts; embroidered with silk in satin and stem stitches; painted details; sleeves: bands of silk, plain weave and of silk and gilt-metal-strip-wrapped silk, plain weave; edging and closures: silk, cotton, and gold-leaf-over-lacquered-paper-strip-wrapped cotton, satin weave with plain interlacings of secondary binding warps and supplementary patterning wefts; lined with silk, satin damask weave; sleeves lined with cotton, plain weave; metal buttons; 156.2 × 200.7 cm (61½ × 79 in.). Gift of the Orientals, 1935.368.

66. Monumental Vase, 1813. Sèvres Porcelain Manufactory (1756–present); model designed by Charles Percier (born France, 1764–1838); decoration designed by Alexandre-Theodore Brogniart (born France, 1739–1813); flowers and ornament painted by Gilbert Drouet (born France, 1785–1825); birds painted by Christophe-Ferdinand Caron (active France, 1792–1815). Enameled and gilded hard-paste porcelain and gilded bronze; 137.2 × 83.2 cm (54 × 32¾ in.). Harold L. Stewart and Harry and Maribel G. Blum endowment funds, 1987.1.

67. Hans Jakob Oeri (Swiss, 1782–1868). *The Twin Brothers Ludwig and Emil Schulthess*, 1818–19. Black chalk on ivory wove paper, fixed; 41.5 × 43.3 cm (16⅜ × 17¹⁄₁₆ in.). Regenstein Endowment Fund, 2024.125.

68. Raphaelle Peale (American, 1774–1825), *Still Life—Strawberries, Nuts, &c.*, 1822. Oil on wood panel; 41.1 × 57.8 cm (16³⁄₁₆ × 22¾ in.). Gift of Jamee J. and Marshall Field, 1991.100.

69. *The Joyous Banquet of Guo Ziyi*, Joseon dynasty (1392–1897), 1800s. Korea. Ink and color on silk; 187.5 × 427.6 cm (73⅞ × 168⅜ in.); Gift of Mrs. William J. Calhoun, 1940.4.

70. Jean-Auguste-Dominique Ingres (French, 1780–1867). *Amédée-David, the Comte de Pastoret*, 1823–26. Oil on canvas; 103 × 83.5 cm (40½ × 32¾ in.). Estate of Dorothy Eckhart Williams; Robert Allerton, Bertha E. Brown, and Major Acquisitions funds, 1971.452.

71. John Philip Simpson (English, 1782–1847). *The Captive Slave (Ira Aldridge)*, 1827. Oil on canvas; 127 × 101.5 cm (50 × 40 in.). Purchased with funds provided by Mary Winton Green, Dan and Sara Green Cohan, Howard and Lisa Green and Jonathan and Brenda Green, in memory of David Green, 2008.188.

72. Eugène Delacroix (French, 1798–1863). *The Combat of the Giaour and Hassan*, 1826. Oil on canvas; 59.6 × 73.4 cm (23½ × 28⅞ in.). Gift of Bertha Palmer Thorne, Rose Movius Palmer, Mr. and Mrs. Arthur M. Wood, and Mr. and Mrs. Gordon Palmer, 1962.966.

73. Joseph Mallord William Turner (English, 1775–1851). *Fishing Boats with Hucksters Bargaining for Fish*, 1837–38. Oil on canvas; 174.5 × 224.9 cm (68¾ × 88½ in.). Mr. and Mrs. W. W. Kimball Collection, 1922.4472.

74. Katsushika Hokusai (Japanese, 1760–1849). Two editions of *The Great Wave off Kanagawa*, from the series *Thirty-Six Views of Mount Fuji*, 1830–33. Color woodblock prints; ōban; each: 25.4 × 37.6 cm (10⅛ × 14¾ in.). Clarence Buckingham Collection, 1925.3245 and 1952.343.

75. William Henry Fox Talbot (English, 1800–1877). *Articles of China*, 1843–44. Salted paper print; 18.7 × 22.4 cm (7⅜ × 8⅝ in.). The Mary and Leigh Block Endowment Fund, 2015.74.

76. Samuel J. Miller (American, 1822–1888). *Frederick Douglass*, 1847–52. Daguerreotype; 15.2 × 24 × 2 cm (6 × 9½ × ¾ in.). Major Acquisitions Centennial Endowment, 1996.433.

77. Lilly Martin Spencer (American, born England, 1822–1902). *This Little Pig Went to Market*, about 1857. Oil on canvas; 61 × 50.8 cm (24 × 20 in.). Roger and J. Peter McCormick Endowment Fund; through prior acquisition of George F. Harding Collection; through prior gift of Chicago Normal School Alumni, 2021.1.

78. David Drake (American, about 1801–1870s); Lewis Miles Stoney Bluff Manufactory (plantation) (American, about 1840–70s). Storage Jar, 1857. Stoneware and glaze; h.: 45.7 cm (18 in.); diam.: 43.2 cm (17 in.). Through prior bequest of Arthur Rubloff; Wesley M. Dixon Jr. Endowment Fund, 2020.58.

79. Robert S. Duncanson (American, 1821–1872). *River Scene*, 1867–71. Oil on canvas; 72.4 × 132.4 cm (28½ × 52⅛ in.). Through prior gift of Rena Buck Robinson, Caroline Buck Sauter, and Frances Buck Taylor in memory of Nelson L. Buck; purchased with funds provided by the bequest of Muriel J. Kogan; Arts of the Americas Discretionary Fund, 2023.3043.

80. Emma Stebbins (American, 1815–1882). *Machinist* and *Machinist's Apprentice*, about 1859. Marble; 74.9 × 29.2 × 29.2 cm (29½ × 11½ × 11½ in.) and 74.9 × 29.9 × 22.9 cm (29½ × 11¾ × 9 in.), respectively. Gift of the Antiquarian Society, 2000.13.1–2.

81. Sideboard and Wine Cabinet, 1859. Designed by William Burges (born England, 1827–1881); made by Harland and Fisher (1845–88); painted by Nathaniel Hubert John Westlake (born England, 1833–1921). Pine, mahogany, paint, gilding, iron, brass, and marble; 126.7 × 151.5 × 57.8 cm (49⅞ × 59⅝ × 22¾ in.). Purchased with funds provided by the James McClintock Snitzler Fund through the Antiquarian Society, Mrs. DeWitt W. Buchanan Jr., Mr. and Mrs. Henry M. Buchbinder, Mr. and Mrs. Stanford D. Marks, Mrs. Eric Oldberg, Harry A. Root, and the Woman's Board in honor of Mrs. Gloria Gottlieb; Harry and Maribel G. Blum Foundation, Richard T. Crane, Ada Turnbull Hertle, Kay and Frederick Krehbiel, Florence L. Notter, Mr. and Mrs. Joseph Varley, and European Decorative Arts Purchase endowment funds; through prior purchase with funds provided by Robert Allerton and the Antiquarian Society; through prior gifts of Mr. and Mrs. James W. Alsdorf and Helen Bibas; Mrs. Emily Crane Chadbourne, Mr. and Mrs. Richard T. Crane Jr., the R. T. Crane, Jr., Memorial Fund; through prior gifts of H. M. Gillen; the George F. Harding Collection, Mrs. John Hooker, and the Kenilworth Garden Club, 1999.262.

82. Herter Brothers (American, 1864–1906), New York. Cabinet, 1878–80. Rosewood with ebonized cherry, maple, walnut, satinwood, marquetry of various woods, brass, gilding, and paint; 134.6 × 180.3 × 40.6 cm (53 × 71 × 16 in.). Purchased with funds provided by the Antiquarian Society through the Capital Campaign, 1986.26.

83. Julia Margaret Cameron (English, 1815–1879). *Mrs. Herbert Duckworth*, 1867. Albumen print; 34.2 × 26.3 cm (13 ½ × 10 ⅜ in.). The Mary and Leigh Block Endowment Fund, 2001.59.

84. Édouard Manet (French, 1832–1883). *The Races at Longchamp*, 1866. Oil on canvas; 44 × 84.2 cm (17 5⁄16 × 33 ⅛ in.). Potter Palmer Collection, 1922.424.

85. James McNeill Whistler (American, 1834–1903). *Nocturne: Blue and Gold—Southampton Water*, 1872. Oil on canvas; 51 × 76.7 cm (20 1⁄16 × 30 3⁄16 in.). Stickney Fund, 1900.52.

86. Gustave Caillebotte (French, 1848–1894). *Paris Street; Rainy Day*, 1877. Oil on canvas; 212.2 × 276.2 cm (83 ½ × 108 ¾ in.). Charles H. and Mary F. S. Worcester Collection, 1964.336.

87. Attributed to Unobhadule (active mid- to late 1800s, Northern Nguni, South Africa). Lidded Container, mid- to late 1800s. Wood; h.: 46 cm (18 ⅛ in.); diam.: 27.9 cm (11 in.). Ada Turnbull Hertle Fund, 1979.539a–b.

88. Punch Bowl, designed 1891, made 1892. Royal Porcelain Manufactory (Königliche Porzellan-Manufaktur or KPM, Berlin, 1763–present); designed by Alexander Kips (born Prussia [now Germany], 1858–1910); modeled by Ernst Wägner (born Austria-Hungary [now Slovenia], active Germany, 1877–1951). Hard-paste porcelain; 87.7 × 78.8 × 80 cm (34 ½ × 31 × 31 ½ in.). Gift of Jack Shear, 2022.164a–b.

89. Edgar Degas (French, 1834–1917). *The Millinery Shop*, 1879–86. Oil on canvas; 100 × 110.7 cm (39 ⅜ × 43 9⁄16 in.). Mr. and Mrs. Lewis Larned Coburn Memorial Collection, 1933.428.

90. Parrot Storage Jar (*Olla*), 1880s. Pueblo of Acoma, New Mexico. Clay and pigment; h.: 42.6 cm (16 ¾ in.); diam.: 46.7 cm (18 ⅜ in.). Ethel T. Scarborough and Major Acquisitions funds; Gladys N. Anderson Endowment Fund, 2006.749.

91. *Strawberry Thief*, design 1883, made 1883–1917. Designed by William Morris (English, 1834–1896); produced by Morris & Co., London (English, 1875–1940). Cotton; plain weave, block printed, wool trim with tassels; 283 × 106 cm (111 ½ × 41 ¾ in.). Purchased with funds provided by John H. Bryan, Hope McCormick, and Patrick G. and Shirley W. Ryan Foundation; and the Textile Society, 1992.396.

92. Pierre-Auguste Renoir (French, 1841–1919). *Two Sisters (On the Terrace)*, 1881. Oil on canvas; 100.4 × 80.9 cm (39 ½ × 31 ⅞ in.). Mr. and Mrs. Lewis Larned Coburn Memorial Collection, 1933.455.

93. Evelyn De Morgan (British, 1855–1919). *The Angel of Death*, 1885. Black pastel and opaque gold paint, over traces of black chalk, on brown wove paper; 46.5 × 38 cm (18 5⁄16 × 15 in.). Regenstein Endowment and Meg and Mark Hausberg funds, 2019.925.

94. James Ensor (Belgian, 1860–1949). *The Temptation of Saint Anthony*, 1887. Colored pencils and scraping, with graphite, charcoal, Conté crayon, and additions in colored chalk and watercolor, selectively fixed, with cut and pasted elements, on 51 sheets of ivory wove paper (discolored to cream), joined, and formerly laid down on canvas; 179.5 × 154.7 cm (70 11⁄16 × 60 15⁄16 in.). Regenstein Endowment and the Louise B. and Frank H. Woods Purchase Fund, 2006.87.

95. Vincent van Gogh (Dutch, 1853–1890). *The Bedroom*, 1889. Oil on canvas; 73.6 × 92.3 cm (29 × 36 ⅝ in.). Helen Birch Bartlett Memorial Collection, 1926.417.

96. Paul Gauguin (French, 1848–1903). *Arlésiennes (Mistral)*, 1888. Oil on jute canvas; 73 × 92 cm (28 ¾ × 36 3⁄16 in.). Mr. and Mrs. Lewis Larned Coburn Memorial Collection, 1934.391.

97. Georges Seurat (French, 1859–1891). *A Sunday on La Grande Jatte—1884*, 1884–86 (border added 1888–89). Oil on canvas; 207.5 × 308.1 cm (81 ¾ × 121 ¼ in.). Helen Birch Bartlett Memorial Collection, 1926.224.

98. Mary Cassatt (American, 1844–1926). *The Child's Bath*, 1893. Oil on canvas; 101.3 × 67.3 cm (39 15⁄16 × 26 ½ in.). Robert A. Waller Fund, 1910.2.

99. George Inness (American, 1825–1894). *Early Morning, Tarpon Springs*, 1892. Oil on canvas; 107.2 × 82.2 cm (42 3⁄16 × 32 ⅜ in.). Edward B. Butler Collection, 1911.32.

100. Winslow Homer (American, 1836–1910). *The Herring Net*, 1885. Oil on canvas; 76.5 × 122.9 cm (30 ⅛ × 48 ⅜ in.). Mr. and Mrs. Martin A. Ryerson Collection, 1937.1039.

101. Käthe Kollwitz (German, 1867–1945). *Self-Portrait*, 1891–92. Brush and opaque black and white watercolor on brown wove paper; 41 × 33 cm (16 3⁄16 × 13 in.). Purchased with funds provided by Margaret Day Blake, Mr. and Mrs. Alan Press, and Prints and Drawings Purchase Fund, 1980.361.

102. Henri de Toulouse-Lautrec (French, 1864–1901). *At the Moulin Rouge*, 1892–95. Oil on canvas; 123 × 141 cm (48 7⁄16 × 55 ½ in.). Helen Birch Bartlett Memorial Collection, 1928.610.

103. Marion Mahony Griffin (American, 1871–1961). Window from Church of All Souls, Evanston, Illinois, 1903 (demolished 1960). Clear and colored lead glass in oak frame; 177.8 × 132.1 cm (70 × 50 in.). Mary Waller Langhorne Endowment Fund; Architecture Purchase Fund, 2021.182.

104. Edvard Munch (Norwegian, 1863–1944). *The Girl by the Window*, 1893. Oil on canvas; 96.5 × 65.4 cm (38 × 25 ¾ in.). Searle Family Trust and Goldabelle McComb Finn endowments; Charles H. and Mary F. S. Worcester Collection, 2000.50.

105. Paul Cezanne (French, 1839–1906). *The Basket of Apples*, about 1893. Oil on canvas, 65 × 80 cm (25 7⁄16 × 31 ½ in.).

Helen Birch Bartlett Memorial Collection, 1926.252.

106. Odilon Redon (French, 1840–1916). *Sita*, about 1893. Pastel, with touches of black Conté crayon, over various charcoals, on cream wove paper altered to a golden tone; 53.6 × 37.7 cm (21 1/8 × 14 7/8 in.). Joseph Winterbotham Collection, 1954.320.

107. Rose Bowl, 1902–3. Designed by Archibald Knox (born Isle of Man, active England, 1864–1933); made by W. H. Haseler Ltd. (Birmingham, England, 1848–1963); retailed by Liberty & Co. (London, founded 1875). Silver, enamel, and turquoise; h.: 19.1 cm (7 1/2 in.); diam.: 35.3 cm (13 7/8 in.). Gift of Crab Tree Farm Foundation, 2024.332a–b.

108. Chest for Photographs, about 1902. Designed by Josef Hoffmann (born Moravia [now Czech Republic], active Austria, 1870–1956); made by W. Müller (active Austria, early 20th century). Wood with palisander and maple veneers, nickel silver; 55.9 × 52.8 × 37.1 cm (22 × 20 13/16 × 14 5/8 in.). Purchased with funds provided by the Antiquarian Society of Mrs. James W. Alsdorf, Mrs. Walter Alexander, Mrs. P. Kelly Armour, Mr. and Mrs. T. Stanton Armour, Mr. John H. Bryan, Mrs. DeWitt W. Buchanan Jr., Mrs. Henry M. Buchbinder, Mrs. George M. Covington, Dr. Edwin J. DeCosta, Quinn E. Delaney, Mr. David P. Earle III, Mr. and Mrs. Gordon R. Ewing, Marshall Field, Mrs. Robert Hixon Glore, Mrs. Fred A. Krehbiel, Dr. Kenneth J. Maier, Mrs. Harold T. Martin, Mrs. Brooks McCormick, Mr. and Mrs. Charles F. Nadler, Mrs. John K. Notz Jr., Mrs. Eric Oldberg, Mrs. James C. Pritchard, Mrs. Edgar J. Uihlein, Mrs. Morris S. Weeden, and Mrs. George B. Young; purchased with funds provided by John H. Bryan and David P. Earle lll, and the Antiquarian Society, in honor of Lynn Springer Roberts, the Eloise W. Martin curator of European Decorative Arts and Sculpture and Classical Art, 1981–1989, 1992.93.

109. Paula Modersohn-Becker (German, 1876–1907). *Woman in Profile, Turned Right*, 1898–99. Charcoal on cream wove paper; 46.7 × 65.4 cm (18 7/16 × 25 3/4 in.). Purchased with funds provided by The Donnelley Family, 1978.26.

110. Vilhelm Hammershøi (Danish, 1864–1916). *Interior. The Music Room, Strandgade 30*, 1907. Oil on canvas; 70 × 59 cm (27 9/16 × 23 1/4 in.). Joseph Winterbotham Collection, 2023.1322.

111. Claude Monet (French, 1840–1926). *Water Lilies*, 1906. Oil on canvas; 89.9 × 94.1 cm (35 3/8 × 37 1/16 in.). Mr. and Mrs. Martin A. Ryerson Collection, 1933.1157.

112. Pablo Picasso (Spanish, active France, 1881–1973). *The Old Guitarist*, late 1903–early 1904. Oil on panel; 122.9 × 82.6 cm (48 3/8 × 32 1/2 in.). Helen Birch Bartlett Memorial Collection, 1926.253.

113. John Singer Sargent (American, 1856–1925). *The Fountain, Villa Torlonia, Frascati, Italy*, 1907. Oil on canvas; 71.4 × 56.5 cm (28 1/8 × 22 1/4 in.). Friends of American Art Collection, 1914.57.

114. Frank Lloyd Wright (American, 1867–1959). *Spindle Cube Chair*, 1902–6. Poplar and leather; 73.7 × 73.7 × 73.7 cm (29 × 29 × 29 in). Purchased with funds provided by the Antiquarian Society; Roger McCormick Purchase, Alyce and Edwin DeCosta and the Walter E. Heller Foundation, Robert Allertun Purchase Income, Ada Turnbull Hertle, and Mary Waller Langhorne Memorial Funds; Robert Allerton Trust; Pauline Seipp Armstrong Fund; Bequest of Ruth Falkenau Fund in memory of her parents; Wendel Fentress Ott Endowment, Bessie Bennett, Elizabeth R. Vaughan, and Gladys N. Anderson funds; Estate of Stacia Fischer; The Goodman Fund; Maurice D. Galleher Endowment; Samuel P. Avery and Charles U. Harris Endowed Acquisition Funds; Estate of Cora Abrahamson; Charles R. and Janice Feldstein Endowment Fund for Decorative Arts, 2007.79.

115. Design attributed to Agnes F. Northrop (American, 1857–1953); made by Tiffany Studios (American, 1902–32). *Hartwell Memorial Window*, 1917. Corona, New York. Leaded glass; 798.7 × 554.7 × 42.5 cm (314 7/16 × 218 3/8 × 16 3/4 in.). Purchased with funds provided by the Antiquarian Society, the Chauncey and Marion Deering McCormick Family Foundation, and Ann and Samuel M. Mencoff; through prior gift of the George F. Harding Collection; Roger and J. Peter McCormick Endowment Fund; American Art Sales Proceeds, Discretionary, and Purchase funds; Jane and Morris Weeden Endowment Fund; Mary Swissler Oldberg Fund; purchased with funds provided by the Davee Foundation, Pamela R. Conant in memory of Louis John Conant, Stephanie Field Harris, the Komarek-Hyde-Soskin Foundation, and Jane Woldenberg; gifts in memory of John H. Bryan, Jr.; Wesley M. Dixon, Jr. Endowment Fund; through prior gift of the Friends of American Art Collection and Mr. and Mrs. Martin A. Ryerson; purchased with funds provided by Jamee J. and Marshall Field, Roxelyn and Richard Pepper, and an anonymous donor; Goodman Endowment Fund; purchased with funds provided by Abbie Helene Roth and Daniel Jesse Roth in memory of Sandra Gladstone Roth, Henry and Gilda Buchbinder Family in memory of John H. Bryan, Jr., Suzanne Hammond and Richard Leftwich, Maureen Tokar in memory of Edward Tokar, Bonnie and Frank X. Henke, III, Erica C. Meyer, Joseph P. Gromacki in memory of John H. Bryan, Jr., Louise Ingersoll Tausché, Mrs. Robert O. Levitt, Christopher and Sara Pfaff, Charles L. and Patricia A. Swisher, Abby and Don Funk, Kim and Andy Stephens, and Dorothy J. Vance; B. F. Ferguson Fund; Jay W. McGreevy, Dr. Julian Archie, Mr. and Mrs. John W. Puth, and Kate S. Buckingham endowment funds, 2018.121.

116. Henri Matisse (French, 1869–1954). *Bathers by a River*, 1909–10, 1913, and 1916–17. Oil on canvas; 260 × 392 cm (102 1/2 × 154 3/16 in.). Charles H. and Mary F. S. Worcester Collection, 1953.158.

117. Ọlọ́wẹ̀ of Isẹ̀ (Yoruba, Nigeria, died 1938). Veranda Post (*Òpó Ògògà*), King and Wife, 1910–14. Wood and pigment; 152.5 × 31.8 × 40.6 cm (60 × 12 1/2 × 16 in.). The Art Institute of Chicago, Major Acquisitions Centennial Fund, 1984.550.

118. Pair of Headdresses (*Ciwara Kunw*), mid-1800s to early 1900s. Bamana; Baninko region, French West Africa or French Sudan (present-day Mali). Wood, metal, brass tacks, and grasses; 98.4 × 40.9 × 10.8 cm (38 3/4 × 16 1/8 × 4 1/4 in.) and 79.4 × 31.8 × 7.6 cm (31 1/4 × 12 1/2 × 3 in.). Ada Turnbull Hertle Endowment, 1965.6–7.

119. Vasily Kandinsky (born Moscow [formerly Russian Empire, now Russia], 1866; died Neuilly-sur-Seine, France, 1944). *Improvisation No. 30 (Cannons)*, 1913. Oil on canvas; 111 × 111.3 cm (43 11/16 × 43 13/16 in.). Arthur Jerome Eddy Memorial Collection, 1931.511.

120. María Blanchard (Spanish, 1881–1932). *Still Life with a Box of Matches*, 1918. Oil, sand, and glass on canvas; 74 × 50 cm (29 × 19 3/4 in.). Joseph Winterbotham Collection, 2022.1493.

121. Suzanne Duchamp (French, 1889–1963). *Broken and Restored Multiplication*, 1918–19. Oil and silver paper on canvas; 61 × 50 cm (24 × 19 11/16 in.). Gift of Mary P. Hines in memory of her mother, Frances W. Pick; through prior acquisitions of Mr. and Mrs. Martin A. Ryerson, H. J. Willing, and Charles H. and Mary F. S. Worcester, 1994.552.

122. Alfred Stieglitz (American, 1864–1946). *Georgia O'Keeffe—Hands and Thimble*, 1919. Palladium print; 24.4 × 19.4 cm (9 5/8 × 7 11/16 in.). Alfred Stieglitz Collection, 1949.745.

123. Piet Mondrian (Dutch, 1872–1944). *Lozenge Composition with Yellow, Black, Blue, Red, and Gray*, 1921. Oil on canvas; 60 × 60 cm (23 5/8 × 23 5/8 in.). Gift of Edgar Kaufmann, Jr., 1957.307.

124. Constantin Brancusi (Romanian, active France, 1876–1957). *Golden Bird*, 1919–20 (base about 1922). Bronze, stone, and wood; 217.8 × 29.9 × 29.9 cm (86 × 11 3/4 × 11 3/4 in.). Partial gift of The Arts Club of Chicago; purchased with funds provided by various donors; through prior bequest of Arthur Rubloff; through prior purchase with funds provided by William E. Hartmann; through prior gift of Mr. and Mrs. Carter H. Harrison, Mr. and Mrs. Arnold H. Maremont through the Kate Maremont Foundation, Woodruff J. Parker, Mrs. Clive Runnells, Mr. and Mrs. Martin A. Ryerson, and various donors, 1990.88.

125. Marcel Duchamp (American, born France, 1887–1968). *Bottle Rack (Porte-bouteilles)*, 1914/1959. Galvanized iron; h.: 59.1 cm (23 1/4 in.); diam. at base: 36.2 cm (14 1/4 in.). Through prior gifts of Mary and Leigh Block, Mr. and Mrs. Maurice E. Culberg, and Mr. and Mrs. James W. Alsdorf; Charles H. and Mary F. S. Worcester Collection Fund; through prior gift of Mary and Earle Ludgin Collection; Sheila Anne Morgenstern in memory of Dorothy O. Morgenstern and William V. Morgenstern; through prior bequests of Joseph Winterbotham and Mima de Manziarly Porter; Ada Turnbull Hertle and Modern Discretionary funds, 2017.422.

126. André Kertész (American, born Hungary, 1894–1985). *Satiric Dancer, Paris (variant)*, 1927. Gelatin silver print; 9 × 7.8 cm (3 1/2 × 3 1/16 in.). Gift of Nicholas and Susan Pritzker, 2009.646.

127. Walter T. Bailey (American, 1882–1941). Facade Panel from the National Pythian Temple, Chicago, Illinois, around 1927 (demolished 1980). Glazed terracotta; 38.1 × 59.7 × 20.3 cm (15 × 23 1/2 × 8 in.). Gift of Matthew and Molly Godfrey, 2020.324.

128. Georgia O'Keeffe (American, 1887–1986). *Black Cross, New Mexico*, 1929. Oil on canvas; 99.1 × 76.2 cm (39 × 30 in.). Art Institute Purchase Fund, 1943.95.

129. László Moholy-Nagy (American, born Hungary, 1895–1946). *Berlin Radio Tower*, 1928. Gelatin silver print; 36 × 25.5 cm (14 3/16 × 10 1/16 in.). Julien Levy Collection, Special Photography Acquisition Fund, 1979.84.

130. Paul Theodore Frankl (American, born Austria, 1886–1958). *Skyscraper Cabinet*, about 1927. Wood and paint; 213.4 × 83.8 × 40 cm (84 × 33 × 15 3/4 in.). Gift of the Antiquarian Society through Mr. and Mrs. Thomas B. Hunter III and Mr. and Mrs. Morris S. Weeden, 1998.567.

131. Ivan Albright (American, 1897–1983). *Into the World There Came a Soul Called Ida*, 1929–30. Oil on canvas; 142.9 × 119.2 cm (56 1/4 × 47 in.). Gift of Ivan Albright, 1977.34.

132. Claude Cahun (French, 1894–1954). *Object*, 1936. Wood, paint, tennis ball, hair, and found objects; 13.7 × 10.7 × 16 cm (5 3/8 × 6 3/8 × 4 in.). Through prior gift of Mrs. Gilbert W. Chapman, 2007.30.

133. José Clemente Orozco (Mexican, 1883–1949). *Zapata*, 1930. Oil on canvas; 198.8 × 122.6 cm (78 1/4 × 48 1/4 in.). Gift of Joseph Winterbotham Collection, 1941.35.

134. Grant Wood (American, 1891–1942). *American Gothic*, 1930. Oil on Beaver Board; 78 × 65.3 cm (30 3/4 × 25 3/4 in.). Friends of American Art Collection, 1930.934.

135. Helmet Mask (Mukenga), possibly late 1800s to mid-1900s. Kuba; Congo Free State or Belgian Congo (now Democratic Republic of the Congo). Wood, glass beads, cowrie shells, feathers, raffia, fur, fabric, thread, monkey hair, and bells; 57.5 × 24.1 × 20.3 cm (22 5/8 × 9 1/2 × 8 in.). Laura T. Magnuson Fund, 1982.1504.

136. Tusk Hat (*Ogut Tigo*), early 1900s. Luo; British East Africa (now Kenya) or Tanganyika (now Tanzania). Glass beads, cotton, rattan, leather, and warthog tusks; 9.5 × 23 × 29 cm (3 3/4 × 9 1/16 × 11 7/16 in.). Gift of the Michael R. Mack Collection, 2024.362.

137. Mary Reynolds (American, 1891–1950); illustrated by Man Ray (Emmanuel Radnitzky) (American, 1890–1976); written by Paul Éluard (French, 1895–1952). *Les mains libres: Dessins de Man Ray, illustrés par les poèmes de Paul Éluard (Free Hands: Drawings by Man Ray, Illustrated by the Poems of Paul Éluard)*, published 1937; rebound 1937–42. Full tan morocco binding; leather gloves onlaid on front and back covers; author and title stamped in palladium on spine; doublures; silk endpapers; top edge gilt; original paper covers bound in; 123 from an edition of 675 printed on chester vergé, 1st edition; 28.8 × 23 × 4.3 cm (11 3/8 × 9 1/16 × 1 3/4 in.). Mary Reynolds Collection, Ryerson and Burnham Libraries, 2019.171.

138. Marc Chagall (French, born Vitebsk [Russian Empire, now Belarus], 1887; died Saint-Paul, France, 1985). *White Crucifixion*, 1938. Oil on canvas; 154.6 × 140 cm (60 7/8 × 55 1/16 in.). Purchased with funds provided by Alfred S. Schuler, 1946.925.

139. Female Caryatid Drum (*Pinge*), about 1930–50. Senufo, Côte d'Ivoire. Wood, hide, and pigment; 122.9 × 49.2 cm (48 3/8 × 19 3/8 in.). Robert J. Hall,

Herbert R. Molner Discretionary, Curator's Discretionary, and African and Amerindian Art Purchase funds; Arnold Crane, Mrs. Leonard Florsheim, O. Renard Goltra, Holly and David Ross, Departmental Acquisitions, Ada Turnbull Hertle, and Marian and Samuel Klasstorner endowments; through prior gifts of various donors, 1990.137.

140. Display Cloth (*Ndop*), 1910–37. Bamum; Foumban, Cameroon Grassfields (in present-day Cameroon). 60 panels joined: cotton, plain weave; resist-dyed; 171.1 × 327 cm (67 3⁄8 × 128 3⁄4 in.). Department of African and Amerindian Curator's Discretionary and Louise A. Lutz Estate funds, 2010.4.

141. Roberto Matta (Chilean, 1911–2002). *The Earth Is a Man*, 1942. Oil on canvas; 182.9 × 243.8 cm (72 × 96 in.). Gift of Mr. and Mrs. Joseph Randall Shapiro (after her death, dedicated to the memory of Jory Shapiro by her husband), 1992.168.

142. Edward Hopper (American, 1882–1967). *Nighthawks*, 1942. Oil on canvas; 84.1 × 152.4 cm (33 1⁄8 × 60 in.). Friends of American Art Collection, 1942.51.

143. Walker Evans (American, 1903–1975). *Untitled (Subway Portrait)*, 1938–41. Gelatin silver print; 12.4 × 18.8 cm (4 15⁄16 × 7 7⁄16 in.). Gift of David C. and Sarajean Ruttenberg, 2002.639.

144. Gordon Parks (American, 1912–2006). *The Invisible Man (Harlem, New York)*, from the series *A Man Becomes Invisible*, 1952. Gelatin silver print; 33.1 × 42 cm (13 1⁄16 × 16 9⁄16 in.). Anonymous gift, 2014.1101.

145. Bruce Goff (American, 1904–1982) and Herb Greene (Herb Greenberg) (American, born 1929). *Eugene and Nancy Bavinger House, Norman, Oklahoma, Elevation*, 1950. Colored pencil with graphite on cream wove paper; 60.5 × 81 cm (23 7⁄8 × 31 15⁄16 in.). Gift of Shin'enKan, Inc., 1990.811.12.

146. Nanna Ditzel (Danish, 1923–2005); Jorgen Ditzel (Danish, 1921–1969); manufactured by Ludvig Pontoppidan (Danish, mid-1900s). Basket Chairs, about 1950. Wicker and teak; each: 74 × 82.5 × 76 cm (29 × 32 1⁄2 × 30 in.). Architecture Purchase Account Fund, 2017.338.1–2.

147. Archibald John Motley Jr. (American, 1891–1981). *Nightlife*, 1943. Oil on canvas; 91.4 × 121.3 cm (36 × 47 3⁄4 in.). Purchased with funds provided by Jamee J. and Marshall Field, Jack and Sandra Guthman, Ben W. Heineman, Ruth Horwich, Lewis and Susan Manilow, Beatrice C. Mayer, Charles A. Meyer, John D. Nichols, and Mr. and Mrs. Edward Byron Smith, Jr.; James W. Alsdorf Memorial Fund; Goodman Endowment Fund, 1992.89.

148. Willem de Kooning (American, born Netherlands, 1904–1997). *Excavation*, 1950. Oil on canvas; 205.7 × 254.6 cm (81 × 100 1⁄4 in.); Mr. and Mrs. Frank G. Logan Purchase Prize Fund; purchased with funds provided by Edgar J. Kaufmann, Jr., and Mr. and Mrs. Noah Goldowsky, 1952.1.

149. Helen Frankenthaler (American, 1928–2011). *10/29/52*, 1952. Oil on unsized, unprimed canvas; 164.8 × 168.3 cm (64 7⁄8 × 66 1⁄4 in.). Gift of the Helen Frankenthaler Foundation; Mr. and Mrs. Frank G. Logan Purchase Prize Fund; through prior gift of Helen Harvey Mills in honor of Natalie, Julian, and Brett; Barbara Neff Smith and Solomon Byron Smith Purchase Fund, 2023.1317.

150. Mark Rothko (Marcus Rothkowitz) (American, born Russia [Russian Empire, now Latvia], 1903–1970). *Untitled (Purple, White, and Red)*, 1953. Oil on canvas; 197.5 × 207.7 cm (77 13⁄16 × 81 13⁄16 in.); Gift of Sigmund E. Edelstone, 1983.509.

151. Ellsworth Kelly (American, 1923–2015). *Red Yellow Blue White and Black II*, 1953. Oil on canvas, 7 joined panels; 99.1 × 351.2 cm (39 × 138 1⁄4 in.). Gift of Anstiss and Ronald Krueck Collection, 2001.157.

152. Ed Clark (American, 1926–2019). *Untitled*, 1957. Oil on canvas and paper, on wood; 116.9 × 139.7 cm (46 × 55 in.). Purchased with funds provided by an anonymous donor; Samuel A. Marx Endowment, 1999.243.

153. Lee Krasner (American, 1908–1954). *Black and White*, 1953. Oil paint, gouache, and cut and torn painted paper, with adhesive residue on cream laid paper; 76.6 × 57.1 cm (30 3⁄16 × 22 1⁄2 in.). Margaret Fisher Endowment Fund, 1994.245.

154. Charles White (American, 1918–1979). *Harvest Talk*, 1953. Charcoal, Wolff's carbon drawing pencil, and graphite, with stumping and erasing, on ivory wood pulp laminate board; 66.1 × 99.2 cm (26 1⁄16 × 39 1⁄16 in.). Purchased with funds provided by Mr. and Mrs. Robert S. Hartman, 1991.126.

155. Robert Rauschenberg (American, 1925–2008). *Short Circuit*, 1955. Oil, fabric, notebook paper, postcard, printed reproductions, concert program, and autograph on canvas, wood supports, and cabinets with paintings by Susan Weil and Elaine Sturtevant; 103.5 × 95.2 × 10.8 cm (41 1⁄2 × 38 1⁄4 × 4 1⁄2 in.). Through prior purchase of the Grant J. Pick purchase fund; through prior bequest of Sigmund E. Edelstone; Frederick W. Renshaw Acquisition fund; Estate of Walter Aitken; Alyce and Edwin DeCosta, Walter E. Heller Foundation, and Ada Turnbull Hertle funds; Wirt D. Walker Trust; Marian and Samuel Klasstorner, Mrs. Clive Runnells, Alfred and May Tiefenbronner Memorial, Boles C. and Hyacinth G. Drechney, Charles H. and Mary F. Worcester Collection, Mary and Leigh Block Endowment, Gladys N. Anderson, Benjamin Argile Memorial, Director's, and Joyce Van Pilsum funds, 2011.247.

156. Shozo Shimamoto (Japanese, 1928–2013). *Untitled*, 1957. Oil on newspaper on wood; 160 × 128.3 cm (63 × 50 1⁄2 in.). Through prior purchase from the Mary and Leigh Block Fund, 2016.60.

157. Joan Mitchell (American, 1925–1992). *City Landscape*, 1955. Oil on linen; 203.2 × 203.2 cm (80 × 80 in.). Gift of Society for Contemporary American Art, 1958.193.

158. Cy Twombly (American, 1928–2011). *The First Part of the Return from Parnassus*, 1961. Oil paint, lead pencil, wax crayon, colored pencil on canvas; 240.7 × 300.7 cm (94 3⁄4 × 118 3⁄8 in.). Through prior gift of Mary and Leigh

Block; Marian and Samuel Klasstorner and Major Acquisitions Endowment Income funds; Wirt D. Walker Trust; Estate of Walter Aitken; Director's Fund; Helen A. Regenstein Endowment; Laura T. Magnuson Acquisition Fund, 2007.63.

159. Jasper Johns (American, born 1930). *Target*, 1961. Encaustic and newspaper on canvas; 167.6 × 167.6 cm (66 × 66 in.). Gift of Edlis Neeson Collection, 2015.119.

160. Claes Oldenburg (American, born Sweden, 1929–2022). *Soft Light Switches—"Ghost Version" II*, 1964–71. Canvas filled with kapok, gesso and pencil; 119.4 × 119.4 × 30.5 cm (47 × 47 × 12 in.). Partial and promised gift of Anstiss and Ronald Krueck, 2020.572.

161. Eva Hesse (American, born Germany, 1936–1970). *Hang Up*, 1966. Acrylic on cloth over wood and acrylic on cord over steel tube; 182.9 × 213.4 × 198.1 cm (72 × 84 × 78 in.). Through prior gifts of Arthur Keating and Mr. and Mrs. Edward Morris, 1988.130.

162. Roy Lichtenstein (American, 1923–1997). *Brushstroke with Spatter*, 1966. Oil and Magna on canvas; 172.7 × 203.2 cm (68 × 80 in.). Barbara Neff Smith and Solomon Byron Smith Purchase Fund, 1966.3.

163. Romare Bearden (American, 1911–1988). *Gray Interior (aka Gray Morning)*, 1969. Collage of cut and pasted printed papers, with graphite and touches of incising, on paperboard, laid down on wood panel; 52.5 × 67.9 cm (20 11⁄16 × 26 3⁄4 in.). Regenstein and Margaret Fisher endowment funds, 2020.29.

164. Faith Ringgold (American, 1930–2024). *Black Light Series #7: Ego Painting*, 1969. Oil on canvas; 76 × 76 cm (30 × 30 in.). Wilson L. Mead Trust Fund; Claire and Gordon Prussian Fund for Contemporary Art; Mr. and Mrs. Frank G. Logan Purchase Prize Fund; Ada S. Garrett Prize, Flora Mayer Witkowsky Purchase Prize, Gordon Prussian Memorial, Emilie L. Wild Prize, William H. Bartels Prize, William and Bertha Clusmann Prize, Max V. Kohnstamm Prize, and Pauline Palmer Prize funds, 2019.184.

165. Ed Ruscha (American, born 1937). *Space*, 1971. Gunpowder and pastel on cream wove paper; 58.4 × 73.7 cm (23 × 29 1⁄16 in.). Gift of the Neisser Family, 2018.752.

166. Gerhard Richter (German, born 1932). *Woman Descending the Staircase (Frau die Treppe herabgehend)*, 1965. Oil on canvas; 198 × 128 cm (79 × 51 in.). Roy J. and Frances R. Friedman Endowment; gift of Lannan Foundation, 1997.176.

167. Charles Harrison (American, 1931–2018); manufactured by GAF Corporation (founded 1929). View-Master (Model G), about 1976. Injection molded plastic; 10.9 x 16.8 x 15 cm (4 5⁄16 x 6 5⁄8 x 5 7⁄8 in.). Gift of John and Ina Beierle, 2010.556.

168. Diane Arbus (American, 1923–1971). *Identical twins, Roselle, N.J. 1966*, 1966. Gelatin silver print; 38 × 37 cm (15 × 14 5⁄8 in.). Gift of Richard Avedon, 1986.2976.

169. David Hockney (English, born 1937). *American Collectors (Fred and Marcia Weisman)*, 1968. Acrylic on canvas; 213.4 × 304.8 cm (83 7⁄8 × 120 in.). Purchased with funds provided by Mr. and Mrs. Frederic G. Pick, 1984.182.

170. Barbara Chase-Riboud (American, born 1939). *Zanzibar / Gold #2*, 1977. Polished bronze and silk; 137.2 × 55 × 25.1 cm (54 × 21 5⁄8 × 9 7⁄8 in.). Through prior purchase from the Mary and Leigh Block Endowment Fund, 2024.286.

171. Suzuki Osamu (Japanese, 1926–2001). *Clay Figure (Dogū)*, 1965. Glazed stoneware; 61 × 25.4 × 21.6 cm (24 × 10 × 8 1⁄2 in.). Purchased with funds provided by Tamara and Michael Root, Japanese Art Shinkokai Fund, 2012.174.

172. Jessie T. Pettway (American, 1929–2023). Housetop Half-Log Cabin Quilt, about 1975. Pieced cotton, polyester, cellulose acetate, silk, rayon and acrylic, plain weaves; some with supplementary warps some forming cut voided pile; some self-patterned by main warp and ground weft floats; some printed; plain weave derived float weave; twill weaves, some printed; satin weave; and machine knitting; backed with cotton, plain weave; quilted with cotton threads; 209.1 × 214 cm (82 3⁄8 × 84 1⁄4 in.). Robert Allerton Endowment, 2002.384.

173. Alma Thomas (American, 1891–1978). *Starry Night and the Astronauts*, 1972. Acrylic on canvas; 152.4 × 134.6 cm (60 × 53 in.). Purchased with funds provided by Mary P. Hines in memory of her mother, Frances W. Pick, 1994.36.

174. Andy Warhol (American, 1928–1987). *Mao*, 1972. Acrylic, silkscreen ink, and pencil on linen; 448.3 × 346.7 cm (176 1⁄2 × 136 1⁄2 in.). Mr. and Mrs. Frank G. Logan Purchase Prize and Wilson L. Mead funds, 1974.230.

175. J.D. 'Okhai Ojeikere (Nigerian, 1930–2014). *Ife Bronze*, from the series *Hairstyles*, 1972. Gelatin silver print; 27.9 × 18 cm (11 × 7 1⁄8 in.). Purchased with funds provided by Robin and Sandy Stuart, 2015.93.

176. Peter Hujar (American, 1934–1987). *Candy Darling on Her Deathbed*, 1973. Gelatin silver print; 26.7 × 26.7 cm (10 1⁄2 × 10 1⁄2 in.). Mary and Leigh Block Endowment and Wentworth Greene Field Memorial Endowment funds, 2024.479.

177. Stanley Tigerman (American, 1930–2019). *The Titanic*, 1978. Photocollage, gelatin silver print, and cardboard; approx. 28 × 35.7 cm (11 × 14 1⁄16 in.). Gift of Stanley Tigerman, 1984.802.

178. Nan Goldin (American, born 1953). *The Ballad of Sexual Dependency*, 1979–2001. Multimedia installation (720 color slides and programmed sound-track); edition 7 of 10; run time: 43 min. Through prior bequest of Marguerita S. Ritman; purchased with funds provided by Dorie Sternberg, the Photography Associates, Mary L. and Leigh B. Block Endowment, Robert and Joan Feitler, Anstiss and Ronald Krueck, Karen and Jim Frank, Martin and Danielle Zimmerman, 2006.158.

179. Martin Kippenberger (German, 1953–1997). *Betty Ford Clinic (Betty Ford Klinik)*, 1985. Oil and lacquer on canvas; 179.8 × 299.8 cm (70 3⁄4 × 118 in.). Joseph Winterbotham Collection, 2024.86.

180. Felix Gonzalez-Torres (American, born Cuba, 1957–1996). *"Untitled" (Portrait of Ross in L.A.)*, 1991. Candies in variously colored wrappers, endless supply; dimensions vary with installation, ideal weight 175 lbs. Gift of Donna and Howard Stone, 2022.343.

181. Olga de Amaral (Colombian, born 1932). *Alquimia III* (*Alchemy III*), 1983. Strips of linen and cotton, plain weave with exposed warps; applied gesso; painted with gold leaf and pigment; joined by knotted extended ground weft fringe; 204.5 × 79.4 cm (80½ × 31¼ in.). Nicole Williams Contemporary Textile Fund, 1986.1006.

182. Ettore Sottsass Jr. (Italian, born Austro-Hungarian Empire [now Austria], 1917–2007); Memphis Furniture, S.R.L. (Italian, founded 1981). *Carlton Room Divider*, 1981. Wood and colored plastic laminate (Formica); 194.3 × 189.8 × 40 cm (76½ × 74¾ × 15¾ in.). Gift of the Antiquarian Society through the 1984 North Italian Trip Fund, 1984.1035.

183. Bruce Nauman (American, born 1941). *Clown Torture*, 1987. 4-channel video installation with 2 projections and 4 monitors, color, sound; approx. 1 hr.; installation dimensions variable. Watson F. Blair Prize, Wilson L. Mead, and Twentieth-Century Purchase funds; through prior gift of Joseph Winterbotham; gift of Lannan Foundation, 1997.162.

184. Diana Thater (American, born 1962). *Delphine*, 1999. 5-channel digital color video, silent (projection), 9-monitor video wall, light filters, and existing architecture; continuous loop; installation dimensions variable; artist's proof, from an edition of 3. Donna and Howard Stone New Media Fund, 2005.93.

185. Lorna Simpson (American, born 1960). *Outline*, 1990. 2 gelatin silver prints with applied plastic plaques; each: 124 × 103.5 cm (48⅞ × 40¾ in.). Gift of Boardroom, Inc., 1992.601a–b.

186. Dawoud Bey (American, born 1953). *Candida and Her Mother, Celia, II*, 1994. 6 internal dye diffusion transfer prints; each frame: 79.7 × 59.1 × 5.8 cm (31⅜ × 23¼ × 2¼ in.). Gladys N. Anderson Endowment, 2002.554a–f.

187. Kerry James Marshall (American, born 1955). *Many Mansions*, 1994. Acrylic on paper mounted on canvas; 289.6 × 342.9 cm (114 × 135 in.). Max V. Kohnstamm Fund, 1995.147.

188. Jeff Wall (Canadian, born 1946). *The Flooded Grave*, 1998–2000. Transparency in light box; 228.6 × 282 cm (90 × 111 in.). Promised gift of Pamela J. and Michael N. Alper; Claire and Gordon Prussian Fund for Contemporary Art; Harold L. Stuart Endowment; through prior acquisitions of the Mary and Leigh Block Collection, 2001.161.

189. Toshiko Takaezu (American, 1922–2011). *Dancing Brush*, 1990. Stoneware and glazes; 91.4 × 55.9 cm (42½ × 22 in.). Gift of Toshiko Takaezu, 2006.240.

190. Yoon Kwang-cho (Korean, born 1946). *Heart Sutra*, 2007. Stoneware with white slip; 55 × 57 × 35 cm (21 11/16 × 22 7/16 × 13¾ in.). Asian Art Council Acquisition Fund, 2018.127.

191. Kukuli Velarde (Peruvian, active United States, born 1962). *La Linda Nasca*, 2011. Low-fire clay, underglazes, glazes, metal, gold leaf, luster, and glass; 111.8 × 58.4 × 63.5 cm (44 × 23 × 25 in.). Arts of the Americas Discretionary Fund, 2021.174a–c.

192. Kelly Church (Match-e-be-nash-she-wish Pottawatomi, Ottawa, and American, born 1967). *Sustaining Traditions—Digital Teachings*, 2018. Black ash, sweetgrass, copper, and Rit dye; medicine pouch containing sage, tobacco, sweetgrass, and cedar; glass vial containing emerald ash borer and isopropyl alcohol; USB flash drive; 19.7 × 10.2 × 10.2 cm (7 13/16 × 4 1/16 × 4 1/16 in.). Mrs. Leonard S. Florsheim Jr. Fund, 2020.389a–d.

193. Jeremy Frey (Passamaquoddy, born 1978). *Nearly Monochrome*, 2022. Black ash, braided ash, cedar bark, and synthetic dye; 79.9 × 41.3 × 41.3 cm (31½ × 16 5/16 × 16 5/16 in.). Mrs. Leonard S. Florsheim Jr. Fund; purchased with funds provided by the bequest of Fred E. Spreitzer, 2022.1824a-b.

194. Bisa Butler (American, born 1973). *The Safety Patrol*, 2018. Cotton, wool, and chiffon, appliquéd and quilted; 210.8 × 229 cm (83 × 90 in.). Cavigga Family Trust Fund, 2019.785.

195. Rosemarie Trockel (German, born 1952). *Grater 2*, 2006. Ceramic and platinum; 322.6 × 259.1 × 5.1 cm (127 × 102 × 2 in.). Gift of Society for Contemporary Art, 2007.363a–ll.

196. Amanda Williams (American, born 1974). *Color(ed) Theory: Flamin' Red Hots* and *Crown Royal Bag*, 2014–15. Inkjet prints on 100% rag photo paper; each: 56 × 81 cm (22 × 32 in.). Funds provided by the Architecture & Design Society, 2016.182.2.

197. Charles Ray (American, born 1953). *Huck and Jim*, 2014. Machined stainless steel; artist's proof, from an edition of 2; overall: 283.3 × 137.2 × 136.6 cm (111½ × 54 × 53¾ in.). Gift of the artist; fabrication supported by Grant J. Pick Purchase Fund, 2022.251.1–2.

198. Simone Leigh (American, born 1967). *Sharifa*, 2022. Bronze; 2 of 2, plus 1 artist's proof; 283 × 104 × 103 cm (111 7/16 × 41 × 40 9/16 in.). Through prior gift of Mrs. Frank R. Lillie; The Lacy Armour Endowment Fund, 2024.3.

Contributors

Guest Authors

Jack Bankowsky, art writer and editor-at-large, *Artforum*

Lee Bey, architecture critic, *Chicago Sun-Times*

Charissa Bremer-David, former curator, Sculpture and Decorative Arts, J. Paul Getty Museum

Gerald A. Brown, multidisciplinary ceramic artist

Bisa Butler, textile artist

Tony Cokes, visual artist and educator

Alex Da Corte, visual artist

Darlene Fukuji, president, Toshiko Takaezu Foundation, and Takaezu's grandniece

Judith Geichman, artist and adjunct professor, School of the Art Institute of Chicago

Wade Guyton, post-conceptual artist

Anne Harris, artist and associate professor, School of the Art Institute of Chicago

Sandra Hindman, professor emerita of art history, Northwestern University, and owner, Les Enluminures galleries in Chicago, New York, and Paris

Sarah Holian, art historian and adjunct professor, DePaul University

Rhonda Holy Bear (Cheyenne River Lakota), multimedia artist

Brook Hsu, painter

Thomas Kelley, partner, Norman Kelley Architecture and Design Collaborative, and associate professor, University of Illinois Chicago School of Architecture

IfeOluwa Nihinlola, writer

Theresa Secord (Penobscot), basketmaker and founding director, Maine Indian Basketmakers Alliance

Maggie Taft, art historian and founding director, Writing Space in Chicago

Brian Vallo (Pueblo of Acoma), former governor, Pueblo of Acoma

Karli Wurzelbacher, chief curator, Heckscher Museum of Art

Art Institute of Chicago Authors

Ellenor Alcorn, former chair and Eloise W. Martin Curator, Applied Arts of Europe

Kris L. Anderson, Buddhism Public Scholar, the Robert H. N. Ho Family Foundation, Arts of Asia

Ashley Arico, associate curator, ancient Egyptian art

Makayla Bava, assistant curator, Modern and Contemporary Art

Mel Becker Solomon, associate research curator, Prints and Drawings

Giampaolo Bianconi, Dittmer Associate Curator, Modern and Contemporary Art

Lois Taylor Biggs (Cherokee Nation/White Earth Ojibwe), Daniel F. and Ada L. Rice Curatorial Fellow in Native American Art

Annika Bohanec, curatorial assistant, Modern and Contemporary Art

Emerson Bowyer, former Searle Curator, Painting and Sculpture of Europe

Chris Brooks, assistant conservator of frames

Molly Bryson, exhibition interpretation specialist

Anna Burckhardt Pérez, Neville Bryan Assistant Curator, Architecture and Design

Antawan I. Byrd, associate curator, Photography and Media

Lisa Ayla Çakmak, Mary and Michael Jaharis Chair and Curator, Arts of Greece, Rome, and Byzantium

Stephanie R. Caruso, assistant curator, Textiles and Arts of Greece, Rome, and Byzantium

Yeonsoo Chee, Korea Foundation Endowed Associate Curator of Korean Art

Nancy Chen, associate director, gallery activation

Jay A. Clarke, Rothman Family Curator, Prints and Drawings

Jacquelyn N. Coutré, Eleanor Wood Prince Curator, Painting and Sculpture of Europe

Grace Deveney, David C. and Sarajean Ruttenberg Associate Curator, Photography and Media

Alison Fisher, Harold and Margot Schiff Curator, Architecture and Design

Emily Fry, executive director, Interpretation

Jamie Gabbarelli, Prince Trust Associate Curator, Prints and Drawings

Madhuvanti Ghose, Alsdorf Associate Curator of Indian, Southeast Asian, and Himalayan Art

Gloria Groom, chair and David and Mary Winton Green Curator, Painting and Sculpture of Europe

Andrew James Hamilton, curator, Arts of the Americas

Caitlin Haskell, Gary C. and Frances Comer Senior Curator, Modern and Contemporary Art, and director, Ray Johnson Collection and Research

Charlotte Healy, senior research associate, Prints and Drawings

Mairead Carney Horton, research associate, Applied Arts of Europe

Alex Jen, assistant curator, Prints and Drawings

Alexandra Kader Herrera, former McMullan Arts Leadership Intern, Photography and Media

Janice Katz, Roger L. Weston Curator of Japanese Art

Kelly Keegan, conservator of paintings

Tamar Kharatishvili, Daniel F. and Ada L. Rice Research Fellow in Modern Art

Craig Lee, assistant curator, Architecture and Design

Rebecca Long, Patrick G. and Shirley W. Ryan Curator, Painting and Sculpture of Europe

Annelise K. Madsen, Gilda and Henry Buchbinder Curator, Arts of the Americas

Sofia Martinez, McMullan Museum Scholar, Arts of the Americas

Christopher Maxwell, chair and Eloise W. Martin Curator, Applied Arts of Europe

Elizabeth McGoey, Ann S. and Samuel M. Mencoff Curator, Arts of the Americas

Emily Mercer, assistant conservator of photography

Andrea Morgan, assistant curator, Painting and Sculpture of Europe

Kate Nesin, curator-at-large, Modern and Contemporary Art

Thea Liberty Nichols, associate research curator, Modern and Contemporary Art

Sarah Kelly Oehler, Field-McCormick Chair and Curator, Arts of the Americas, and vice president of curatorial strategy

Seung Hee Oh, assistant curator of Chinese art

Constantine Petridis, Rita Knox Chair and Curator, Arts of Africa

Charles Pietraszewski, assistant conservator of frames

Paulina Pobocha, chair and curator, Modern and Contemporary Art

Elizabeth I. Pope, senior research associate, Arts of the Americas and Textiles

Kate Tierney Powell, executive director, communications and research

Janet Marion Purdy, associate curator, Textiles

Katharine A. Raff, Elizabeth McIlvaine Curator, Arts of Greece, Rome, and Byzantium

Michal Raz-Russo, former associate curator, Photography and Media, now programs director, Gordon Parks Foundation

Kloie Rush-Spratt, educator, learning partnerships and resources, Patrick G. and Shirley W. Ryan Learning Center

Kevin Salatino, chair and Anne Vogt Fuller and Marion Titus Searle Curator, Prints and Drawings

Castor Santee, former collections assistant, Research Center

Elizabeth Siegel, former curator, Photography and Media, now chief of curatorial affairs, Milwaukee Art Museum

Irene Sunwoo, John H. Bryan Chair and Curator, Architecture and Design

Ginia Shubik Sweeney, director, Interpretation

Jonathan Tavares, Amy and Paul Carbone Curator, Applied Arts of Europe

Megan True, former curatorial assistant, Painting and Sculpture of Europe

Giovanni Verri, conservation scientist

Felipe Villada Ruiz, senior research associate, Prints and Drawings

Tacy Wagner, research associate, Modern and Contemporary Art

Isabel Waring, curatorial associate, Modern and Contemporary Art

Melinda Watt, chair and Christa C. Mayer Thurman Curator, Textiles

Grant Williams-Yackel, former Dangler Intern, Photography and Media

Matthew S. Witkovsky, Richard and Ellen Sandor Chair and Curator, Photography and Media, and vice president of strategic art initiatives

Loren Wright, assistant director, Interpretation

Yechen Zhao, Karen Frank Assistant Curator, Photography and Media

Index of Artists and Cultures

Note: Page numbers in *italics* refer to illustrations.

Photography Credits

Unless otherwise noted, photographs of artworks in the collection are copyrighted by the Art Institute of Chicago. Photography by Nathan Keay, Robert Lifson, Jonathan Mathias, Juan Molina Hernández, and Joe Tallarico. Postproduction by Hayley Hinsberger and Kaitlyn Fultz-Campion.

Unless otherwise noted, archival photographs are from the Art Institute of Chicago Archives.

The Art Institute of Chicago makes reasonable efforts to identify and contact copyright holders when necessary, but also asserts its fair use rights in the reproduction of applicable illustrations in its publications. We adhere to the standards set by the Association of Art Museum Directors' Guidelines for the Use of Copyrighted Materials and Works of Art by Art Museums. We make every reasonable attempt to ensure the accuracy of credit and caption information for each image. Any uncredited creators or rights holders are encouraged to contact the Art Institute of Chicago. The following credits apply to all images in this book for which separate acknowledgment is due.

Foreword
P. 5, fig. 1: Building and Renovation Files, Design and Construction, Institutional Archives, IM022577; p. 6, fig. 2: Board of Trustees and Committee Files, Secretary's Office, Institutional Archives, J30755; p. 7, fig. 3: © The Felix Gonzalez-Torres Foundation.

A Chronology of the Art Institute of Chicago
P. 10, right: photo by J.W. Taylor, Institutional Photography Archive, E28476; p. 11, left: South Lion (1893.1a), Institutional Photography Archive, D10380_26; p. 12, left: Institutional Photography Archive, J9309; p. 12, right: photo by John W. Barriger III, courtesy of Barriger Library at University of Missouri–St. Louis; p. 13, left: photo by Frances Kinsley Hutchinson, Institutional Photography Archive, E02187; p. 14, left: © 2025 Estate of Hale Woodruff / Licensed by VAGA at Artists Rights Society (ARS), NY; p. 14, right: Institutional Photography Archive, C12330; p. 15, left: Institutional Photography Archive, C13315; p. 15, right: Institutional Photography Archive, E05987; p. 17, left: photo by the Chicago Tribune, Institutional Photography Archive, E28276; p. 17, right: photo by the Chicago Tribune, Institutional Photography Archive, G20204; p. 18, left: photo by Mike Schwartz; p. 18, right: Institutional Photography Archive, D11299_22; p. 19: © 2026 Artists Rights Society (ARS), New York / ADAGP, Paris; p. 20, left: photos by CBS via Getty Images © Paramount Pictures; p. 20, right: Institutional Photography Archive, D11438A_029; p. 21, left: Institutional Photography Archive, D48700_002; p. 22, left: © Paul Warchol; p. 22, right: photo by Michael Litchfield; p. 23, left: © 2026 The Andy Warhol Foundation for the Visual Arts, Inc. / Licensed by Artists Rights Society (ARS), New York; p. 23, right: © SEPS licensed by Curtis Licensing, all rights reserved.

Works (by entry number)
13: © 2017 Ana De Orbegoso; 101: © Käthe Kollwitz Museum Köln, www.kollwitz.de; 112: © 2026 Estate of Pablo Picasso / Artists Rights Society (ARS), New York; 114: © 2026 Frank Lloyd Wright Foundation. All Rights Reserved. Licensed by Artists Rights Society; 116: © 2026 Succession H. Matisse / Artists Rights Society (ARS), New York; 121: © Suzanne Duchamp / Artists Rights Society (ARS), New York / ADAGP, Paris 2026; 124: © Succession Brancusi - All rights reserved (ADAGP) 2026; 125: © Association Marcel Duchamp / ADAGP, Paris / Artists Rights Society (ARS), New York 2026; 126: © Estate of André Kertész; 128: © The Art Institute of Chicago; 129: © 2026 Estate of László Moholy-Nagy / Artists Rights Society (ARS), New York; 133: © 2026 Artists Rights Society (ARS), New York / SOMAAP, Mexico City; 138: © 2026 Artists Rights Society (ARS), New York / ADAGP, Paris; 141: © 2026 Artists Rights Society (ARS), New York / ADAGP, Paris; 143: © Walker Evans Archive, The Metropolitan Museum of Art; 144: © The Gordon Parks Foundation; 147: © Estate of Archibald John Motley Jr. All reserved rights 2026 / Bridgeman Images; 148: © 2026 The Willem de Kooning Foundation / Artists Rights Society (ARS), New York; 149: © 1952 Helen Frankenthaler; 150: © 1998 Kate Rothko Prizel & Christopher Rothko / Artists Rights Society (ARS), New York; 152: © The Estate of Ed Clark. Courtesy of the Estate and Hauser & Wirth; 153: © 2026 The Pollock-Krasner Foundation / Artists Rights Society (ARS), New York; 154: © The Charles White Archives; 155: © 2026 Robert Rauschenberg Foundation / Licensed by VAGA at Artists Rights Society (ARS), NY; 156: © Associazione Shōzō Shimamoto; 157: © Estate of Joan Mitchell; 158: © Cy Twombly Foundation; 159: © 2026 Jasper Johns / Licensed by VAGA at Artists Rights Society (ARS), NY; 161: © The Estate of Eva Hesse. Courtesy of Hauser & Wirth; 162: © 2026 Estate of Roy Lichtenstein/DACS; 163: © 2026 Romare Bearden Foundation / Licensed by VAGA at Artists Rights Society (ARS), NY; 164: © 2026 Anyone Can Fly Foundation / Artists Rights Society (ARS), New York; 165: © Ed Ruscha; 166: © Gerhard Richter; 168: © The Estate of Diane Arbus; 169: © David Hockney; 170: © Barbara Chase-Riboud; 172: © 2026 Jessie T. Pettway / Artists Rights Society (ARS), New York; 173: © 2026 Estate of Alma Thomas (Courtesy of the Hart Family) / Artists Rights Society (ARS), New York; 174: © 2026 The Andy Warhol Foundation for the Visual Arts, Inc. / Licensed by Artists Rights Society (ARS), New York; 176: © 2026 The Peter Hujar Archive / Artists Rights Society (ARS), New York; 177: © 1978 Stanley Tigerman; 178: © Nan Goldin; 179: © Estate of Martin Kippenberger, Galerie Gisela Capitain, Cologne; 180: Courtesy of The Felix Gonzalez-Torres Foundation © Estate Felix Gonzalez-Torres; 181: © 1983 Olga de Amaral; 182: © erede Ettore Sottsass / Artists Rights Society, New York, 2026; 183: © 2026 Bruce Nauman / Artists Rights Society (ARS), New York; 184: Photo by Roman Mensing © Diana Thater. Courtesy of the artist and David Zwirner; 185: © Lorna Simpson. Courtesy of the artist and Hauser & Wirth; 186: © Dawoud Bey; 188: Courtesy of the artist; 189: © The Family of Toshiko Takaezu, courtesy of the Toshiko Takaezu Foundation; 191: © 2011 Kukuli Velarde; 192: © 2018 Kelly Church; 193: © 2022 Jeremy Frey; 194: © Bisa Butler; 195: © 2026 Artists Rights Society (ARS), New York / VG Bild-Kunst, Bonn; 196: © Amanda Williams; 197: © Charles Ray, Courtesy of Matthew Marks Gallery; 198: © Simone Leigh.

Essays
P. 107, fig. 4: © Estate of Onchi Kōshirō; p. 174, fig. 3: © 2026 Artists Rights Society (ARS), New York / VG Bild-Kunst, Bonn; p. 175, fig. 5: © Jeanne Gang; p. 188, fig. 1: © 2026 Artists Rights Society (ARS), New York / ADAGP, Paris; p. 189, fig. 2: © 2026 Salvador Dalí, Fundació Gala-Salvador Dalí, Artists Rights Society; p. 190, fig. 3: © 2026 The Joseph and Robert Cornell Memorial Foundation / Licensed by VAGA at Artists Rights Society (ARS), NY; p, 191, fig. 4: © 2026 Remedios Varo, Artists Rights Society (ARS), New York / VEGAP, Madrid; p. 205, fig. 1: Courtesy of the Estate of Karl Wirsum; Corbett vs. Dempsey, Chicago; and Derek Eller Gallery, New York; p. 206, fig. 2: Courtesy of the Estate of Christina Ramberg and Corbett vs. Dempsey, Chicago; p. 207, fig. 3: © 2026 The Richard Hunt Trust / Artists Rights Society (ARS), NY; pp. 247–48, figs. 2–3: © 2026 Rhonda Holy Bear, Wakah Wayuphika Win, Making with Exceptional Skills Woman.